Visual Basic
Power Programming

Visual Basic
Power Programming

Namir C. Shammas

Windcrest®/McGraw-Hill

FIRST EDITION
FIRST PRINTING

© 1992 by **Namir C. Shammas**.
Published by Windcrest Books, an imprint of TAB Books.
TAB Books is a division of McGraw-Hill, Inc.
The name "Windcrest" is a registered trademark of TAB Books.

Library of Congress Cataloging-in-Publication Data

Shammas, Namir Clement, 1954-
    Visual basic power programming / by Namir C. Shammas.
        p.   cm.
    Includes index.
    ISBN 0-8306-3962-4 (h)   ISBN 0-8306-3963-2 (p)
    1. Visual programming (Computer science) 2. BASIC (Computer
program language)   I. Title.
QA76.65.S52   1992
005.26'2—dc20   91-41351
                                        CIP

TAB Books offers software for sale. For information and a catalog, please contact
TAB Software Department, Blue Ridge Summit, PA 17294-0850.

Acquisitions Editor: Brad J. Schepp
Book Editor: Mark Vanderslice
Managing Editor: Sandra L. Johnson
Book Design: Jaclyn J. Boone
Director of Production: Katherine G. Brown
Paperbound Cover: Sandra Blair Design and Brent Blair Photography,
                Harrisburg, PA.   WP1

To the Holy Enabler

Contents

_____**PART ONE**_____

PROGRAMMING TOOLS

_____PART TWO_____

THE CALCULATOR FORMS

Acknowledgments

This book is the fruit of the support and encouragement of several people. I would like to thank Brad Schepp of TAB Books for his backing, encouragement, and shared vision for the project. I also would like to thank Matt Wagner of Waterside Productions, my literary agent, for his support in making this project come to light. I also thank managing editor Sandra Johnson and book editor Mark Vanderslice for their efforts in shaping up the book. Finally, I would like to thank Ethan Winer, president of Crescent Software, for allowing me to include parts of his fine product, QuickPak Professional for Windows.

Introduction

Visual Basic is considered by many to be a landmark product for programming in Windows. The Microsoft implementation has brought Basic programming with a HyperCard twist to the Windows' programmers. Consequently, with that much interest in Visual Basic, there is a flurry of books on the topic. This is my second Visual Basic book with TAB/McGraw-Hill. The first one introduces the readers to programming with Visual Basic. This sequel offers you modules and reusable forms that you can incorporate in your own Visual Basic applications.

The book is divided into four parts. Part one includes chapters 1 through 9 and offers modules for data structures that build on the versatile Visual Basic list box control. Part two includes chapters 10 through 12 and offers reusable forms that implement three types of calculators. Part three includes chapters 13 through 19 and offers modules and reusable forms that allow you to select and process files. Part four includes chapters 20 through 24 and contains practical utilities. After this very brief introduction to the various parts of the book, let me introduce you to the individual chapters.

The chapters in the first part are highly modular. You should first read or browse through chapters 1 and 2. You can then read the other chapters in any order you like.

Chapter 1 looks at the Visual Basic list box control and its properties and methods. If you are already familiar with the list box, you can move to chapter 2.

Chapter 2 presents the GENERIC.BAS module, a general-purpose module that offers routines commonly used by the other data structure modules.

Chapter 3 offers the STACK.BAS module which implements a dynamic stack using the list box control. The module includes basic stack operations, such as clear, push, pop, swap, roll up, and roll down.

Chapter 4 presents the QUEUE.BAS module, which implements an extended version of the queue structure. This implementation allows you to insert and remove data from either end of the queue.

Chapter 5 discusses list-based dynamic arrays. These arrays need not be predimensioned and can be expanded "on the fly." The DYNARR.BAS module offers array operations such as storing, recalling, sorting, and searching.

Chapter 6 offers the SPARR.BAS module, which implements sparse arrays using list box controls. The implementation offers a storage scheme for sparse arrays that removes the spaces of unused array elements.

Chapter 7 presents the SPMAT.BAS module, which implements sparse matrices. Like their sparse array cousins, sparse matrices require space only for those elements that are used to store data.

Chapter 8 offers the TABLE.BAS module implementing table structures. These are dynamic arrays with string-typed indices.

Chapter 9 ends the first part by presenting the module HASHTABL.BAS, which implements the versatile hash table. This structure is known for its fast search speed. The module offers a flexible version of the hash table that you can use in various applications.

Part two offers three chapters containing reusable forms for different calculators. Chapter 10 presents a programmer's calculator that performs the four basic math operations, has a memory register, and can be set to show integers in different bases (decimal, hexadecimal, octal, and binary).

Chapter 11 presents a scientific algebraic calculator form. The implementation has a 100-register memory, performs a variety of math functions, and supports open- and close-parenthesis operations.

Chapter 12 offers a Reverse Polish Notation (RPN) scientific calculator. The emulated machine has a 100-register memory, math functions, a stack manipulation function, and statistical linear regression functions.

Part three focuses on modules and reusable forms that enable you to build Visual Basic applications for selecting and processing files.

Chapter 13 presents the DIRFILES.BAS and FILESLIB.BAS modules. The DIRFILES.BAS module maintains information on the directory tree map of a disk drive. The module contains routines that enable you to obtain the entire directory tree map and query the parent, sibling, and children directories. The FILESLIB.BAS module contains power routines that manipulate a single file or a group of selected files. The module supports operations such as copying, moving, deleting, and printing files.

Chapter 14 offers the SELFILE.FRM and WHEREIS.FRM reusable forms, which allow you to select a group of files. The SELFILE.FRM form quickly searches for files in a currently selected directory. The WHEREIS.FRM form is able to search for files in the entire directories of a drive, or starting from the currently selected directory, or only in the currently selected directory. The files you select using either form are stored in a special data file that is read by other forms presented in this part of the book.

Chapter 15 presents the reusable form FILEVIEW.FRM, which allows you to view the files you select using either the SELFILE.FRM or the WHEREIS.FRM forms. The form allows you to search for strings in the viewed files.

Chapter 16 offers the form EDITFILE.FRM, which enables you to edit the files you select using either the SELFILE.FRM or the WHEREIS.FRM forms. The forms allow you to search and replace strings in the edited files.

Chapter 17 presents the FASTFIND.FRM form, which allows you to quickly search for the same text in the files you select using either the SELFILE.FRM or the WHEREIS.FRM forms.

Chapter 18 offers the FASTEDIT.FRM form that enables you to efficiently and quickly replace a common block of text in all of the files you select using the SELFILE.FRM or WHEREIS.FRM forms. This form frees you from having to load, edit, and save each file individually.

Chapter 19 is a sample Visual Basic application that uses the modules and reusable forms presented in chapters 13 through 18. This powerful shell program allows you to copy, move, print, delete, view, and edit a selection of files.

Part four presents Visual Basic utilities that perform text and file processing. Chapter 20 presents a program that arranges the procedures of Visual Basic text listings in an ascending order. The resulting listings enable you to quickly locate a routine.

Chapter 21 offers a utility that lets you attach one-line notes to the files in a directory. The utility also allows you to view and edit these notes, as well as rename a file while maintaining the attached note.

Chapter 22 introduces a cross-referencing utility that allows you to generate a cross-reference list for a Visual Basic text listing file. The utility allows you to define the set of keywords to exclude from the generated cross-reference lists.

Chapter 23 offers a program that strips comments from a Visual Basic text listing file. The file is then reloaded into the source Visual Basic application and compiled to yield the smallest possible .EXE file.

Chapter 24 presents the QuickPak Professional for Windows package from Crescent Software. The chapter discusses the various libraries in the package and presents two utilities. The first utility allows you to back up files from a directory into a single disk. The backup utility gives you the options of adding new files to the backup disk, updating existing files on the backup disk, and deleting old files from the backup disk. The second utility displays a list of the selected files along with their sizes, date stamps, and time stamps. The utility also allows you to delete, print, and view the selected files.

Part One

Programming tools

This part of the book presents data structures that use the extremely powerful Visual Basic list box control. The chapters in this part introduce you to the stack, queue, dynamic array, sparse array, sparse matrix, table, and hash table structures. All of these structures can be emulated by the Visual Basic list box control.

1
The power of lists

The first part of the book explores the great potential of Visual Basic list box controls. This chapter discusses why these lists are special and versatile. You can learn about the power of Visual Basic lists, and about list box properties and methods.

The power of Visual Basic lists

One of the limitations of the BASIC language (including Visual Basic) is the lack of pointers like the ones used in Pascal or C. A *pointer* is a special variable that stores the address and the data type of information in memory. Therefore, you can say that a pointer, as the name suggests, points to a specific memory location containing particular data. This memory location can be accessed by the pointer to read and write data. The power of a pointer lies in its ability to change its address and therefore point to another memory location.

Pointers are used to access both existing static data and dynamically allocated data. Existing data are available as variables set either by the program (during compile time) or by the operating system. Dynamically allocated data represents new variables and arrays that are created at run time. Pointers are needed to access these dynamic variables. Visual Basic supports a limited type of dynamic data that allows you to redimension arrays at run time. This process is executed without using explicit pointers; however, pointers are used internally by Visual Basic.

Linked lists are popular data structures in Pascal, C, and many other languages that support pointers and dynamic allocations. They are somewhat similar to dynamically expanded arrays and are made up of *nodes* that are linked together using pointers. Unlike array elements, linked list nodes are not always stored in a contiguous area of the memory. Instead, list nodes can be scattered throughout the heap area of the memory. This is why nodes use pointers to establish the proper links between them. A typical linked list is shown in FIG. 1-1. Typical linked lists also differ from arrays in that they cannot be indexed. Thus, accessing data in linked lists resembles accessing data in sequential files—you must scroll to the leading items to get to a specific data item.

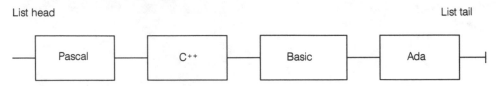

1-1   A typical linked list.

Interestingly, while Visual Basic does not offer the basic ingredients necessary to build linked lists, it does offer "prepackaged" lists. The list box control implements an indexable dynamic list. This control can be used to emulate other interesting data structures, such as stacks, queues, dynamic arrays, sparse arrays, sparse matrices, table structures, and hash tables. These structures are explored in the later chapters in this part. The power of Visual Basic list boxes is that they offer the best of both arrays and traditional linked lists. List box controls can be used as hidden controls by setting the Visible property of the list box to False. Thus, invisible list boxes can be used to implement behind-the-scenes versions of the data structures I mentioned.

List box properties and methods

This section discusses the properties and methods of list boxes that are relevant to this book. If you are already familiar with list boxes, you might want to skip this section.

The list box controls have a number of properties that enable you to maintain and select items from their lists. These items are stored as an array of strings with the lower index of 0. The properties that manage list selections follow.

The Sorted property determines whether or not the list items are alphabetically sorted. The Sorted property can be set only during design time. The general syntax for this run-time read-only property is:

[form.]listBox.Sorted

The Sorted property returns a Boolean True (–1) or False (0). If the Sorted property is set to True at design time, the list items are maintained in ascending order.

The Text property specifies the currently selected text. The general syntax for the Text property is:

*[form.]listBox.*Text = *[stringExpression$]*

Visual Basic limits the content of the Text property during design time to an empty string.

The List property represents an array of strings that contain the list data. The general syntax for the List property is:

*[form.]listBox.*List*(index%) [* = *stringExpression$]*

By using the List property, you can overwrite a current list item.

🕱 **Warning!**   Overwriting list items when the Sorted property is True can corrupt the order of the list. Consequently, you need to include sorting procedures that reorder the items in the list before you add new data items.

The ListIndex property indicates the index of the currently selected item. The value of the ListIndex for a list box ranges from − 1 to the number of data items minus one, or ListCount − 1. The − 1 indicates that there is no current selection. The general syntax for this run-time read-only property is:

*[form.]listBox.*ListIndex

The ListCount property maintains the current number of items in the list. The general syntax for this run-time read-only property is:

*[form.]listBox.*ListCount

The list boxes have several methods that are used to add and remove items from the lists. The AddItem method inserts new data items in the list. The general syntax for the AddItem method is:

*[form.]listBox.*AddItem *item$ [,index%]*

The index% is optional. If it is omitted and the Sorted property is False, the new item is appended to the list. If the Sorted property is True, the new item is inserted in its proper place.

🕱 **Warning!**   When the Sorted property is True, you must omit the index% value, or you will corrupt the order of the items in the list.

When the Sorted property is False, the value of index% can be in the range of 0 to ListCount. If the value of index% is less than ListCount, the list items are shifted upwards from the index% location.

The RemoveItem method removes an item from the list. The general syntax for the RemoveItem method is:

*[form.]listBox.*RemoveItem *index%*

The values for the index% range from 0 to ListCount − 1.

Opening the door

Lists are powerful data structures. In fact, LISP is a list-oriented programming language that came out of MIT in the 1950s. Lists in general and the Visual Basic list boxes in particular are able to emulate other data structures. The next chapter presents a code module that is used in emulating stacks, queues, arrays, and the other data structures that I mentioned earlier. Chapters 3 through 9 present the various data structures.

2
The generic module

This chapter presents the GENERIC.BAS module, which contains procedures used by the other modules to emulate the various data structures. I discuss the various procedures in the GENERIC.BAS module. Testing these routines is included in testing the data structures that are presented in the next chapters.

☞ The GENERIC.BAS module, shown in Listing 2-1, declares three constants: True, False, and BIG_SIZE. The familiar constants True and False are declared in this module rather than the global module. As a rule, every data structure module in this book declares its own version of True and False constants. This approach avoids using the global module as much as possible; consequently, you are free to use your own global module when you incorporate these modules in a Visual Basic application.

The BIG_SIZE constant is used as a default value for selecting the remaining part of a string.

The procedures in the GENERIC.BAS module are presented next.

The ClearList procedure removes the members of a list box. This action may be needed, for example, before copying the members of one list into another list, or before reading the list members for a data file.

The ShellSort procedure performs a Shell-Metzner sort on the list members. The parameter St& specifies the first character of the list members that forms the sort key. When the argument for St& is 1, the entire list member is used as a sort key.

The Combsort procedure implements the Combsort algorithm to order the list members. The parameter St& specifies the first character of the list members that forms the sort key. When the argument for St& is 1, the entire list member is used as a sort key.

Listing 2-1 The code attached to the GENERIC.BAS module.

```
Const True = -1, False = 0
Const BIG_SIZE = 65535

Sub ClearList (L As Control)
' Clears the list
  ' loop to delete list elements
  Do While L.ListCount ' > 0 (test not required)
    L.RemoveItem 0
  Loop
End Sub

Sub ShellSort (L As Control, ByVal St&)
' Performs a Shell-Metzner sort on the items in the list box L.
' The St& parameter determines the portion of the list members
' that are used as sorting keys.
  Dim N As Integer
  Dim Skip As Long
  Dim InOrder As Integer
  Dim I As Integer, J As Integer
  Dim TempStr As String
  N = L.ListCount
  Skip = N ' set the skip factor to N
  Do While Skip > 1
    Skip = Skip * 2 \ 3
    If Skip < 1 Then Skip = 1
    Do
      InOrder = True ' set order flag to true
      ' compare elements that are Skip members apart
      For J = 0 To N - 1 - Skip
        I = J + 1
        If Mid$(L.List(J), St&) > Mid$(L.List(I), St&) Then
          ' swap elements
          InOrder = False
          TempStr = L.List(I)
          L.List(I) = L.List(J)
          L.List(J) = TempStr
        End If
      Next J
    Loop Until InOrder
  Loop
End Sub

Sub CombSort (L As Control, ByVal St&)
' Performs the Combsort on the elements of a list
  Dim N As Integer
  Dim Skip As Integer
  Dim InOrder As Integer ' Boolean sort flag
  Dim I As Integer, J As Integer
  Dim TempStr As String

  N = L.ListCount ' get the list size
  Skip = N
  ' sorting loop
  Do
    ' adjust the Skip factor
    Skip = Skip * 8 \ 11
    If Skip < 0 Then Skip = 1
    InOrder = True
    ' loop to compare elements that are Skip members apart
    For I = 0 To N - 1 - Skip
      J = I + Skip
      If Mid$(L.List(I), St&) > Mid$(L.List(J), St&) Then
        ' swap elements I and J
        InOrder = False
        TempStr = L.List(I)
```

Listing 2-1 Continued.

```
            L.List(I) = L.List(J)
            L.List(J) = TempStr
        End If
      Next I
   Loop Until InOrder And (Skip = 1)
End Sub

Sub QuickSort (L As Control, ByVal St&)
' Master procedure that triggers the QuickSort method
' by invoking the QSort procedure
   QSort L, 0, L.ListCount - 1, St&
End Sub

Sub QSort (L As Control, ByVal Low%, ByVal High%, ByVal St&)
' Recursive procedure to implement the QuickSort algorithm
   Dim X As String, Y As String
   Dim I As Integer, J As Integer

   ' initialize index I and J
   I = Low%
   J = High%
   ' select the median
   X = Mid$(L.List((Low% + High%) \ 2), St&)
   Do
      Do While Mid$(L.List(I), St&) < X
         I = I + 1
      Loop
      Do While X < Mid$(L.List(J), St&)
         J = J - 1
      Loop
      If I <= J Then
         Y = L.List(I)
         L.List(I) = L.List(J)
         L.List(J) = Y
         I = I + 1
         J = J - 1
      End If
   Loop Until I > J
   If Low% < J Then QSort L, Low%, J, St&
   If I < High% Then QSort L, I, High%, St&
End Sub

Function LinSearch (L As Control, ByVal Find$, ByVal Occur%, ByVal
CaseSense%, ByVal St&, ByVal Size&) As Integer
' Searches for the substring Find$ to match a member of
' list L.   The search looks for the Occur% matching member.   The
' CaseSense% parameter determines if the search is case-sensitive.
' The St& and Size& parameters specify the first string character
' and number of characters to compare.
' The function returns the index of the first mathing element
' or -1 if no match is found.
   Dim N As Integer
   Dim I As Integer
   Dim FoundMatch As Integer
   ' adjust Size& argument
   If Size& < 1 Then Size& = BIG_SIZE
   If Occur% < 1 Then Occur% = 1
   N = L.ListCount - 1
   FoundMatch = False ' set found flag
   If CaseSense% Then ' is search case sensitive?
      ' search the list members
      For I = Occur% To N
         If Find$ = Mid$(L.List(I), St&, Size&) Then
            Occur% = Occur% - 1
            If Occur% = 0 Then
               FoundMatch = True
```

Listing 2-1 Continued.

```
            Exit For ' exit loop
        End If
      End If
    Next I
  Else
    ' make search string into uppercase
    FindStr$ = UCase$(FindStr$)
    ' search the list members
    For I = Occur% To N
      If Find$ = UCase$(Mid$(L.List(I), St&, Size&)) Then
        Occur% = Occur% - 1
        If Occur% = 0 Then
          FoundMatch = True
          Exit For ' exit loop
        End If
      End If
    Next I
  End If
  If FoundMatch Then ' found a match?
    LinSearch = I ' Yes! Return idndex I
  Else
    LinSearch = -1 ' No! Return -1
  End If
End Function

Function BinSearch (L As Control, ByVal Find$, ByVal Occur%, ByVal St&,
ByVal Size&) As Integer
' Performs binary search by calling the BinLocate function.
' The Occur% parameter specifies the sought occurence.
' If the list members are unique, supply an Occur% with
' an argument of 1.
  Dim Median As Integer
  ' adjust Size& parameter
  If Size& < 1 Then Size& = BIG_SIZE
  ' adjust Occur% parameter
  If Occur% = 0 Then Occur% = 1
  Median = BinLocate(L, Find$, St&, Size&) ' get the matching location
  ' doe sthe search string match the element at index Median
  If Find$ = Mid$(L.List(Median), St&, Size&) Then
    If Occur% = 1 Then
      ' return the index of the matching element
      BinSearch = Median
    Else
      ' find first matching element by examining the
      ' list members before the Median element
      I = Median
      Do While (I >= 0) And (Find$ = Mid$(L.List(I), St&, Size&))
        I = I - 1
      Loop
      ' adjust the value of index I?
      If Find$ <> Mid$(L.List(I), St&, Size&) Then
        ' reset I to index the first matching element
        I = I + 1
      End If
      ' I now points to the first matching element
      ' is sought occurrence out-of-range?
      If (I + Occur% - 1) > L.ListCount Then
        BinSearch = -1
      End If
      ' does element I+Occur%-1 match Find$?
      If Find$ = Mid$(L.List(I + Occur% - 1), St&, Size&) Then
        ' Yes! Returns that index
        BinSearch = I + Occur% - 1
      Else
        ' No! Return - 1
        BinSearch = -1
```

Listing 2-1 Continued.

```
            End If
        End If
    Else
        BinSearch = -1 ' return -1 to indicate that no match is found
    End If
End Function


Sub CopyList (Source As Control, Target As Control)
' copy list Source into list Target
    Dim I As Integer
    ClearList Target ' clear target list first
    ' copy the individual list members
    For I = 0 To Source.ListCount - 1
        Target.AddItem Source.List(I), I
    Next I
End Sub


Function LinFind (L As Control, ByVal Find$, ByVal Occur%, ByVal
CaseSense%, ByVal St&, ByVal Size&) As Integer
' Searches for the substring Find$ anywhere in a member of
' list L.  The search looks for the Occur% matching member.  The
' CaseSense% parameter determines if the search is case-sensitive.
' The St& and Size& parameters specify the first string character
' and number of characters to compare.
' The function returns the index of the first mathing element
' or -1 if no match is found.
    Dim N As Integer
    Dim I As Integer
    Dim FoundMatch As Integer
    ' adjust Size& argument
    If Size& < 1 Then Size& = BIG_SIZE
    If Occur% < 1 Then Occur% = 1
    N = L.ListCount - 1
    FoundMatch = False ' set found flag
    If CaseSense% Then ' is search case sensitive?
        ' search the list members
        For I = 0 To N
            If InStr(Mid$(L.List(I), St&, Size&), Find$) > 0 Then
                Occur% = Occur% - 1
                If Occur% = 0 Then
                    FoundMatch = True
                    Exit For ' exit loop
                End If
            End If
        Next I
    Else
        ' make search string into uppercase
        Find$ = UCase$(Find$)
        ' search the list members
        For I = 0 To N
            If InStr(UCase$(Mid$(L.List(I), St&, Size&)), Find$) > 0 Then
                Occur% = Occur% - 1
                If Occur% = 0 Then
                    FoundMatch = True
                    Exit For ' exit loop
                End If
            End If
        Next I
    End If
    If FoundMatch Then ' found a match?
        LinFind = I ' Yes! Return index I
    Else
        LinFind = -1 ' No! Return -1
    End If
End Function
```

Listing 2-1 Continued.

```
Function WriteList (L As Control, ByVal Filename$) As Integer
' Writes the list members to the file Filename$.
' The function returns True if the file output was
' successful.  Otherwise the function returns False.
  Dim FileNum As Integer
  Dim I As Integer
  On Error GoTo BadWriteList
  FileNum = FreeFile ' get next handle number
  ' open file for output
  Open Filename$ For Output As #FileNum%
  ' write the list members
  For I = 0 To L.ListCount - 1
    Print #FileNum, L.List(I)
  Next I
  Close #FileNum
  On Error GoTo 0
  WriteList = True
  Exit Function

BadWriteList:
  WriteList = False
  Resume ExitWriteList
ExitWriteList:
End Function

Function ReadList (L As Control, ByVal Filename$, ByVal Merge%) As Integer
' Reads the list members from the file Filename$.
' The function returns True if the file input was
' successful.  Otherwise the function returns False.
' The Merge% file specifies whether the data is merged
' with the current list box or not.
  Dim FileNum As Integer
  Dim I As Integer
  Dim TextLine As String
  On Error GoTo BadReadList
  ' get the next file handle
  FileNum = FreeFile
  ' open the file for input
  Open Filename$ For Input As #FileNum%
  If Not Merge% Then ClearList L ' clear the list
  I = L.ListCount - 1' set the line counter
  ' loop to read the text lines
  Do While Not EOF(FileNum)
    I = I + 1
    Line Input #FileNum, TextLine
    L.AddItem TextLine, I
  Loop
  Close #FileNum
  On Error GoTo 0
  ReadList = True
  Exit Function

BadReadList:
  ReadList = False
  Resume ExitReadList
ExitReadList:
End Function

Sub InsertSort (ByVal Elem$, L As Control, ByVal St&, ByVal Size&)
' Insert Elem$ in list L such that the order
' in the list is maintained
  Dim I As Integer
  Dim TheKey As String
  If Size& < 1 Then Size& = BIG_SIZE
  If L.ListCount > 0 Then
    ' obtain the insertion key
```

Listing 2-1 Continued.

```
    TheKey = Mid$(Elem$, St&, Size&)
    ' list is not empty: insert in proper location
    I = BinLocate(L, TheKey, St&, Size&)
    If TheKey <= Mid$(L.List(I), St&, Size&) Then
      L.AddItem Elem$, I
    Else
      L.AddItem Elem$, I + 1
    End If
  Else
    ' list is empty: insert as the first list member
    L.AddItem Elem$, 0
  End If
End Sub

Function BinLocate (L As Control, ByVal Find$, ByVal St&, ByVal Size&) As
Integer
' Function locates the index of a list member that is either
' suitable for inserting or recalling data.  The function
' assumes that the list members are sorted.
  Dim Low As Integer
  Dim High As Integer
  Dim Median As Integer
  If Size& < 1 Then Size& = BIG_SIZE
  ' set limits for search
  Low = 0
  High = L.ListCount - 1
  ' start search loop
  Do
    Median = (Low + High) \ 2 ' calculate the median
    ' compare the search string with the median list element
    If Find$ < Mid$(L.List(Median), St&, Size&) Then
      High = Median - 1 ' update upper limit
    Else
      Low = Median + 1 ' update lower limit
    End If
  Loop Until (Find$ = Mid$(L.List(Median), St&, Size&)) Or (Low > High)
  BinLocate = Median ' return function result
End Function

Sub HighlightTextBox (T As Control)
' highlight the text in a text box
  If TypeOf T Is TextBox Then
    T.SelStart = 0
    T.SelLength = Len(T.Text)
  End If
End Sub
```

The QuickSort and QSort procedures order the list members using the recursive QuickSort method. You should invoke the QuickSort procedure, which in turn calls the recursive QSort procedure to perform the actual sorting. The St& parameter in procedure QuickSort specifies the first character of the list members as the sort key. When the argument for St& is 1, the entire list member is used as the sort key.

The InsertSort procedure inserts a new member in an ordered list. If the list is not empty, the procedure calls BinLocate to find the proper insertion index. Otherwise, the first member is inserted at index 0. The parameter St& specifies the first character of the list members as the sort key. When the argument for St& is 1, the entire list member is used as a sort key.

The LinSearch function performs a case-sensitive linear search for the specified occurrence of list member. The Occur% parameter specifies the sought occurrence, which is usually 1. The CaseSense% parameter is a Boolean flag that indicates whether or not to conduct a case-sensitive search. The St& and Size& parameters determine the portion of the list members that is used in searching for string Find$. If the argument for Size& is 0, then Size% is assigned constant BIG_SIZE to select the rest of the string. A match is found when Find$ equals the entire specified portion of the list member (case sensitivity depends on the value of the CaseSense% flag). The procedure searches the list members starting with the first one. When a match is found, the Occur% argument is decreased by 1 and then compared with 0. If the value of Occur% is 0, the sought occurrence of string Find$ is located. The function returns the index of Occur% occurrence of the matching element, or −1 if no match is found.

The LinFind function is similar to the LinSearch procedure. The difference is that a match is found when the Find$ string matches any part of the specified list member portion. As with LinSearch, case sensitivity depends on the CaseSense% flag.

☞ The BinLocate function searches for any occurrence of the string Find$ in an ordered list. It is your responsibility to make sure that the list is in order. This procedure implements the efficient binary search to locate the index value of where Find$ might be located or might be inserted. The St& and Size& parameters determine the portion of the list members that are compared with string Find$. If the argument for Size& is 0, then Size% is assigned constant BIG_SIZE to select the rest of the string.

☞ The BinSearch function searches for the Occur% occurrence of the string Find$ in an ordered list. It is up to you to make sure that the list is in order. The St& and Size& parameters determine the portion of the list members that are compared with string Find$. If the argument for Size& is 0, then Size% is assigned constant BIG_SIZE to select the rest of the string. The BinSearch function calls procedure BinLocate to obtain a preliminary index for the possible location of the sought element. If the list member at the specified preliminary index does not match string Find$, the function returns −1. This value indicates that no match was found. If the list member at the specified preliminary index matches string String$, the procedure searches for the first element that matches Find$. Once that element is found, the next Occur%−1 element is compared with Find$. If the two strings match, the function returns the index of the matching list member; otherwise, the function returns −1.

The WriteList function writes the list members to the text file Filename$. Each list member is written on a separate line. If the file output is successful, the function returns True; otherwise, the function returns False.

The ReadList function reads the list members from the text file Filename$. Each list member is read from a separate line. If the file input is successful, the function returns True; otherwise, the function returns False.

The third function parameter is a Boolean flag that determines whether or not the data from the file is merged.

The CopyList procedure copies the members of one list into another. The target list is cleared before receiving copies of the source list members.

The HighlightTextBox procedure highlights the contents of a text box. It is usually invoked in a TextBox_GetFocus event-handling procedure, and it verifies that the control argument is a text box.

☞ I chose to write the list handling procedures without checking that the control argument is a list box. If you feel that such argument checking is required, then by all means insert the required If statement. A sample If-Then-Else statement is shown below:

```
If TypeOf L Is ListBox Then
Else
   Exit Sub
End If
```

Storing user-defined types

The generic routines store strings in the list boxes. Each member of the list box contains a variable-length string. This storage scheme is very suitable for string-typed data. But what about storing user-defined data types? The basic strategy is to convert all of the fields of a user-defined data type into a string, and vice versa. Let me explain this concept using a simple example. Consider the following user-defined data type:

```
Type PersonRec
   LastName As String     * 10
   FirstName As String    * 10
   Age As Integer
   Weight As Single
End Type
```

The LastName and FirstName fields are fixed-length strings. Storing them in a list box member is straightforward. The Age data field is an integer. Integers have values that range between – 32,768 and 32,767. However, in this case the values assigned to the Age field typically range between 0 and 150 (a maximum of three digits). Consequently, a three-character string is used to convert the numeric Age field into a string. Using the Format$ function requires the following form:

```
AgeStr as String *3
AgeStr = Format$(Age, "000")
```

The above form produces an AgeStr string with leading zeros if Age is less than 100. Using zeros in the format string is preferred over using # characters, since the leading zeros will cause the number of characters occupied by the string image of a number to remain fixed.

The Weight field is a floating-point numeric field. In this case, the field has one significant decimal place. The integer part of the field might range from 0 to 300 (another three-digit maximum). Consequently, a five-character string can store the Weight using the "000.0" format string.

An example of how the fields of a PersonRec variable are written to a list member is shown here:

```
Person As PersonRec
RecordString As String
AgeStr As String * 3
WeightStr As String * 5

GetData(Person)
' store the first two fields
RecordString = Person.LastName + Person.FirstName
AgeStr = Format$(Person.Age, "000")
' store the string image of the Age field
RecordString = RecordString + AgeStr
WeightStr = Format$(Person.Weight, "000.0")
' store the string image of the Weight field
RecordString = RecordString + WeightStr
' insert in the list
The ListBox.AddItem RecordString
```

The variable RecordString contains the concatenation of the fields and/or their string images. Figure 2-1 contains the map of RecordString that shows where each field or its string image is stored. The figure also shows the size of each substring.

Substring	Index	Size
LastName	1	10
FirstName	11	10
Age	21	3
Weight	24	5

2-1 The map of the concatenated substrings in the *RecordString* variable.

Figure 2-1 shows a typical example of information of a user-defined type whose fields are stored in list box members. Using the values of the indicated indices and sizes, you can then sort and search the list box members using a specific data field.

3
Stacks

The first data structure that I emulate using the list box controls is the stack. A stack is a simple yet highly versatile data structure that serves to queue incoming and outgoing information in a specific way. A typical stack is shown in FIG. 3-1. Stacks can be emulated using arrays or lists.

Top of stack

C++	Last element inserted
SmallTalk	
Basic	
AWK	Stack growth direction
Oberon	
Modula-2	
Pascal	
Ada	First element inserted

Bottom of stack

3-1 A typical stack.

Arrays commonly implement fixed-sized arrays, while lists usually implement dynamic stacks. Stacks arrange data using the last in, first out (LIFO) queue model. The more recently an item is pushed onto a stack, the sooner it is popped off the stack. Stacks have a bottom and a top (at least logical ones) and grow toward the top.

Basic stack operations

Figure 3-1 shows a typical stack with bottom, top, and intermediate members. When you use a list to emulate the stack, you can make the first list member (the one with index 0) either the top or the bottom of the stack. The highest list member becomes the other end of the stack. I chose to implement the emulated stack so that the bottom stack member is element 0 of the list. This method leads to a visually inverted stack, where the bottom of the stack is the first list member. Either visual orientation is fine, as long as it correctly represents the logical stack.

Basic stack operations include the following:

- Clearing the stack.
- Pushing data in the stack. Each new item is placed at the top of the stack.
- Popping off data from the stack. This operation removes data from the top of the stack.
- Swapping the two topmost elements.
- Rolling up the stack. This operation moves the top member to the bottom and moves every other element upward, toward the top. Figure 3-2 shows an example of rolling up a stack.
- Rolling down the stack. This operation moves the bottom member to the top and moves every other element downward. Figure 3-3 shows an example of rolling down a stack.

The data stored in the stack can be either simple variable-length strings or strings that store the fields or string images of a user-defined type. Since the stack operations do not include searching and sorting, the information for mapping the stack members is not significant to the stack operations themselves.

The STACK.BAS module

Listing 3-1 shows the code in the module STACK.BAS. The module contains the procedures that implement the stack operations described in the previous section.

The ClearStack procedure clears the stack by invoking the ClearList procedure in the GENERIC.BAS module.

The PushStack procedure pushes the argument for X$ into the stack S, using a single S.AddItem statement to perform the required operation.

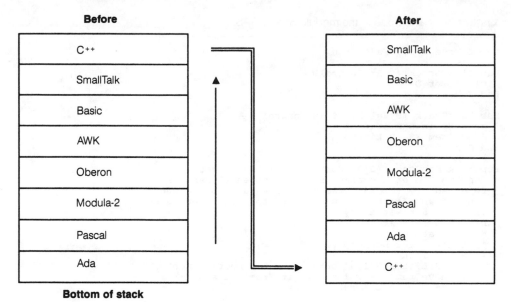

3-2 Rolling up a sample stack.

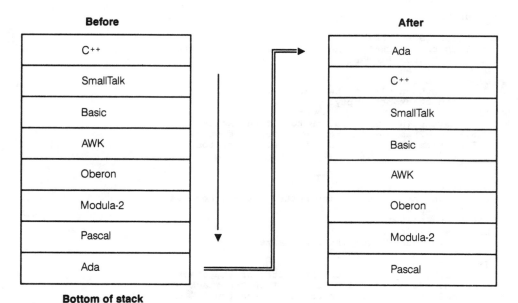

3-3 Rolling down a sample stack.

The Boolean PopStack function pops off the top stack member and stores it in the argument of parameter X$. The function returns True if the operation is successful and yields False if is not. The basic code for popping the top stack member consists of two statements. The first statement assigns the last list member, which represents the top of the stack, to the

Listing 3-1 The code in the module STACK.BAS.

```
Const True = -1, False = 0

Sub ClearStack (S As Control)
   ClearList S
End Sub

Sub PushStack (ByVal X$, S As Control)
' push X$ in the stack S
   S.AddItem X$, S.ListCount
End Sub

Function PopStack (S As Control, X$) As Integer
' Pop the top of the stack S.  The popped element is
' returned  by the X$ parameter.  The function returns
' True if an element was popped off the stack, or False
' if the stack was empty.
   Dim N As Integer
   N = S.ListCount
   ' is the stack not empty?
   If N > 0 Then
      X$ = S.List(N - 1) ' obtain the top most element
      S.RemoveItem N - 1 ' remove it from the stack
      PopStack = True ' return True
   Else
      X$ = "" ' dummy value
      PopStack = False ' returns False
   End If
End Function

Sub RollUp (S As Control)
' Roll up the stack S.  The old top element becomes
' the new bottom element.
   Dim N As Integer
   Dim X As String
   N = S.ListCount ' get the stack size
   ' is the stack not empty?
   If N > 0 Then
      X = S.List(N - 1) ' obtain top of the stack
      S.RemoveItem N - 1 ' remove it from the stack
      S.AddItem X, 0     ' insert it at the bottom
   End If
End Sub

Sub RollDown (S As Control)
' Roll down the stack S.  The bottom element becomes
' the new top element.
   Dim N As Integer
   Dim X As String
   N = S.ListCount ' get the stack size
   ' is the stack not empty?
   If N > 0 Then
      X = S.List(0)      ' obtain bottom of the stack
      S.RemoveItem 0     ' remove it from the stack
      S.AddItem X, N - 1 ' insert it at the top
   End If
End Sub

Sub SwapTopStack (S As Control)
' Swaps the two topmost stack members
   Dim X As String
   Dim N As Integer
   N = S.ListCount ' get the stack size
   ' are there more than one stack members?
   If N > 1 Then
      ' swap topmost members
```

Listing 3-1   Continued.

```
    X = S.List(N - 1)
    S.List(N - 1) = S.List(N - 2)
    S.List(N - 2) = X
  End If
End Sub
```

parameter X$. The second statement removes the top stack member using the RemoveItem method. The value returned by parameter X$ in function PopStack is meaningful only if the function result is True.

The SwapTopStack procedure swaps the two top stack members. The procedure first verifies that there are at least two stack members. If that condition is true, the procedure swaps the top members (at index N-1 and N-2) using the following code:

```
X = S.List(N - 1)
S.List(N - 1) = S.List(N - 2)
S.List(N - 2) = X
```

The Rollup procedure rolls up the stack. The procedure first verifies that there are at least two stack members. If that condition is true, the procedure stores the top stack member in the local variable X, removes the top member, and then inserts the string of variable X at the stack bottom (index 0), as shown in the code below:

```
X = S.List(N - 1)         '  obtain top of the stack
S.RemoveItem N - 1        '  remove it from the stack
S.AddItem X, 0            '  insert it at the bottom
```

The Rolldown procedure rolls down the stack. The procedure first verifies that there are at least two stack members. If that condition is true, the procedure stores the bottom stack member in the local variable X, removes the bottom member, and then inserts the string of variable X at the stack top (at index N – 1), as shown in this code:

```
X = S.List(0)            '  obtain the bottom of the stack
S.RemoveItem 0           '  remove it from the stack
S.AddItem X, N - 1       '  insert it at the top
```

The operations presented here represent a minimal set. You may add other procedures to perform additional stack operations, such as duplicating the top stack member, swapping the top of the stack with other stack members, or rolling up or down a specified number of stack members.

The stack test program

Let's look at a test program to exercise the various procedures in module STACK.BAS. Figures 3-4 to 3-6 show the specifications for the TSSTACK .MAK project file and the TSSTACK.FRM form file. The program has com-

Application name: Stack test program
Application code name: TSSTACK

Version: 1.0   Date created: August 12, 1991
Programmer(s): Namir Clement Shammas

List of filenames

Storage path: \ VB \ VBXTOOL
Project   TSSTACK.MAK
Global   GLOBAL.BAS
Form 1   TSSTACK.FRM
Module 1   GENERIC.BAS
Module 2   STACK.BAS

3-4 The basic specifications for the TSSTACK.MAK project file.

Form #1   Form filename: TSSTACK.FRM
Version: 1.0   Date: August 12, 1991

Control object type	Default CtlName	Purpose
Command button	Command1	Exits the test program
	Command2	Pushes an item in the stack
	Command3	Pops the top stack member
	Command4	Clears the stack
	Command5	Rolls up the stack
	Command6	Rolls down the stack
	Command7	Swaps the two top stack members
Text box	Text1	Input/Output text box
List box	List1	Visible stack emulator
Label	Label1	Stack label
	Label2	Text box label

3-5 The list of controls in the TSSTACK.FRM form file.

Application (code) name: TSSTACK
Form #1
Version: 1.0   Date: August 12, 1991

Original control name	Property	New setting
Form	Caption	Stack Test Program
Command1	CtlName	QuitBtn
	Caption	&Quit
Command2	CtlName	PushBtn
	Caption	P&ush
Command3	CtlName	PopBtn
	Caption	P&op

3-6 The customized settings for the TSSTACK.FRM form.

Original control name	Property	New setting
Command4	CtlName	ClearBtn
	Caption	&Clear
Command5	CtlName	RollUpBtn
	Caption	Roll &Up
Command6	CtlName	RollDownBtn
	Caption	Roll &Down
Command7	CtlName	SwapBtn
	Caption	S&wap
Text1	CtlName	TextBox
	Text	(empty string)
List1	CtlName	StackLst
Label1	CtlName	StackLbl
	Caption	The Inverted Stack
Label2	CtlName	IOLbl
	Caption	Input/Output Text Box

3-6 Continued.

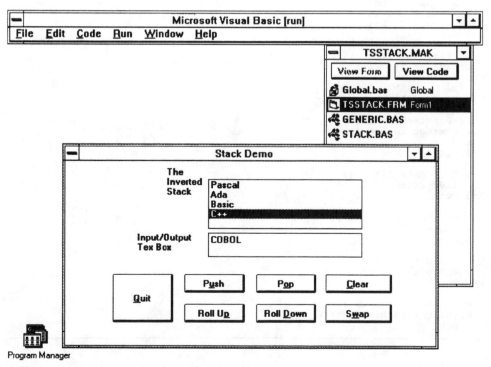

3-7 A sample session with the stack test program.

mand buttons to push, pop, roll up, roll down, and clear the stack, as well as swap the top two stack members. To push a string in the stack, you key in the string characters in the text box, then click on the Push button. To pop off the top member of the stack, just click the Pop button. The popped stack member appears in the text box.

The test program shows a visible inverted stack for the sake of the demonstration. You can set the Visible property of the list box to False and then run the program. Figure 3-7 (on the previous page) shows a sample session with the stack test program.

Listing 3-2 shows the code attached to the controls of form TSSTACK .FRM. The code in the event-handling procedure is very simple. The event-handling procedures serve as simple shells that execute the stack manipulation procedures exported by module STACK.BAS.

Listing 3-2   The code attached to form TSSTACK.FRM.

```
Sub QuitBtn_Click ()
   End
End Sub

Sub PushBtn_Click ()
   Dim S As String
   S = TextBox.Text
   PushStack S, StackLst
End Sub

Sub ClearBtn_Click ()
   ClearList StackLst
End Sub

Sub PopBtn_Click ()
   Dim S As String
   If PopStack(StackLst, S) Then
      TextBox.Text = S
   End If
End Sub

Sub RollUpBtn_Click ()
   RollUp StackLst
End Sub

Sub RollDownBtn_Click ()
   RollDown StackLst
End Sub

Sub SwapBtn_Click ()
   SwapTopStack StackLst
End Sub

Sub TextBox_GotFocus ()
   HighlightTextBox TextBox
End Sub
```

4
Queues

When you stand in line to pay for an item in a store or in a fast food restaurant, you are a member of a queue. Queue data structures are akin to stacks and serve to exchange data using the first in, first out (FIFO) operating model. The Windows operating environment uses the queue data structure to store and process various events.

A queue has a front end and a back end. Data are pushed (or enqueued) at the back end, and are popped off (or dequeued) at the front end. There are several types of queues. First, there is the *simple queue*. This data structure strictly adheres to the FIFO operating model—no data can jump ahead in the queue. The second type of queue is the *priority queue*, which assigns a priority level to every item entering in the queue. Using priority levels means that an item can instantly move to the front end of the queue if it has the highest priority level. The third type of queue is the *bidirectional* queue, which allows data to be enqueued and dequeued from either end of the queue. This version of the queue can behave both as a simple queue or as a stack. This chapter implements the third type.

Basic queue operations

The basic operations of a queue are clearing the queue; enqueueing data at either end of the queue; and dequeueing data at either end of the queue. These operations are amazingly versatile. For example, you can implement a roll-down or roll-up operation that works like a stack, by dequeueing an item from one end and enqueueing it at the other end. Other stack-like operations can be similarly implemented.

The QUEUE.BAS module

The three basic queue operations are implemented in the QUEUE.BAS module, whose code is shown in Listing 4-1. The module contains the procedures described in the next several paragraphs.

Listing 4-1 The code in the QUEUE.BAS module.

```
Const True = -1, False = 0

Sub ClearQue (Q As Control)
' Clears the queue Q.
  ClearList Q
End Sub

Sub EnQue (Q As Control, ByVal X$, ByVal Back%)
' Inserts the data item X$ in the queue Q.  The
' Back% parameter is a flag that specifies whether
' to insert the new item at the back end (when -1)
' or at the front end (when 0).
  If Back% Then
    Q.AddItem X$, Q.ListCount
  Else
    Q.AddItem X$, 0
  End If
End Sub

Function DeQue (Q As Control, X$, ByVal Front%) As Integer
' Remove an item from the queue Q.  The parameter X$
' returns the removed element.  The Front% parameter is
' a flag that specifies whether the item is removed from
' the front of the queue (when -1) or from the back of
' of the queue (when 0).
' The function returns True when an element is removed from
' the queue.  Otherwise, the function yields a False result.
  Dim N As Integer
  N = Q.ListCount
  ' Is the queue not empty?
  If N > 0 Then
    ' Remove from the front?
    If Front% Then
      ' remove from the front end
      X$ = Q.List(0)
      Q.RemoveItem 0
    Else
      ' remove from the tail end
      X$ = Q.List(N - 1)
      Q.RemoveItem N - 1
    End If
    DeQue = True
  Else
    X$ = ""
    DeQue = False
  End If
End Function
```

The ClearQue procedure clears the list box Q, which emulates a queue. The procedure calls the ClearList procedure that is exported by the GENERIC.BAS module.

The EnQue procedure inserts the data item X$ in the queue Q. The Boolean Back% parameter determines where to insert the new data. It is inserted at the back end when the argument for Back% is True (− 1), or at the front end when the argument for Back% is False (0). In either case the procedure uses the AddItem method to insert the new data. The argument for AddItem is equal to Q.ListCount when Back% is True, and is equal to 0 when Back% is False.

The DeQue function removes an item from either end of the queue and returns that item via the argument of parameter X. The Boolean Front% parameter determines whether to dequeue an item from the front end (when the argument for Front% is True) or from the back end (when the argument for Front% is False). In either case, the procedure uses the Remove Item method to remove the dequeued data. The argument for RemoveItem is equal to 0 when Front% is True and is equal to Q.ListCount − 1 when Back% is False.

The queue can store either simple variable-length strings or the fields (or their string images) of a user-defined type. Since the queue operations do not include searching and sorting, the information for mapping the queue members is not significant to the queue operations themselves.

The queue test program

Let's look at a program to test the basic queue operations. I wrote the next program to demonstrate these operations. For the sake of demonstration I made the list box visible. You may choose to make the list box invisible; changing the visibility of the list box does not affect the operations of the test program. If you add to the routines in module QUEUE.BAS, then this program can also serve as a starting point for your own test program.

The test program contains a list box that emulates the queue, an Input/Output text box, labels, and a collection of command buttons. The command buttons allow you to exit, enqueue data, dequeue data, clear the queue, and select the other end to enqueue or dequeue data. The latter command button has the caption INV. Normally, when you click on the EnQue button you insert the string in the text box at the back end of the queue. If you click on the INV button and then click on the EnQue button, you insert the contents of the text box at the front end of the queue. The INV button works in a similar way with the DeQue button. Normally, when you click on the DeQue button you remove an item from the front end of the queue. Using the INV button, the DeQue button removes an item from the back end of the queue. The text box is used to supply strings for enqueued data. The text box also receives dequeued strings.

Figures 4-1 to 4-3 contain the specifications for the TSQUE.MAK project file and the TSQUE.FRM form file and its controls. Figure 4-4 shows a sample session with the queue test program.

Application name: Stack test program
Application code name: TSQUE

Version: 1.0   Date created: August 13, 1991
Programmer(s): Namir Clement Shammas

List of filenames

Storage path: \ VB \ VBXTOOL
Project   TSQUE.MAK
Global   GLOBAL.BAS
Form 1   TSQUE.FRM
Module 1   GENERIC.BAS
Module 2   QUEUE.BAS

4-1 The basic specifications for the TSQUE.MAK project file.

Form #1   Form filename: TSQUE.FRM
Version: 1.0   Date: August 13, 1991

Control object type	Default CtlName	Purpose
Command button	Command1	Exits the test program
	Command2	Enqueues an item
	Command3	Dequeues an item
	Command4	INVerse operation button
	Command5	Clears the queue
Text box	Text1	Input/Output text box
List box	List1	Visible queue emulator
Label	Label1	Front end label
	Label2	Back end label
	Label3	Text box label

4-2 The list of controls in the TSQUE.FRM form file.

Application (code) name: TSQUE
Form #1
Version: 1.0   Date:August 13, 1991

Original control name	Property	New setting
Form	Caption	Queue Test Program
Command1	CtlName	QuitBtn
	Caption	&Quit
Command2	CtlName	EnQueBtn
	Caption	&EnQue
Command3	CtlName	DeQueBtn
	Caption	&DeQue
Command4	CtlName	INVBtn
	Caption	&INV
Command5	CtlName	ClearBtn
	Caption	&Clear

4-3 The customized settings for the TSQUE.FRM form.

Original control name	Property	New setting
Text1	CtlName	TextBox
	Text	(empty string)
List1	CtlName	QueLbl
Label1	CtlName	FrontLbl
	Caption	The Front End
Label2	CtlName	BackLbl
	Caption	The Back End
Label3	CtlName	IOLbl
	Caption	Input/Output Text Box

4-3 Continued.

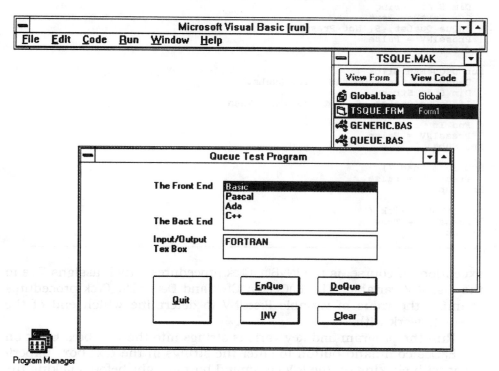

4-4 A sample session with the queue test program.

Listing 4-2 shows the code attached to the TSQUE.FRM form. The event-handling procedures contain code that triggers the queue manipulation procedures in the GENERIC.BAS module. Of interest is the variable PressINV declared in the general declarations section. This variable is initialized by the Form_Load procedure to False. The majority of the procedures that handle the Click events assign False to the PressINV variable. The

Listing 4-2 The code attached to the TSQUE.FRM form.

```
Const True = -1, False = 0
Dim PressINV As Integer

Sub QuitBtn_Click ()
   End
End Sub

Sub ClearBtn_Click ()
   ClearList QueLst
   PressINV = False
End Sub

Sub TextBox_GotFocus ()
   HighlightTextBox TextBox
End Sub

Sub EnQueBtn_Click ()
' Enque a data item in the queue QueLst
   Dim S As String
   S = TextBox.Text
   EnQue QueLst, S, Not PressINV
   PressINV = False
End Sub

Sub DeQueBtn_Click ()
' Deque an item from the queue QueLst
   Dim S As String
   If DeQue(QueLst, S, Not PressINV) Then
      TextBox.Text = S
   End If
   PressINV = False
End Sub

Sub Form_Load ()
   PressINV = False
End Sub

Sub INVBtn_Click ()
   PressINV = True
End Sub
```

exception, of course, is the INVBtn_Click procedures which assigns True to the PressINV variable. The EnQueBtn_Click and DeQueBtn_Click procedures examine the value of variable PressINV to determine which end of the queue to work with.

Run the program and key various strings into the text box. Click on the EnQue command button to enter the strings in the text box. Experiment with clicking on the INV command button right before clicking the EnQue button, and watch where the new data item is inserted.

Use the DeQue command button to remove data from the queue. The removed items appear in the text box. Experiment with clicking the INV button just before you click the DeQue button; the data item will be removed from the back end and appear in the text box.

5
Dynamic arrays

Visual Basic supports dynamic arrays that can be resized and retyped. However, these dynamic arrays lose their contents when they are resized. To resize a dynamic array and maintain its data usually requires a second dynamic array that stores the data of the main dynamic array while it is being redimensioned. Once the main dynamic array is resized, it restores its data from the second array. This is a typical technique used to perform a nondestructive resizing of a dynamic array. The Visual Basic list box control, however, is able to emulate dynamic arrays that can be expanded *without* losing their data. In fact, the emulated dynamic arrays do not require you to declare any dimension size, since they expand as needed during run time. This chapter presents a module that uses a list box to implement the basic operations of a dynamic array.

Basic array operations

The basic operations of any kind of array include storing and recalling array elements. All other operations build upon these. The list of the basic and important operations for a dynamic array are:

- Storing data in a dynamic array element. This operation may require expansion of the array if the specified index exceeds the current highest index.
- Recalling data from an array element. The index of the sought element must be in the range of 0 to ListCount − 1.
- Swapping two array elements. The indices of the swapped elements must be in the range of 0 to ListCount − 1.

- Sorting the array. The elements of the dynamic array are ordered by using a portion or all of the characters of an element.
- Searching for an array element. This operation can use a binary search procedure if the array is sorted. If the array is not sorted, the search uses a linear method.
- Writing the array elements to a text file. Each array member is written on a separate text line. This allows you to edit, change, add, and delete array elements using your favorite text editor.
- Reading the array elements from a text file. These elements either overwrite or merge with the elements of the current dynamic array.

The data stored in the dynamic arrays can be either simple variable-length strings or strings that store the fields of a user-defined type. Because the dynamic array operations include searching and sorting, the information for mapping the array members is very significant to the array operations.

The DYNARR.BAS module

The procedures that support the dynamic arrays are located in the GENERIC.BAS and the DYNARR.BAS modules. The GENERIC.BAS module contains procedures and functions that allow you to sort dynamic arrays and search for array elements. The DYNARR.BAS module offers procedures to store, recall, and swap array elements. Listing 5-1 shows the code of the DYNARR.BAS module. Its routines are described next.

Listing 5-1   The code in the DYNARR.BAS module.

```
Sub StoreInArray (A As Control, ByVal X$, ByVal I%)
' Store string X$ at the I% index of array A.
' The arguments for I% range from 0 to 32767.
' The dynamic array is automatically expanded if
' i >= A.ListCount.
  Dim N As Integer
  Dim J As Integer
  If I% > -1 Then
    ' get the highest index
    N = A.ListCount - 1
    ' does I% exceed the highest index?
    If I% > N Then
      ' Expand dynamic array
      For J = N + 1 To I%
        A.AddItem "", J
      Next J
    End If
    A.List(I%) = X$
  End If
End Sub

Function RecallFromArray (A As Control, ByVal I%) As String
' Recall element at index I%.  The values for I% range from
' 0 to array_size-1.  If the argument of I% is out of range,
' the function returns an empty string.
  If (I% > -1) And (I% < A.ListCount) Then
```

Listing 5-1   Continued.

```
      RecallFromArray = A.List(I%)
   Else
      RecallFromArray = ""
   End If
End Function

Sub SwapArrayElems (A As Control, ByVal I%, ByVal J%)
' Swap elements I% and J% of the dynamic array.  Both
' indices must be within the range 0 to A.ListCount-1.
   Dim X As String
   Dim N As Integer
   N = A.ListCount - 1
   ' is I% out of range?
   If (I% < 0) Or (I% > N) Then Exit Sub
   ' is J% out of range?
   If (J% < 0) Or (J% > N) Then Exit Sub
   ' are I% and J% different?
   If (I% <> J%) Then
      ' swap the elements at indices I% and J%
      X = A.List(I%)
      A.List(I%) = A.List(J%)
      A.List(J%) = X
   End If
End Sub
```

The StoreInArray procedure stores the string X$ at the I% element of the dynamic array A. The valid range for the arguments of I% is 0 to 32,767. The procedure verifies that the index I% is not negative, obtains the current highest index of the dynamic array A. If the specified index I% exceeds the current highest index, the procedure expands the array by adding elements with empty strings. Finally, it stores the string X$ in the I% element of the array.

The RecallFromArray function returns the string stored at the index I%. The valid range for the arguments of I% is 0 to 32,767. If the argument for I% is in the range of 0 to A.ListCount − 1, the function returns the corresponding element. Otherwise, it returns an empty string.

The SwapArrayElems swaps the elements I% and J% of the dynamic array A. The procedure verifies that the arguments for both I% and J% are within the valid range. The corresponding elements are swapped when the arguments for I% and J% are not equal.

The dynamic array test program

Using the procedures from the GENERIC.BAS and the DYNARR.BAS modules, let's build a test program for the dynamic arrays. The program contains several important controls.

A visible list box emulates the dynamic array. An Input/Output text box is used to type strings and save them in the array. The text box is also used to display array members that are recalled.

Two text boxes store the primary index I and the secondary index J. The primary index is used in storing, recalling, and swapping array elements. The secondary index is used only in swapping elements.

Two vertical scroll bars allow you to quickly change the values of the primary and secondary indices. Each vertical scroll bar has the default value range of 0 to 32,767. This happens to be the same range of dynamic arrays.

A number of command buttons are used to store, recall, swap, and search for elements; sort the dynamic array; write the array to a text file; read the array from a text file; and exit the test program.

When you select an element and double click, the index of that element appears in the Index I text box and the string of the selected element is copied into the Input/Output text box.

Application name: Dynamic array test program
Application code name: TSDYNARR

Version: 1.0   Date created: August 13, 1991
Programmer(s): Namir Clement Shammas

List of filenames

Storage path: \ VB \ VBXTOOL
Project   TSDYNARR.MAK
Global   GLOBAL.BAS
Form 1   TSDYNARR.FRM
Module 1   GENERIC.BAS
Module 2   DYNARR.BAS

5-1   The basic specifications for the TSDYNARR.MAK project file.

Form # 1   Form filename: TSDYNARR.FRM
Version: 1.0   Date: August 13, 1991

Control object type	Default CtlName	Purpose
Command button	Command1	Stores an element in the array
	Command2	Recalls an array element
	Command3	Swaps two array elements
	Command4	Writes the array to a text file
	Command5	Sorts the array elements
	Command6	Search for an array element
	Command7	Exits the test program
	Command8	Reads the array elements from a file
Text box	Text1	Input/Output text box
	Text2	Maintains the first Index I
	Text3	Maintains the second index J
Vertical scroll bar	VScroll1	Scroll bar for Text2
	VScroll2	Scroll bar for Text3
List box	List1	Dynamic array emulator
Label	Label1	Label for the dynamic array
	Label2	Label for the Input/Output text box
	Label3	Label for Index I text box
	Label4	Label for Index J text box

5-2   The list of controls in the TSDYNARR.FRM form file.

Figures 5-1 to 5-3 show the specifications for the TSDYNARR.MAK project file and the TSDYNARR.FRM form file. Figure 5-4 shows a sample session with the dynamic array test program.

Application (code) name: TSDYNARR
Form # 1
Version: 1.0   Date: August 13, 1991

Original control name	Property	New setting
Form	CtlName	Test Dynamic Arrays
Command1	CtlName	StoreBtn
	Caption	&Store
Command2	CtlName	RecallBtn
	Caption	&Recall
Command3	CtlName	SwapBtn
	Caption	Swa&p
Command4	CtlName	WriteBtn
	Caption	&Write
Command5	CtlName	SortBtn
	Caption	S&ort
Command6	CtlName	SearchBtn
	Caption	S&earch
Command7	CtlName	QuitBtn
	Caption	&Quit
Command8	CtlName	ReadBtn
	Caption	Rea&d
Text1	CtlName	TextBox
	Text	(empty string)
Text2	CtlName	IBox
	Text	(empty string)
Text3	CtlName	JBox
	Text	(empty string)
VScroll1	CtlName	IScl
VScroll2	CtlName	JScl
List1	CtlName	ArrayLst
Label1	CtlName	ArrayLbl
	Caption	Array
Label2	CtlName	IOLbl
	Caption	Input/Output
Label3	CtlName	IndexILbl
	Caption	Index I
Label4	CtlName	IndexJLbl
	Caption	Index J

5-3 The customized settings for the TSDYNARR.FRM form.

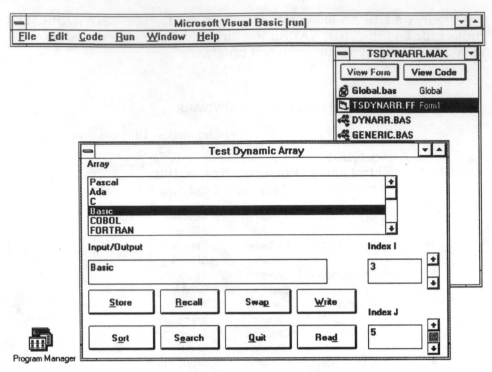

5-4 A sample session with the dynamic array test program.

Listing 5-2 contains the code attached to the TSDYNARR.FRM form. The form contains a declaration of the IsSorted variable. This variable keeps track of the order-status of the array. The Form_Load procedure initializes the IsSorted variable to False.

Listing 5-2 The code attached to the TSDYNARR.FRM form.

```
Const True = -1, False = 0

Dim IsSorted As Integer
Dim Filename As String

Sub StoreBtn_Click ()
' Store the contents of the text box in dynamic array.
' The Index I box provides the storage index
  Dim I As Integer
  Dim X As String
  If TextBox.Text <> "" And IBox.Text <> "" Then
    ' obtain the storage index
    I = Val(IBox.Text)
    ' obtain the data to store
    X = TextBox.Text
    ' store the data in the dynamic array
    StoreInArray ArrayLst, X, I
    IsSorted = False ' clear sort flag
```

Listing 5-2 Continued.

```
      End If
End Sub

Sub QuitBtn_Click ()
   End
End Sub

Sub RecallBtn_Click ()
' Recall an array element.  The Index I text box provides
' the index of the rcalled element.  That element is
' appears in the text box.
   Dim I As Integer
    ' is there something in the Index I text box?
   If IBox.Text <> "" Then
      ' obtain the index from the Index I text box
      I = Val(IBox.Text)
      ' Put the recalled element in the text box
      TextBox.Text = RecallFromArray(ArrayLst, I)
   End If
End Sub

Sub SwapBtn_Click ()
' Swap the elements of the dynamic array.  The Index I
' box and the Index J box provide the indices of the
' swapped elements.
   Dim I As Integer
   Dim J As Integer
    ' is there something in both index boxes
   If (IBox.Text <> "") And (JBox.Text <> "") Then
      ' get the index of Index I text box
      I = Val(IBox.Text)
      ' get the index of Index J text box
      J = Val(JBox.Text)
      ' swap the elements
      SwapArrayElems ArrayLst, I, J
      IsSorted = False ' clear the sort flag
   End If
End Sub

Sub Form_Load ()
   IsSorted = False ' set sort flag to false
    ' assign the default data filename
   Filename = "\vb\vbxtool\tsdynarr.dat"
End Sub

Sub SortBtn_Click ()
' sort the dynamic array
    ' is the array unordered?
   If Not IsSorted Then
      ' use the Combsort method
      CombSort ArrayLst, 1
      IsSorted = True ' array is now sorted
   End If
End Sub

Sub SearchBtn_Click ()
' Search the array for a string that matches the contents
' of the text box.
   Dim S As String
   Dim I As Integer
    ' Is there something to search for?
   If TextBox.Text <> "" Then
      S = TextBox.Text
      ' Is the array sorted?
      If IsSorted Then
         ' use the binary search function
```

Listing 5-2 Continued.

```
      I = BinSearch(ArrayLst, S, 1, 1, 0)
    Else
      ' use the linear search function
      I = LinSearch(ArrayLst, S, 1, True, 1, 0)
    End If
    ' ease the contents of the Index I box
    IBox.Text = Format$(I, "")
  End If
End Sub

Sub ArrayLst_DblClick ()
' Recall the index and content of the selected element
  IBox.Text = Format$(ArrayLst.ListIndex, "")
  TextBox.Text = ArrayLst.Text
End Sub

Sub TextBox_GotFocus ()
  HighlightTextBox TextBox
End Sub

Sub IBox_GotFocus ()
  HighlightTextBox IBox
End Sub

Sub JBox_GotFocus ()
  HighlightTextBox JBox
End Sub

Sub WriteBtn_Click ()
' Store the dynamic array in a text file.
  Dim S As String
  ' prompt for output filename
  S = InputBox$("Enter filename", "File Output", Filename)
  ' if the response is not Cancel
  If S <> "" Then
    Filename = S
    ' write the data to the file
    If Not WriteList(ArrayLst, Filename) Then
      MsgBox "File output error", 64, "I/O Error"
    End If
  End If
End Sub

Sub ReadBtn_Click ()
' Read the elements of a dynamic array from a text file.
' The previous elements are lost.
  Dim S As String
  Dim OK As Integer
  S = InputBox$("Enter filename", "File Input", Filename)
  If S <> "" Then
    Filename = S
    If Not ReadList(ArrayLst, Filename, False) Then
      MsgBox "Error in reading data file", 64, "I/O Error"
    End If
    IsSorted = Not OK
  End If
End Sub

Sub IScl_Change ()
  IBox.Text = Format$(IScl.Value, "")
End Sub

Sub JScl_Change ()
  JBox.Text = Format$(JScl.Value, "")
End Sub
```

The form contains a number of relevant procedures. The StoreBtn_Click procedure stores the contents of the Input/Output text box in the dynamic array. The Index I text box provides the index of the target array element. The procedure verifies that neither text box is empty before storing the sought element. The procedure converts the contents of the Index I text box into the storage index. If the Index I text box does not contain the string image of a properly formatted number, the Val function returns a value of 0. The contents of the Input/Output text box are stored in the local variable X. The procedure then calls the StoreInArray procedure to store the characters of the string variable X at element I of array A. Because storing a new element in an array will corrupt the existing order of the array, the StoreBtn _Click procedure assigns False to the IsSorted variable.

The RecallBtn_Click procedure recalls the array element whose index is specified in the Index I text box. The procedure first ensures that the Index I text box is not empty. If this condition is true, the procedure converts the string in the text box to a numeric index. This index is used in calling the RecallFromArray function and storing the function result into the Input/Output text box. Because recalling an array element does not disturb the existing order of the array, the procedure does not assign any new value to the IsSorted variable.

The SwapBtn_Click procedure swaps the array elements whose indices are indicated by the two index text boxes. The procedure first makes sure that both index text boxes are not empty. Then the procedure converts the string in the index text boxes to numeric indices. Next, the procedure invokes the SwapArrayElems procedure to swap the two elements. Swapping elements will disturb the existing order of the array, so the procedure assigns False to the IsSorted variable.

The Form_Load procedure initializes the program by assigning False to the IsSorted variable and assigning \ vb \ vbxtool \ tsdynarr.dat to the variable Filename.

The SortBtn_Click procedure sorts the array. The procedure performs the sorting only if the IsSorted variable is False; this prevents the unnecessary sorting of an already ordered array. The CombSort procedure is invoked to order the array. You can replace this procedure with either the QuickSort or the ShellSort procedure. This change allows you to get an idea of the actual speed of each sorting method. Because the test program stores variable-length strings, the argument for the St& parameter of CombSort is 1. Consequently, the entire string of an array element is used as the sort key.

The SearchBtn_Click procedure searches for the array element that matches the contents of the Input/Output text box. The search is case-sensitive and compares the entire characters of the array members and the Input/Output text box. The procedure uses the IsSorted variable to determine whether to call the binary search function (for sorted arrays) or the linear search function (for unordered arrays). The index returned by either search function appears in the Index I text box.

The ArrayLst_DblClick procedure retrieves the index and contents of the selected element. The index appears in the Index I text box, whereas the string of the selected element appears in the Input/Output text box.

The WrittenBtn_Click procedure writes the elements of the dynamic array to a text file. A dialog box appears with the current default filename, obtained from the Filename variable. If you accept the default or edited filename, the procedure invokes the WriteList function to write the array to the file Filename. If the WriteList function returns False, a message box appears to inform you that there was an error in the file operation. This error may be attributed either to supplying a bad or invalid filename or to a write error, like one resulting from a full disk.

The ReadBtn_Click procedure reads the elements of the dynamic array from a text file. A dialog box appears with the current default filename, obtained from the variable Filename. If you accept the default or edited filename, the procedure invokes the ReadList function to read the array from the file Filename. If the ReadList function returns False, a message box appears to inform you that there was an error in the file operation. This error may be attributed either to supplying a bad or invalid filename or to a read error.

The IScl_Change procedure writes the current value of the IScl vertical scroll to the Index I text box. The JScl_Change procedure writes the current value of the JScl vertical scroll to the Index J text box.

Run the test program to experiment with the various aspects of dynamic arrays. The companion disk includes the TSDYNARR.DAT file, which contains a small sample dynamic array. The unordered array contains the name of programing languages. Click on the Read button to read the array from the above data file. This step quickly provides you with a nucleus array that you can manipulate further. Experiment with sorting the array, searching for particular elements, and recalling elements. You can also swap elements or store new ones. You can either type in the indices or use the vertical scroll bars. In addition, you can double click on an array member. This operation results in putting the index of the selected member in the Index I text box, while the data in the selected member appears in the input/output text box.

When you have finished working with the program you may want to save the updated array by clicking on the Write command button. You can use the default filename or type in a new one. Exit the program by clicking on the Quit button.

6
Sparse arrays

Chapter 5 presented dynamic arrays that are implemented using list box controls. These arrays do not need a declared dimension size, since they expand as needed during run time. However, these arrays have two limitations. The first is that their upper index range cannot exceed 32,767. The second limitation is that they may contain blocks of elements with empty strings. Such blocks appear when you store data in a high index in a non-sequential manner. For example, you might store data in elements 0, 1, 2, and then 1000. This creates a block of elements in the index range of 3 to 999 that store empty strings. The space occupied by this block is wasted, especially if you never need to use these array elements.

This situation actually describes a *sparse array*, in which the meaningful data is scattered in noncontiguous array elements. The Visual Basic list box can be used to implement a sparse array. This chapter briefly discusses sparse arrays and presents the Visual Basic module that implements the basic sparse array operations.

The basics of sparse arrays

When you store data in a normal array, you typically insert data gradually starting at the element with the lowest index. This data storage scheme creates two regions in the array. The first is made up of the leading elements that store the data you have inserted so far, the second is made up of the trailing elements that have not yet been used. Figure 6-1 shows a normal array with these two regions. When you first create an array, it has only unused elements. Once you start storing data in the array, you create the two regions. If the array is deliberately oversized, so that the actual number of data items to be stored is less than the available space, the two

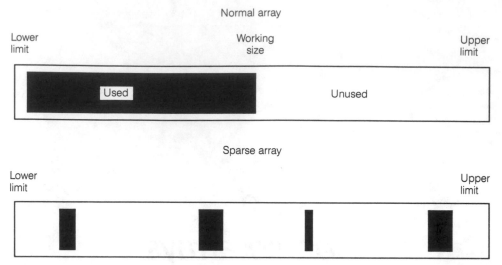

6-1 A typical normal and a sparse array.

regions will always exist. By contrast, if the size of the array is exactly matched to the number of data items, the second region eventually disappears.

Figure 6-1 also shows a sparse array. The used elements have a dark background. Notice that the elements of a sparse array are scattered—there are multiple regions of unused elements. To avoid wasting space by storing the unused regions, sparse arrays should be stored in special data structures that eliminate the unused regions. The Visual Basic list box control offers a suitable structure for emulating sparse arrays.

☞   To store the elements of a sparse array in a contiguous sequence, you need to store the indices along with the sparse array data. I will call these indices the *existing* indices, since they refer to existing sparse array elements. Moreover, the sparse array elements should be stored in the order of ascending (or descending) indices. This scheme enables the use of a binary search procedure to quickly determine whether or not an array element with a specific index exists.

Basic sparse array operations

Visual Basic allows you to use list box controls to implement sparse arrays that have an index range of 0 to 2,147,483,648. The limitations on sparse arrays are that you cannot store more than 32,768 elements, and you cannot exceed the storage capacity of a list box control.

I mentioned in the last section that the index of the sparse array must be stored with the data. In chapter 2, I discussed how to pack the fields of a user-defined type in a string-typed list member. The same technique applies here. Since the upper limit of the sparse array index is

2,147,483,648, a 10-character string is required. The general format for storing a sparse array element in a list box member is:

DDDDDDDDDDSSSSSSSSSSSSSSSSSS...SS

where D represents a numeric character (0 to 9), and S represents the string characters. Sparse arrays can store simple variable-length strings or strings that contain user-defined data fields. In the latter case, you need to take into account that the character indices for the string images of the data fields must be increased by 10, the size of the sparse array index.

The basic operations of sparse arrays are:

- Storing data in an element whose index is specified. The index is converted into a string image using the 0000000000 string format. If there is already an element with the same specified index, that element must be first removed before inserting the new data. Elements of a sparse array are stored according to ascending indices.
- Recalling data from an element whose index is specified. If the sought element does not exist, the operation returns an empty string.
- Visiting the first and next members. These operations sequentially retrieve the data stored in a list box control and yield both the index and the data of each accessed array member. If the data contains string images of user-defined types, then further processing is needed to produce the information in a useable form.

🕱 **Warning!** If you need to maintain the elements of the sparse array in an ascending or a descending order, you need to use a separate array of indices. You must **not** use the sorting procedures found in the GENERIC.BAS module.

The SPARRAY.BAS module

The basic sparse array operations described in the previous section are implemented in the SPARRAY.BAS module, as shown in Listing 6-1. The general declarations section defines the constant SP_INDEX as the string format for the array indices, and declares the VisitIndex variable, which maintains the index of the visited list box member. This index is different from the indices of the sparse array members. The procedures of the SPARRAY.BAS module follow.

The CreateSparseArray procedure clears the list box control that emulates the sparse array.

The StoreInSpArray procedure stores the string X$ at the index I& of the sparse array A. The procedure obtains the string image of the index I& and stores it in the local string variable Idx. Then it checks whether the sparse array is empty. If the array is empty, the string X$ is inserted as the first

Listing 6-1   The code in the SPARRAY.BAS module.

```
Const True = -1, False = 0
Const SP_INDEX = "00000000000"

Dim VisitIndex As Integer

Sub CreateSparseArray (A As Control)
  ClearList A ' clear list emulating the sparse array
End Sub

Sub StoreInSpArray (A As Control, ByVal X$, ByVal I&)
' store item X$ in the index I& of the sparse array A
  Dim Idx As String
  Dim J As Integer
  ' get the string image of the index
  Idx = Format$(I&, SP_INDEX)
  ' is array not empty?
  If A.ListCount > 0 Then
    ' search for candidate array index that may contain
    ' the same spare array index
    J = BinLocate(A, Idx, 1, Len(Idx))
    ' is there a matching index?
    If Idx = Mid$(A.List(J), 1, Len(Idx)) Then
      ' remove old item
      A.RemoveItem J
      ' insert element X$ in sparse array
      A.AddItem Idx + X$, J
    ElseIf Idx < Mid$(A.List(J), 1, Len(Idx)) Then
      ' insert element X$ before A.List(J)
      A.AddItem Idx + X$, J
    Else
      ' insert element X$ after A.List(J)
      A.AddItem Idx + X$, J + 1
    End If
  Else
    ' insert sparse array element as the first list member
    A.AddItem Idx + X$, 0
  End If
End Sub

Function RecallFromSpArray (A As Control, ByVal I&) As String
' Recall the element I& of the sparse array A.  If the sought
' element is not in the sparse array, an empty string is
' returned.
  Dim Idx As String
  Dim Index As Integer
  ' get the string image of the index
  Idx = Format$(I&, SP_INDEX)
  ' search for the sought element using the string
  ' image of the index
  Index = BinSearch(A, Idx, 1, 1, Len(Idx))
  If Index > -1 Then ' Found a match?
    ' Yes!  Return the array element
    RecallFromSpArray = Mid$(A.List(Index), Len(Idx) + 1)
  Else
    ' No! Return an empty string
    RecallFromSpArray = ""
  End If
End Function

Function GetVisitIndex () As Integer
' Return the value of the module-level variable VisitIndex
  GetVisitIndex = VisitIndex
End Function
```

Listing 6-1 Continued.

```
Sub SetVisitIndex (ByVal NewVisitIndex%)
' Sets the value of the module-level variable VisitIndex
  VisitIndex = NewVisitIndex
End Sub

Function VisitFirstSpArrayElem (A As Control, X$, I&) As Integer
' Visits the first member of the sparse array and
' obtains its index and data
  Dim Elem As String
  ' is array not empty?
  If A.ListCount > 0 Then
    VisitIndex = 0 ' set the VisitIndex
    Elem = A.List(0) ' get the first element
    ' extract the index and string of the first array element
    GetSpArrayElemData Elem, I&, X$
    ' return a True function result
    VisitFirstSpArrayElem = True
  Else
    ' the values assigned to I& and X$ are meaningless
    I& = 0
    X$ = ""
    ' return a False function result
    VisitFirstSpArrayElem = False
  End If
End Function

Function VisitNextSpArrayElem (A As Control, X$, I&) As Integer
' Visits the next member of the sparse array and
' obtains its index and data
  Dim Elem As String
  ' Is VisitIndex in the valid range?
  If VisitIndex < (A.ListCount - 1) Then
    VisitIndex = VisitIndex + 1 ' increment the visit index
    Elem = A.List(VisitIndex) ' get the sought element
    ' extract the index and string of the sought array element
    GetSpArrayElemData Elem, I&, X$
    ' return a True function result
    VisitNextSpArrayElem = True
  Else
    ' the values assigned to I& and X$ are meaningless
    I& = 0
    X$ = ""
    ' return a False function result
    VisitNextSpArrayElem = False
  End If
End Function

Sub GetSpArrayElemData (ByVal SpArrayElem$, I&, X$)
' Extract the index and string from a string
' representing the selected text of a sparse array
  I& = Val(Mid$(SpArrayElem$, 1, Len(SP_INDEX)))
  X$ = Mid$(SpArrayElem$, Len(SP_INDEX) + 1)
End Sub

Function SearchSpArray (A As Control, ByVal X$, ByVal Occur%, ByVal
CaseSense%, ByVal St&, ByVal Size&) As Integer
' searches the sparse array A for Occur% occurrence of the
' string X$.  The St& and Size& parameters determine the
' portions of the sparse array data that are included in
' the search
  SearchSpArray = LinSearch(A, X$, Occur%, CaseSense%, St&, Size&)
End Function
```

member in the list box. If the array is not empty, the procedure invokes the BinLocate function to obtain the list box index for inserting the string X$.

If the list box index contains an array member with index I&, the routine removes that list box member before inserting the new data. If the list box index does not contain a member with the index I&, the procedure inserts string X$ at that list member or immediately after it, depending on how the variable Idx compares with the string image of the target list box member.

The RecallFromSpArray function recalls the sparse array element at index I&. The function obtains the string image of the index I& and uses it to search for a matching index string image. The function invokes the Bin Search function to determine whether or not there is an element with the specified string image index. The function returns the data of the sought element, or an empty string if that element does not exist.

The Boolean VisitFirstSpArrayElem function visits the first member of the list box control. The function returns True if the list box emulating the sparse array is not empty, otherwise, the function returns False. The parameters X$ and I& return the data and index, respectively, of the sparse array stored in A.List(0). If the function result is False, the values returned by these parameters are meaningless. The VisitFirstSpArrayElem function invokes the GetSpArrayElemData routine to extract the values for the X$ and I& parameters. The function sets the VisitIndex variable to 0, preparing it for subsequent calls to function VisitNextSpArrayElem.

The Boolean VisitNextSpArrayElem function visits the next member of the list box control. The function returns True if variable VisitIndex has not exceeded the highest current index of the list box emulating the sparse array; otherwise, it returns False. The parameters X$ and I& return the data and index, respectively, of the sparse array stored in A.List(VisitIndex). If the function result is False, the values returned by these parameters are meaningless. The VisitNextSpArrayElem function invokes the GetSpArrayElemData routine to extract the values for the X$ and I& parameters. The function increments the variable VisitIndex to index the next list box member.

The GetVisitIndex function returns the value stored in the VisitIndex variable. The SetVisitIndex procedure assigns the value of its argument, NewVisitIndex, to the VisitIndex variable. This procedure enables you to revisit specific elements without having to reset the value of VisitIndex by calling the VisitFirst SpArrayElem and VisitNextSpArrayElem routines.

☠ **Warning!**   The purpose of the GetVisitIndex function and the SetVisitIndex procedure is to enable you to alternately visit multiple sparse arrays. The following steps are used for this operation:

- Begin visiting each sparse array by calling the function VisitFirstSp ArrayElem.
- Inspect the next array of the same sparse array using the function VisitNextSpArrayElem.

- Switch from one sparse array to another by using the GetVisitIndex function to store the contents of the variable VisitIndex in a separate variable. There is only one instance of the VisitIndex variable.
- Then use the SetVisitIndex procedure to restore the appropriate value of VisitIndex for the other sparse array. This step is needed only if you are visiting the next element of the other sparse array.

Warning! Use the SetVisitIndex routine with care. Passing incorrect arguments throws off the inspection of array elements.

The GetSpArrayElemData procedure extracts the index and string from a string representing the selected text of a sparse array. The SearchSpArray function searches for the specified occurrence of the string X$. The parameters St& and Size& specify the portion of an array element that are compared with the X$. The Boolean CaseSense% parameter determines whether or not the search is case-sensitive.

The sparse array test program

I modified the dynamic array test program to obtain a similar test program for the sparse array. This test program uses the procedures from the GENERIC.BAS and the SPARRAY.BAS modules.

The program contains several controls. A visible list box emulates the sparse array. An Input/Output text box is used to type in strings and save them in the sparse array, and to display array members that are recalled. An Index text box displays the selected index string, and a number of command buttons are used. These buttons store, recall, and visit the array elements; clear the sparse array; write the sparse array to a text file; read the array from a text file; and exit the test program.

When you select an element and double click, the index of that element appears in the Index I text box, and the string of the selected element is copied into the Input/Output text box.

Figures 6-2 to 6-4 show the specifications for the TSSPARR.MAK project file and the TSSPARR.FRM form file. Figure 6-5 shows a sample session with the sparse array test program. Listing 6-2 contains the code attached to the TSSPARR.FRM form. A description of this form's procedures and functions follows.

The StoreBtn_Click procedure stores the contents of the Input/Output text box in the sparse array. The Index I text box provides the index of the target array element. The procedure verifies that neither text box is empty before storing the element. The procedure converts the contents of the Index I text box into the storage index. If the Index I text box does not contain the string image of a properly formatted number, the Val function returns a value of 0. The contents of the Input/Output text box are stored in the local variable X. The procedure then calls the StoreInSpArray procedure to store the characters of the string variable X at element I of the sparse array A.

Application name: Sparse array test program
Application code name: TSSPARR

Version: 1.0   Date created: August 14, 1991
Programmer(s): Namir Clement Shammas

List of filenames

Storage path: \VB\VBXTOOL
Project   TSSPARR.MAK
Global   GLOBAL.BAS
Form 1   TSSPARR.FRM
Module 1   GENERIC.BAS
Module 2   SPARRAY.BAS

6-2 The basic specifications for the TSSPARR.MAK project file.

Form # 1   Form filename: TSSPARR.FRM
Version: 1.0   Date: August 14, 1991

Control object type	Default CtlName	Purpose
Command button	Command1	Stores an element in the array
	Command2	Recalls an array element
	Command3	Clears the sparse array
	Command4	Writes the array to a text file
	Command5	Visits the first array element
	Command6	Visits the next array element
	Command7	Exits the test program
	Command8	Reads the array elements from a file
Text box	Text1	Input/Output text box
	Text2	Maintains the index I
List box	List1	Sparse array emulator
Label1	Label1	Label for the sparse array
	Label2	Label for the Input/Output text box
	Label3	Label for Index I text box

6-3 The list of controls in the TSSPARR.FRM form file.

Application (code) name: TSSPARR
Form # 1
Version: 1.0   Date: August 14, 1991

Original control name	Property	New setting
Form	CtlName	Test Sparse Arrays
Command1	CtlName	StoreBtn
	Caption	&Store
Command2	CtlName	RecallBtn
	Caption	&Recall

6-4 The customized settings for the TSSPARR.FRM form.

Original control name	Property	New setting
Command3	CtlName	ClearBtn
	Caption	&Clear
Command4	CtlName	WriteBtn
	Caption	&Write
Command5	CtlName	VisitFirstBtn
	Caption	Visit &First
Command6	CtlName	VisitNextBtn
	Caption	Visit &Next
Command7	CtlName	QuitBtn
	Caption	&Quit
Command8	CtlName	ReadBtn
	Caption	Rea&d
Text1	CtlName	TextBox
	Text	(empty string)
Text2	CtlName	IBox
	Text	(empty string)
List1	CtlName	ArrayLst
Label1	CtlName	ArrayLbl
	Caption	Sparse Array
Label2	CtlName	IOLbl
	Caption	Input/Output
Label3	CtlName	IndexILbl
	Caption	Index I

6-4 Continued.

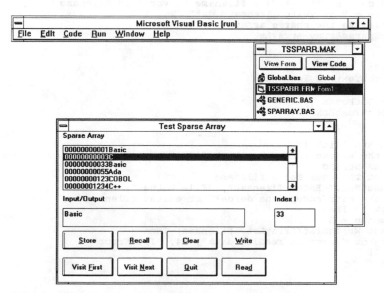

6-5 A sample session with the sparse array test program.

Listing 6-2 The code attached to the TSSPARR.FRM form.

```
Const True = -1, False = 0

Dim IsSorted As Integer
Dim Filename As String

Sub StoreBtn_Click ()
' Store the string in TextBox in the sparse array
  Dim I As Long
  Dim X As String
  ' does the Index I test box contain any text?
  If (TextBox.Text <> "") And (IBox.Text <> "") Then
    ' obtain the numeric index
    I = Val(IBox.Text)
    ' copy the string of the input/output text box into X
    X = TextBox.Text
    ' store X at element I of the sparse array
    StoreInSpArray ArrayLst, X, I
  End If
End Sub

Sub QuitBtn_Click ()
  End
End Sub

Sub RecallBtn_Click ()
' Recall an array element
  Dim I As Long
  ' doe sthe Index I text box contain any text?
  If IBox.Text <> "" Then
    ' obtain the numeric index
    I = Val(IBox.Text)
    ' store the recalled element in TextBox
    TextBox.Text = RecallFromSpArray(ArrayLst, I)
  End If
End Sub

Sub Form_Load ()
  ' asssign the default data filename to varibale Filename
  Filename = "\vb\vbxtool\tssparr.dat"
  ' initialize the sparse array
  CreateSparseArray ArrayLst
End Sub

Sub TextBox_GotFocus ()
  HighlightTextBox TextBox
End Sub
Sub IBox_GotFocus ()
  HighlightTextBox IBox
End Sub

Sub WriteBtn_Click ()
' Write the sparse array to a text file
  Dim S As String
  ' prompt the user for a filename
  S = InputBox$("Enter filename", "File Output", Filename)
  ' did the user accept the defualt or edited filename
  If S <> "" Then
    Filename = S
    If Not WriteList(ArrayLst, Filename) Then
      MsgBox "Error in reading data", 64, "I/O Error"
    End If
  End If
End Sub
```

Listing 6-2 Continued.

```
Sub ReadBtn_Click ()
' Read the the sparse array from a text file
   Dim S As String
   ' prompt for a filename
   S = InputBox$("Enter filename", "File Input", Filename)
   ' did the user accept the efualt or edited filename?
   If S <> "" Then
     Filename = S
     If Not ReadList(ArrayLst, Filename, False) Then
       MsgBox "Error in reading data", 64, "I/O Error"
     End If
   End If
End Sub

Sub VisitFirstBtn_Click ()
' Visit the first element of the sparse array and
' obtain the index and the data of that element
   Dim X As String
   Dim I As Long
   ' is there a first element to visit?
   If VisitFirstSpArrayElem(ArrayLst, X, I) Then
     ' copy the contents of X into TextBox
     TextBox.Text = X
     ' store the string image of index I in the Index I
     ' text box
     IBox.Text = Format$(I, "")
   Else
     ' clear the input/output and Index I text boxes
     TextBox.Text = ""
     IBox.Text = ""
   End If
End Sub

Sub VisitNextBtn_Click ()
   Dim X As String
   Dim I As Long
   ' is there another element to visit?
   If VisitNextSpArrayElem(ArrayLst, X, I) Then
     ' copy the contents of X into TextBox
     TextBox.Text = X
     ' store the string image of index I in the Index I
     ' text box
     IBox.Text = Format$(I, "")
   Else
     ' clear the input/output and Index I text boxes
     TextBox.Text = ""
     IBox.Text = ""
   End If
End Sub

Sub ClearBtn_Click ()
   ClearList ArrayLst
End Sub

Sub ArrayLst_DblClick ()
' Obtain the index and the data of the selected list item
   Dim X As String
   Dim S As String
   Dim I As Long
   ' is there a selected text?
   If ArrayLst.ListIndex > -1 Then
     S = ArrayLst.Text ' copy the selected text into S
     ' obtain the index I and the data X from S
     GetSpArrayElemData S, I, X
```

Listing 6-2 Continued.

```
    TextBox.Text = X ' write X to TextBox
    IBox.Text = Format$(I, "") ' write I to Index I text box
  End If

End Sub
```

The RecallBtn_Click procedure recalls the array element whose index is specified in the Index I text box. The procedure first checks that the Index I text box is not empty; if it is not, the procedure converts the string in the Index text box to a numeric index. This index is used in calling the RecallFrom SpArray function and in storing the function result in the Input/Output text box.

The ClearBtn_Click procedure clears the sparse array by invoking the ClearList procedure in module GENERIC.BAS.

The Form_Load procedure initializes the program by assigning the string \ vb \ vbxtool \ tssparr.dat to the variable Filename.

The WriteBtn_Click procedure writes the elements of the sparse array to a text file. A simple dialog box appears with the current default filename, which is stored in the variable Filename. If you accept the default or edited filename, the procedure invokes the WriteList function to write the array in the file Filename.

If the WriteList function returns False, a message box appears to inform you that there was an error in the file operation. This error may be caused by supplying an invalid filename, or by a write error, like one resulting from a full disk.

The ReadBtn_Click procedure reads the elements of the sparse array from a text file. A dialog box appears with the current default filename, obtained from the variable Filename. If you accept the default or edited filename, the procedure invokes the ReadList function to read the array from the file Filename. If the ReadList function returns False, a message box appears to inform you that there was an error in the file operation. This error may be caused by using an invalid filename, or by a read error.

The VisitFirstBtn_Click procedure visits the first sparse array element, invoking the function VisitFirstSpArrayElem. If the function returns True, the index and contents of the first sparse array element are displayed in the Input/Output and Index I text boxes, respectively. Otherwise, these boxes are cleared.

The VisitNextBtn_Click procedure visits the next sparse array element. The procedure invokes the function VisitNextSpArrayElem. If the function returns True, the index and contents of the first sparse array element are displayed in the Input/Output and Index I text boxes, respectively. If it returns False, these boxes are cleared.

The ArrayLst_DblClick procedure retrieves the index and contents of the selected sparse array element. The index appears in the Index I text box, and the selected element appears in the Input/Output text box.

Run the test program to experiment with the various aspects of sparse arrays. The companion disk includes the TSSPARR.DAT file, which contains a small sample sparse array containing the names of programming languages. Click on the Read button to read the array from the data file. This provides you with a nucleus array that you can further manipulate.

Experiment with visiting the array elements, and recalling elements. You can also store new elements in the array; try inserting data with new indices and then with currently used indices. In addition, double click on an array member. This operation results in putting the index of the selected member in the Index I text box, while the data in the selected member appears in the Input/Output text box.

When you are finished working with the program, you might want to save the updated array using the Write button. You can use the default filename or type in a new one. Finally, exit the program by clicking on the Quit button.

7
Sparse matrices

The previous chapter discussed sparse arrays. The same programming concepts and techniques can be expanded to two other similar data structures, sparse matrices and tables. This chapter discusses the sparse matrices and presents a module that implements the related procedures.

The basics of sparse matrices

Sparse matrices are extensions of sparse arrays, just as normal matrices are extensions of normal arrays. In fact sparse matrices are more commonly used than sparse arrays, because sparse matrices save a considerable amount of memory. For example, consider a matrix with 100 rows and 100 columns. If you only use 10 rows and 10 columns, you are saving the space of 9900 elements, calculated by $(100 * 100) - (10 * 10)$.

Storing a sparse matrix in a list box control requires the same approach as with a sparse array. The row and column indices of the sparse matrix are converted into string images. Both of these indices range from 0 to 2,147,483,648. The general form is:

    RRRRRRRRRR,CCCCCCCCCCSSSSSSSSSSSSSSS...SS

where the R represents the characters of the string image for the row index. Similarly, C depicts the characters of the string image for the column index, and S represents the characters for the matrix data. I have separated the R and C strings with a comma, which is optional and serves to enhance the readability of the string storing the sparse matrix. The string images for the row and column indices are 10 characters long. The string format 0000000000 is used to convert the matrix row or column to the required string image.

The basic operations of a sparse matrix are very similar to those of the sparse array, covered in chapter 6. The main difference is that you are dealing with two indices instead of one.

The SPMAT.BAS module

The SPMAT.BAS module exports the procedures that implement the sparse matrix. Listing 7-1 shows the code in the SPMAT.BAS module. The procedures in this module are very similar to the ones in the SPARRAY .BAS modules. In the SPMAT.BAS module, however, the various types of references to the sparse array are replaced with the sparse matrix. For example, the parameter A that represents a sparse array is replaced with the parameter M. Likewise, the name of the procedures reflect that you are dealing with a matrix and not an array. Another difference is that the procedures handle the row and column indices of the sparse matrix, and the sparse array Index I is replaced with the matrix parameters Row and Col.

Listing 7-1   The code in the SPMAT.BAS module.

```
Const True = -1, False = 0
Const SP_INDEX = "0000000000"

Dim VisitIndex As Integer

Sub CreateSparseMat (M As Control)
  CLearList M
End Sub

Sub StoreInSpMat (M As Control, ByVal X$, ByVal Row&, ByVal Col&)
' store item X$ in the index (Row&, Col&) of the sparse matrix M
  Dim Idx As String
  Dim J As Integer
  ' get the string image of the row and column indices
  Idx = Format$(Row&, SP_INDEX) + "," + Format$(Col&, SP_INDEX)
  ' is the matrix not empty?
  If M.ListCount > 0 Then
    ' search for candidate matrix indices that may contain
    ' the same sparse matrix row and column indices
    J = BinLocate(M, Idx, 1, Len(Idx))
    ' is there a matching index?
    If Idx = Mid$(M.List(J), 1, Len(Idx)) Then
      ' remove old item
      M.RemoveItem J
      ' insert new item
      M.AddItem Idx + X$, J
    ElseIf Idx < Mid$(M.List(J), 1, Len(Idx)) Then
      ' insert new item before M.List(J)
      M.AddItem Idx + X$, J
    Else
      ' insert new item after M.List(J)
      M.AddItem Idx + X$, J + 1
    End If
  Else
    ' insert new item as the first matrix member
    M.AddItem Idx + X$, 0
  End If
End Sub
```

Listing 7-1 Continued.

```
Function RecallFromSpMat (M As Control, ByVal Row&, ByVal Col&) As String
' Recall the element (Row&, Col&) of the sparse matrix M.  If the sought
' element is not in the sparse matrix, an empty string is
' returned.
  Dim Idx As String
  Dim Elem As String
  Dim Index As Integer
  ' get the string image of the row and column indices
  Idx = Format$(Row&, SP_INDEX) + "," + Format$(Col&, SP_INDEX)
  ' search for the sought element using the string
  ' image of the row and column indices
  Index = BinSearch(M, Idx, 1, 1, Len(Idx))
  If Index > -1 Then ' Found a match?
    ' Yes! Return the matrix element
    Elem = M.List(Index)
    RecallFromSpMat = Mid$(Elem, Len(Idx) + 1)
  Else
    ' No! Return an empty string
    RecallFromSpMat = ""
  End If
End Function


Function GetVisitIndex () As Integer
' Return the value of the module-level variable VisitIndex
  GetVisitIndex = VisitIndex
End Function


Sub SetVisitIndex (ByVal NewVisitIndex%)
' Sets the value of the module-level variable VisitIndex
  VisitIndex = NewVisitIndex
End Sub


Function VisitFirstSpMatElem (M As Control, X$, Row&, Col&) As Integer
' Visits the first member of the sparse matrix and
' obtains its indices and data
  Dim Elem As String
  Dim LenSP As Integer
  ' is the matrix not empty?
  If M.ListCount > 0 Then
    VisitIndex = 0 ' set the visit index
    LenSP = Len(SP_INDEX)
    Elem = M.List(0) ' get the first element
    ' extract the row and column indices, and the string
    ' of the first sparse matrix element
    GetSpMatElemData Elem, Row&, Col&, X$
    ' returns a True function result
    VisitFirstSpMatElem = True
  Else
    ' the values assigned to Row&, Col&, and X$ are meaningless
    Col& = 0
    Row& = 0
    X$ = ""
    ' return a False function result
    VisitFirstSpMatElem = False
  End If
End Function

Function VisitNextSpMatElem (M As Control, X$, Row&, Col&) As Integer
    ' Visits the next member of the sparse matrix and
    ' obtains its indices and data
    Dim Elem As String
    Dim LenSP As Integer
    ' are there more elements to visit?
    If VisitIndex < (M.ListCount - 1) Then
```

Listing 7-1 Continued.

```
      VisitIndex = VisitIndex + 1 ' increment the visit index
      LenSP = Len(SP_INDEX)
      Elem = M.List(VisitIndex) ' get the sought element
      ' extract the row nad column indices, and the string
      ' of the sought sparse matrix element
      GetSpMatElemData Elem, Row&, Col&, X$
      ' return a True function result
      VisitNextSpMatElem = True
   Else
      ' the values assigned to Row&, Col&, and X$ are meaningless
      Row& = 0
      Col& = 0
      X$ = ""
      ' return a False function result
      VisitNextSpMatElem = False
   End If
End Function

Sub GetSpMatElemData (ByVal SpMatElem$, Row&, Col&, X$)
' Extract the indices and data from a string
' representing the selected text of a sparse matrix
   Dim StrLen As Long
   StrLen = Len(SP_INDEX)
   Row& = Val(Mid$(SpMatElem$, 1, StrLen))
   Col& = Val(Mid$(SpMatElem$, StrLen + 2, StrLen))
   X$ = Mid$(SpMatElem$, 2 * StrLen + 2)
End Sub

Function SearchSpMat (M As Control, ByVal X$, ByVal Occur%, ByVal
CaseSense%, ByVal St&, ByVal Size&) As Integer
' searches the sparse matrix M for Occur% occurrence of the
' string X$.  The St& and Size& parameters determine the
' portions of the sparse matrix data that are included in
' the search
   SearchSpMat = LinSearch(M, X$, Occur%, CaseSense%, St&, Size&)
End Function
```

Next we look at the module's procedures and functions, which are described in the following paragraphs.

The CreateSparseMatrix procedure clears the list box control that emulates the sparse matrix.

The StoreInSpMatrix procedure stores the string X$ at the indices Row& and Col& of matrix M. The procedure obtains the string image of the row and column indices and stores them in the local string variable Idx. It then checks whether or not the matrix is empty. If it is empty, the string X$ is inserted as the first member in the list box. If not, procedure then invokes the BinLocate function to obtain the list box index for inserting the string X$. If the list box index already contains a member with the same index, the existing member is removed before inserting the new member. If not, the string X$ is inserted either at that index or immediately after, depending on how the variable Idx compares with the string image of the target list box member.

The RecallFromSpMatrix function recalls the sparse matrix element at the Row& and Col& indices. The function obtains the string image of these indices and uses it to search for the matching index, then invokes the Bin Search function to determine whether or not there is an element with these indices. The function returns the data of the sought element, or an empty string if no such element exists.

The Boolean VisitFirstSpMatrixElem function visits the first member of the list box control. The function returns True if the list box is not empty; otherwise, it returns False. The parameters X$, Row&, and Col& return the data and indices, respectively, of the member stored in M.List(0). If the function result is False, the values returned by these parameters are meaningless. The VisitFirstSpMatrixElem function invokes GetSpMatrixElemData to extract the values for the X$, Row&, and Col& parameters, and sets the VisitIndex variable to 0, preparing it for the subsequent VisitNextSpMatrixElem calls.

The Boolean VisitNextSpMatrixElem function visits the next member of the list box control. The function returns True if variable VisitIndex has not exceeded the highest current index of the list box emulating the matrix. Otherwise, the function returns False. The parameters X$, Row&, and Col& return the data and indices of the member stored in M.List(VisitIndex). If the function result is False, the values returned by these parameters are meaningless. the VisitNextSpMatrixElem function invokes the GetSpMatrixElemData routine to extract the values for the X$, Row&, and Col& parameters. The function increments the variable VisitIndex to derive the index of the next list box member.

The GetVisitIndex function returns the value stored in the VisitIndex variable.

The SetVisitIndex procedure assigns the value of its argument, NewVisit Index, to the VisitIndex variable. This procedure enables you to revisit specific elements without having to reset the value of VisitIndex by calling the VisitFirstSpMatrixElem and VisitNextSpMatrixElem routines.

⚠ **Warning!** The purpose of the GetVisitIndex function and the Set VisitIndex procedure is to enable you to alternately visit multiple sparse matrices. To do this, you must use the following procedure:

- Begin visiting each sparse matrix by calling the function VisitFirst SpMatrixElem.
- Inspect the next member of the same sparse matrix using the function VisitNextSpMatrixElem.
- Switch from one matrix to the other by using the GetVisitIndex function to store the contents of the variable VisitIndex in a separate variable. Then use the SetVisitIndex procedure to restore the appropriate value of VisitIndex for the other matrix. (This step is needed only if you are visiting the next element of the other matrix.)

⚠ **Warning!** Use the SetVisitIndex routine with care! Passing incorrect arguments throws off the inspection of matrix elements.

The GetSpMatrixElemData procedure extracts the row and column indices and the data from the string representing the selected member of a sparse matrix.

The SearchSpMat function searches for the specified occurrence of the string X$. The parameters St& and Size& specify the portion of a matrix element that is compared with the X$. The Boolean CaseSense% parameter determines whether or not the search is case-sensitive.

The sparse matrix test program

The sparse matrix test program is very similar to the sparse array test program. The differences are:

- There are now two index boxes: one for the row index and the other for the column index.
- Some of the labels have been adjusted to fit the sparse matrix test program.
- Some of the CtlName properties have been renamed to reflect the fact that the program handles sparse matrices.

The operation of the test program is very similar to that of the sparse array test program except that it must deal with both row and column indices in the various operations.

Figures 7-1 to 7-3 show the specifications for the TSSPMAT.MAK project file and the TSSPMAT.FRM form file. Figure 7-4 shows a sample session with the sparse matrix test program.

Application name: Sparse matrix test program
Application code name: TSSPMAT

Version: 1.0   Date created: August 14, 1991
Programmer(s): Namir Clement Shammas

7-1   The basic specifications for the TSSPMAT.MAK project file.

List of filenames

Storage path: \ VB \ VBXTOOL
Project   TSSPMAT.MAK
Global   GLOBAL.BAS
Form 1   TSSPMAT.FRM
Module 1   GENERIC.BAS
Module 2   SPMAT.BAS

Form # 1   Form filename: TSSPMAT.FRM
Version: 1.0   Date: August 14, 1991

Control object type	Default CtlName	Purpose
Command button	Command1	Stores an element in the matrix
	Command2	Recalls an matrix element
	Command3	Clears the sparse matrix
	Command4	Writes the matrix to a text file
	Command5	Visits the first matrix element
	Command6	Visits the next matrix element

7-2   The list of controls in the TSSPMAT.FRM form file.

Control object type	Default CtlName	Purpose
	Command7	Exits the test program
	Command8	Reads the matrix elements from a file
Text box	Text1	Input/Output text box
	Text2	Maintains the row index
	Text3	Maintains the column index
List box	List1	Sparse matrix emulator
Label	Label1	Label for the sparse matrix
	Label2	Label for the Input/Output text box
	Label3	Label for Row index text box
	Label4	Label for Column index text box

7-2   Continued.

Application (code) name: TSSPMAT
Form # 1
Version: 1.0   Date: August 14, 1991

Original control name	Property	New setting
Form	CtlName	Test Sparse Matrices
Command1	CtlName	StoreBtn
	Caption	&Store
Command2	CtlName	RecallBtn
	Caption	&Recall
Command3	CtlName	ClearBtn
	Caption	&Clear
Command4	CtlName	WriteBtn
	Caption	&Write
Command5	CtlName	VisitFirstBtn
	Caption	Visit &First
Command6	CtlName	VisitNextBtn
	Caption	Visit &Next
Command7	CtlName	QuitBtn
	Caption	&Quit
Command8	CtlName	ReadBtn
	Caption	Rea&d
Text1	CtlName	TextBox
	Text	(empty string)
Text2	CtlName	RowBox
	Text	(empty string)
Text3	CtlName	ColBox
	Text	(empty string)
List1	CtlName	MatLst

7-3   The customized settings for the TSSPMAT.FRM form.

Original control name	Property	New setting
Label1	CtlName	MatLbl
	Caption	Sparse Matrix
Label2	CtlName	IOLbl
	Caption	Input/Output
Label3	CtlName	RowLbl
	Caption	Row
Label4	CtlName	ColLbl
	Caption	Column

7-3 Continued.

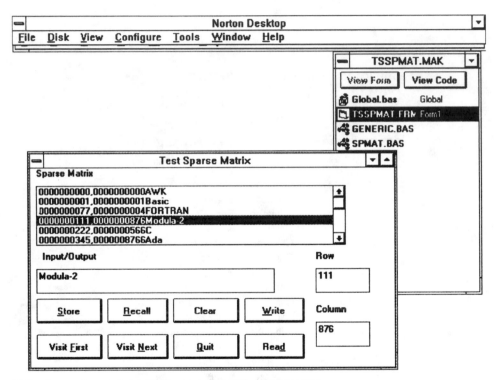

7-4 A sample session with the sparse matrix test program.

Listing 7-2 contains the code attached to the TSSPMAT.FRM form; its procedures greatly resemble their counterparts in Listing 6-2. Descriptions of the procedures follow.

The StoreBtn_Click procedure stores the contents of the Input/Output text box in the sparse matrix. The Row and Column text boxes provide the indices of the target matrix element. The procedure verifies that all of the text boxes are not empty before storing the sought element. The procedure converts the contents of the Row and Column text boxes into the string image of the storage indices. The contents of the Input/Output text box are

Listing 7-2   The code attached to the TSSPMAT.FRM form.

```
Const True = -1, False = 0

Dim Filename As String

Sub StoreBtn_Click ()
' Store the contents of TextBox in the matrix element specified
' by the row and column index boxes
  Dim Row As Long, Col As Long
  Dim X As String
  ' are both the row and column index boxes not empty?
  If (RowBox.Text <> "") And (ColBox.Text <> "") Then
    Row = Val(RowBox.Text) ' obtain the numeric row index
    Col = Val(ColBox.Text) ' obtain the numeric column index
    X = TextBox.Text ' copy the contents of TextBox in X
    ' store the strng in X at sparse matrix (row, Col)
    StoreInSpMat MatLst, X, Row, Col
  End If
End Sub

Sub QuitBtn_Click ()
  End
End Sub

Sub RecallBtn_Click ()
' Recall the sparse matrix at indices specified by the
' row and column index boxes.  If the matrix element
' exists, its data is copied in TextBox.  Otherwise,
' the TextBox is cleared.
  Dim Row As Long, Col As Long
  ' are both the row and column index boxes not empty?
  If (RowBox.Text <> "") And (ColBox.Text <> "") Then
    Row = Val(RowBox.Text) ' obtain the numeric row index
    Col = Val(ColBox.Text) ' obtain the numeric column index
    ' recall the sought matrix element and copy its data in TextBox
    TextBox.Text = RecallFromSpMat(MatLst, Row, Col)
  End If
End Sub

Sub Form_Load ()
  ' assign the default data filename
  Filename = "\vb\vbxtool\tsspmat.dat"
  CreateSparseMat MatLst
End Sub

Sub TextBox_GotFocus ()
  HighlightTextBox TextBox
End Sub

Sub WriteBtn_Click ()
' Writes the sparse matrix elements to a text file
  Dim S As String
  ' prompt the user for an output data filename
  S = InputBox$("Enter output filename", "File Output", Filename)
  ' did the user accept the default or the edited filename?
  If S <> "" Then
    Filename = S
    ' was there a file output error?
    If Not WriteList(MatLst, Filename) Then
      MsgBox "Error in writing data", 64, "I/O Error"
    End If
  End If
End Sub

Sub ReadBtn_Click ()
```

Listing 7-2 Continued.

```
    Dim S As String
    ' prompt the user for an input filename
    S = InputBox$("Enter input filename", "File Input", Filename)
    ' did the user accept the default ot the edited filename?
    If S <> "" Then
      Filename = S
      ' were there any file I/O errors?
      If Not ReadList(MatLst, Filename, False) Then
        MsgBox "Error in reading data", 64, "I/O Error"
      End If
    End If
End Sub

Sub VisitFirstBtn_Click ()
' Visit the first sparse matrix elements.  The row and column
' indices of that element appear in the row and column index
' boxes.  The TextBox displays the data stores at the first
' sparse matrix element
    Dim X As String
    Dim Row As Long, Col As Long
    ' is there a first matrix element to visit?
    If VisitFirstSpMatElem(MatLst, X, Row, Col) Then
      TextBox.Text = X ' copy matrix data to TextBox
      ' write the matrix row to the row index box
      RowBox.Text = Format$(Row, "")
      ' write the matrix column to the column index box
      ColBox.Text = Format$(Col, "")
    Else
      ' clear TextBox and the row and column index text boxes
      TextBox.Text = ""
      RowBox.Text = ""
      ColBox.Text = ""
    End If
End Sub

Sub VisitNextBtn_Click ()
' Visit the next sparse matrix elements.  The row and column
' indices of that element appear in the row and column index
' boxes.  The TextBox displays the data stores at the next
' sparse matrix element
    Dim X As String
    Dim Row As Long, Col As Long
    ' is there a next matrix element to visit?
    If VisitNextSpMatElem(MatLst, X, Row, Col) Then
      TextBox.Text = X ' copy matrix data to TextBox
      ' write the matrix row to the row index box
      RowBox.Text = Format$(Row, "")
      ' write the matrix colum to the column index box
      ColBox.Text = Format$(Col, "")
    Else
      ' clear TextBox and the row and column index text boxes
      TextBox.Text = ""
      RowBox.Text = ""
      ColBox.Text = ""
    End If
End Sub

Sub ClearBtn_Click ()
    CLearList MatLst
End Sub

Sub MatLst_DblClick ()
' extract the data and the row and column indices of
' the selected element
    Dim X As String
```

Listing 7-2 Continued.

```
Dim S As String
Dim Row As Long, Col As Long
' is there a selected text?
If MatLst.ListIndex > -1 Then
  S = MatLst.Text ' copy the selected text into S
  ' extract the Row and Col indices and the string X from S
  GetSpMatElemData S, Row, Col, X
  TextBox.Text = X ' write X to the TextBox
  ' write Row to the row text box
  RowBox.Text = Format$(Row, "")
  ' write Col to the column text box
  ColBox.Text = Format$(Col, "")
End If
End Sub

Sub ColBox_GotFocus ()
  HighlightTextBox ColBox
End Sub

Sub RowBox_GotFocus ()
  HighlightTextBox RowBox
End Sub
```

stored in the local variable X. The procedure then calls the StoreInSpMatrix procedure to store the characters of the string variable X at element (Row, Col) of the sparse matrix M.

The RecallBtn_Click procedure recalls the matrix element whose indices are specified in the Row and Column text boxes. The procedure first ensures that both of these text boxes are not empty. If this condition is true, the procedure converts the strings in the text boxes to their respective numeric indices. These indices are then used to call the RecallFromSpMatrix function and store the function result into the Input/Output text box.

The ClearBtn_Click procedure clears the sparse matrix by invoking the ClearList procedure in module GENERIC.BAS.

The Form_Load procedure initializes the program by assigning string \ vb \ vbxtool \ tsspmat.dat to the variable Filename.

The WriteBtn_Click procedure writes the elements of the sparse matrix to a text file. A dialog box appears with the current default filename, obtained from the variable Filename. If you accept the default or edited filename, the procedure invokes the WriteList function to write the matrix to the file Filename. If the WriteList function returns False, a message box appears to inform you that there was an error in the file operation. This error might be attributed either to supplying a bad or invalid filename, or to a write error, such as one resulting from a full disk.

The ReadBtn_Click procedure reads the elements of the sparse matrix from a text file. A simple dialog box appears with the current default filename, which is obtained from the variable Filename. If you accept the default or edited filename, the procedure invokes the ReadList function to read the matrix from the file Filename. If the ReadList function returns False, a message box appears to inform you that there was an error in the file operation. This error may be attributed either to supplying a bad or invalid filename, or to a read error.

The VisitFirstBtn_Click procedure visits the first sparse matrix element. The procedure invokes the function VisitFirstSpMatrixElem. If the function returns True, the contents and indices of the first element are displayed in the Input/Output and indices text boxes, respectively. Otherwise, the procedure clears these text boxes.

The VisitNextBtn_Click procedure visits the next sparse matrix element. The procedure invokes the function VisitNextSpMatrixElem. If the function returns True, the contents and index of the first sparse matrix element are displayed in the Input/Output and indices text boxes, respectively. Otherwise, the procedure clears these text boxes.

The MatrixLst_DblClick procedure retrieves the index and contents of the selected sparse matrix element. The row and column indices appear in their respective text boxes, and the data of the selected element appears in the Input/Output text box.

Run the test program to experiment with the various aspects of sparse matrices. The companion disk includes the TSSPMAT.DAT file, which contains a small sample sparse matrix. The sparse matrix contains the names of programming languages. Click on the Read button to read the matrix from the above data file. This step quickly provides you with a nucleus matrix which you can further manipulate.

Experiment with visiting the matrix elements, and recalling elements. You can also store new elements in the matrix. Try inserting data with new indices and then with currently used indices. Also, double click on a matrix member. This puts the indices of the selected member in the Row and Column text boxes, while the data in the selected member appears in the Input/Output text box.

When you are finished with the program, you might want to save the updated matrix by clicking on the Write command button. You can either use the default filename or type a new one. Exit the program by clicking on the Quit button.

8
Tables

Tables are arrays that have string indexes. They are special data structures that are commonly offered in programming languages geared toward text processing, such as ICON and AWK. This chapter discusses how to use list box controls to implement tables, in a manner similar to that of implementing sparse arrays. The chapter also includes a module containing the routines that implement table operations.

The basics of tables

Tables are special and convenient data structures that make up the simplest kinds of records. Arrays of user-defined types can be used to implement tables. For example, consider the following user-defined type:

```
Type TableType
    StrIndex As String  * 40
    StrData As String  * 30
End Type
```

The StrIndex data field is a fixed-length string that represents the index of a table element. To create a table, you declare an array of TableType, as shown next.

```
TheTable(1 To TABLE_SIZE) As TableType
```

The array TheTable can then store data. The array elements should be ordered using the values of the StrIndex field. This can be done either directly or using a second indexing array.

☞ The Visual Basic list box controls offer another way to implement a dynamic version of the table structure. In fact, the list boxes allow for the table elements to store variable-length strings. In addition, the table can be dynamically expanded at run time.

The list box stores the table and its index in the same list member. As with sparse arrays, the leading part of a list member stores the string index of the member, while the trailing part stores the data. The general form used to store a table element is given next:

    IIIIIIII...IIISSSSSSSSSSSSSSSSSSSSSSSS...SSS

The Is represent the fixed number of characters reserved for the string index. The Ss depict the characters that store the element's data. Since the index of a table is a string, you have a lot of flexibility (and responsibility) in specifying the maximum length of the string index.

☞   The power of the string-type indices comes to light when you can use them to emulate multidimensional arrays. In fact, you can have the table contain string images of indices that represent multidimensional arrays with a varying number of dimensions. Examples of such indices are:

    0001
    0001,0001
    0002,0003,0003
    0010,0004,0008,0002,002

This programming method allows a table to emulate a sophisticated sparse multidimensional array, which adds new dimensions on the fly. In fact, tables can easily emulate sparse arrays and sparse matrices. Converting from numerical indices to string-typed indices is a task that must be carried out by the applications, using tables to emulate these sparse arrays and matrices.

Basic table operations

The basic operations of tables are very similar to those of sparse arrays and sparse matrices. These operations are:

- Storing data at a specified index. The string index is used to insert the new table element in its proper location in the list box. If there is already an element with the same index, that element must first be removed before inserting the new data. Elements of a table are stored in ascending index order.
- Recalling data from a specified index. If the sought element does not exist, the operation returns an empty string.
- Visiting the first and next members. These operations sequentially retrieve the data stored in the list box controls, and yield both the index and the data of the accessed array member. If the data contains string images of user-defined types, then further processing is needed to put the information into a suitable form.

Warning! If you need to maintain the elements of the table in ascending or descending order, you must use a separate array of indices. You must *not* use the sorting procedures found in the GENERIC.BAS module.

The TABLE.BAS module

The basic table operations described in the previous section are implemented in the TABLE.BAS module, shown in Listing 8-1. The general declarations section defines the constant TABLE_SIZE_LEN, which specifies the maximum length of the string index. The same module section declares the VisitIndex variable, which maintains the index of the visited list box member. This index is different from the indices of the table members. The module's procedures are described next.

Listing 8-1   The code in the TABLE.BAS module.

```
Const True = -1, False = 0
Const TABLE_INDEX_LEN = 40

Dim VisitIndex As Integer

Sub CreateTable (A As Control)
   ClearList A ' clear list emulating the table
End Sub

Sub StoreInTable (T As Control, ByVal X$, ByVal I$)
' store item X$ in the index I$ of the table T
   Dim Idx As String * TABLE_INDEX_LEN
   Dim J As Integer
   ' get the string index
   Idx = I$
   ' is table not empty?
   If T.ListCount > 0 Then
      ' search for candidate table index that may contain
      ' the same table index
      J = BinLocate(T, Idx, 1, TABLE_INDEX_LEN)
      ' is there a matching index?
      If Idx = Mid$(T.List(J), 1, TABLE_INDEX_LEN) Then
         ' remove old item
         T.RemoveItem J
         ' insert element X$ in table
         T.AddItem Idx + X$, J
      ElseIf Idx < Mid$(T.List(J), 1, TABLE_INDEX_LEN) Then
         ' insert element X$ before T.List(J)
         T.AddItem Idx + X$, J
      Else
         ' insert element X$ after T.List(J)
         T.AddItem Idx + X$, J + 1
      End If
   Else
      ' insert table element as the first list member
      T.AddItem Idx + X$, 0
   End If
End Sub

Function RecallFromTable (T As Control, ByVal I$) As String
' Recall the element I$ of the table T.  If the sought
```

Listing 8-1 Continued.

```
      ' element is not in the table, an empty string is
      ' returned.
        Dim Idx As String * TABLE_INDEX_LEN
        Dim Index As Integer
        ' get the string index
        Idx = I$
      ' search for the sought element using the string index
      Index = BinSearch(T, Idx, 1, 1, TABLE_INDEX_LEN)
      If Index > -1 Then ' Found a match?
        ' Yes!  Return the table element
        RecallFromTable = Mid$(T.List(Index), TABLE_INDEX_LEN + 1)
      Else
        ' No! Return an empty string
        RecallFromTable = ""
      End If
End Function

Function GetVisitIndex () As Integer
' Return the value of the module-level variable VisitIndex
  GetVisitIndex = VisitIndex
End Function

Sub SetVisitIndex (ByVal NewVisitIndex%)
' Sets the value of the module-level variable VisitIndex
  VisitIndex = NewVisitIndex
End Sub

Function VisitFirstTableElem (T As Control, X$, I$) As Integer
' Visits the first member of the table and
' obtains its index and data
  Dim Elem As String
  ' is table not empty?
  If T.ListCount > 0 Then
    VisitIndex = 0 ' set the VisitIndex
    Elem = T.List(0) ' get the first element
    ' extract the index and string of the first table element
    GetTableElemData Elem, I$, X$
    ' return a True function result
    VisitFirstTableElem = True
  Else
    ' the values assigned to I$ and X$ are meaningless
    I$ = ""
    X$ = ""
    ' return a False function result
    VisitFirstTableElem = False
  End If
End Function

Function VisitNextTableElem (T As Control, X$, I$) As Integer
' Visits the next member of the table and
' obtains its index and data
  Dim Elem As String
  ' Is VisitIndex in the valid range?
  If VisitIndex < (T.ListCount - 1) Then
    VisitIndex = VisitIndex + 1 ' increment the visit index
    Elem = T.List(VisitIndex) ' get the sought element
    ' extract the index and string of the sought table element
    GetTableElemData Elem, I$, X$
    ' return a True function result
    VisitNextTableElem = True
  Else
    ' the values assigned to I$ and X$ are meaningless
    I$ = ""
    X$ = ""
    ' return a False function result
    VisitNextTableElem = False
```

Listing 8-1 Continued.

```
  End If
End Function

Sub GetTableElemData (ByVal TableElem$, I$, X$)
' Extract the index and string from a string
' representing the selected text of a table
  I$ = RTrim$(Mid$(TableElem$, 1, TABLE_INDEX_LEN))
  X$ = Mid$(TableElem$, TABLE_INDEX_LEN + 1)
End Sub

Function SearchTable (T As Control, ByVal X$, ByVal Occur%, ByVal
CaseSense%, ByVal St&, ByVal Size&) As Integer
' searches the sparse table for Occur% occurrence of the
' string X$.  The St& and Size& parameters determine the
' portions of the table data that are included in the search
  SearchTable = LinSearch(T, X$, Occur%, CaseSense%, St&, Size&)
End Function
```

The CreateTable procedure clears the list box control which emulates the table data structure.

The StoreInTable procedure stores the string X$ at index I$ of table T. The procedure obtains the variable-length string index I$ and stores it in the local fixed-length string variable Idx. Next, the procedure determines whether the table is not empty. If it is empty, the string X$ is inserted as the first member in the list box.

The procedure next invokes the BinLocate function to obtain the list box index for inserting the string X$. If the list box index already contains a table element with index I$, that list box member is removed before inserting the new data. If not, the string X$ is inserted at that list member or immediately after it, depending on how the variable Idx compares with the string index of the target list box member.

The RecallFromTable function recalls the table element at index I$. The function obtains the string index I$ and uses it to search for the matching index. The function invokes the BinSearch function to determine whether or not there is an element with the specified index. The function returns the data of the sought element, or an empty string if that element does not exist.

The Boolean VisitFirstTableElem function visits the first member of the list box control. The function returns True if the list box emulating the table is not empty; otherwise, it returns False. The parameters X$ and I$ return the data and index of the element stored in T.List(0). If the function result is False, the values returned by these parameters are meaningless. The VisitFirstTableElem function invokes the GetTableElemData to extract the values for the X$ and I$ parameters, and sets the VisitIndex variable to 0, preparing it for the subsequent VisitNextTableElem calls.

The Boolean VisitNextTableElem function visits the next member of the list box control. The function returns True if variable VisitIndex has not exceeded the highest current index of the list box emulating the table; otherwise, it returns False. Parameters X$ and I$ return the data and index of the element stored in A.List(VisitIndex). If the function result is False, the values returned are meaningless. The VisitNextTableElem function invokes the Get TableElemData to extract the values for the X$ and I$ parameters, and increments the variable VisitIndex to index the next list box member.

The GetVisitIndex function returns the value stored in the VisitIndex variable.

The SetVisitIndex procedure assigns the value of its argument, NewVisit Index, to the VisitIndex variable. This procedure enables you to revisit specific elements without having to reset the value of VisitIndex by calling the Visit FirstSpTableElem and VisitNextSpTableElem routines.

◼ **Warning!**   The GetVisitIndex function and the SetVisitIndex procedure enable you to alternately visit multiple tables. The following steps are used for this operation:

1. Begin visiting each table by calling the function VisitFirstSpTableElem.
2. Inspect the next element of the same table using the function Visit-NextSpTableElem.
3. Switch from one table to another using the GetVisitIndex function to store the content of the variable VisitIndex in a separate variable. Then use the SetVisitIndex procedure to restore the appropriate value of VisitIndex for the other table. This step is needed only if you are visiting the next element of the other table.

◼ **Warning!**   Use the SetVisitIndex routine with care! Passing incorrect arguments throws off the inspection table elements.

The GetTableElemData procedure extracts the index and data from a string representing the selected element of a table.

The SearchTable function searches for the occurrence of the specified string X$. The parameters St& and Size& specify the portion of a table element that are compared with X$. The Boolean CaseSense% parameter determines whether or not the search is case-sensitive.

The table test program

The sparse array test program can be modified to obtain a smaller test program for the table. This test program uses the procedures from the GENERIC.BAS and the TABLE.BAS modules. The program contains the following controls:

- A visible list box that emulates the table.
- An Input/Output text box. This control is used to type in strings and then save them in the table. The text box is used to display table members that are recalled.
- A string index text box.

- A number of command buttons to store, recall, and visit the table elements; clear the table; write the table to a text file; read the table from a text file; and exit the test program.

When you select a table element and double click, the index of that element appears in the Index I text box and the data of the selected element is copied into the Input/Output text box.

Figures 8-1 to 8-3 show the specifications for the TSTABLE.MAK project file and the TSTABLE.FRM form file. Figure 8-4 shows a sample session with the table test program.

Application name: Table test program
Application code name: TSTABLE

8-1 The basic specifications for the TSTABLE.MAK project file.

Version: 1.0   Date created: August 14, 1991
Programmer(s): Namir Clement Shammas

List of filenames

Storage path: \ VB \ VBXTOOL
Project   TSTABLE.MAK
Global   GLOBAL.BAS
Form 1   TSTABLE.FRM
Module 1   GENERIC.BAS
Module 2   TABLE.BAS

Form # 1   Form filename: TSTABLE.FRM
Version: 1.0   Date: August 14, 1991

Control object type	Default CtlName	Purpose
Command button	Command1	Stores an element in the table
	Command2	Recalls a table element
	Command3	Clears the table
	Command4	Writes the table to a text file
	Command5	Visits the first table element
	Command6	Visits the next table element
	Command7	Exits the test program
	Command8	Reads the table elements from a file
Text box	Text1	Input/Output text box
	Text2	Maintains the index I
List box	List1	Table emulator
Label	Label1	Label for the table
	Label2	Label for the Input/Output text box
	Label3	Label for Index I text box

8-2 The list of controls in the TSTABLE.FRM form file.

Application (code) name: TSTABLE
Form # 1
Version: 1.0   Date: August
                                            14, 1991

Original control name	Property	New setting
Form	CtlName	Test Tables
Command1	CtlName	StoreBtn
	Caption	&Store
Command2	CtlName	RecallBtn
	Caption	&Recall
Command3	CtlName	ClearBtn
	Caption	&Clear
Command4	CtlName	WriteBtn
	Caption	&Write
Command5	CtlName	VisitFirstBtn
	Caption	Visit &First
Command6	CtlName	VisitNextBtn
	Caption	Visit &Next
Command7	CtlName	QuitBtn
	Caption	&Quit
Command8	CtlName	ReadBtn
	Caption	Rea&d
Text1	CtlName	TextBox
	Text	(empty string)
Text2	CtlName	IBox
	Text	(empty string)
List1	CtlName	TableLst
Label1	CtlName	TableLbl
	Caption	Table
Label2	CtlName	IOLbl
	Caption	Input/Output
Label3	CtlName	IndexILbl
	Caption	Index I

8-3 The customized settings for the TSTABLE
.FRM form.

Listing 8-2 contains the code attached to the TSTABLE.FRM form.
Descriptions of the form's procedures follow.

The StoreBtn_Click procedure stores the contents of the Input/Output text
box in the table. The Index I text box provides the index of the target table
element; the procedure verifies that the text box is not empty before storing the element. The procedure stores the contents of the Index I text box in
the variable Idx, and the contents of the Input/Output text box in the local variable X. The procedure then calls the StoreInTable procedure to store the
characters of the string variable X at element Idx of table T.

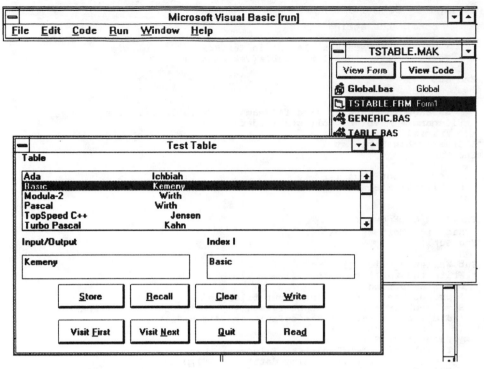

8-4 A sample session with the table test program.

Listing 8-2 The code attached to the TSTABLE.FRM form.

```
Const True = -1, False = 0

Dim Filename As String

Sub StoreBtn_Click ()
' Store the string in TextBox in the table
  Dim I As String
  Dim X As String
  ' does the Index I test box contain any text?
  If IBox.Text <> "" Then
    ' obtain the string index
    I = IBox.Text
    ' copy the string of the input/output text box into X
    X = TextBox.Text
    ' store X at element I of the table
    StoreInTable TableLst, X, I
  End If
End Sub

Sub QuitBtn_Click ()
  End
End Sub

Sub RecallBtn_Click ()
' Recall an table element
  Dim I As String
  ' doe sthe Index I text box contain any text?
  If IBox.Text <> "" Then
```

Listing 8-2 Continued.

```
                    ' obtain the string index
                    I = IBox.Text
                    ' store the recalled element in TextBox
                    TextBox.Text = RecallFromTable(TableLst, I)
               End If
          End Sub

          Sub Form_Load ()
               ' asssign the default data filename to variable Filename
               Filename = "\vb\vbxtool\tstable.dat"
               ' initialize the table
               CreateTable TableLst
          End Sub

          Sub TextBox_GotFocus ()
               HighlightTextBox TextBox
          End Sub

          Sub IBox_GotFocus ()
               HighlightTextBox IBox
          End Sub

          Sub WriteBtn_Click ()
          ' Write the table to a text file
               Dim S As String
               ' prompt the user for an output filename
               S = InputBox$("Enter output filename", "File Output", Filename)
               ' did the user accept the default or edited filename
               If S <> "" Then
                    Filename = S
                    If Not WriteList(TableLst, Filename) Then
                         MsgBox "Error in writing data", 64, "I/O Error"
                    End If
               End If
          End Sub

          Sub ReadBtn_Click ()
          ' Read the the table from a text file
               Dim S As String
               ' prompt for an input filename
               S = InputBox$("Enter input filename", "File Input", Filename)
               ' did the user accept the default or edited filename?
               If S <> "" Then
                    Filename = S
                    If Not ReadList(TableLst, Filename, False) Then
                         MsgBox "Error in reading data", 64, "I/O Error"
                    End If
               End If
          End Sub

          Sub VisitFirstBtn_Click ()
          ' Visit the first element of the table and
          ' obtain the index and the data of that element
               Dim X As String
               Dim I As String
               ' is there a first element to visit?
               If VisitFirstTableElem(TableLst, X, I) Then
                    ' copy the contents of X into TextBox
                    TextBox.Text = X
                    ' store the string image of index I in the Index I
                    ' text box
                    IBox.Text = I
               Else
                    ' clear the input/output and Index I text boxes
                    TextBox.Text = ""
                    IBox.Text = ""
```

Listing 8-2 Continued.

```
  End If
End Sub

Sub VisitNextBtn_Click ()
  Dim X As String
  Dim I As String
  ' is there another element to visit?
  If VisitNextTableElem(TableLst, X, I) Then
    ' copy the contents of X into TextBox
    TextBox.Text = X
    ' store the string image of index I in the Index I
    ' text box
    IBox.Text = I
  Else
    ' clear the input/output and Index I text boxes
    TextBox.Text = ""
    IBox.Text = ""
  End If
End Sub

Sub ClearBtn_Click ()
  CLearList TableLst
End Sub

Sub TableLst_DblClick ()
' Obtain the index and the data of the selected list item
  Dim X As String
  Dim S As String
  Dim I As String
  ' is there a selected text?
  If TableLst.ListIndex > -1 Then
    S = TableLst.Text ' copy the selected text into S
    ' obtain the index I and the data X from S
    GetTableElemData S, I, X
    TextBox.Text = X ' write X to TextBox
    IBox.Text = I ' write I to Index I text box
  End If
End Sub
```

The RecallBtn_Click procedure recalls the array element with the index specified in the Index I text box. The procedure first ensures that the Index I text box is not empty; if this condition is true, it stores the variable-length string index into the fixed-length index Idx. This index is then used in calling the RecallFromTable function and storing the function result in the Input/Output text box.

The ClearBtn_Click procedure clears the table by invoking the ClearList procedure in module GENERIC.BAS.

The Form_Load procedure initializes the program by assigning string \ vb \ vbxtool \ tstable.dat to the variable Filename.

The WriteBtn_Click procedure writes the elements of the table to a text file. A dialog box appears with the current default filename, obtained from the variable Filename. If you accept the default or edited filename, the procedure invokes the WriteList function to write the array in the file Filename. If the WriteList function returns False, a message box appears to inform you that there was an error in the file operation. This error may be attributed either to supplying a bad or invalid filename, or to a write error, like one resulting from a full disk.

The ReadBtn_Click procedure reads the elements of the table from a text file. A dialog box appears with the current default filename, obtained from the variable Filename. If you accept the default or edited filename, the procedure invokes the ReadList function to read the array from the file Filename. If the ReadList function returns False, a message box appears saying that there was an error in the file operation. This error may be attributed either to supplying a bad or invalid filename, or to a read error.

The VisitFirstBtn_Click procedure visits the first table element. The procedure invokes the function VisitFirstTableElem; if the function returns True, the string index and contents of the first table element are displayed in the Input/Output and Index I text boxes, respectively. Otherwise, these boxes are cleared.

The VisitNextBtn_Click procedure visits the next table element. The procedure invokes the function VisitNextTableElem. If the function returns True, the string index and contents of the next table element are displayed in the Input/Output and Index I text boxes. If the function returns False, these boxes are cleared.

The ArrayLst_DblClick procedure retrieves the index and contents of the selected table element. The index appears in the Index I text box, and the element data appears in the Input/Output text box.

Run the test program to gain experience with the various aspects of tables. The companion disk includes the TSTABLE.DAT file which contains a small sample table. The table contains the names of programming languages. Click on the Read button to read the table from the data file. This quickly provides you with a nucleus table which you can further manipulate.

Experiment with visiting the table elements, and recalling elements. You can also store new elements in the table; try inserting data with new indices and then with currently used indices. Also double click on a table member. This operation places the index of the selected member in the Index I text box, and the data in the Input/Output text box.

When you are finished working with the program, you might want to save the updated table by clicking on the Write command button. You can use the default filename or type in a new one. Exit the program by clicking on the Quit button.

9
Hash tables

The previous chapter presented the table data structure—a form of array that uses a string-typed index. The sparse array, sparse matrix, and table structure share the same fundamental approach, which converts the numerical indices into strings. These string indices are concatenated with the string-typed data and are stored in the same list box member. Most of the operations for these data structures seek specific indices using either binary or linear search methods. This chapter presents a faster form of the table structure: the hash table. In brief, hash tables convert all of their data into a storage index. Consequently, the linear and binary search methods are not needed.

The basics of hash tables

The power and potency of a hash table stems from the fact that all or part of its data, which is usually string-typed, is converted into an index. The index is more commonly called an *address* when dealing with hash tables. Because of this addressing scheme, hash tables do not require the use of an external index to access their elements. Hash tables also make linear or binary searches obsolete, because they achieve faster search speeds. What is the basic principle behind the powerful hash tables? How can the hash table order data more efficiently than the table structure?

The answer lies, surprisingly, in perfect chaos. Hash tables work so well because they use the data itself to create unique storage addresses. This conversion is performed using a *hashing function*, which takes the string-typed data and returns a random number which serves as the hash table address.

If you think that using hash tables sounds too good to be true, you are right. Hash tables, like other data structures, have their limitations and peculiar features. The first is that the size of the hash table must be preassigned. Also, the hashing functions rarely, if ever, return an absolutely unique address for every possible string. As a result, different strings might yield the same address. This phenomenon is known as *collision*, since multiple strings are mapped to the same hash table address. Collision is influenced by the size of the hash table, the number of actual records in the hash table, and the randomness of the numbers generated by the hashing function. The ratio of the number of records to the hash table size is known as the *loading factor*. The lower the loading factor, the less likely a collision is.

Another peculiarity is that the elements in a hash table are unordered. To maintain the data in any kind of order, you need to use external arrays or lists.

The process of implementing a hash table is not complete without taking into consideration the collision phenomenon that I mention above. No matter how good you think a hashing function is, you can be certain that it will yield the same address for at least two strings. Computer scientists have proposed various techniques to deal with this. The most effective method is *chaining*. This method is easily implemented with the list box controls that emulate the hash tables. Chaining resolves collision of two or more data items by storing them in the same list member. In the case of the Visual Basic list boxes, colliding elements are simply concatenated in the same list box member. Naturally, a special character must be used to delimit the chained data. A high ASCII character, such as Chr$(255), is a suitable delimiter since it is rarely used in string-typed data.

☞ The next step in implementing the hash table is defining the basic format of a data record. Each hash table element may contain any number of records. Earlier it was mentioned that a hash table may use all or part of its data to obtain a hash table address. This is an important point. Hash tables that store simple data items typically use the entire string of these items to obtain the hash table addresses. For more complex data, only part of a data item is converted into an address. Such data items are made up of a *primary data string* and a *secondary data string*. Only the primary data string is converted into the hash table address. The secondary data string contains auxiliary (though important) information. The primary data string *must* be unique.

Organizing the hash table record into a primary and a secondary string requires that these strings be delimited by a special character. Using such a delimiter is more flexible than storing the record's strings in fixed-length characters. Thus, the record contains two strings and two delimiters, as shown in this general format:

RPPPPPPP...PPPPKSSSSSSSSSSSSSSSS...SSSR

In this format, R is the record delimiter character, and K is the key delimiter character separating the primary data string (depicted by P) from the secondary data string (indicated by S). Surrounding the primary and secondary strings with special delimiters ensures that using the Visual Basic InStr function does not erroneously pick a matching substring of another record in the same hash table entry.

The above organization enables the hash table to store both simple and complex data. In the case of simple data, which uses the entire data string to calculate the address, the secondary data strings are simply empty strings.

Basic hash table operations

Having discussed the basic design of hash tables, let's focus now on their basic operations which are as follows:

Initializing the hash table. This creates a hash table with a specified size. Usually, the hash table entries are empty; however, using the standard hash record format makes it advisable to store a single record delimiter character in each hash table entry. When you insert a hash record in the hash table entry, you automatically insert the primary data string, the key delimiter, the secondary data string (which may be an empty string), and the trailing record delimiter character. This scheme ensures that each hash record is surrounded by a pair of record delimiter characters.

Using the hashing function. The hashing function converts a string into a random number that is in the range of the hash table entries. The most popular random number generator uses the Modulo operator in the following general formula:

$$h(C) = K1 * ASC(C) \; Mod \; K2$$

where $h(C)$ is the hashing function for the single character C. K1 and K2 are prime numbers that are used to generate the random number.

This formula can be integrated in the following pseudocode that converts all of the characters of an input string into a hash table address:

```
let Sum = 0
For i = 1 To length of input string
   C = character i of the input string
   Sum = (Sum + 13 * Asc(C) Mod 17) Mod hash_table_size
Next I
Hashing function address = Sum
```

The first instance of the Mod operator calculates the required random number, using the prime numbers 13 and 17. The second instance ensures that the random number is mapped onto the hash table indices, ranging from 0 to hash_table_size − 1.

Determining if an element is in the hash table. This two-step operation first obtains the hash table address from the primary data string, then searches the target hash table entry for the occurrence of the sought element.

Inserting data in the hash table. If the hash table already contains a record with the same primary data string, the operation is aborted. This measure ensures that primary data strings remain unique in the hash table, and that you don't accidentally overwrite existing data with the same primary data string.

Deleting data from the hash table. This operation removes an existing hash table record using its primary data string.

Recalling the secondary data string of an existing record. This procedure requires the primary data string to locate the required string.

Visiting the first and next records. This operation visits the specified hash table record in the same or in a different hash table entry.

The HASHTABL.BAS module

The basic hash table operations are implemented by the procedures and functions of module HASHTABL.BAS. Listing 9-1 contains the code for this module, which declares a number of constants:

- The True and False constants.
- The RECORD_DELIM constant specifies the ASCII code for the record delimiter character.
- The KEY_DELIM constant designates the ASCII code for the key delimiter that separates the primary and secondary data strings of a hash table record.

Listing 9-1   The code in the HASHTABL.BAS module.

```
Const True = -1, False = 0
Const RECORD_DELIM = 255
Const KEY_DELIM = 254

Dim RecDelim As String * 1
Dim KeyDelim As String * 1
Dim VisitIndex As Integer
Dim CharIndex As Long

Sub CreateHashTable (T As Control, ByVal TableSize%)
' create a hash table with TableSize% entries
  CLearList T
  ' initialize record delimiter
  RecDelim = Chr$(RECORD_DELIM)
  ' initialize key delimiter
  KeyDelim = Chr$(KEY_DELIM)
  ' create the hash table records
  Do While TableSize% > 0
    ' initialize each record with the record delimiter
    T.AddItem RecDelim
    ' decrease the table size variable
    TableSize% = TableSize% - 1
  Loop
End Sub

Function InsertInHashTable (T As Control, ByVal Hash$, ByVal Rec$) As
Integer
' Insert the strings Hash$ and Rec$ in the hash table
```

Listing 9-1 Continued.

```
  Dim HashAddr As Integer
  Dim S As String
  ' get the hash address
  HashAddr = Hash1(T, Hash$)
  S = T.List(HashAddr)
  ' test if Hash$ is not already in the hash table
  If InStr(S, RecDelim + Hash$ + KeyDelim) = 0 Then
    ' append record
    S = S + Hash$ + KeyDelim + Rec$ + RecDelim
    T.List(HashAddr) = S ' insert in the hash table
    ' return the function result
    InsertInHashTable = True
  Else
    ' return the function result
    InsertInHashTable = False
  End If
End Function

Function IsInHashTable (T As Control, ByVal Hash$) As Integer
' Boolean function that determines whether or not the
' string Hash$ is in the hash table.
  Dim HashAddr As Integer
  HashAddr = Hash1(T, Hash$)
  If InStr(T.List(HashAddr), RecDelim + Hash$ + KeyDelim) > 0 Then
    IsInHashTable = True
  Else
    IsInHashTable = False
  End If
End Function

Function Hash1 (T As Control, ByVal X$) As Integer
' A sample hash function. The string X$ is converted
' into a hash table address in the range of 0 to
' T.ListCount-1.
  Dim I As Integer
  Dim R As Integer

  R = 0
  ' process every character in string X$
  For I = 1 To Len(X$)
    R = (R + 13 * Asc(Mid$(X$, I, 1)) Mod 17) Mod T.ListCount
  Next I
  ' return hash table function result
  Hash1 = R
End Function

Sub DeleteFromHashTable (T As Control, ByVal Hash$)
' Delete a record from the hash table.  The Hash$
' parameter provides the hash address of the deleted
' record
  Dim HashAddr As Integer
  Dim I As Long, J As Long, K As Long
  Dim S As String, R As String
  ' get the hash table address
  HashAddr = Hash1(T, Hash$)
  S = T.List(HashAddr) ' get the taget element
  ' find the index to the matching element
  I = InStr(S, RecDelim + Hash$ + KeyDelim)
  ' is Hash$ in the hash table?
  If I > 0 Then
    ' find the index of the next trailing record delimiter
    J = InStr(I + 1, S, RecDelim)
    R = "" ' initialize updated entry string
    ' Loop to extract undeleted characters
    For K = 1 To Len(S)
      If (K <= I) Or (K > J) Then
```

Listing 9-1 Continued.

```
      R = R + Mid$(S, K, 1)
   End If
Next K
      ' update the hash table entry
      T.List(HashAddr) = R
   End If
End Sub

Function VisitFirstHashTableElem (T As Control, Hash$, Rec$) As Integer
' Visits the first entry in the first hash table address.
   Dim NotFound As Integer
   Dim LastIndex As Long
   Dim S As String
   NotFound = True ' set not-found flag to true
   ' assign default values for the Hash$ and Rec$ strings
   Hash$ = ""
   Rec$ = ""
   VisitIndex = 0 ' set index to list member 0
   CharIndex = 1 ' set the character index
   ' start searching for the first element in the hash table
   Do While NotFound And (VisitIndex < T.ListCount)
      LastIndex = CharIndex + 1
      ' get the index to the second occurrence of
      ' the hash table record delimiter
      CharIndex = InStr(LastIndex, T.List(VisitIndex), RecDelim)
      ' found the record delimiter?
      If CharIndex > 0 Then
         ' obtain the first hash table entry
         S = Mid$(T.List(VisitIndex), LastIndex, CharIndex - LastIndex)
         GetHashRecData S, Hash$, Rec$
         NotFound = False
      Else
         VisitIndex = VisitIndex + 1
         CharIndex = 1
      End If
   Loop
   ' return function result
   VisitFirstHashTableElem = Not NotFound
End Function

Function VisitNextHashTableElem (T As Control, Hash$, Rec$) As Integer
' Visits the next entry in the first hash table address.
   Dim NotFound As Integer
   Dim LastIndex As Long
   Dim S As String
   NotFound = True ' set not-found flag to true
   ' assign default values to the Hash$ and Rec$ strings
   Hash$ = ""
   Rec$ = ""
   ' start searching for the next element in the hash table
   Do While NotFound And (VisitIndex < T.ListCount)
      LastIndex = CharIndex + 1
      ' get the index to the second occurrence of
      ' the hash table record delimiter
      CharIndex = InStr(LastIndex, T.List(VisitIndex), RecDelim)
      ' found the record delimiter?
      If CharIndex > 0 Then
         ' obtain the next hash table entry
         S = Mid$(T.List(VisitIndex), LastIndex, CharIndex - LastIndex)
         GetHashRecData S, Hash$, Rec$
         NotFound = False
      Else
         VisitIndex = VisitIndex + 1
         CharIndex = 1
```

Listing 9-1 Continued.

```
      End If
 Loop
   ' return function result
   VisitNextHashTableElem = Not NotFound
 End Function

Function RecallFromHashTable (T As Control, ByVal Hash$, Rec$) As Integer
 ' Recall the secondary data from a hash table entry, given
 ' the primary hash string Hash$.  The function returns True
 ' if it found a hash record that contains the Hash$ primary
 ' data string.  Otherwise, the function returns False.
 ' The Rec parameter returns the secondary data string of
 ' the located hash record.
   Dim HashAddr As Integer
   Dim I As Integer, J As Integer
   Dim S As String
   ' set the default value of the secondary data string
   Rec$ = ""
   ' get the hash address
   HashAddr = Hash1(T, Hash$)
   S = T.List(HashAddr) ' recall the hash table entry
   ' obtain the index to the matching hash string
   I = InStr(S, RecDelim + Hash$ + KeyDelim)
   ' found a match?
   If I > 0 Then
     ' obtain the index to the next trailing record delimiter
     J = InStr(I + 1, S, RecDelim)
     ' obtain the secondary data string
     GetHashRecData Mid$(S, I + 1, J - I - 1), Hash$, Rec$
     RecallFromHashTable = True
   Else
     RecallFromHashTable = False
   End If
 End Function

Sub GetHashRecData (ByVal HashRec$, Hash$, Rec$)
 ' extracts the has string and the auxiliary data
 ' from a HashRec$.  The HashRec$ string may only
 ' contain the KeyDelim character, but not the
 ' RecDelim characters.
   Dim I As Long

   I = InStr(HashRec$, KeyDelim)
   If I > 0 Then
     ' split the HasRec$ string
     ' obtain the Hash$
     If I > 1 Then
       Hash$ = Mid$(HashRec$, 1, I - 1)
     Else
       Hash$ = ""
     End If
     ' obtain the Rec$
     If I < Len(HashRec$) Then
       Rec$ = Mid$(HashRec$, I + 1)
     Else
       Rec$ = ""
     End If
   Else
     ' copy HasRec$ into Hash$
     Hash$ = HasRec$
     ' assign an empty string to Rec$
     Rec$ = ""
   End If
 End Sub
```

The module also declares the following module-level variables:

- The RecDelim variable is a single-character string that is assigned Chr$(RECORD_DELIM) by the procedure that creates the hash table. Using the RecDelim variable speeds up the hash table search, because recalling the contents of a variable is faster than calling the function Chr$(RECORD_DELIM).
- The KeyDelim variable is a single-character string that is assigned Chr$(KEY_DELIM) by the procedure that creates the hash table. Using the KeyDelim variable speeds up the hash table search by recalling the variable contents rather than calling the function Chr$(KEY_DELIM).
- The VisitIndex variable is the index to the hash table entry being visited.
- The CharIndex variable is the index to the hash table record being visited.

The HASHTABL.BAS module declares the procedures which are described in the following paragraphs.

The CreateHashTable procedure creates a hash table with TableSize% entries. The procedure clears the list box that emulates the hash table, assigns the delimiter characters to the RecDelim and KeyDelim variables, and assigns the RecDelim variable (which stores the Chr$(255) character) to each hash table entry.

The Hash1 hashing function converts the argument of X$ into a hash table address in the range of 0 to T.ListCount − 1. The hashing function is based on the pseudocode shown earlier in this chapter.

The Boolean InsertInHashTable function inserts the primary data string Hash$ and the secondary data string Rec$ in a hash table entry. The function returns True if the primary and secondary data strings are inserted. Otherwise, the function yields False. The function carries out several tasks. First, it calculates the hash table address using the hashing function Hash1; then it copies the hash table entry with the target address into variable S. The function then searches for the occurrence of the primary data string Hash$ in the string S; the Visual Basic InStr function is used to perform a quick search. The arguments for the InStr function are S (the copy of the hash table entry) and the expression RecDelim + Hash$ + Key Delim. This expression ensures that the InStr function does not erroneously pick another record (in the same hash table entry) that contains the characters of Hash$.

If this search indicates that there is no matching primary data string in the hash table entry, the function appends the expression Hash$ + Key Delim + Rec$ + RecDelim to the string variable S, and then copies the updated contents of string S to the target table entry, and assigns True to the function result. However, if the search signals that there is a hash record with the same primary data string, the function does not insert any data in the hash table and returns False.

☞ The implementation of the various hash table routines in module HASHTABL.BAS supports case-sensitive primary data strings. This means that strings like "Basic" and "BASIC" produce different hash table addresses. You can make the routines support case-insensitive primary data strings by consistently using the Visual Basic UCase$ or LCase$ functions with the arguments of the primary data string. These functions maintain the primary data strings in either uppercase or lowercase.

The Boolean IsInHashTable function determines whether the hash table contains a record with the Hash$ primary data string. The function obtains the hash table address using the Hash1 hashing function. Then, the routine uses the Visual Basic InStr function to search for the primary data string in the target hash table entry. If the InStr function yields a positive value, the function returns True, since a matching primary data string is located. Otherwise, the function returns False.

The DeleteFromHashTable procedure removes the entire hash record (both the primary and secondary data strings) that contains the Hash$ primary data string. The procedure obtains the hash table address using the Hash1 hashing function, copies the targeted hash table entry into the local string variable S, and searches for the matching primary data string using the Visual Basic InStr function. This function scans the string S for the first occurrence of the string expression RecDelim + Hash$ + KeyDelim.

If the above search locates a matching primary data string, the procedure deletes the target hash record. The deletion involves locating the trailing record delimiter and then extracting the undeleted characters from string S. A For-Next loop copies the undeleted characters of variable S into variable R. The contents of R are then copied back into the target hash table entry.

The Boolean VisitFirstHashTableElem function visits the first element in the hash table, starting with the hash table address 0. Keep in mind that the hash table entry at address 0 may not contain any record. The function returns True if a hash record is located and False if the hash table is empty. The parameters Hash$ and Rec$ return the primary and secondary data strings, respectively, of the first visited element. If the function returns False, the Hash$ and Rec$ parameters return empty strings.

The visiting function initializes the NotFound search flag, the Hash$ string, the Rec$ string, the module-level variable VisitIndex, and the module-level variable CharIndex. The VisitIndex is initialized with 0, the starting hash table address. The CharIndex variable is assigned 1, which is the index of the first character of a hash table entry. The first character for all hash table entries is Chr$(255).

The function then starts a Do-While loop to search for the first hash record. The loop iterates as long as the Boolean variable NotFound is True and the variable VisitIndex is within the range of valid hash table addresses. Each loop iteration searches for any hash record in the current hash table entry. If a hash record is located, its primary and secondary data strings are passed to the caller through the Hash$ and Rec$ parameters. Also, the NotFound variable is assigned False.

If the current table entry contains no hash records, the index VisitIndex is increased by 1 to index the next hash table entry. In addition, the CharIndex variable is reassigned 1 to index the first character of the next hash table entry.

Finally, the function returns its result, which is equal to the Boolean expression Not NotFound when an entry is located.

The Boolean VisitNextHashTableElem function searches for the next hash record. This function contains code that is similar to that of the VisitFirstHashTableElem function. The difference is that VisitNextHashTableElem uses the values of VisitIndex and CharIndex that been previously set by the VisitFirstHashTableElem function or by previous calls to VisitNextHashTableElem.

The Boolean RecallFromHashTable function recalls the secondary data string (using the Rec$ parameter) from a hash record that contains the primary data string Hash$. The function returns True if a matching hash record was found; otherwise, it returns False.

RecallFromHashTable assigns an empty string to parameter Rec$, which is the default value to be returned by Rec$ if no matching hash record is located. The function then obtains the table address using the Hash1 hashing function, and copies the targeted hash table entry into the local string variable S. Next, it searches for the Hash$ primary data string in the string S. If the search finds a matching record, the secondary data string Rec$ is extracted by calling the GetHashRecData procedure. The function then returns True. If no matching record is found, the function returns False.

The GetHashRecData procedure extracts the primary data string Hash$ and the secondary data string Rec$ from the hash record string HashRec$. Note that the HashRec$ string might only contain the KeyDelim character.

The hash table test program

Let's look at a program that tests the various hash table procedures in the HASHTABL.BAS module. This test program contains the following controls:

- A visible list box that emulates the hash table. I made the list box visible for the sake of the demonstration. You can set the Visible property of the list box to False at design time, and still use the test program.
- Two text boxes, one for the primary data string and the other for the secondary data strings. The test program uses both text boxes for input and output.
- A number of command buttons to store, recall, delete, and visit the hash table entries; clear the hash table; write the hash table to a text file; read the hash table from a text file; and exit the test program.

Figures 9-1 to 9-3 show the specifications for the TSHASH.MAK project file and the TSHASH.FRM form file. Figure 9-4 shows a sample session with the table test program.

Application name: Hash table test program
Application code name: TSHASH

9-1 The basic specifications for the TSHASH.MAK project file.

Version: 1.0   Date created: August 16, 1991
Programmer(s): Namir Clement Shammas

List of filenames

Storage path: \ VB \ VBXTOOL
Project   TSHASH.MAK
Global   GLOBAL.BAS
Form 1   TSHASH.FRM
Module 1   GENERIC.BAS
Module 2   HASHTABL.BAS

Form # 1   Form filename: TSHASH.FRM
Version: 1.0   Date: August 16, 1991

Control object type	Default CtlName	Purpose
Command button	Command1	Stores a record in the hash table
	Command2	Recalls a hash table record
	Command3	Clears the hash table
	Command4	Writes the hash table to a text file
	Command5	Visits the first hash table record
	Command6	Visits the next hash table record
	Command7	Exits the test program
	Command8	Reads the hash table elements from a text file
	Command9	Deletes a hash table record
Text box	Text1	Primary Data String text box
	Text2	Secondary Data String text box
List box	List1	Table emulator
Label	Label1	Label for the table
	Label2	Label for the Primary Data String text box
	Label3	Label for the Secondary Data String text box

9-2 The list of controls in the TSHASH.FRM form file.

Listing 9-2 contains the code attached to the TSHASH.FRM form. The form's procedures are presented in the next several paragraphs.

The StoreBtn_Click procedure stores the contents of the text boxes in the hash table. The contents of the primary data string text box are used to obtain the hash address for the target table entry. The procedure verifies that the primary data text box is not empty before storing the data in the hash table. The procedure then calls the StoreInHashTable procedure to store the strings Hash and Rec in hash table T.

Application (code) name: TSHASH
Form # 1
Version: 1.0   Date: August 16, 1991

Original control name	Property	New setting
Form	CtlName	Test Hash Table
Command1	CtlName	StoreBtn
	Caption	&Store
Command2	CtlName	RecallBtn
	Caption	&Recall
Command3	CtlName	ClearBtn
	Caption	&Clear
Command4	CtlName	WriteBtn
	Caption	&Write
Command5	CtlName	VisitFirstBtn
	Caption	Visit &First
Command6	CtlName	VisitNextBtn
	Caption	Visit &Next
Command7	CtlName	QuitBtn
	Caption	&Quit
Command8	CtlName	ReadBtn
	Caption	Rea&d
Command9	CtlName	DeleteBtn
	Caption	Dele&te
Text1	CtlName	PrimaryDataStringBox
	Text1	(empty string)
Text2	CtlName	SecondaryDataStringBox
	Text	(empty string)
List1	CtlName	TableLst
Label1	CtlName	TableLbl
	Caption	Hash Table
Label2	CtlName	PrimaryDataStringLbl
	Caption	Primary Data String
Label3	CtlName	SecondaryDataStringLbl
	Caption	Secondary Data String

9-3 The customized settings for the TSHASH.FRM form.

The RecallBtn_Click procedure recalls the secondary data string associated with the contents of the primary data string text box. The procedure first ensures that the primary data string text box is not empty. If this is true, the procedure calls the RecallFromHashTable function, and stores the contents of arguments Hash and Rec in the primary and secondary data string text boxes, respectively.

The ClearBtn_Click procedure clears the hash table by invoking the ClearList procedure in module GENERIC.BAS.

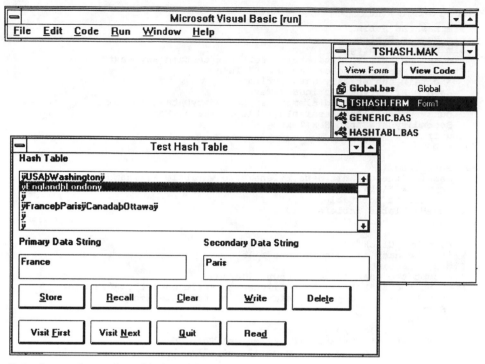

9-4 A sample session with the table test program.

Listing 9-2 The code attached to the TSHASH.FRM form.

```
Const True = -1, False = 0

Dim Filename As String

Sub StoreBtn_Click ()
' Store the string in SecondaryDataStringBox in the table
  Dim Hash As String
  Dim Rec As String
  ' does the primary data string test box contain any text?
  If PrimaryDataStringBox.Text <> "" Then
    ' obtain the primary data string
    Hash = PrimaryDataStringBox.Text
    ' copy the string of the secondary data string
    ' text box into Rec
    Rec = SecondaryDataStringBox.Text
    ' insert strings Hash and Rec in the table
    If Not InsertInHashTable(TableLst, Hash, Rec) Then
      MsgBox "Cannot insert data with duplicate hash keys", 64, "Error"
    End If
  End If
End Sub

Sub QuitBtn_Click ()
  End
End Sub

Sub RecallBtn_Click ()
' Recall a hash table element
```

Listing 9-2 Continued.

```
    Dim Hash As String
    Dim Rec As String
    Dim Dummy As Integer
    ' does the primary data string text box contain any text?
    If PrimaryDataStringBox.Text <> "" Then
        ' obtain the primary data string
        Hash = PrimaryDataStringBox.Text
        ' store the recalled element in SecondaryDataStringBox
        Dummy = RecallFromHashTable(TableLst, Hash, Rec)
        SecondaryDataStringBox.Text = Rec
    End If
End Sub

Sub Form_Load ()
    ' asssign the default data filename to varibale Filename
    Filename = "\vb\vbxtool\tshash.dat"
    ' initialize the table
    CreateHashTable TableLst, 10
End Sub

Sub WriteBtn_Click ()
' Write the hash table to a text file
    Dim S As String
    ' prompt the user for an output filename
    S = InputBox$("Enter output filename", "File Output", Filename)
    ' did the user accept the default or edited filename
    If S <> "" Then
        Filename = S
        ' did any file I/O error occur
        If Not WriteList(TableLst, Filename) Then
            MsgBox "Error in writing data", 64, "I/O Error"
        End If
    End If
End Sub

Sub ReadBtn_Click ()
' Read the the hash table from a text file
    Dim S As String
    ' prompt for an input filename
    S = InputBox$("Enter input filename", "File Input", Filename)
    ' did the user accept the defualt or edited filename?
    If S <> "" Then
        Filename = S
        ' did any file I/O error occur?
        If Not ReadList(TableLst, Filename, False) Then
            MsgBox "Error in reading data", 64, "I/O Error"
        End If
    End If
End Sub

Sub VisitFirstBtn_Click ()
' Visit the first hash record of the table and
' obtain the primary and secondary data strings from
' that hash record.
    Dim Hash As String
    Dim Rec As String
    ' is there a first element to visit?
    If VisitFirstHashTableElem(TableLst, Hash, Rec) Then
        ' copy the contents of Rec into secondary data
        ' string text box
        SecondaryDataStringBox.Text = Rec
        ' store the string Has in the primary data string
        ' text box
        PrimaryDataStringBox.Text = Hash
    Else
        ' clear the text boxes
```

Listing 9-2 Continued.

```
    SecondaryDataStringBox.Text = ""
    PrimaryDataStringBox.Text = ""
  End If
End Sub

Sub VisitNextBtn_Click ()
  Dim Hash As String
  Dim Rec As String
  ' is there another element to visit?
  If VisitNextHashTableElem(TableLst, Hash, Rec) Then
    ' copy the contents of Rec into the secondary data
    ' string text box
    SecondaryDataStringBox.Text = Rec
    ' store the string Hash in the primary data string
    ' text box
    PrimaryDataStringBox.Text = Hash
  Else
    ' clear the text boxes
    SecondaryDataStringBox.Text = ""
    PrimaryDataStringBox.Text = ""
  End If
End Sub

Sub ClearBtn_Click ()
  CLearList TableLst
End Sub

Sub DeleteBtn_Click ()
' delete a hash table record that matches the string
' in the primary data string text box.
  Dim Hash As String
  ' is th eprimary data string text box not empty?
  If PrimaryDataStringBox.Text <> "" Then
    ' copy the string of the primary data string text
    ' box into string Hash
    Hash = PrimaryDataStringBox.Text
    ' delete the target record
    DeleteFromHashTable TableLst, Hash
  End If
End Sub

Sub SecondaryDataStringBox_GotFocus ()
  HighlightTextBox SecondaryDataStringBox
End Sub

Sub PrimaryDataStringBox_GotFocus ()
  HighlightTextBox PrimaryDataStringBox
End Sub
```

The Form_Load procedure initializes the program by creating the hash table and assigning \ vb \ vbxtool \ tshash.dat to the variable Filename. I purposely made the program create a small hash table with 10 entries. The small table size prevents scrolling through a large list box, and also shows how colliding records are chained.

The WriteBtn_Click procedure writes the hash table entries to a text file. A simple dialog box appears with the current default filename, which is stored in the variable Filename. If you accept the default or edited filename, the procedure invokes the WriteList function to write the array to the file Filename. If the WriteList function returns False, a message box appears to inform you that there was an error in the file operation. This error might be attributed either to supplying a bad or invalid filename, or to a write error, such as one resulting from writing to a full disk.

The ReadBtn_Click procedure reads the hash table entries from a text file. A simple dialog box appears with the current default filename, stored in the variable Filename. If you accept the default or edited filename, the procedure invokes the ReadList function to read the array from the file Filename. If the ReadList function returns False, a message box appears saying that there was an error in the file operation, which might be attributed either to supplying a bad or invalid filename or to a read error.

The VisitFirstBtn_Click procedure visits the first hash table record. The procedure invokes the function VisitFirstTableElem; if the function returns True, the string variables Hash and Rec are copied into the text boxes.

The VisitNextBtn_Click procedure visits the next hash table record. The procedure invokes the function VisitNextTableElem. If the function returns True, the variables Hash and Rec are copied into the text boxes.

Run the test program and experiment with the various aspects of the hash table. The companion disk includes the TSHASH.DAT file which contains a small sample hash table containing the names of programming languages. Click on the Read button to read the hash table from the data file.

Try visiting and recalling the hash table records. You can also store new records in the hash table. Try inserting new data in the hash table, and notice where the new data appears.

When you finish working with the program, you might want to save the updated hash table, using the default filename or a new one. Finally, exit the program by clicking on the Quit button.

Part Two

The calculator forms

This part presents three kinds of calculators that you can easily incorporate in your applications. These calculators are the programmer's calculator, the algebraic scientific calculator, and the Reverse Polish Notation (RPN) scientific calculator. Each calculator is coded in a separate form that you can use in your own application simply by loading it.

10
The programmer's calculator

This chapter presents a simple four-function programmer's calculator. The simulated algebraic calculator handles positive integers in decimal, hexadecimal, octal, or binary bases. Negative integers are limited to the decimal base. You will learn about the various aspects of designing a simple calculator, including setting the specifications, drawing the controls, and attaching the code to the various controls.

The version of the programmer's calculator presented here is rather simple in design; this simplicity enables you to easily understand the dynamics of the basic four-function calculator. In the next chapter, I present an algebraic scientific calculator that is a significant superset of the four-function calculator.

All types of calculators are essentially state machines. The state of the calculator changes as you click on different buttons. The core of emulating a calculator lies in managing the calculator's state.

Design specifications

Let's look at the specifications and operations of the programmer's calculator, whose form is shown in FIG. 10-1. The basic operations and features of the calculator are:

- Handling integers ranging from minus 2 billion to 2 billion, or $2^{31} - 1$. This applies to the decimal base only; if you plan to convert integers between the different bases, avoid negative decimal numbers.
- Displaying numbers in decimal, hexadecimal, octal, and binary mode. When you switch from one mode to another, the currently

displayed number is changed to the new base. Base conversion supports only non-negative integers.
- Performing the four basic math operations. All operators have the same precedence.
- Storing numbers in one memory register. You can add a number to the register, recall a number from the register, and clear the memory register.
- Clearing the machine by resetting the internal registers, the display, and any pending operations.

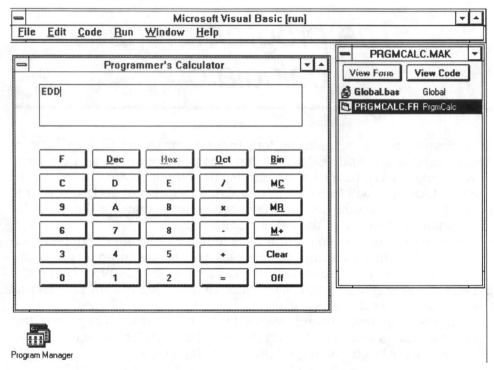

10-1 A sample session with the programmer's calculator.

☞ Figure 10-2 shows the various systems in the programmer's calculator. The Processing system performs the mathematical operations and maintains the internal registers and the pending operator. The Display system controls the display, while the Digits system offers input to the Display/Processing system when you key in a new number.

The Base system influences the Display/Processing and the Digits systems. The Base system specifies the base used in displaying integers, and specifies those digit buttons that are enabled and disabled for the current base.

The Operators system influences the Display/Processing system by specifying the sequence of operators that you invoke. The Memory Regis-

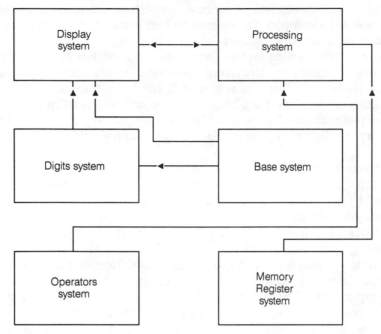

10-2 The various systems in the programmer's calculator.

ter system interacts with the Display/Processing system by storing and recalling the contents of the single-memory register.

In the next paragraphs I explain these systems in more detail.

The Processing system

The heart of the calculator is the Processing system, which is responsible for monitoring the flow of operands and operators, and for performing the math operations. The Processing system works closely with the Display system and receives feedback from the Operators and Memory Register systems. The processing system maintains information on the new-number state, the last pending operator, and the two internal numeric registers, which I will call X and Y.

☞ How does the processing system execute the sequence of operations? The answer lies in monitoring the two states of the machine. These states are:

- The new-number state, which is a flag that signals whether or not the calculator user is in the process of keying in a new number.
- The last pending operator state, which specifies the last pending operator, if any. When the calculator form is first loaded or when you click on the Clear button, the last pending operator is cleared.

I will explain the dynamics of executing math operations by walking you through a short example. This scenario can occur either after the form is first loaded or after you click on the Clear button.

The calculator states and registers start out with a clear new-number state, which is equivalent to setting the state to False. There is no last pending operator, and the internal registers X and Y contain zeros.

You start keying in a number, the first operand. As soon as you enter a digit, the new-number flag is set. The number you key in may be made up of one or more digits; any subsequent digits do not alter the new-number state.

Next you select the first operator. Since there is no pending operator, this operator becomes the last pending operator. The first operand that you keyed in is stored in register X, and the new-number flag is cleared.

When you key in the second operand, the first digit entered sets the new-number flag, telling the display to clear its previous contents and show the digits of the second operand.

You now choose a second operator. This action terminates keying in the second operand, clears the new-number flag, and executes the last pending operation. This involves copying the contents of register X into register Y, copying the second operand into register X, and then executing the last pending operator. The result is placed both in register X and in the display. Finally, the second operator is made the last pending operator.

Next you key in a third number. Once again, the first digit you enter sets the new-number flag, clearing the previous contents of the display and showing the digits of the third number.

You now select the = button to end the sequence of operations. This action terminates keying in the third number, clears the new-number state, and executes the last pending operation. The contents of register X are copied into register Y, the third number is copied into register X, and the last pending operator is executed. The result is placed both in register X and in the display. Finally, the last pending operator is cleared.

The Display system

The Display system is responsible for displaying a number (usually the contents of a register X) in the current base.

The Digits system

The Digits system permits you to enter a number either by keying numbers in the display text box or by clicking on the digit buttons with the mouse. The current base mode determines which digits from 0 to 9 and from A to F are acceptable. If you are keying a number in the text box, the KeyPress event handler makes sure that only the valid digits appear in the display text box. If you use the digit command buttons, the matter is resolved more easily, since the illegal digit buttons are disabled.

The Base system

The Base system selects and manages the various bases. When you select a new base, the Base system disables the button for the selected base and enables the other base buttons. You can tell which base is in effect by the disabled base button.

The Base system then converts the number in the display into the new base. It enables and disables the appropriate digit buttons for the selected base. Figure 10-3 lists the digit buttons that are enabled and disabled for the various bases. Also, the system sets the base mode that is used by Processing and Display systems.

		Digit command buttons	
Base	**Value range**	**Enabled**	**Disabled**
Hexadecimal	0 to F	2 to F	None
Decimal	0 to 9	2 to 9	A to F
Octal	0 to 7	2 to 7	8 to F
Binary	0 to 1	None*	2 to F

*The 0 and 1 digit command buttons are always enabled.

10-3 The list of digit command buttons that are enabled and disabled.

The Operators system

The Operators system feeds the queue of operators to the Processing system. The system manages the four base math operators, the Clear button, and the = button.

The Memory Register system

The Memory Register system manages storing, recalling, and clearing the contents of the single memory register.

The programmer's calculator controls

Figures 10-4 to 10-6 show the specifications for the PRGMCALC.MAK project file and the PRGMCALC.FRM form. The form file is the object of primary interest. Figures 10-5 and 10-6 list the various command buttons that make up the programmer's calculator, including the DigitBtn control array that represents the digit command buttons.

The programmer's calculator code

Having seen the specifications for the calculator's control objects, let's look now at the code attached to the PRGMCALC.FRM form, shown in

Application name: Programmer's calculator
Application code name: PRGMCALC

Version: 1.0   Date created: August 21, 1991   **10-4**   The basic
Programmer(s): Namir Clement Shammas   specifications for the
List of filenames   PRGMCALC.MAK
                                                                                 project file.
Storage path: \ VB/VBXTOOL
Project   PRGMCALC.MAK
Global   GLOBAL.BAS (not used)
Form 1   PRGMCALC.FRM

Form # 1   Form filename: PRGMCALC.FRM
Version: 1.0   Date: August 21, 1991

Control object type   **Default CtlName**   **Purpose**

Command button   Command1   Exits the form
                          Command2   The digit button control array

	Index	Digit emulated
	0	0
	1	1
	2	2
	3	3
	4	4
	5	5
	6	6
	7	7
	8	8
	9	9
	10	A
	11	B
	12	C
	13	D
	14	E
	15	F

                          Command3   Adds two numbers
                          Command4   Subtracts two numbers
                          Command5   Multiplies two numbers
                          Command6   Divides two numbers
                          Command7   The equals operator
                          Command8   Clears the calculator
                          Command9   Adds to the memory register
                          Command10   Recalls the memory register
                          Command11   Clears the memory register
                          Command12   Selects the decimal base
                          Command13   Selects the hexadecimal base
                          Command14   Selects the octal base
                          Command15   Selects the binary base

Text box   Text1   The Display text box

10-5   The list of controls in the PRGMCALC.FRM form file.

Application (code) name: PRGMCALC
Form # 1
Version: 1.0   Date: August 21, 1991

Original control name	Property	New setting	
Form	CtlName	Programmer's Calculator	
	FormName	PrgmCalc	
Command1	CtlName	OffBtn	
	Caption	Off	
Command2	CtlName	DigitBtn	
	Caption	0 for Index	0
		1 " "	1
		2 " "	2
		3 " "	3
		4 " "	4
		5 " "	5
		6 " "	6
		7 " "	7
		8 " "	8
		9 " "	9
		A " "	10
		B " "	11
		C " "	12
		D " "	13
		E " "	14
		F " "	15
Command3	CtlName	AddBtn	
	Caption	*	
Command4	CtlName	SubBtn	
	Caption	–	
Command5	CtlName	MulBtn	
	Caption	*	
Command6	CtlName	DivBtn	
	Caption	/	
Command7	CtlName	EqualBtn	
	Caption	=	
Command8	CtlName	ClearBtn	
	Caption	Clear	
Command9	CtlName	MaddBtn	
	Caption	&M +	
Command10	CtlName	MrecallBtn	
	Caption	M&R	
Command11	CtlName	MclearBtn	
	Caption	M&C	
Command12	CtlName	DecBtn	
	Caption	&Dec	
Command13	CtlName	HexBtn	
	Caption	&Hex	

10-6 The customized settings for the PRGMCALC.FRM form.

Original control name	Property	New setting
Command14	CtlName	OctBtn
	Caption	&Oct
Command15	CtlName	BinBtn
	Caption	&Bin
Text1	CtlName	DspText
	Text	(empty string)

10-6 Continued.

Listing 10-1. The form declares a number of constants, variables, event-handling procedures, and other procedures.

The form declares the following constants:

- The Boolean True and False.
- The DECMODE, HEXMODE, OCTMODE, and BINMODE constants represent integer values for the various base modes.
- The BITS_IN_LONG constant that is assigned 32, the number of bits in a long integer type.

Listing 10-1 The code attached to the PRGMCALC.FRM form.

```
Const True = -1, False = 0
' Declare constants for the various bases
Const DECMODE = 1, HEXMODE = 2, OCTMODE = 3, BINMODE = 4
Const BITS_IN_LONG = 32

' Declare form-level variables
Dim Memory As Long ' memory register
Dim RegY As Long    ' first operand
Dim RegX As Long    ' second operand
Dim BaseMode As Integer 'base mode
Dim NewNum As Integer ' Boolean numeric entry state
Dim LastOp As String * 1

Sub AddBtn_Click ()
' Handle pressing the + button
  SetPendOp "+"
End Sub

Function Bin$ (N As Long)
' Function converts the argument for N into a string image of
' a binary number
  Dim S As String * BITS_IN_LONG
  Dim BitNum As Integer
  ' fill the variable that stores the function result with
  ' BITS_IN_LONG "0" characters
  S = String$(BITS_IN_LONG, "0")
  ' loop for bits 0 to BITS_IN_LONG
  For BitNum = 0 To BITS_IN_LONG - 2
    ' is bit number BitNum set?
    If N And 2 ^ BitNum Then
      ' replace the "0" with a "1" at the character that
      ' maps the BitNum bit
```

Listing 10-1 Continued.

```
        Mid$(S, BITS_IN_LONG - BitNum, 1) = "1"
      End If
   Next BitNum
   ' is N negative?
   If N < 0 Then Mid$(S, 1, 1) = "1"
   Bin$ = S ' return the function result
End Function

Sub BinBtn_Click ()
' Select the binary base mode
   Dim I As Integer
   Dim X As Long
   ' convert the string in the display text box into a number
   X = GetNumber()
   ' disable the Bin button and enable all of the other base buttons
   DecBtn.Enabled = True
   HexBtn.Enabled = True
   OctBtn.Enabled = True
   BinBtn.Enabled = False
   BaseMode = BINMODE ' set the current base mode to binary
   ' convert the number X into the string image of the current
   ' base mode
   PutNumber X
   NewNum = False ' clear the NewNum state
   ' clear the digit buttons 2 to F
   For I = 2 To 15
      DigitBtn(I).Enabled = False
   Next I
End Sub

Function BinVal () As Long
' Convert the string image of a binary number in
' the display text box into a long integer
   Dim X As Long
   Dim BitNum As Integer
   Dim S As String * BITS_IN_LONG
   X = 0 ' initialize the function result
   ' add leading zeros to the binary number?
   Do While Len(DspBox.Text) < BITS_IN_LONG
      DspBox.Text = "0" + DspBox.Text
   Loop
   S = DspBox.Text
   ' loop for bits 0 to 30
   For BitNum = 0 To BITS_IN_LONG - 2
      ' is the image of bit BitNum a "1"?
      If Mid$(S, BITS_IN_LONG - BitNum, 1) = "1" Then
         ' add to value of bit BitNum to X
         X = X + 2 ^ BitNum
      End If
   Next BitNum
   ' is the number positive?
   If Left$(S, 1) = "0" Then
      BinVal = X ' return the function result
   Else
      BinVal = -X ' return the function result
   End If
End Function

Sub ClearBtn_Click ()
' Clear the calculator
   ' reset the RegX and RegY registers
   RegX = 0
   RegY = 0
   ' clear the display text box
   DspBox.Text = ""
   ' turn off the NewNum status
```

Listing 10-1 Continued.

```
    NewNum = False
    ' assign a space to the last operator variable
    LastOp = " "
End Sub

Sub DecBtn_Click ()
' Select the decimal base mode
    Dim I As Integer
    Dim X As Long
    ' convert the string in the display text box into a number
    X = GetNumber()
    ' disable the Dec button and enable all of the other base buttons
    DecBtn.Enabled = False
    HexBtn.Enabled = True
    OctBtn.Enabled = True
    BinBtn.Enabled = True
    BaseMode = DECMODE ' set the current base mode to decimal
    ' convert the number X into the string image of the current
    ' base mode
    PutNumber X
    NewNum = False ' clear the NewNum state
    ' enable the digit buttons 2 to 9
    For I = 2 To 9
      DigitBtn(I).Enabled = True
    Next I
    ' disable the digit buttons A to F
    For I = 10 To 15
      DigitBtn(I).Enabled = False
    Next I
End Sub

Sub DigitBtn_Click (Index As Integer)
' Enter a digit in the display text box
    ' is the NewNum state False?
    If Not NewNum Then
      DspBox.Text = "" ' clear the display text box
    End If
    ' set the NewNum state to True
    NewNum = True
    ' append the corresponding digit.
    DspBox.Text = DspBox.Text + DigitBtn(Index).Caption
End Sub

Sub DivBtn_Click ()
' Handle pressing the / button
    SetPendOp "/"
End Sub

Sub DspBox_Change ()
' Set the NewNum state to True when the display text box is changed
    NewNum = True
End Sub

Sub DspBox_KeyPress (KeyAScii As Integer)
' Monitor the keys pressed in the display text box and filter
' out illegal characters.  The set of legal characters depends
' on the current base mode
    Const BACKSPACE = 8
    If KeyAScii = BACKSPACE Then Exit Sub
    Select Case BaseMode
      Case DECMODE:
        ' in the decimal mode the characters 0 to 9 are valid.
        ' is the input not in the valid set of characters?
        If InStr("-0123456789", Chr$(KeyAScii)) = 0 Then
          KeyAScii = 0 ' filter input out
        End If
```

Listing 10-1 Continued.

```
      Case HEXMODE:
        ' in the hexadecimal mode the characters 0 to 9 and A to F
        ' are valid.
        ' is the input not in the valid set of characters?
        If InStr("0123456789ABCEF", Chr$(KeyAScii)) = 0 Then
          KeyAScii = 0  ' filter input out
        End If
      Case OCTMODE:
        ' in the octal mode the characters 0 to 7 are valid.
        ' is the input not in the valid set of characters?
        If InStr("01234567", Chr$(KeyAScii)) = 0 Then
          KeyAScii = 0  ' filter input out
        End If
      Case BINMODE:
        ' in the binary mode the characters 0 and 1 are valid.
        ' is the input not in the valid set of characters?
        If InStr("01", Chr$(KeyAScii)) = 0 Then
          KeyAScii = 0  ' filter input out
        End If
  End Select
End Sub

Sub DspBox_LostFocus ()
' Handle the LostFocus event for the display text box.
  Dim S As String
  S = DspBox.Text
  ' is the number in the display text box negative?
  If Mid$(S, 1, 1) = "-" Then
    ' remove the leading "-"
    S = Mid$(S, 2)
    ' update the display text box
    DspBox.Text = S
  End If
End Sub

Sub EqualBtn_Click ()
' Terminate the chain of operator evaluations
  ExecLastOp ' execute the last pending operation
  LastOp = " " ' clear the last operator
  NewNum = False ' set the NewNum state to False
End Sub

Sub ExecLastOp ()
' Execute the last operator
  ' turn on the error trapping
  On Error GoTo BadOp
  ' copy register RegX into register RegY
  RegY = RegX
  ' obtain the number in the display text box and write it to RegX
  RegX = GetNumber()
  ' execute the pending operation
  Select Case LastOp
    Case "+"
      RegX = RegY + RegX
    Case "-"
      RegX = RegY - RegX
    Case "/"
      RegX = RegY / RegX
    Case "*"
      RegX = RegY * RegX
  End Select
  On Error GoTo 0 ' turn off the error trap
  PutNumber RegX
  Exit Sub
  '********************** Error Handler **********************
BadOp:
```

Listing 10-1 Continued.

```
     ' display an error message box
     MsgBox "Error in " + LastOp + " operation", 64, "Error"
     ClearBtn_Click ' clear the calculator
     Resume ExitOp
ExitOp:
End Sub

Sub Form_Load ()
' Initialize the form PrgmCalc when loaded
   ClearBtn_Click ' clear the operands
   DecBtn_Click   ' select decimal base mode
   LastOp = " "   ' clear the last operator
End Sub

Function GetNumber () As Long
' Convert the string in the display text box into a positive long
' integer.
   Dim X As Long
   ' turn on the error trap
   On Error GoTo OverFlowErr
   ' convert DspBox.Text into a long integer, based on the
   ' current base mode
   Select Case BaseMode
      Case DECMODE: X = Val(DspBox.Text + "&")
      Case HEXMODE: X = Val("&H" + DspBox.Text + "&")
      Case OCTMODE: X = Val("&O" + DspBox.Text + "&")
      Case BINMODE: X = BinVal() ' call the BinVal function
   End Select
   GetNumber = X ' return the function value
   ' turn off the error trap
   On Error GoTo 0
   Exit Function
   '********************** Error Handler **********************
OverFlowErr:
   ' display the error message box
   MsgBox "Overflow error", 64, "Error"
   ClearBtn_Click ' clear the calculator
   Resume ExitGetNumber
ExitGetNumber:
End Function

Sub HexBtn_Click ()
' Select the hexadecimal base mode
   Dim I As Integer
   Dim X As Long
   ' convert the string in the display text box into a number
   X = GetNumber()
   ' disable the Hex button and enable all of the other base buttons
   DecBtn.Enabled = True
   HexBtn.Enabled = False
   OctBtn.Enabled = True
   BinBtn.Enabled = True
   BaseMode = HEXMODE ' set the current base mode to hexadecimal
   ' convert the number X into the string image of the current
   ' base mode
   PutNumber X
   NewNum = False  ' clear the NewNum state
   ' enable the digit buttons 2 to F
   For I = 2 To 15
      DigitBtn(I).Enabled = True
   Next I
End Sub

Sub MaddBtn_Click ()
' Add the number whose image is in the display text box to the
' current contents of the memory register
```

Listing 10-1 Continued.

```
    Dim X As Long
    ' convert the string in the display text box into a number
    X = GetNumber()
    ' add X to Memory
    Memory = Memory + X
    NewNum = False ' set the NewNum state to false
End Sub

Sub MclearBtn_Click ()
' Clear the memory register
    Memory = 0
End Sub

Sub MrecallBtn_Click ()
' Recall the contents of the memory register
    ' copy the contents of memory register to the display text box
    PutNumber Memory
    NewNum = False ' set the NewNum state to False
End Sub

Sub MulBtn_Click ()
' Handle pressing the * button
    SetPendOp "*"
End Sub

Sub OctBtn_Click ()
' Select the octal base
    Dim I As Integer
    Dim X As Long
    ' convert the string in the display text box into a number
    X = GetNumber()
    ' disable the Oct button and enable all of the other base buttons
    DecBtn.Enabled = True
    HexBtn.Enabled = True
    OctBtn.Enabled = False
    BinBtn.Enabled = True
    BaseMode = OCTMODE ' set the current base mode to octal
    ' convert the number X into the string image of the current
    ' base mode
    PutNumber X
    NewNum = False ' clear the NewNum state
    ' enable the digit buttons 2 to 7
    For I = 2 To 7
        DigitBtn(I).Enabled = True
    Next I
    ' disable the digit buttons 8 to F
    For I = 8 To 15
        DigitBtn(I).Enabled = False
    Next I
End Sub

Sub OffBtn_Click ()
' Unload the PrgmCalc form
    Unload PrgmCalc
End Sub

Sub PutNumber (X As Long)
' Convert the argument of X into the string image of an integer
' using the current base mode
    Select Case BaseMode
        Case DECMODE: DspBox.Text = Format$(X)
        Case HEXMODE: DspBox.Text = Hex$(X)
        Case OCTMODE: DspBox.Text = Oct$(X)
        Case BINMODE: DspBox.Text = Bin$(X) ' call the module
                                            ' Bin$ function
    End Select
End Sub
```

Listing 10-1 Continued.

```
Sub SetPendOp (ByVal OpStr As String)
' Execute the current pending operator and set the new
' pending operator to OpStr
  ' no pending operations?
  If LastOp = " " Then
    ' obtain the number in the display text box and write it to RegX
    RegX = GetNumber()
  Else
    ' execute the current pending operator
    ExecLastOp
  End If
  ' set the new pending operator to OpStr
  LastOp = OpStr
  NewNum = False ' clear the NewNum state
End Sub

Sub SubBtn_Click ()
' Handle pressing the - button
  SetPendOp "-"
End Sub
```

The form also declares the following set of variables:

- The variable Memory represents the memory register of the calculator.
- The RegX and RegY variables model the internal X and Y registers.
- The BaseMode variable stores the current base mode. This variable is assigned one of the xxxMODE constants.
- The Boolean NewNum variable represents the new-number state.
- The single-character string LastOp variable stores the last pending operator.

Processing system procedures

The form contains a number of auxiliary procedures that make up the Processing system of the calculator. These procedures are called by the various event-handling procedures.

The Bin$ function converts a long integer into a string that contains the binary image of that integer. The function uses the local fixed-length string variable S to build the image of the sought binary number. The string is initialized with the 0 characters. A For-Next loop examines the bits 0 to BITS_IN_LONG – 2. Each loop iteration ANDs the argument of N with the expression 2^BitNum. If the ANDed expression is true, the character that corresponds to the tested bit is replaced with 1. The loop iterates from 0 to BITS_IN_LONG – 2. The number 2 is subtracted from the BITS _IN_LONG for two reasons. First, the highest bit of a long integer is bit number 31. Second, the highest bit deals with the minus sign of a long integer. Thus the loop iterates from bit 0 to bit 30. The procedure assigns 1 to the first character of variable S, if the converted long integer is negative.

The BinVal function converts the image of the binary number in the display text box into a long integer. The function uses the local variable X to iteratively refine the function result. Initially, the variable X is assigned 0, and the contents of the display text box are copied into a local fixed-length string S. The function uses a For-Next loop to examine the characters of S that map bits 0 to 30. If the examined character is 1, the variable X is increased by 2^BitNum, the value of the examined bit. If the first character of variable S is 1, the function returns a negative long integer.

The ExecLastOp procedure executes the last pending operator. The procedure sets the error trap to handle mathematical overflow errors, copies the value of RegX into RegY, and converts the string in the display text box into a long integer, assigning that integer to variable RegX. The procedure then executes the pending operation using a Select Case statement that compares the single-character string variable LastOp with the various literal strings that represent the supported operators. Each Case clause performs a specific math operation and assigns the result back to RegX. Next, the code turns off the error trap and writes the image of RegX into the display text box. The procedure also manages any run-time error by displaying an error message and then clearing both the calculator state and the internal registers.

The GetNumber function converts the string image of the display text box into a long integer. The function turns on the error trap to handle run-time conversion errors due to a bad string image. It then converts the contents of the display text box into the local variable X using a Select Case statement. This statement examines the value of the BaseMode variable and selects the proper type of conversion. In the case of the binary mode, the GetNumber function uses the BinVal function. The procedure then assigns the function value, turns off the error trap, and exits the function. Any run-time errors are managed by displaying an error message and then clearing both the calculator state and registers.

The PutNumber procedure converts its long integer parameter X into the string image stored in the display text box. The procedure converts the parameter X into a string using a Select Case statement that examines the value of the BaseMode variable. The procedure uses the built-in Format$, Hex$, and Oct$ functions, as well as the form function Bin$ to convert X into the string image of a decimal, hexadecimal, octal, or binary number, respectively.

The SetPendOp procedure executes the currently pending operation and sets a new one. If the variable LastOp is empty, the procedure assigns the result of function GetNumber into the RegX variable; otherwise, the procedure invokes the ExecLastOp procedure to execute any pending operation. The procedure then assigns the argument for OpStr to the variable LastOp. The routine also assigns False to the new-number state variable NewNum.

Display system procedures

The Display system is made up of two event-handling procedures.

The DspBox_Change procedure sets the new-number state to True. The DspBox_LostFocus procedure checks the display text box for the presence of the string image of a negative number typed by the user. If such an item is detected, the negative sign is removed.

Digit system procedures

The form contains the following procedures that make up the Digit system.

The DigitBtn_Click procedure enters a digit in the display text box. The value of the parameter Index determines which digit button was clicked. The procedure tests if the new-number state is False; if it is, the procedure clears the display text box to make way for a new number. Then it sets the new-number state to True. This action appends the subsequent digits that are part of the new number when this procedure is called again. Finally, the procedure appends the single-character caption of DigitBtn(Index) to the string in the display text box.

The DspBox_KeyPress procedure monitors the keys that you press while typing directly into the text box. The procedure uses a Case Select statement to examine the value in the BaseMode variable and determine which set of characters form legal digits. Each Case clause uses the Visual Basic Instr function to determine whether or not the character you type is part of the string of legal digits. If the value of the InStr function is 0, the procedure filters out the character you just typed.

Base system procedures

The form also contains the following procedures that belong to the Base system.

The BinBtn_Click procedure selects the binary base mode. The procedure converts the string image in the display text box into a long integer and assigns that integer to the local variable X. It disables the Bin button and enables all of the other base buttons, then assigns the constant BIN MODE to the variable BaseMode. The procedure then writes the string image of X to the display text box using the PutNumber procedure. This step displays a binary image of X. Finally, it sets the new-number state to False and disables the digit buttons 2 to 15 (this includes the hexadecimal buttons A to F).

The DecBtn_Click procedure selects the decimal base mode. The procedure converts the string in the display text box into a long integer and assigns that integer to the local variable X. Next, the procedure disables the Dec button and enables all of the other base buttons, and assigns the constant DECMODE to the variable BaseMode. The procedure then writes the string image of X to the display text box using the PutNumber procedure, which causes a decimal image of X to be displayed. Finally, the procedure sets the new-number state to False, enables the digit buttons 2 to 9, and disables the digit buttons 10 to 15 (representing the hexadecimal buttons A to F).

The HexBtn_Click procedure selects the hexadecimal base mode. This procedure converts the string image in the display text box into a long integer and assigns that integer to the local variable X. It disables the Hex button and enables all of the other base buttons, and assigns the constant HEXMODE to the variable BaseMode. Then it writes the string image of X to the display text box using the PutNumber procedure, which displays the hexadecimal image of X. Before terminating, the procedure sets the new-number state to False and enables the digit buttons 2 to 15 (including the hexadecimal buttons A to F).

The OctBtn_Click procedure selects the octal base mode. Like the other procedures, this procedure converts the string image in the display text box into a long integer and assigns that integer to the local variable X. It disables the Oct button, enables all of the other base buttons, and assigns the constant OCTMODE to the variable BaseMode. The procedure then writes the string image of X to the display text box using the PutNumber procedure. The octal image of X is displayed. Finally, the procedure sets the new-number state to False, enables the digit buttons 2 to 7, and disables the digit buttons 8 to 15 (including the hexadecimal buttons A to F).

Operators system procedures

The form contains procedures described next that make up the Operators system:

The AddBtn_Click procedure sends the + operator to the Processing system.

The ClearBtn_Click procedure clears the calculator state. The routine assigns 0 to the variables RegX and RegY, clears the display text box, clears the new-number state, and clears the last pending operator.

The DivBtn_Click procedure sends the / operator to the Processing system.

The EqualBtn_Click procedure terminates the chain of operations. The routine invokes the ExecLastOp to execute any pending operations, then clears both the last pending operation and the new-number state.

The MulBtn_Click procedure sends the * operator to the Processing system.

The SubBtn_Click procedure sends the – operator to the Processing system.

Memory register system procedures

The procedures described here make up the Memory Register system.

The MaddBtn_Click procedure adds the number displayed in the text box to the memory register, represented by the variable Memory.

The MclearBtn_Click procedure clears the memory register by assigning 0 to the Memory variable.

The MrecallBtn_Click procedure recalls the contents of the memory register which are in variable Memory. The routine puts the value of the variable Memory in the display text box by calling the PutNumber procedure.

Run the program and experiment with the various calculator features. Switch between base modes and watch the display change numeric formats.

11
The scientific calculator

The last chapter presented a programmer's calculator; this chapter introduces a scientific calculator. This calculator adds various mathematical functions and includes 100 memory registers. I will discuss the design and specifications of a scientific calculator form that you can load and unload in your custom Visual Basic programs.

Design specifications

The scientific calculator that I offer, which is shown in FIG. 11-1, has the following features and capabilities:

- A set of numeric entry buttons that includes the digits 0 to 9, the decimal point, a change sign button, and an exponent button.
- A group of buttons for mathematical operations, including addition, subtraction, multiplication, division, and exponentiation. All of the operators have equal precedence, unless you employ the parentheses.
- A group of buttons that supports various trigonometric and transcendental functions. The current list of functions includes:
  - ~Trigonometric functions: sine, cosine, tangent, and their inverses. The calculator supports angles in radians and degrees.
  - ~Logarithmic functions: natural and common logarithms and their inverses.
  - ~Hyperbolic functions: hyperbolic sine, hyperbolic cosine, hyperbolic tangent, and their inverses.
  - ~Other math functions: square, cube, square root, cube root, absolute, pi, and reciprocal.

- 100 memory registers, which are managed by a group of buttons that store, accumulate, recall, and clear data in the memory registers.
- An operator stack that stores pending operators and numbers.
- A text box that allows you to enter a new number.

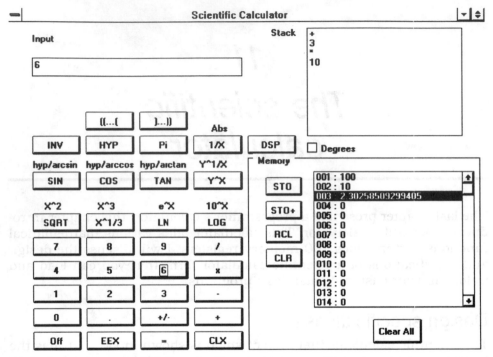

11-1 A sample session with the scientific calculator.

☞ The scientific calculator is made up of several systems, shown in FIG. 11-2. The Processing system handles the execution of the operators and mathematical functions. The Display system manages the direct input of a number into the display text box. This system also maintains the current format string. The Memory Registers system manages the operations of 100 memory registers. The Operators system requests that the Processing system execute an operation which requires two operands. The Digits system manages keying in a new number in the display text box. The Functions system requests that the Processing system evaluate a specified mathematical function which takes one argument.

The Processing system

The calculator's Processing system is a superset of the Processing system of the programmer's calculator presented in chapter 10. The system evaluates the requested mathematical functions and executes the pending

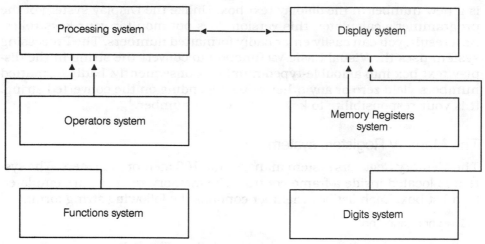

11-2 The systems of the scientific calculator form.

operators. The Processing system uses the form-level variables RegX, RegY, and LastOp to manage and execute the pending operators. The evaluation of mathematical functions is handled somewhat differently. First, the system evaluates the specified mathematical function; then the evaluation is carried out such that the RegX and RegY are not involved.

In evaluating a math function, the system reads the number in the display text box and uses that number as the argument to evaluate the designated function. It then evaluates the function with the obtained argument, and writes the result of the function evaluation back to the display text box. These steps ensure that the function evaluation disturbs neither the pending operation nor the internal registers.

To evaluate an expression with a function, you must specify the function's argument before you invoke the function. For example, to evaluate the Visual Basic expression:

    2 * Sin(45)

you enter and execute the following sequence of numbers, operators, and functions:

    2 * 45 SIN

This example shows that the scientific calculator does not use pure algebraic logic. Instead it employs a hybrid logic that combines the algebraic and Reverse Polish logics. I'll discuss Reverse Polish logic in the next chapter.

The Display system

The Display system of the scientific calculator is very simple. Its main purpose is to update the format string and to inform other systems that there is a new number in the display text box. Unlike the Display system of the programmer's calculator, this version does not monitor your keystrokes. As a result, you can easily enter badly formatted numbers. The Processing system uses the Visual Basic Val function to convert the string in the display text box into a double-typed number. Consequently, badly formatted numbers yield zero or any other value depending on the converted string. It is your responsibility to key in the correct number.

The Memory Registers system

The Memory Registers system manages the 100 memory registers. The system is located inside a frame control. The memory registers are emulated by a list box. Each list box member contains the following string format:

    iii : nnnnnnn...nn

where iii is a three-digit memory register index. The n characters represent the string image of a number stored in a memory register. You can inspect the various memory registers by using the vertical scroll bar of the list box.

The Memory Registers system uses the STO and STO+ buttons to store and accumulate the value of the display text box in a selected memory register. The string of the display text box is stored into the selected memory register. The default memory register is the first memory register. The system also supports writing the contents of a selected memory register to the display text box. Again, the first memory register is the default.

Other operations include clearing a selected register (there are no default memory registers for this operation) and clearing all of the registers. The system assigns one or more zeros to clear one or more memory registers.

The Operators system

The Operators system becomes active when you click on one of the operator buttons. These include the buttons with captions +, −, *, /, Y^X, and Y^1/X. The Operators system requests that the Processing system perform the designated operation. The = button requests the execution of all pending operators. Since the various operators have the same precedence, you may want to use the open and close parentheses. For example, to evaluate the Visual Basic expression:

    2 + 3 * 4

you must enter the following sequence of numbers and operators:

    2 + (3 * 4)

The (operator pushes the number 2 and the + operator in the operators stack, resets the internal registers, and clears the pending operator value stored in LastOp. When you enter the 3 * 4 sequence, the Processing system places these items in the internal registers and the LastOp variable. So far no operator has been executed, but this condition changes when you invoke the) operator. At this point, a number of tasks are carried out. First, the pending expression 3 * 4 is evaluated. Next, the number 2 and the + operator are popped off the operators stack. Finally, the result of 3 * 4 is added to the operand 2 to give the final result. In effect the above sequence is equivalent to:

    3 * 4 + 2

The Functions system

The Functions system becomes active when you click on a math function button. This system asks the Processing system to evaluate the designated function.

☞ The scientific calculator uses the INV and HYP buttons (see FIG. 11-1) with the SIN, COS, and TAN buttons to offer inverse trigonometric, hyperbolic, and inverse hyperbolic functions. For example, to calculate the hyperbolic sine, click the INV button and then the SIN button. The INV button also works with other buttons that have labels located above the buttons. For example, to obtain the cube of a number, click the INV button and then the X^1/3 button. I have coded the routines of the scientific calculator such that all of the buttons automatically clear the INV and HYP buttons— whether or not they work with these two buttons. This feature implements the "use it or lose it" principle.

The Digits system

The Digits system manages entering a new number using the digit command buttons. You begin entering a new number by clicking one of the 0 to 9 digit buttons, or by clicking the decimal point button. The Digits system allows you to toggle the sign of the number you are keying and permits you to enter an exponent part. The system uses an input dialog box to enter the exponent. Once you enter the exponent, the Digits system considers the number entry to be completed.

The scientific calculator controls

Figures 11-3 to 11-5 show the specifications for the SCICALC.MAK project file and the SCICALC.FRM form. The form file is the object of primary interest. Figures 11-4 and 11-5 list the various command buttons that make up the scientific calculator, including the DigitBtn control array that represents the digit command buttons.

Application name: Scientific calculator
Application code name: SCICALC

Version: 1.0   Date created: August 22, 1991   **11-3** The basic
Programmer(s): Namir Clement Shammas   specifications for the
List of filenames   SCICALC.MAK project
                                                                 file.
Storage path: \VB\VBXTOOL
Project   SCICALC.MAK
Global   GLOBAL.BAS (not used)
Form 1   SCICALC.FRM

Form # 1   Form filename: SCICALC.FRM
Version: 1.0   Date: August 22, 1991

Control object type	Default CtlName	Purpose
Command button	Command1	Unloads the form
	Command2	The control array for the digit buttons 0 to 9
	Command3	Inserts a decimal point
	Command4	Changes the sign of a number
	Command5	Inserts an exponent
	Command6	Clears the operands and operators
	Command7	Executes the pending operations
	Command8	Adds numbers
	Command9	Subtract numbers
	Command10	Multiplies numbers
	Command11	Divides numbers
	Command12	Returns the square root or the square of a number
	Command13	Returns the cube root or the cube of a number
	Command14	Returns the natural logarithm or the exponential of a number
	Command15	Returns the common logarithm or the power-of-ten of a number
	Command16	Returns the sine, arc sine, hyperbolic sine, or inverse hyperbolic sine values
	Command17	Returns the cosine, arc cosine, hyperbolic cosine, or inverse hyperbolic cosine values
	Command18	Returns the tangent, arc tangent, hyperbolic tangent, or inverse hyperbolic tangent values
	Command19	Returns the power or roots of two numbers
	Command20	Sets the INV state to obtain the inverse trigonometric functions
	Command21	Sets the HYP state to obtain hyperbolic functions or their inverses

11-4 The list of controls in the SCICALC.FRM form file.

Control object type	Default CtlName	Purpose
	Command22	Returns the value of pi
	Command23	Returns the reciprocal or absolute value of numbers
	Command24	Specifies the display format string
	Command25	Pushes an operation in the operators stack
	Command26	Executes the next operation in the operators stack
	Command27	Store the display text box in a selected memory register
	Command28	Adds the value of display text box in the selected memory register
	Command29	Copies the contents of the selected memory register to the display text box
	Command30	Clears the selected memory register
	Command31	Clears all the memory registers
Text box	Text1	The Input text box
List box	List1	The operations stack
	List2	The emulated memory registers
Check box	Check1	Specifies the degree or radian angle mode
Frame	Frame1	The frame that contains the controls for the memory registers
Label	Label1	Input text box label
	Label2	Stack label
	Label3	Sine button label
	Label4	Cosine button label
	Label5	Tangent button label
	Label6	Power button label
	Label7	Reciprocal button label

11-4 Continued.

Application (code) name: SCICALC
Form # 1
Version: 1.0   Date: August 22, 1991

Original control name	Property	New setting
Form	Caption	Scientific Calculator
	FormName	SciCalc
Command1	CtlName	OffBtn
	Caption	Off
Command2	CtlName	DigitBtn
	Caption	(the string image of the control index)

11-5 The customized settings for the SCICALC.FRM form.

Original control name	Property	New setting
Command3	CtlName	DecimalBtn
	Caption	.
Command4	CtlName	ChsBtn
	Caption	+/−
Command5	CtlName	EexBtn
	Caption	EEX
Command6	CtlName	ClxBtn
	Caption	CLX
Command7	CtlName	EqualBtn
	Caption	=
Command8	CtlName	AddBtn
	Caption	+
Command9	CtlName	SubBtn
	Caption	−
Command10	CtlName	MulBtn
	Caption	*
Command11	CtlName	DivBtn
	Caption	/
Command12	CtlName	SqrtBtn
	Caption	SQRT
Command13	CtlName	CubeRootBtn
	Caption	$X^{1/3}$
Command14	CtlName	LnBtn
	Caption	LN
Command15	CtlName	LogBtn
	Caption	LOG
Command16	CtlName	SinBtn
	Caption	SIN
Command17	CtlName	CosBtn
	Caption	COS
Command18	CtlName	TanBtn
	Caption	TAN
Command19	CtlName	PowerBtn
	Caption	Y^X
Command20	CtlName	InvBtn
	Caption	INV
Command21	CtlName	HypBtn
	Caption	HYP
Command22	CtlName	PiBtn
	Caption	SIN
Command23	CtlName	ReciprocalBtn
	Caption	1/X
Command24	CtlName	DspBtn
	Caption	DSP
Command25	CtlName	OpenParenBtn
	Caption	((...(

11-5 Continued.

Original control name	Property	New setting
Command26	CtlName	CloseParenBtn
	Caption	)...))
Command27	CtlName	StoBtn
	Caption	STO
Command28	CtlName	StoPluBtn
	Caption	STO +
Command29	CtlName	RclBtn
	Caption	RCL
Command30	CtlName	ClrBtn
	Caption	CLR
Command31	CtlName	ClearAllBtn
	Caption	Clear All
Text1	CtlName	DspBox
	Text	(empty string)
List1	CtlName	StackLst
List2	CtlName	MemLst
Check1	CtlName	DegreesChk
	Caption	Degrees
Frame1	Caption	Memory
Label1	CtlName	InputLbl
	Caption	Input
Label2	CtlName	StackLbl
	Caption	Stack
Label3	CtlName	SinLbl
	Caption	hyp/arcsin
Label4	CtlName	CosLbl
	Caption	hyp/arccos
Label5	CtlName	TanLbl
	Caption	hyp/arctan
Label6	CtlName	PowerLbl
	Caption	Y^1/X
Label7	CtlName	ReciprocalLbl
	Caption	Abs

11-5 Continued.

The scientific calculator code

The lengthy code for the scientific calculator is shown in Listing 11-1. The SCICALC.FRM form contains a number of module-level constants and variables. The constants are:

- The True and False constants.
- The MAX_MEM constant, which designates the number of memory registers. You can change the value of this constant to any other

positive integer. High values may cause the system to run out of memory.

- A series of constants that are assigned various error messages and error-related numeric codes.

Listing 11-1   The code attached to the SCICALC.FRM form.

```
Const True = -1, False = 0
' maximum number of memory registers
Const MAX_MEM = 100
' declare constants for various error messages
Const ERROR_TITLE = "Error!"
Const OVERFLOW_ERR = "Overflow error"
Const ARGUMENT_ERR = "Bad function argument"
Const BOX_MODE = 64 ' the second argument for the MsgBox statement

' Declare form level variables
Dim Frmt As String
Dim NewNum As Integer ' new number flag
Dim PressINV As Integer ' INV key flag
Dim PressHYP As Integer ' HYP key flag
' Operands variables
Dim RegX As Double, RegY As Double
' Angle conversion factor
Dim AngleCF As Double
Dim LastOp As String

Sub AddBtn_Click ()
' Add the two numbers
  SetPendOp "+"
End Sub

Sub ChsBtn_Click ()
' Change the sign of the number in the display box
  Dim S As String
  Dim OldNewNum As Integer
  OldNewNum = NewNum ' copy the NewNum state
  PressHYP = False
  PressINV = False
  S = DspBox.Text ' copy the display text box into variable S
  ' is the first character in the text box not a - sign
  If Left$(S, 1) <> "-" Then
    ' is the first character a + sign?
    If Left$(S, 1) = "+" Then
      Mid$(S, 1, 1) = "-" ' replace + with -
    Else
      ' prepend a - sign
      S = "-" + S
    End If
  Else
    S = Mid$(S, 2)
  End If
  ' update the display text box
  DspBox.Text = S
  ' restore the old NewNum value to override the procedure
  ' DspBox_Change
  NewNum = OldNewNum
End Sub

Sub ClearAllBtn_Click ()
' Clear the memory registers by assigning 0s to their
' contents.  The number of the memory registers is not
' altered.
  Dim I As Integer
```

Listing 11-1 Continued.

```
    PressHYP = False
    PressINV = False
    ' are there elements in the MemLst list box?
    If MemLst.ListCount > 0 Then
      For I = 1 To MemLst.ListCount
        MemLst.RemoveItem 0
      Next I
    End If
    ' insert the new set of list members
    For I = 1 To MAX_MEM
      ' assign the string using the format "iii : 0"
      MemLst.AddItem Format$(I, "000") + " : 0"
    Next I
End Sub

Sub CloseParenBtn_Click ()
' Drop the next pending operation.
    ' doses the operators stack have at least two members
    If StackLst.ListCount > 1 Then
      ' is the last operation a valid one?
      If LastOp <> " " Then
        ExecLastOp ' execute the last operation
        ' if there was an error in the above
        ' call, the operators stack would be
        ' cleared by ClxBtn_Click
        If StackLst.ListCount = 0 Then Exit Sub
      End If
      ' copy the operation at the top of the stack to LastOp
      LastOp = StackLst.List(0)
      ' shift the internal registers
      RegY = RegX
      ' copy the numeric equivalent of the next top stack
      ' member to RegX
      RegX = Val(StackLst.List(1))
      ' remove the two topmost stack members
      StackLst.RemoveItem 0
      StackLst.RemoveItem 0
      ' execute the operation that was popped off the stack
      ExecLastOp
      LastOp = " " ' clear the last operation
    End If
End Sub

Sub ClrBtn_Click ()
' Clear the selected memory register
    Dim I As Integer
    PressHYP = False
    PressINV = False
    ' get the index of the selected memory register
    I = MemLst.ListIndex
    ' is there a no selected memory register?
    If I < 0 Then Exit Sub
    ' reset the contents of the selected memory register
    MemLst.List(I) = Format$(I + 1, "000") + " : 0"
End Sub

Sub ClxBtn_Click ()

    DspBox.Text = "" ' clear display text box
    ' reset the internal registers
    RegX = 0
    RegY = 0
    LastOp = " " ' clear the last operation
    PressHYP = False
    PressINV = False
    ' clear the operators stack by removing every stack member
```

Listing 11-1 Continued.

```
  Do While StackLst.ListCount > 0
    StackLst.RemoveItem 0
  Loop
End Sub

Sub CosBtn_Click ()
' Handle the calls to the cosine, arc cosine, hyperbolic cosine,
' and inverse hyperbolic cosine functions.
  If PressHYP And PressINV Then
    ExecFunction "ArcCosh"
  ElseIf PressHYP Then
    ExecFunction "Cosh"
  ElseIf PressINV Then
    ExecFunction "ArcCos"
  Else
    ExecFunction "Cos"
  End If
End Sub

Sub CubeRootBtn_Click ()
' Handle the cube and cube root functions.
  If PressINV Then
    ExecFunction "X^3"
  Else
    ExecFunction "CubeRoot"
  End If
End Sub

Sub DecimalBtn_Click ()
' Insert a decimal in a number being keying in, or start a new
' number with a decimal point.
  PressHYP = False
  PressINV = False
  ' is the user in the process of keying in a number?
  If NewNum Then
    ' append a decimal if there is not one already
    If InStr(DspBox.Text, ".") = 0 Then
      DspBox.Text = DspBox.Text + "."
    End If
  Else
    ' start keying in a new number with the decimal point
    DspBox.Text = "0."
    NewNum = True
  End If
End Sub

Sub DegreesChk_Click ()
' Handle the degrees check box
  ' is the degrees check box marked?
  If DegreesChk.Value = 1 Then
    ' the current angle mode handles degrees
    AngleCF = 4 * Atn(1) / 180
  Else
    ' the current angle mode handles radians
    AngleCF = 1
  End If
End Sub

Sub DigitBtn_Click (Index As Integer)
' Emulate keying in a digit in the display text box
  ' is NewNum state False
  If Not NewNum Then
    ' clear the display text box
    DspBox.Text = ""
  End If
  NewNum = True ' set the NewNum state to True
```

Listing 11-1 Continued.

```
    PressHYP = False
    PressINV = False
    ' append the keyed in digit using the Index of the
    ' array of command button controls that represents
    ' the digits' buttons
    DspBox.Text = DspBox.Text + Format$(Index)
End Sub

Sub DivBtn_Click ()
' Divide two numbers
    SetPendOp "/"
End Sub

Sub DspBox_Change ()
' Set the NewNum state to True if the display box is changed.
' This procedure is often overridden.
    NewNum = True
End Sub

Sub DspBtn_Click ()
' Select a new format string
    Dim S As String
    Dim OK As Integer
    Dim Z As Double
    OK = True ' assign the default value
    Do
        ' prompt the user for a new format string
        S = InputBox$("Enter display format", "Input", Frmt)
        ' did the user accepted the current or edited format string?
        If S <> "" Then
            Frmt = S ' update the format string
            ' test if the format is correct
            Z = 10 ^ (4 * Atn(1))
            On Error GoTo BadDsp ' turn on error trap
            S = Format$(Z, Frmt) ' test conversion
            On Error GoTo 0 ' turn off error trap
        End If
    Loop Until OK
    Exit Sub
    '****************** Error Handler ******************
BadDsp:
    OK = False
    MsgBox "Bad format string", BOX_MODE, ERROR_TITLE
    Resume Next
End Sub

Sub EexBtn_Click ()
' Append an exponent to a number being keyed in and terminate
' the number entry
    Dim S As String
    ' if there is no number being keyed in exit
    If Not NewNum Then Exit Sub
    ' is the display text box void from a current exponent?
    If InStr(DspBox.Text, "D") = 0 Then
        ' prompt the user to enter the exponent
        S = InputBox$("Enter exponent ", "Input", "D+000")
        ' did the user accept the default or the edited exponent?
        If S <> "" Then
            ' append the exponent to the string in the display text box
            DspBox.Text = DspBox.Text + S
            NewNum = False ' set the NewNum state to False
            Push
        End If
    End If
    PressHYP = False
    PressINV = False
End Sub
```

Listing 11-1 Continued.

```
Sub EqualBtn_Click ()
' Execute the pending operations
  ' is the operators stack empty
  If StackLst.ListCount = 0 Then
    ' execute the last pending operation
    ExecLastOp
    LastOp = " " ' clear the last operation
  Else
    ' execute the pending operations
    Do While StackLst.ListCount > 0
      CloseParenBtn_Click
    Loop
  End If
End Sub

Sub ExecFunction (ByVal FunctionName As String)
' Evaluation the function FunctionName
  Dim Z As Double
  Dim X As Double
  ' set the error trap
  On Error GoTo BadFunction
  ' convert the string of the display text box into a number and
  ' assign it to the variable X
  X = Val(DspBox.Text)
  ' convert the function name to uppercase
  FunctionName = UCase$(FunctionName)
  ' use nested Select Case statements to invoke the sought function.
  ' The outer Select Case examines the length of the function name
  Select Case Len(FunctionName)
    ' process 2-character function names
    Case 2
      Select Case FunctionName
        Case "LN"
          X = Log(X)
      End Select

    ' process 3-character function names
    Case 3
      Select Case FunctionName
        Case "SIN"
          X = Sin(AngleCF * X)
        Case "COS"
          X = Cos(AngleCF * X)
        Case "TAN"
          X = Tan(AngleCF * X)
        Case "1/X"
          X = 1 / X
        Case "X^2"
          X = X ^ 2
        Case "LOG"
          X = Log(X) / Log(10)
        Case "X^3"
          X = X ^ 3
        Case "EXP"
          X = Exp(X)
      End Select

    ' process 4-character function names
    Case 4
      Select Case FunctionName
        Case "SQRT"
          X = Sqr(X)
        Case "10^X"
          X = 10 ^ X
        Case "SINH"
          X = (Exp(X) - Exp(-X)) / 2
```

Listing 11-1 Continued.

```
          Case "COSH"
            X = (Exp(X) + Exp(-X)) / 2
          Case "TANH"
            Z = Exp(X)
            X = (Z - 1 / Z) / (Z + 1 / Z)
      End Select

    ' process 6-character function names
    Case 6
      Select Case FunctionName
        Case "ARCSIN"
          X = Atn(X / Sqr(1 - X * X)) / AngleCF
        Case "ARCCOS"
          X = 2 * Atn(1) - Atn(X / Sqr(1 - X * X))
          X = X / AngleCF
        Case "ARCTAN"
          X = Atn(X) / AngleCF
      End Select

    ' process 7-character function names
    Case 7
      Select Case FunctionName
        Case "ARCSINH"
          X = Log(X + Sqr(X * X + 1))
        Case "ARCCOSH"
          X = Log(X + Sqr(X * X - 1))
        Case "ARCTANH"
          X = Log((1 + X) / (1 - X)) / 2
      End Select

    ' process other function names
    Case Else
      Select Case FunctionName
        Case "CUBEROOT"
          X = X ^ (1 / 3)
      End Select
  End Select
  ' turn off error trap
  On Error GoTo 0
  ' convert the result X into a string and store the string in the
  ' display text box
  DspBox.Text = Format$(X, Frmt)
  NewNum = False
  PressINV = False
  PressHYP = False
  Exit Sub
  ' ******************** Error Handler ******************
BadFunction:
  ' display error message
  MsgBox "Error in " + FunctionName + " function", 64, "Error"
  ClxBtn_Click ' clear the calculator
  Resume ExitExecFunction
ExitExecFunction:
End Sub

Sub ExecLastOp ()
' Execute the last operation.
  ' turn on error trap
  On Error GoTo BadOp
  ' shift the internal registers
  RegY = RegX
  ' convert the string in the display text box into a number
  ' and store that number in the internal register RegX
  RegX = Val(DspBox.Text)
  ' select the operator to execute
  Select Case UCase$(LastOp)
```

Listing 11-1   Continued.

```
      Case "+"
        RegX = RegY + RegX
      Case "-"
        RegX = RegY - RegX
      Case "/"
        RegX = RegY / RegX
      Case "*"
        RegX = RegY * RegX
      Case "Y^X"
        RegX = RegY ^ RegX
      Case "Y^1/X"
        RegX = RegY ^ (1 / RegX)
    End Select
    ' turn off the error trap
    On Error GoTo 0
    ' convert the result X into a string and store the string in the
    ' display text box
    DspBox.Text = Format$(RegX, Frmt)
    NewNum = False
    PressINV = False
    PressHYP = False
    Exit Sub
    ' ******************** Error Handler ******************
BadOp:
    ' display an error message
    MsgBox "Error in " + LastOp + " operation", 64, "Error"
    ClxBtn_Click ' clear the calculator
    Resume ExecLastOp
ExecLastOp:
End Sub

Sub Form_Load ()
' Initialize the SciCalc form
    WindowState = 2 ' maximize the window
    Frmt = "" ' set the initial format string
    AngleCF = 1 ' the initial angle conversion factor is 1, since
                ' the initial angle mode is in radians
    ClearAllBtn_Click ' clear the memory registers
    ClxBtn_Click ' clear the internal registers
End Sub

Sub HypBtn_Click ()
' Set the PressHYP state to True
    PressHYP = True
End Sub

Sub InvBtn_Click ()
' Set the PressINV state to True
    PressINV = True
End Sub

Sub LnBtn_Click ()
' Handle the natural logarithm and exponential functions.
    If PressINV Then
      ExecFunction "Exp"
    Else
      ExecFunction "Ln"
    End If
End Sub

Sub LogBtn_Click ()
' Handle the common logarithm and power of 10 functions.
    If PressINV Then
      ExecFunction "10^X"
    Else
      ExecFunction "Log"
```

Listing 11-1 Continued.

```
      End If
End Sub

Sub MulBtn_Click ()
' Multiply two numbers
   SetPendOp "*"
End Sub

Sub OffBtn_Click ()
' Unload the form
   Unload SciCalc
End Sub

Sub OpenParenBtn_Click ()
' Push an operand and operation in the operator stack.
   ' is the pending operation valid?
   If LastOp <> " " Then
      ' push the string image of RegX in the stack
      StackLst.AddItem Format$(RegX, Frmt), 0
      RegX = 0 ' clear the internal register RegX
      ' push the operator in the stack
      StackLst.AddItem LastOp, 0
   End If
   LastOp = " " ' clear the pending operation
End Sub

Sub PiBtn_Click ()
' Writes the string image of Pi in the display text box
   PressINV = False
   PressHYP = False
   If NewNum Then Push
   DspBox.Text = Format$(4 * Atn(1), Frmt)
End Sub

Sub PowerBtn_Click ()
' Handle the raising of powers operators.
   If PressINV Then
      SetPendOp "Y^1/X"
   Else
      SetPendOp "Y^X"
   End If
End Sub

Sub Push ()
' Shift the internal registers and copy number of the display
' text in the RegX register.
   RegY = RegX
   RegX = Val(DspBox.Text)
   NewNum = False
End Sub

Sub RclBtn_Click ()
' Recall the number stored in the selected memory register and
' write it to the display text box.
   Dim I As Integer
   Dim S As String
   PressHYP = False
   PressINV = False
   ' get the index of the selected memory register
   I = MemLst.ListIndex
   ' if there is no selected memory register, then select
   ' the first memory register
   If I < 0 Then I = 0
   ' write the string image of the number in the selected memory
   ' register to the display text box
   DspBox.Text = Mid$(MemLst.List(I), 7)
End Sub
```

Listing 11-1 Continued.

```
Sub ReciprocalBtn_Click ()
' Handle the reciprocal and absolute functions.
  ExecFunction "1/X"
End Sub

Sub SetPendOp (ByVal OpStr As String)
' Set the pending operator.
  ' push any pending new number?
  If NewNum Then Push
  ' no pending operations?
  If LastOp = " " Then
    ' convert the string image of the display text box into
    ' a number and store that number in RegX
    RegX = Val(DspBox.Text)
  Else
    ' execute the last pending operator
    ExecLastOp
  End If
  ' OpStr is the new pending operator
  LastOp = OpStr
  NewNum = False
  PressINV = False
  PressHYP = False
End Sub

Sub SinBtn_Click ()
' Handle the calls to the sine, arc sine, hyperbolic sine, and
' inverse hyperbolic sine functions.
  If PressHYP And PressINV Then
    ExecFunction "ArcSinh"
  ElseIf PressHYP Then
    ExecFunction "Sinh"
  ElseIf PressINV Then
    ExecFunction "ArcSin"
  Else
    ExecFunction "Sin"
  End If
End Sub

Sub SqrtBtn_Click ()
' Handle the square and square root functions.
  If PressINV Then
    ExecFunction "X^2"
  Else
    ExecFunction "Sqrt"
  End If
End Sub

Sub StoBtn_Click ()
' Store the string of the display text box in the selected memory
' register.  The default selected memory register is the first one.
  Dim X As Double
  Dim I As Integer
  PressHYP = False
  PressINV = False
  NewNum = False
  ' get the index of the selected memory register
  I = MemLst.ListIndex
  ' if there is no selected register then select the first
  ' memory register
  If I < 0 Then I = 0
  X = Val(DspBox.Text)
  MemLst.List(I) = Format$(I + 1, "000") + " : " + Format$(X, Frmt)
End Sub

Sub StoPlusBtn_Click ()
' Add the number in the display text box to the selected memory
```

Listing 11-1 Continued.

```
' register.  The default selected memory register is the first one.
  Dim I As Integer
  Dim X As Double, Y As Double
  Dim S As String
  PressHYP = False
  PressINV = False
  NewNum = False
  ' get the index of the selected memory register
  I = MemLst.ListIndex
  ' if there is no selected register then select the first
  ' memory register
  If I < 0 Then I = 0
  ' convert the string of the display box into a number and
  ' store that number in variable X
  X = Val(DspBox.Text)
  ' convert the string of the selected memory register into a
  ' number and store that number in variable Y
  Y = Val(Mid$(MemLst.List(I), 7))
  ' obtain the string for the new memory register
  S = Format$(I + 1, "000") + " : " + Format$(X + Y, Frmt)
  ' store the string S in the selected memory register
  MemLst.List(I) = S
End Sub

Sub SubBtn_Click ()
' Subtract two numbers.
  SetPendOp "-"
End Sub

Sub TanBtn_Click ()
' Handle the calls to the tangent, arc tangent, hyperbolic tangent,
' and inverse hyperbolic tangent functions.
  If PressHYP And PressINV Then
    ExecFunction "ArcTanh"
  ElseIf PressHYP Then
    ExecFunction "Tanh"
  ElseIf PressINV Then
    ExecFunction "ArcTan"
  Else
    ExecFunction "Tan"
  End If
End Sub
```

The form also declares the following variables:

- The Frmt variable, which contains the format string.
- The Boolean NewNum variable, which stores the new-number state.
- The Boolean PressINV variable, which contains the press-INV state.
- The Boolean variable PressHYP, which maintains the press-HYP state.
- The RegX and RegY variables, which represent the internal registers.
- The AngleCF variable, which maintains the angle conversion factor for radians and degrees.

The procedures attached to the SCICALC.FRM form are arranged alphabetically in Listing 11-1. Figure 11-6 gives you a brief alphabetized summary of the procedures along with their related systems. Figure 11-7

Routine name	System
AddBtn_Click	Operators
ChsBtn_Click	Digits
ClearAllBtn_Click	Memory
CloseParenBtn_Click	Operators
ClrBtn_Click	Memory
ClxBtn_Click	Processing
CosBtn_Click	Functions
CubeRootBtn_Click	Functions
DecimalBtn_Click	Digits
DegreesChk_Click	Functions
DigitBtn_Click	Digits
DivBtn_Click	Operators
DspBox_Change	Display
DspBtn_Click	Display
ExecLastOp	Processing
EexBtn_Click	Digits
EqualBtn_Click	Operators
ExecFunction	Processing
Form_Load	none
HypBtn_Click	Functions
InvBtn_Click	Functions
LnBtn_Click	Functions
LogBtn_Click	Functions
MulBtn_Click	Operators
OffBtn_Click	none
OpenParenBtn_Click	Operators
PiBtn_Click	Functions
PowerBtn_Click	Operators
Push	Processing
RclBtn_Click	Memory
ReciprocalBtn_Click	Functions
SetPendOp	Processing
SinBtn_Click	Functions
SqrtBtn_Click	Functions
StoBtn_Click	Memory
StoPlusBtn_Click	Memory
SubBtn_Click	Operators
TanBtn_Click	Functions

11-6 The list of alphabetized procedures and functions in the SCICALC.FRM form.

shows the same list sorted by the systems. These figures offer two ways for cross-referencing the procedures. I will present the procedures by system affiliation, beginning with those that initialize and unload the SciCalc form.

Initializing procedures

The Form_Load procedure initializes the form. It begins by maximizing the window, which gives the form the needed size. Then the procedure initializes the angle conversion factor to 1, since the default angles are in radians, and proceeds to clear the operators stack and the memory registers.

The OffBtn_Click unloads the SciCalc form.

Routine name	System
ChsBtn_Click	Digits
DecimalBtn_Click	Digits
DigitBtn_Click	Digits
EexBtn_Click	Digits
DspBox_Change	Display
DspBtn_Click	Display
CosBtn_Click	Functions
CubeRootBtn_Click	Functions
DegreesChk_Click	Functions
HypBtn_Click	Functions
InvBtn_Click	Functions
LnBtn_Click	Functions
LogBtn_Click	Functions
PiBtn_Click	Functions
ReciprocalBtn_Click	Functions
SinBtn_Click	Functions
SqrtBtn_Click	Functions
TanBtn_Click	Functions
ClearAllBtn_Click	Memory
ClrBtn_Click	Memory
RclBtn_Click	Memory
StoBtn_Click	Memory
StoPlusBtn_Click	Memory
Form_Load	none
OffBtn_Click	none
AddBtn_Click	Operators
DivBtn_Click	Operators
CloseParenBtn_Click	Operators
EqualBtn_Click	Operators
MulBtn_Click	Operators
OpenParenBtn_Click	Operators
PowerBtn_Click	Operators
SetPendOp	Processing
SubBtn_Click	Operators
ClxBtn_Click	Processing
ExexFunction	Processing
ExecLastOp	Processing
Push	Processing

11-7 The functions and procedures in form SCICALC.FRM listed by system affiliation.

Digits system procedures

The procedures which make up the Digits system are described next.

The ChsBtn_Click procedure toggles the sign of the number in the display box.

The DecimalBtn_Click procedure inserts or appends a decimal point to the string in the text box. If the number in the display box is being keyed in, the procedure first makes sure that there isn't already a decimal point. If this condition is true, the procedure appends a decimal point. If the number in the display text box is not a new number, the procedure begins a new number by writing the string 0. to the display text box and then setting the NewNum variable to True.

The DigitBtn_Click procedure appends a digit in the display. If the NewNum variable is False, the procedure first clears the display text box to remove the previous number; then it sets NewNum to True and appends the caption of the DigitBtn(Index) control.

The EexBtn_Click procedure appends an exponent to the number being entered in the display text box. The procedure verifies that the NewNum variable is True and that there is no exponent already in the text box; it uses the Visual Basic InStr function to detect the letter D in the text box. If these conditions are true, the procedure invokes the InpuBox$ function to prompt for an exponent. The default exponent in the dialog box is D + 000. If you accept the default or the edited exponent, it is appended to the string in the display text box. In addition, the procedure sets the NewNum variable to False, thus ending the entry of the new number.

Display system procedures

The following procedures make up the Display system.

The DspBox_Change procedure sets the NewNum variable to True when the display text box is altered. This step is regarded as a default action. The procedures that alter the display text box often reset the NewNum variable to False, overriding the action of DspBox_Change.

The DspBtn_Click procedure invokes the InputBox$ function to prompt you for a new format string. The form-level variable Frmt maintains the current format string. The InputBox$ function uses the variable Frmt to display the current format string. If you accept the current or the edited format string, the Frmt variable is updated. The procedure also tests the format string; if it generates an error, you are prompted to enter a new format string.

Functions system procedures

The form has the following procedures that are associated with the Functions system. All of these procedures test whether you were entering a new number just before invoking a math function.

The CosBtn_Click procedure handles the cosine, inverse cosine, hyperbolic cosine, and inverse hyperbolic cosine functions. The procedure examines the Boolean values of the PressHYP and PressINV variables to select the proper version of the ExecFunction call.

The CubeRootBtn_Click procedure handles the cube and cube root functions. The procedure examines the Boolean value of the variable PressINV to determine the proper call to the ExecFunction function.

The DegreesChk_Click procedure updates the angle conversion factor based on the current Value property of the DegreeChk check box.

The HypBtn_Click procedure assigns True to the variable PressHYP. This assignment turns on the hyperbolic mode.

The InvBtn_Click procedure assigns True to the variable PressINV. This assignment turns on the inverse mode.

The LnBtn_Click procedure handles the natural and exponential functions. The procedure examines the Boolean value of the variable PressINV to determine the proper call to ExecFunction.

The LogBtn_Click procedure handles the common logarithm and power of ten functions. The procedure examines the Boolean value of the variable PressINV to choose the proper call to ExecFunction.

The PiBtn_Click procedure inserts the value of Pi in the display text box.

The ReciprocalBtn_Click procedure handles the reciprocal and the absolute value functions. The procedure examines the Boolean value of the variable PressINV to select the call to the ExecFunction function.

The SinBtn_Click procedure handles the sine, inverse sine, hyperbolic sine, and inverse hyperbolic sine functions. The procedure examines the Boolean values of the PressHYP and PressINV variables to select the proper version of the ExecFunction call.

The SqrtBtn_Click procedure handles the square root and the square functions. The procedure examines the Boolean value of the variable PressINV to determine the proper call to the ExecFunction function.

The TanBtn_Click procedure handles the tangent, inverse tangent, hyperbolic tangent, and inverse hyperbolic tangent functions. The procedure examines the Boolean values of the PressHYP and PressINV variables to select the proper version of the ExecFunction call.

Memory system procedures

The form contains the following procedures that implement the operations of the Memory Registers system.

The ClearAllBtn_Click procedure clears all of the memory registers by assigning them the string image of 0.

The ClearBtn_Click procedure clears the selected memory register by assigning it the string image of 0. The procedure performs no operation if there is no selected memory register.

The RclBtn_Click procedure writes the selected memory register to the display text box. The default memory register is the first one.

The StoBtn_Click procedure copies the display text box to the selected memory register. Again, the default memory register is the first one.

The StoPlusBtn_Click procedure is similar to StoBtn_Click, except that it adds the number in the display text box to the selected memory register.

Operators system procedures

The form includes the following procedures that are part of the Operators system.

The AddBtn_Click procedure invokes the SetPendOp function with the + argument to add two top stack members. If there is a pending new number, that number is used as one of the two required operands.

The CloseParenBtn_Click procedure executes the next operation in the operators stack. The procedure verifies that the operators stack contains at least two members, then checks whether there is a pending operation. If there is, the procedure invokes ExecLastOp. If ExecLastOp experiences a math error, the operators stack is cleared. At this point the procedure tests if the stack size is 0 and exits if that condition is true.

The procedure next copies the first pending operator from the stack to the variable LastOp, copies the contents of RegX into RegY, and converts the first pending operand in the stack into a number, storing it in RegX. The procedure then removes the two top stack members, executes the operation that was popped off the operators stack, and finally clears the last operator.

The DivBtn_Click procedure calls the SetPendOp function with the / argument to divide two top stack members. If there is a pending new number, that number is used as one of the two required operands.

The EqualBtn_Click procedure executes any pending operation. The procedure compares the stack size with zero. If that condition is true, the procedure calls ExecLastOp to execute the only pending operation, otherwise, the procedure executes the pending operations in the operators stack. The routine uses a Do-While loop that makes one or more calls to procedure CloseParenBtn_Click. Each iteration executes the next pending operation in the stack.

The MulBtn_Click procedure invokes the SetPendOp function with the * argument to multiply the two top stack members. If there is a pending new number, that number is used as one of the two required operands.

The OpenParenBtn_Click procedure pushes the string image of the variable RegX and the string variable LastOp into the operators stack. The pending operator is cleared by assigning a single space to the variable LastOp.

The PowerBtn_Click procedure invokes the SetPendOp function with the Y^X argument to take the power of the top stack members. If there is a pending new number, that number is used as one of the two required operands.

The SubBtn_Click procedure invokes the SetPendOp function with the − argument to subtract the two top stack members. If there is a pending new number, that number is used as one of the two required operands.

Processing system procedures

The form contains the following procedures that comprise the Processing system.

The ClxBtn_Click procedure resets the internal registers and clears both the last operator and the operators stack. This enables you to start evaluating a new expression.

The ExecFunction procedure evaluates mathematical functions. The procedure turns on an error trap, which jumps to the BadFunction label if activated. There, the procedure invokes the ClxBtn_Click procedure. This method is very efficient, because it uses one error trap to deal with errors related to all the various function calls.

If there is no error condition, the procedure converts the string of the display box into a number and stores it in the local variable X. It then converts the characters stored in the FunctionName argument into uppercase, and uses a nested Select Case statement to speed up selecting the proper function evaluation. The outer Select Case statement examines the length of the FunctionName string, allowing the functions to be grouped by length of function name.

At this point, the procedure turns off the error trap, writes the string image of the function result to the display text box, and sets the NewNum variable to False.

The ExecLastOp procedure executes the pending operation. The procedure first turns on an error trap, which if activated resumes at the BadOp label. There, the procedure invokes the ClxBtn_Click procedure. If there is no error condition, the procedure copies the contents of RegX into RegY, converts the string of the display box into a number, and stores that number in RegX. It next uses a Select Case statement to compare the expression UCase$(LastOp) with the various Case clauses; the matching Case clause invokes the proper operation.

Before exiting, the procedure turns off the error trap, writes the string image of the result to the display text box, and sets the NewNum variable to False.

The Push procedure copies the value of RegX into RegY, converts the string of the display text box into a number, and stores that number in RegX. It then sets the NewNum variable to False.

The SetPendOp procedure executes any current pending operation and sets up a new one. The procedure pushes any new pending number in the internal registers; then, if there is no last pending operation, it copies the numeric equivalent of the display text box in RegX. Otherwise, the procedure executes the current pending operation. It then assigns the new pending operator to the LastOp variable, and sets the NewNum, PressINV, and PressHYP variables to False.

12
The RPN calculator

The previous chapter presented an algebraic scientific calculator; this chapter presents a Reverse Polish Notation (RPN) calculator. RPN calculators have been made popular by the Hewlett-Packard Company. In this chapter I discuss the design specifications of an RPN calculator form that you can load and unload in your custom Visual Basic programs.

RPN logic

If you are familiar with RPN logic you can skip this section. The original Polish notation, devised by a Polish mathematician, handles the simple math expressions by first specifying the operator; then the operands. For example, to add 10 and 5, Polish notation uses the following expression:

+ 10 5

Notice that Polish notation seems to be structured the same way we state an operation. The above Polish notation expression is read, "add the number 10 and the number 5." To evaluate a simple function, for example, the logarithm of 20, the following Polish notation expression is used:

Log 20

Again the above expression seems to translate to the phrase, "take the logarithm of the number 20."

More complex mathematical expressions have to specify their operators in the reverse order of execution. For example, the Polish notation equivalent of the following algebraic expression:

(3 + 5) * (6 − 4)

is:

> * + 3 5 − 6 4

The result of the addition is pushed into a stack before the subtraction is carried out, then the subtraction result is pushed into the stack. Finally the multiplication is carried out using the two results in the stack.

Reverse Polish Notation, as the name might suggest, puts the operator after the operands. Thus the above algebraic expression becomes the following RPN expression:

> 3 5 + 6 4 − *

RPN is more logical than Polish notation—you get the operands and then execute a math operation. Implementing RPN in calculators is also easier than Polish notation and algebraic notation, since the operators themselves act as number terminators.

RPN calculators are noted for the following features:

- The absence of an Equal Sign key.
- The presence of an Enter key, which is used to delimit two operands that are keyed in sequentially.
- The use of a stack to push and pop numbers and intermediate results.

Design specifications

The RPN calculator presented in this chapter is shown in FIG. 12-1. It has the following features and capabilities:

- A dynamic stack that stores numbers. The stack is made up of registers and is visually oriented such that the logical top of the stack is the top visual member of the emulating list box (index 0).
- A set of 100 memory registers. These registers are managed by a group of buttons that store, accumulate, recall, and clear data in the memory registers.
- A set of numeric entry buttons that includes the digits 0 to 9, the decimal point, a change sign button, and an exponent button.
- A family of math operator buttons that performs various operations, such as addition, subtraction, multiplication, division, and exponentiation.
- A group of buttons that support various trigonometric and transcendental functions. The current list of functions includes:
  - ~ Trigonometric functions: sine, cosine, tangent, and their inverses. The RPN calculator supports angles in radians and degrees.
  - ~ Logarithmic functions: natural and common logarithms, and their inverses.

~Hyperbolic functions: hyperbolic sine, hyperbolic cosine, hyperbolic tangent, and their inverses.

~Other math functions: square, cube, square root, cube root, absolute, pi, and reciprocal.

- A family of buttons that manipulate the stack. These operations include swapping the two top stack members, rolling down the stack, rolling up the stack, recalling the last top-of-stack value, popping off the top of the stack, and clearing the entire stack.
- A set of buttons that perform statistical linear regression and projections.
- A text box that allows you to enter a new number.

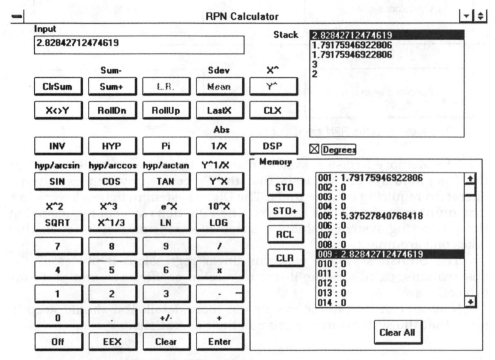

12-1 A sample session with the RPN calculator.

Like the calculators in the previous chapters, the RPN calculator is made up of several systems, shown in FIG. 12-2. The Processing system handles the execution of the operators and mathematical functions. This system is also responsible for pushing and popping off numbers from the stack in the course of executing an operation or evaluating a math function. The Display system manages the direct input of a number into the display text box, and maintains the current format string. The RPN Stack system manages the stack operations triggered by the stack manipulating buttons.

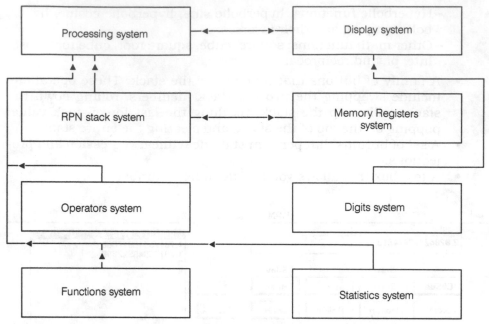

12-2 The systems of the RPN calculator form.

The Memory Registers system manages the memory registers, while the Operators system requests that the Processing system execute an operation requiring two operands. The Digits system manages keying in a new number in the display text box. The Functions system requests that the Processing system evaluate a specified mathematical function that takes one argument.

The Statistics system performs linear regression. It processes the observations, calculates the linear regression coefficients, and performs projections.

Now we can look at the systems in more detail. You should keep in mind that the systems may overlap in their operations.

The Processing system

The Processing system of the RPN calculator is quite different from that of the algebraic scientific calculator in chapter 11. An RPN calculator does not store any operations; all of the operators are promptly executed as long as the stack can provide two operands. Likewise, all of the functions are immediately evaluated.

When you click an operator or a math function command button, the Processing system pushes any new number in the display text box into the stack, and pops off the required number of operands from the stack. If there aren't enough operands, the Processing system displays an error message. If there are, it executes the operation or evaluates the math function. If an error occurs at this point, the Processing system pushes the operands back in the stack and displays an error message. If not, it pushes the result in the stack and also writes it to the display text box.

The Display system

The Display system of the RPN calculator is quite simple. Its main purpose is to update the format string and inform other systems that there is a new number in the display text box. Unlike the Display system of the programmer's calculator, this version does not monitor your keystrokes. As a result, you can easily enter badly formatted numbers. The Processing system uses the Visual Basic Val function to convert the string in the display text box into a double-typed number. Consequently, badly formatted numbers yield 0 or any other value depending on the converted string. It is your responsibility to key in the correct number.

The RPN Stack system

The RPN Stack system performs several operations as needed. It pushes a new number into the stack, swaps the top stack members, rolls the stack up or down, pushes the last top-of-stack value into the stack, pops off the top stack elements, and clears the stack. Other stack manipulating operations such as recalling a number from a memory register, popping off operands, and pushing in results are delegated to other systems.

The Memory Registers system

The Memory Registers system manages the 100 memory registers, and is located inside a frame control. The memory registers are emulated by a list box, each member of which contains the following string format:

iii : nnnnnnn...nn

where iii is a three-digit memory register index and the ns represent the string image of a number stored in a memory register. You can inspect the various memory registers by using the vertical scroll bar of the list box.

The Memory Registers system uses the STO and STO+ buttons to store and accumulate the value of a stack member in a selected memory register. You can select a stack member by clicking on it with the mouse; the top number is the default selection. The stack member is stored into the selected memory register, with the default being the first memory register. The system also supports pushing the contents of a selected memory register into the stack. Again, the first memory register is the default selection.

Other operations include clearing a selected register and clearing all of the registers. The system assigns one or more zeros to clear one or more memory registers.

The Operators system

The Operators system becomes active when you click on an operator button. This includes the buttons with the captions +, −, *, /, Y^X, and Y^1/X. The Operators system requests that the Processing system perform the designated operation.

The Functions system

The Functions system becomes active when you click on a math function button, and requests that the Processing system evaluate the designated function.

☞ The RPN calculator uses the INV and HYP buttons (see FIG. 12-1) with the SIN, COS, and TAN buttons to offer inverse trigonometric, hyperbolic, and inverse hyperbolic functions. For example, to calculate the hyperbolic sine, you would click the INV button and then the SIN button. The INV button also works with other buttons that have labels located right above the buttons. To obtain the cube of a number, click the INV button and then the X^1/3 button. I have coded the routines of the RPN calculator such that all of the buttons automatically clear the INV and HYP buttons, whether or not they work with these two buttons.

The Digits system

The Digits system manages entering a new number using the digit buttons. You begin entering a new number by clicking a digit button from 0 to 9, or by clicking the decimal point button. The Digits system allows you to toggle the sign of the number you are keying in, and to enter an exponent. The system uses an input dialog box to enter the exponent; once you enter the exponent, the Digits system considers the number entry completed.

The Statistics system

The Statistics system manages the linear regression included in the RPN calculator. The system uses a set of form-level variables to store the statistical summations and results of the linear regression. The linear regression correlates the observations of an independent variable X with a dependent variable Y, using the following equation:

$$Y = A + B * X$$

Where A is the intercept and B is the slope of the best line that fits the pair of (X,Y) observations. The correlation coefficient, R^2, measures the quality of the fit. The values of the correlation coefficient vary between one (a perfect fit) and zero (absolutely no correlation). In a perfect fit, the above equation is able to account for 100% of the variation between the observed values of X and Y.

The Statistics system accumulates the observations in the statistical summations. At least two observations are required to perform a linear regression, although more observations are recommended to obtain more meaningful results. When the number of observations is less than two, the L.R., Mean, and Y^ buttons are disabled. When the number of observations is two or more, the L.R. button is enabled.

The system also allows you to remove statistically "bad" or erroneously entered observations. Again, if the number of observations falls below two, the L.R., Mean, and Y^ buttons are disabled.

Another task of the Statistics system is performing linear regression. This operation pushes the regression slope, intercept, and correlation coefficient into the stack. In addition, the system enables the Mean and Y^ buttons, which offer post-regression statistics.

The system obtains the mean and standard deviation statistics, and also handles two types of projection. It projects X on Y, predicting the value of Y for a given value of X based on the current values of the regression slope and intercept. The system also can project Y on X, predicting the value of X for a given value of Y based on the current values of the regression slope and intercept.

☞   The Statistics system has three states. In the first state, the statistical summations are either cleared or lack the minimum number of observations to perform a linear regression. In this state, the L.R., Mean, and Y^ buttons are disabled. The system shifts to the second state when the summations have accumulated at least two observations. In this state, the system is ready to perform a linear regression; consequently, the L.R. button is enabled. The system shifts to the third state when the linear regression calculations are performed. The other statistical buttons are then enabled, since the intermediate results which these buttons need are now available.

The RPN calculator controls

Figures 12-3 to 12-5 show the specifications for the RPNCALC.MAK project file and the RPNCALC.FRM form; the form file is the object of primary interest. Figures 12-4 and 12-5 list the various command buttons that make up the RPN calculator, including the DigitBtn control array, which represents the digit command buttons.

Application name: Reverse Polish Notation scientific calculator
Application code name: RPNCALC

12-3 The basic
specifications for the
RPNCALC.MAK
project file.

Version: 1.0   Date created: August 22, 1991
Programmer(s): Namir Clement Shammas

List of filenames

Storage path: \ VB \ VBXTOOL
Project   RPNCALC.MAK
Global   GLOBAL.BAS (not used)
Form 1   RPNCALC.FRM

Form # 1   Form filename: RPNCALC.FRM
Version: 1.0   Date: August 22, 1991

Control object type	Default CtlName	Purpose
Command button	Command1	Unloads the form
	Command2	The control array for the digit buttons 0 to 9
	Command3	Inserts a decimal point
	Command4	Changes the sign of a number
	Command5	Inserts an exponent
	Command6	Pushes a number in the stack
	Command7	Clears the stack
	Command8	Adds numbers
	Command9	Subtract numbers
	Command10	Multiplies numbers
	Command11	Divides numbers
	Command12	Returns the square root or the square of a number
	Command13	Returns the cube root or the cube of a number
	Command14	Returns the natural logarithm or the exponential of a number
	Command15	Returns the common logarithm or the power-of-ten of a number
	Command16	Returns the sine, arc sine, hyperbolic sine, or inverse hyperbolic sine values
	Command17	Returns the cosine, arc cosine, hyperbolic cosine, or inverse hyperbolic cosine values
	Command18	Returns the tangent, arc tangent, hyperbolic tangent, or inverse hyperbolic tangent values
	Command19	Returns the power or roots of two numbers
	Command20	Sets the INV state to obtain the inverse trigonometric functions
	Command21	Sets the HYP state to obtain hyperbolic functions or their inverses
	Command22	Returns the value of pi
	Command23	Returns the reciprocal or absolute value of numbers
	Command24	Specifies the display format string
	Command25	Swaps the two top stack members
	Command26	Rolls down the stack
	Command27	Rolls up the stack
	Command28	Retrieves the last top of the stack
	Command29	Drops the top stack member
	Command30	Clears the statistical summations
	Command31	Updates the statistical summations
	Command32	Performs linear regression

12-4   The list of controls in the RPNCALC.FRM form file.

Control object type	Default CtlName	Purpose
	Command33	Returns the mean or standard deviation values
	Command34	Project X on Y or Y on X
	Command35	Store a stack member in a selected memory register
	Command36	Adds the value of a stack register in the selected memory register
	Command37	Pushes the contents of the selected memory register into the stack
	Command38	Clears the selected memory register
	Command39	Clears all the memory registers
Text box	Text1	The Input text box
List box	List1	The emulated stack
	List2	The emulated memory registers
Check box	Check1	Specifies the degree or radian angle mode
Frame	Frame1	The frame that contains the controls for the memory registers
Label	Label1	Input text box label
	Label2	Stack label
	Label3	Sine button label
	Label4	Cosine button label
	Label5	Tangent button label
	Label6	Power button label
	Label7	Reciprocal button label
	Label8	Update sums button label
	Label9	Statistical mean button label
	Label10	Statistical projections button label

12-4 Continued.

Application (code) name: RPNCALC
Form # 1
Version: 1.0   Date: August 22, 1991

Original control name	Property	New setting
Form	Caption	RPN Calculator
	FormName	RPNCalc
Command1	CtlName	OffBtn
	Caption	Off
Command2	CtlName	DigitBtn
	Caption	(the string image of the control index)
Command3	CtlName	DecimalBtn
	Caption	

12-5 The customized settings for the RPNCALC.FRM form.

Original control name	Property	New setting
Command4	CtlName	ChsBtn
	Caption	+/−
Command5	CtlName	EexBtn
	Caption	EEX
Command6	CtlName	EnterBtn
	Caption	Enter
Command7	CtlName	ClearBtn
	Caption	Clear
Command8	CtlName	AddBtn
	Caption	+
Command9	CtlName	SubBtn
	Caption	−
Command10	CtlName	MulBtn
	Caption	*
Command11	CtlName	DivBtn
	Caption	/
Command12	CtlName	SqrtBtn
	Caption	SQRT
Command13	CtlName	CubeRootBtn
	Caption	X^1/3
Command14	CtlName	LnBtn
	Caption	LN
Command15	CtlName	LogBtn
	Caption	LOG
Command16	CtlName	SinBtn
	Caption	SIN
Command17	CtlName	CosBtn
	Caption	COS
Command18	CtlName	TanBtn
	Caption	TAN
Command19	CtlName	PowerBtn
	Caption	Y^X
Command20	CtlName	InvBtn
	Caption	INV
Command21	CtlName	HypBtn
	Caption	HYP
Command22	CtlName	PiBtn
	Caption	SIN
Command23	CtlName	ReciprocalBtn
	Caption	1/X
Command24	CtlName	DspBtn
	Caption	DSP
Command25	CtlName	SwapBtn
	Caption	X< >Y
Command26	CtlName	RollDnBtn
	Caption	RollDn

12-5 Continued.

Original control name	Property	New setting
Command27	CtlName	RollUpBtn
	Caption	RollUp
Command28	CtlName	LastXBtn
	Caption	LastX
Command29	CtlName	ClxBtn
	Caption	CLX
Command30	CtlName	ClrSumBtn
	Caption	ClrSum
Command31	CtlName	SumBtn
	Caption	Sum +
Command32	CtlName	LRBtn
	Caption	L.R.
Command33	CtlName	MeanBtn
	Caption	Mean
Command34	CtlName	YhatBtn
	Caption	Y^
Command35	CtlName	StoBtn
	Caption	STO
Command36	CtlName	StoPluBtn
	Caption	STO +
Command37	CtlName	RclBtn
	Caption	RCL
Command38	CtlName	ClrBtn
	Caption	CLR
Command39	CtlName	ClearAllBtn
	Caption	Clear All
Text1	CtlName	DspBox
	Text	(empty string)
List1	CtlName	StackLst
List2	CtlName	MemLst
Check1	CtlName	DegreesChk
	Caption	Degrees
Frame1	Caption	Memory
Label1	CtlName	InputLbl
	Caption	Input
Label2	CtlName	StackLbl
	Caption	Stack
Label3	CtlName	SinLbl
	Caption	hyp/arcsin
Label4	CtlName	CosLbl
	Caption	hyp/arccos
Label5	CtlName	TanLbl
	Caption	hyp/arctan

12-5 Continued.

Original control name	Property	New setting
Label6	CtlName	PowerLbl
	Caption	Y^1/X
Label7	CtlName	ReciprocalLbl
	Caption	Abs
Label8	CtlName	SumLbl
	Caption	Sum −
Label9	CtlName	MeanLbl
	Caption	Sdev
Label10	CtlName	YhatLbl
	Caption	X^

12-5 Continued.

The RPN calculator code

The code for the RPN calculator is shown in Listing 12-1. The RPN-CALC.FRM form contains a number of module-level constants and variables. The constants are:

- The True and False constants.
- The MAX_MEM constant, which designates the number of memory registers. You can change the value of this constant to any other positive integer. High values may cause the system to run out of memory.
- A series of constants that are assigned various error messages and error-related numeric codes.

Listing 12-1 The code attached to the RPNCALC.FRM form.

```
Const True = -1, False = 0
' maximum number of memory registers
Const MAX_MEM = 100
' declare constants for various error messages
Const ERROR_TITLE = "Error!"
Const OVERFLOW_ERR = "Overflow error"
Const STACK_SIZE_ERR = "Insufficient stack elements"
Const ARGUMENT_ERR = "Bad function argument"
Const FORMAT_ERR = "Enter a correct format string"
Const BOX_MODE = 64 ' the second argument for the MsgBox statement

' Declare form level variables
Dim LastX As Double ' LastX value
Dim Frmt As String ' current format string
Dim NewNum As Integer ' new number flag
Dim PressINV As Integer ' INV key flag
Dim PressHYP As Integer ' HYP key flag
' Operands variables
Dim X As Double, Y As Double
' Angle conversion factor
Dim AngleCF As Double

' Statistical summations
Dim Sum As Double        ' sum of observations
Dim SumX As Double       ' sum of X data
Dim SumY As Double       ' sum of Y data
Dim SumXX As Double      ' sum of X^2 data
```

Listing 12-1 Continued.

```
Dim SumYY As Double          ' sum of Y^2 data
Dim SumXY As Double          ' sum of X * Y data
Dim MeanX As Double          ' mean of X data
Dim MeanY As Double          ' Mean of Y data
Dim SdevX As Double          ' standard deviation of X data
Dim SdevY As Double          ' standard deviation of Y data
Dim Slope As Double          ' linear regression slope
Dim Intercept As Double      ' linear regression intercept
Dim R2 As Double             ' correlation coefficient

Sub AddBtn_Click ()
' Add the two topmost stack members
  BinaryOp "+"
End Sub

Sub BinaryOp (ByVal OpStr As String)
' Perform a binary operation.  The string OpStr specifies the
' operator to execute
  ProcessPendingNewNumber
  PressHYP = False
  PressINV = False
  ' does the stack contain at least two elements?
  If StackLst.ListCount > 1 Then
    Pop ' pop the two top stack members into variables X and Y
    ' set the error trap for a bad math operation
    On Error GoTo BadBinaryOp
    ' select the proper operation to execute
    Select Case UCase$(OpStr)
      Case "+"
        Y = Y + X
      Case "-"
        Y = Y - X
      Case "*"
        Y = Y * X
      Case "/"
        Y = Y / X
      Case "Y^X"
        Y = Y ^ X
      Case "Y^1/X"
        Y = Y ^ (1 / X)
    End Select
    On Error GoTo 0 ' turn off error trap
    LastX = X ' assign the last value of X to LastX
    ' assign the string image of the result to the
    ' display text box
    DspBox.Text = Format$(Y, Frmt)
    Push ' push the result in the stack
  Else
    MsgBox STACK_SIZE_ERR, BOX_MODE, ERROR_TITLE
  End If
  NewNum = False
  Exit Sub
  '****************** Error Handler *********************
BadBinaryOp:
  ' push the numbers in X and Y back in the stack
  StackLst.AddItem Format$(Y, Frmt), 0
  DspBox.Text = Format$(X, Frmt)
  Push
  NewNum = False
  ' display an error message
  MsgBox OVERFLOW_ERR, BOX_MODE, ERROR_TITLE
  Resume ExitBinaryOp
ExitBinaryOp:
End Sub

Sub ChsBtn_Click ()
' Change the sign of the number in the display box and possibly
' the top of the RPN stack
```

Listing 12-1 Continued.

```
  Dim S As String
  Dim OldNewNum As Integer
  OldNewNum = NewNum ' copy the NewNum state
  PressHYP = False
  PressINV = False
  S = DspBox.Text ' copy the display text box into variable S
  ' is the first character in the text box not a - sign
  If Left$(S, 1) <> "-" Then
    ' is the first character a + sign?
    If Left$(S, 1) = "+" Then
      Mid$(S, 1, 1) = "-" ' replace + with -
    Else
      ' prepend a - sign
      S = "-" + S
    End If
  Else
    S = Mid$(S, 2)
  End If
  ' update the display text box
  DspBox.Text = S
  ' restore the old NewNum value to override the procedure
  ' DspBox_Change
  NewNum = OldNewNum
  If Not NewNum Then
    ' change the sign of the top stack element
    StackLst.RemoveItem 0
    Push
  End If
End Sub

Sub ClearAllBtn_Click ()
' Clear the memory registers by assigning 0s to their
' contents.  The number of the memory registers is not
' altered.
  Dim I As Integer
  PressHYP = False
  PressINV = False
  ' are there elements in the MemLst list box?
  If MemLst.ListCount > 0 Then
    ' remove them
    For I = 1 To MemLst.ListCount
      MemLst.RemoveItem 0
    Next I
  End If
  ' insert the new set of list members
  For I = 1 To MAX_MEM
    ' assign the string using the format "iii : 0"
    MemLst.AddItem Format$(I, "000") + " : 0"
  Next I
End Sub

Sub ClearBtn_Click ()
' Clear the RPN stack registers
  ' delete the stack elements
  Do While StackLst.ListCount > 0
    StackLst.RemoveItem 0
  Loop
  ' clear the display text box
  DspBox.Text = ""
  NewNum = False
End Sub

Sub ClrBtn_Click ()
' Clear the selected memory register
  PressHYP = False
  PressINV = False
```

Listing 12-1 Continued.

```
' get the index of the selected memory register
I = MemLst.ListIndex
' is there a no selected memory register?
If I < 0 Then Exit Sub
' reset the contents of the selected memory register
MemLst.List(I) = Format$(I + 1, "000") + " : 0"
End Sub

Sub ClrSumBtn_Click ()
' Clear the statistical summations and disable some of the
' linear regression command buttons
ProcessPendingNewNumber
PressHYP = False
PressINV = False
NewNum = False
' assign zeros to the statistical summations
Sum = 0
SumX = 0
SumY = 0
SumXX = 0
SumYY = 0
SumXY = 0
' disable the LR button
LRBtn.Enabled = False
' disable the Mean button
MeanBtn.Enabled = False
' disable the Y^ button
YhatBtn.Enabled = False
End Sub

Sub ClxBtn_Click ()
' Drop off the top of the stack
DspBox.Text = "" ' clear display text box
' is the stack not empty?
If StackLst.ListCount > 0 Then
  ' delete the top of the stack
  StackLst.RemoveItem 0
  ' is the updated stack not empty
  If StackLst.ListCount > 0 Then
    ' copy the new top of the stack into the display text box
    DspBox.Text = StackLst.List(0)
  End If
End If
NewNum = False
PressHYP = False
PressINV = False
End Sub

Sub CosBtn_Click ()
' Handle the calls to the cosine, arc cosine, hyperbolic cosine,
' and inverse hyperbolic cosine functions.
If PressHYP And PressINV Then
  FunctionOp "ArcCosh"
ElseIf PressHYP Then
  FunctionOp "Cosh"
ElseIf PressINV Then
  FunctionOp "ArcCos"
Else
  FunctionOp "Cos"
End If
End Sub

Sub CubeRootBtn_Click ()
' Handle the cube and cube root functions.
If PressINV Then
  FunctionOp "X^3"
```

Listing 12-1 Continued.

```
   Else
      FunctionOp "CubeRoot"
   End If
End Sub

Sub DecimalBtn_Click ()
' Insert a decimal in a number being keying in, or start a new
' number with a decimal point.
   PressHYP = False
   PressINV = False
   ' is the user in the process of keying in a number?
   If NewNum Then
      ' append a decimal if there is not one already
      If InStr(DspBox.Text, ".") = 0 Then
         DspBox.Text = DspBox.Text + "."
      End If
   Else
      ' start keying in a new number with the decimal point
      DspBox.Text = "0."
      NewNum = True
   End If
End Sub

Sub DegreesChk_Click ()
' Handle the degrees check box
   ' is the degrees check box marked?
   If DegreesChk.Value = 1 Then
      ' the current angle mode handles degrees
      AngleCF = 4 * Atn(1) / 180
   Else
      ' the current angle mode handles radians
      AngleCF = 1
   End If
End Sub

Sub DigitBtn_Click (Index As Integer)
' Emulate keying in a digit in the display text box
   ' is NewNum state False
   If Not NewNum Then
      ' clear the display text box
      DspBox.Text = ""
   End If
   NewNum = True ' set the NewNum state to True
   PressHYP = False
   PressINV = False
   ' append the keyed in digit using the Index of the
   ' array of command button controls that represents
   ' the digits' buttons
   DspBox.Text = DspBox.Text + Format$(Index)
End Sub

Sub DivBtn_Click ()
' Divide the two topmost stack members
   BinaryOp "/"
End Sub

Sub DspBox_Change ()
' Set the NewNum state to True if the display box is changed.
' This procedure is often overridden.
   NewNum = True
End Sub

Sub DspBtn_Click ()
' Select a new format string
   Dim S As String
   Dim OK As Integer
```

Listing 12-1 Continued.

```
    Dim Z As Double
    OK = True ' assign the default value
    Do
        ' prompt the user for a new format string
        S = InputBox$("Enter display format", "Input", Frmt)
        ' did the user accepted the current or edited format string?
        If S <> "" Then
            Frmt = S ' update the format string
            ' test if the format is correct
            Z = 10 ^ (4 * Atn(1))
            On Error GoTo BadDsp ' turn on error trap
            S = Format$(Z, Frmt) ' test conversion
            On Error GoTo 0 ' turn off error trap
        End If
    Loop Until OK
    Exit Sub
    '****************** Error Handler ******************
BadDsp:
    OK = False
    MsgBox "Bad format string", BOX_MODE, ERROR_TITLE
    Resume Next
End Sub

Sub EexBtn_Click ()
' Append an exponent to a number being keyed in and terminate
' the number entry
    Dim S As String
    ' if there is no number being keyed in exit
    If Not NewNum Then Exit Sub
    ' is the display text box void from a current exponent?
    If InStr(DspBox.Text, "D") = 0 Then
        ' prompt the user to enter the exponent
        S = InputBox$("Enter exponent ", "Input", "D+000")
        ' did the user accept the default or the edited exponent?
        If S <> "" Then
            ' append the exponent to the string in the display text box
            DspBox.Text = DspBox.Text + S
            NewNum = False ' set the NewNum state to False
            Push
        End If
    End If
    PressHYP = False
    PressINV = False
End Sub

Sub EnterBtn_Click ()
' Terminate the data entry of a new number and explicitly push
' in the RPN stack.
    Dim X As Double
    PressHYP = False
    PressINV = False
    NewNum = False ' set the NewNum state to False
    ' convert the string in the display text box into a number
    X = Val(DspBox.Text)
    ' set the error trap for a possible bad format string
    On Error GoTo BadEnter
    ' push the string image of X in the stack
    StackLst.AddItem Format$(X, Frmt), 0
    On Error GoTo 0 ' turn off the error trap
    Exit Sub
    '****************** Error Handler ********************
BadEnter:
    ' prompt the user to enter a new format string
    Frmt = InputBox$(FORMAT_ERR, "Input", Frmt)
    ' resume at the offending statement
    Resume 0
```

Listing 12-1 Continued.

```
End Sub

Sub Form_Load ()
' Initialize the RPNCalc form
  WindowState = 2 ' maximize the window
  Frmt = "" ' set the initial format string
  AngleCF = 1 ' the initial angle conversion factor is 1, since
              ' the initial angle mode is in radians
  ClearBtn_Click ' clear the RPN stack
  ClearAllBtn_Click ' clear the memory registers
  ClrSumBtn_Click ' clear the statistical summations
End Sub

Sub FunctionOp (ByVal OpStr As String)
' Perform a math function evaluation
  Dim Z As Double
  ProcessPendingNewNumber
  ' is the stack not empty?
  If StackLst.ListCount > 0 Then
    PopX ' pop the top stack member
    ' convert the characters in parameter OpStr into uppercase
    OpStr = UCase$(OpStr)
    ' set the error trap
    On Error GoTo BadFunctionOp
    ' select the proper operation
    Select Case Len(OpStr)

       ' select 2-character functions
       Case 2
         Select Case OpStr
           Case "LN"
              Y = Log(X)
         End Select

       ' select 3-character functions
       Case 3
         Select Case OpStr
           Case "ABS"
             Y = Abs(X)
           Case "SIN"
             Y = Sin(AngleCF * X)
           Case "COS"
             Y = Cos(AngleCF * X)
           Case "TAN"
             Y = Tan(AngleCF * X)
           Case "1/X"
             Y = 1 / X
           Case "X^2"
             Y = X ^ 2
           Case "LOG"
             ' calculate Log base 10
             Y = Log(X) / Log(10)
           Case "X^3"
             Y = X ^ 3
           Case "EXP"
             Y = Exp(X)
         End Select

       ' select 4-character functions
       Case 4
         Select Case OpStr
           Case "SQRT"
             Y = Sqr(X)
           Case "10^X"
             Y = 10 ^ X
           Case "SINH" ' hyperbolic sine
             Y = (Exp(X) - Exp(-X)) / 2
```

Listing 12-1 Continued.

```
            Case "COSH" ' hyperbolic cosine
              Y = (Exp(X) + Exp(-X)) / 2
            Case "TANH" ' hyperbolic tangent
              Z = Exp(X)
              Y = (Z - 1 / Z) / (Z + 1 / Z)
          End Select

        ' select 6-character functions
        Case 6
          Select Case OpStr
            Case "ARCSIN" ' arc sine
              Y = Atn(X / Sqr(1 - X * X)) / AngleCF
            Case "ARCCOS" ' arc cosine
              Y = 2 * Atn(1) - Atn(X / Sqr(1 - X * X))
              Y = Y / AngleCF
            Case "ARCTAN" ' arc tangent
              Y = Atn(X) / AngleCF
          End Select

        ' select 7-character functions
        Case 7
        Select Case OpStr
          Case "ARCSINH" ' inverse hyperbolic sine
            Y = Log(X + Sqr(X * X + 1))
          Case "ARCCOSH" ' inverse hyperbolic cosine
            Y = Log(X + Sqr(X * X - 1))
          Case "ARCTANH" ' inverse hyperbolic tangent
            Y = Log((1 + X) / (1 - X)) / 2
        End Select

      ' select function names that are longer than 7 characters
      Case Is > 7
        Select Case OpStr
          Case "CUBEROOT"
            Y = X ^ (1 / 3)
        End Select
    End Select
    ' turn off error trap
    On Error GoTo 0
    LastX = X ' store the last value of X
    ' convert numeric result of Y into a string image and
    ' store it in the display text box
    DspBox.Text = Format$(Y, Frmt)
    Push ' push the result in the stack
  Else
    MsgBox STACK_SIZE_ERR, BOX_MODE, ERROR_TITLE
  End If
ExitFunctionOp:
  NewNum = False
  PressHYP = False
  PressINV = False
  Exit Sub
  '********************** Error Handler ******************
BadFunctionOp:
  ' write the string image of X in the display text box and
  ' push the value of X back into the stack
  DspBox.Text = Format$(X, Frmt)
  Push
  ' display error message box
  MsgBox OVERFLOW_ERR, BOX_MODE, ERROR_TITLE
  Resume ExitFunctionOp
End Sub

Sub HypBtn_Click ()
' Set the PressHYP state to True
  PressHYP = True
End Sub
```

Listing 12-1 Continued.

```
Sub InvBtn_Click ()
' Set the PressINV state to True
  PressINV = True
End Sub

Sub LastXBtn_Click ()
' Recall the value stored by the variable LastX
  ProcessPendingNewNumber
  ' copy the string image of LastX into the display text box
  DspBox.Text = Format$(LastX, Frmt)
  Push ' push the LastX value in the stack
  NewNum = False
  PressHYP = False
  PressINV = False
End Sub

Sub LnBtn_Click ()
' Handle the natural logarithm and exponential functions.
  If PressINV Then
    FunctionOp "Exp"
  Else
    FunctionOp "Ln"
  End If
End Sub

Sub LogBtn_Click ()
' Handle the common logarithm and power of 10 functions.
  If PressINV Then
    FunctionOp "10^X"
  Else
    FunctionOp "Log"
  End If
End Sub

Sub LRBtn_Click ()
' Perform linear regression calculations
  ProcessPendingNewNumber
  ' are there least than 2 observations?
  If Sum < 2 Then
    MsgBox "Insufficient statistical data", BOX_MODE, ERROR_TITLE
    Exit Sub
  End If
  NewNum = False
  PressHYP = False
  PressINV = False
  ' calculate the mean value for the X observations
  MeanX = SumX / Sum
  ' calculate the mean value for the Y observations
  MeanY = SumY / Sum
  ' calculate the std. deviation value for the X observations
  SdevX = Sqr((SumXX - SumX ^ 2 / Sum) / (Sum - 1))
  ' calculate the std. deviation value for the Y observations
  SdevY = Sqr((SumYY - SumY ^ 2 / Sum) / (Sum - 1))
  ' calculate the linear regression slope
  Slope = (SumXY - MeanX * MeanY * Sum) / SdevX ^ 2 / (Sum - 1)
  ' calculate the regression coefficient
  R2 = (Slope * SdevX / SdevY) ^ 2
  ' calculate the linear regression intercept
  Intercept = MeanY - Slope * MeanX
  ' push the linear regression slope, intercept, and regression
  ' coefficient in the stack
  StackLst.AddItem Format$(R2, Frmt), 0
  StackLst.AddItem Format$(Slope, Frmt), 0
  StackLst.AddItem Format$(Intercept, Frmt), 0
  ' enable the Mean button
  MeanBtn.Enabled = True
```

Listing 12-1 Continued.

```
   ' enable the Y^ button
   YhatBtn.Enabled = True
End Sub

Sub MeanBtn_Click ()
' Push the mean of std. deviation statistics in the stack
   ProcessPendingNewNumber
   NewNum = False
   PressHYP = False
   ' was the INV button clicked?
   If PressINV Then
      ' push the std. deviation for the X and Y data in the stack
      StackLst.AddItem Format$(SdevY, Frmt), 0
      StackLst.AddItem Format$(SdevX, Frmt), 0
   Else
      ' push the mean of the X and Y data in the stack
      StackLst.AddItem Format$(MeanY, Frmt), 0
      StackLst.AddItem Format$(MeanX, Frmt), 0
   End If
   PressINV = False
End Sub

Sub MulBtn_Click ()
' Multiply the two topmost stack members
   BinaryOp "*"
End Sub

Sub OffBtn_Click ()
' Unload the form
   Unload RPNCalc
End Sub

Sub PiBtn_Click ()
' Push the value of Pi into the RPN stack
   PressINV = False
   PressHYP = False
   ProcessPendingNewNumber
   ' push Pi in the stack
   ' set the error trap for a possible bad format string
   On Error GoTo BadPi
   StackLst.AddItem Format$(4 * Atn(1), Frmt), 0
   On Error GoTo 0 ' turn off the error trap
   Exit Sub
   '******************* Error Handler **********************
BadPi:
   ' prompt the user to enter a new format string
   Frmt = InputBox$(FORMAT_ERR, "Input", Frmt)
   ' resume at the offending statement
   Resume 0
End Sub

Sub Pop ()
' Pop off the two topmost stack members into the form-level
' variables X and Y.
   ' pop off the top two stack members into X and Y
   X = Val(StackLst.List(0))
   StackLst.RemoveItem 0 ' remove the top of the stack
   Y = Val(StackLst.List(0))
   StackLst.RemoveItem 0 ' remove the top of the stack
End Sub

Sub PopX ()
' Pop off the top stack element.  The caller routine must verify
' that the stack is not empty.
   ' get the number stored in the top stack register
   X = Val(StackLst.List(0))
```

Listing 12-1 Continued.

```
' remove the top of the stack member
StackLst.RemoveItem 0
End Sub

Sub PowerBtn_Click ()
' Handle the raising of powers operators.
    If PressINV Then
        BinaryOp "Y^1/X"
    Else
        BinaryOp "Y^X"
    End If
End Sub

Sub ProcessPendingNewNumber ()
    ' is there a new number pending in the display text box?
    If NewNum Then Push ' push it in the stack
    NewNum = False ' set the NewNum state to False
End Sub

Sub Push ()
' Push the string in the display text box into the stack.  The
' procedure first converts the contents of the text box into
' a number and them pushes the string image of that number
' in the stack.
    ' convert the contents of the display text box into a number
    X = Val(DspBox.Text)
    ' set the error trap for bad format strings
    On Error GoTo BadPush
    ' push the string image of X into the stack
    StackLst.AddItem Format$(X, Frmt), 0
    On Error GoTo 0 ' turn off the error trap
    Exit Sub
    '
BadPush:
    '****************** Error Handler ********************
    ' prompt the user to enter a new format string
    Frmt = InputBox$(FORMAT_ERR, "Input", Frmt)
    ' resume at the offending statement
    Resume 0
End Sub

Sub RclBtn_Click ()
' Recall the number stored in the selected memory register and
' push that number in the RPN stack.
    Dim I As Integer
    Dim S As String
    PressHYP = False
    PressINV = False
    ProcessPendingNewNumber
    ' get the index of the selected memory register
    I = MemLst.ListIndex
    ' if there is no selected memory register, then select
    ' the first memory register
    If I < 0 Then I = 0
    ' push the string image of the number in the selected memory
    ' register into the stack
    StackLst.AddItem Mid$(MemLst.List(I), 7), 0
    DspBox.Text = StackLst.List(0)
End Sub

Sub ReciprocalBtn_Click ()
' Handle the reciprocal and absolute functions.
    If PressINV Then
        FunctionOp "Abs"
    Else
        FunctionOp "1/X"
```

Listing 12-1 Continued.

```
   End If
End Sub

Sub RollDnBtn_Click ()
' Roll down the stack.  The pervious bottom stack member becomes the
' new top member.  Every other member is moved downward in the
' stack.
  Dim L As Integer
  ProcessPendingNewNumber
  PressHYP = False
  PressINV = False
  ' obtain the height of the stack
  L = StackLst.ListCount
  ' is there at more than one member in the stack?
  If L > 1 Then
    ' copy the bottom of the stack into X (with data conversion)
    X = Val(StackLst.List(L - 1))
    ' remove the old bottom element
    StackLst.RemoveItem L - 1
    ' insert old bottom as the new top of the stack
    StackLst.AddItem Format$(X, Frmt), 0
    ' display the new top of the stack in the display text box
    DspBox.Text = StackLst.List(0)
    NewNum = False
  End If
End Sub

Sub RollUpBtn_Click ()
' Roll up the stack.  The pervious top stack member becomes the
' new bottom member.  Every other member is moved upward in the
' stack.
  ProcessPendingNewNumber
  PressHYP = False
  PressINV = False
  ' is there at more than one member in the stack?
  If StackLst.ListCount > 1 Then
    PopX ' pop off the top of the stack
    ' move the old top to the bottom of the stack
    StackLst.AddItem Format$(X, Frmt), StackLst.ListCount
    ' display the new top of the stack in the display text box
    DspBox.Text = StackLst.List(0)
    NewNum = False
  End If
End Sub

Sub SinBtn_Click ()
' Handle the calls to the sine, arc sine, hyperbolic sine, and
' inverse hyperbolic sine functions.
  If PressHYP And PressINV Then
    FunctionOp "ArcSinh"
  ElseIf PressHYP Then
    FunctionOp "Sinh"
  ElseIf PressINV Then
    FunctionOp "ArcSin"
  Else
    FunctionOp "Sin"
  End If
End Sub

Sub SqrtBtn_Click ()
' Handle the square and square root functions.
  If PressINV Then
    FunctionOp "X^2"
  Else
    FunctionOp "Sqrt"
  End If
```

Listing 12-1 Continued.

```
End Sub

Sub StoBtn_Click ()
' Store a stack register in the selected memory register.  By
' default the top of the stack is stored in the selected memory
' register.  The default selected memory register is the first one.
  Dim I As Integer
  Dim S As String
  PressHYP = False
  PressINV = False
  ProcessPendingNewNumber
  ' get the index of the selected memory register
  I = MemLst.ListIndex
  ' if there is no selected register then select the first memory register
  If I < 0 Then I = 0
  ' is the RPN stack empty?
  If StackLst.ListCount = 0 Then Exit Sub ' exit
  ' is there a selected stack register?
  If StackLst.ListIndex >= 0 Then
    ' store the number of the selected register in X
    X = Val(StackLst.Text)
  Else
    ' store the top of the stack in X
    X = Val(StackLst.List(0))
  End If
  ' obtain the string image of the target memory register
  S = Format$(I + 1, "000") + " : " + Format$(X, Frmt)
  ' store the data in the selected memory register
  MemLst.List(I) = S
End Sub

Sub StoPlusBtn_Click ()
' Add the number in the selected stack register to the content
' of the selected memory register.  By default, the selected
' stack register is the top of the stack.
  Dim I As Integer
  Dim S As String
  PressHYP = False
  PressINV = False
  ProcessPendingNewNumber
  ' get the index of the selected memory register
  I = MemLst.ListIndex
  ' if there is no selected register then select the first memory register
  If I < 0 Then I = 0
  ' is the RPN stack empty
  If StackLst.ListCount = 0 Then Exit Sub ' exit
  ' is there a selected stack register?
  If StackLst.ListIndex >= 0 Then
    ' store the number of the selected register in X
    X = Val(StackLst.Text)
  Else
    ' store the top of the stack in X
    X = Val(StackLst.List(0))
  End If
  ' obtain the number from the current memory register
  Y = Val(Mid$(MemLst.List(I), 7))
  ' obtain the string image of the target memory register
  S = Format$(I + 1, "000") + " : " + Format$(X + Y, Frmt)
  ' store the updated data in the selected memory register
  MemLst.List(I) = S
End Sub

Sub SubBtn_Click ()
' Subtract the two topmost stack members
  BinaryOp "-"
End Sub
```

Listing 12-1 Continued.

```
Sub SumBtn_Click ()
' Update the statistical summations
  ProcessPendingNewNumber
  ' is there more than one stack member?
  If StackLst.ListCount > 1 Then
    Pop ' pop the two topmost stack registers
    ' was the INV button clicked?
    If PressINV Then
      ' delete the observation (X, Y) from the
      ' statistical summations
      Sum = Sum - 1
      SumX = SumX - X
      SumY = SumY - Y
      SumXX = SumXX - X * X
      SumYY = SumYY - Y * Y
      SumXY = SumXY - X * Y
    Else
      ' add the observations (X, Y) to the
      ' statistical summations
      Sum = Sum + 1
      SumX = SumX + X
      SumY = SumY + Y
      SumXX = SumXX + X * X
      SumYY = SumYY + Y * Y
      SumXY = SumXY + X * Y
    End If
    ' are there more than 1 observations?
    If Sum > 1 Then
      LRBtn.Enabled = True ' enable the LR button
    Else
      ' disable the LR button
      LRBtn.Enabled = False
      ' disable the Mean button
      MeanBtn.Enabled = False
      ' disable the Y^ button
      YhatBtn.Enabled = False
    End If
    ' display the current value of Sum in the display text box
    DspBox.Text = Str$(Sum)
    NewNum = False
  Else
    MsgBox STACK_SIZE_ERR, BOX_MODE, ERROR_TITLE
  End If
  NewNum = False
  PressHYP = False
  PressINV = False
End Sub

Sub SwapBtn_Click ()
' Swap the two topmost stack registers
  ProcessPendingNewNumber
  ' does the stack contain more than one elements?
  If StackLst.ListCount > 1 Then
    Pop ' pop off the two topmost stack elements
    ' reinsert these elements in the reverse order
    ' first push the data of variable X
    StackLst.AddItem Format$(X, Frmt), 0
    ' then, push the data of variable Y
    DspBox.Text = Format$(Y, Frmt)
    Push
  End If
  NewNum = False
  PressHYP = False
  PressINV = False
End Sub

Sub TanBtn_Click ()
```

Listing 12-1 Continued.

```
' Handle the calls to the tangent, arc tangent, hyperbolic tangent,
' and inverse hyperbolic tangent functions.
  If PressHYP And PressINV Then
    FunctionOp "ArcTanh"
  ElseIf PressHYP Then
    FunctionOp "Tanh"
  ElseIf PressINV Then
    FunctionOp "ArcTan"
  Else
    FunctionOp "Tan"
  End If
End Sub

Sub YhatBtn_Click ()
' Project X on Y r Y on X
  ProcessPendingNewNumber
  ' is the stack not empty?
  If StackLst.ListCount > 0 Then
    PopX ' pop the top stack element
    ' set the error trap
    On Error GoTo BadYhat
    ' was the INV button clicked?
    If PressINV Then
      ' project X on Y
      Y = (X - Intercept) / Slope
    Else
      ' project Y on X
      Y = Intercept + Slope * X
    End If
    On Error GoTo 0  ' turn off error trap
    ' push the result in the stack
    DspBox.Text = Format$(Y, Frmt)
    Push
  Else
    MsgBox STACK_SIZE_ERR, BOX_MODE, ERROR_TITLE
  End If
ExitYhat:
  NewNum = False
  PressHYP = False
  PressINV = False
  Exit Sub
  '******************** Error Handler *********************
BadYhat:
  ' push X back into the stack
  DspBox.Text = Format$(X, Frmt)
  Push
  ' display an error message box
  MsgBox OVERFLOW_ERR, BOX_MODE, ERROR_TITLE
  Resume ExitYhat
End Sub
```

The form also declares the following variables:

- The LastX variable, which stores the value of the top stack member before the last function or operation.
- The Frmt variable, which contains the format string.
- The Boolean NewNum variable, which stores the new-number state.
- The Boolean PressINV variable, which contains the press-INV state.
- The Boolean PressHYP variable, which maintains the press-HYP state.

- The double-precision floating point X and Y variables, which are used frequently by the various procedures.
- The AngleCF variable, which maintains the angle conversion factor for radians or degrees.

  The Sum, SumX, SumY, SumXX, SumYY, and SumXY variables, which represent the statistical summations.

  The MeanX, MeanY, SdevX, SdevY, Slope, Intercept, and R2 variables, which store statistics related to linear regression.

The procedures attached to the RPNCALC.FRM form are listed alphabetically in Listing 12-1. Figure 12-6 gives you a brief alphabetized summary of the procedures along with their related systems. Figure 12-7 shows the same procedures sorted by the various systems. These figures offer two ways for cross-referencing the procedures. I will discuss the procedures by system affiliation, and begin with the procedures that initialize and unload the RPNCalc form.

Initializing procedures

The Form_Load procedure initializes the form. To do this, it first maximizes the window, giving the form the needed size. Then it initializes the angle conversion factor to 1, since the default angles are in radians, and then clears the RPN stack. At this point the procedure clears the memory registers, clears the statistical summations, and disables the L.R., Mean, and Y^ buttons.

The OffBtn_Click procedure unloads the RPNCalc form.

Digits system procedures

The procedures which make up the Digits system are described in the following paragraphs.

The ChsBtn_Click procedure toggles the sign of the number in the display box. If the number in the display box is not being keyed in, the sign of the top stack member is also toggled.

The DecimalBtn_Click procedure inserts or appends a decimal point to the string in the text box. If the number in the display box is being keyed in, the procedure first makes sure that there isn't already a decimal point; If not, the procedure appends a decimal point. If the number in the display text box is not a new number, the procedure begins a new number by writing the string 0. to the display text box and then setting the NewNum variable to True.

The DigitBtn_Click procedure appends a digit in the display. If the NewNum variable is False, the procedure first clears the display text box to remove the previous number, then sets NewNum to True and appends the caption of the DigitBtn(Index) control.

The EexBtn_Click procedure appends an exponent to the number being

Routine name	System
AddBtn_Click	Operators
BinaryOp	Processing
ChsBtn_Click	Digits
ClearAllBtn_Click	Memory
ClearBtn_Click	Stack
ClrBtn_Click	Memory
ClrSumBtn_Click	Statistics
ClxBtn_Click	Stack
CosBtn_Click	Functions
CubeRootBtn_Click	Functions
DecimalBtn_Click	Digits
DegreesChk_Click	Functions
DigitBtn_Click	Digits
DivBtn_Click	Operators
DspBox_Change	Display
DspBtn_Click	Display
EexBtn_Click	Digits
EnterBtn_Click	Stack
Form_Load	none
FunctionOp	Processing
HypBtn_Click	Functions
InvBtn_Click	Functions
LastXBtn_Click	Stack
LnBtn_Click	Functions
LogBtn_Click	Functions
LRBtn_Click	Statistics
MeanBtn_Click	Statistics
MulBtn_Click	Operators
OffBtn_Click	none
PiBtn_Click	Functions
Pop	Processing
PopX	Processing
PowerBtn_Click	Operators
ProcessPendingNewNumber	Processing
Push	Processing
RclBtn_Click	Memory
ReciprocalBtn_Click	Functions
RollDnBtn_Click	Stack
RollUpBtn_Click	Stack
SinBtn_Click	Functions
SqrtBtn_Click	Functions
StoBtn_Click	Memory
StoPlusBtn_Click	Memory
SubBtn_Click	Operators
SumBtn_Click	Statistics
SwapBtn_Click	Stack
TanBtn_Click	Functions
YhatBtn_Click	Statistics

12-6 The list of alphabetized procedures and functions in the RPNCALC.FRM form.

Routine name	System
ChsBtn_Click	Digits
DecimalBtn_Click	Digits
DigitBtn_Click	Digits
EexBtn_Click	Digits
DspBox_Change	Display
DspBtn_Click	Display
CosBtn_Click	Functions
CubeRootBtn_Click	Functions
DegreesChk_Click	Functions
HypBtn_Click	Functions
InvBtn_Click	Functions
LnBtn_Click	Functions
LogBtn_Click	Functions
PiBtn_Click	Functions
ReciprocalBtn_Click	Functions
SinBtn_Click	Functions
SqrtBtn_Click	Functions
TanBtn_Click	Functions
ClearAllBtn_Click	Memory
ClrBtn_Click	Memory
RclBtn_Click	Memory
StoBtn_Click	Memory
StoPlusBtn_Click	Memory
Form_Load	none
OffBtn_Click	none
AddBtn_Click	Operators
DivBtn_Click	Operators
MulBtn_Click	Operators
PowerBtn_Click	Operators
SubBtn_Click	Operators
BinaryOp	Processing
FunctionOp	Processing
Pop	Processing
PopX	Processing
ProcessPendingNewNumber	Processing
Push	Processing
ClearBtn_Click	Stack
ClxBtn_Click	Stack
EnterBtn_Click	Stack
LastXBtn_Click	Stack
RollDnBtn_Click	Stack
RollUpBtn_Click	Stack
SwapBtn_Click	Stack
ClrSumBtn_Click	Statistics
LRBtn_Click	Statistics
MeanBtn_Click	Statistics
SumBtn_Click	Statistics
YhatBtn_Click	Statistics

12-7 The functions and procedures in form RPNCALC.FRM listed by system affiliation.

entered in the display text box. The procedure verifies that the NewNum variable is True and that there is no exponent already in the text box. The procedure uses the Visual Basic InStr function to detect the letter D in the display text box. If these conditions are favorable, the procedure invokes the InputBox$ function to prompt for an exponent. The default exponent in the dialog box is D + 000. If you accept the default or the edited exponent, it is appended to the string in the display text box. Finally, the procedure sets the NewNum variable to False, ending the entry of the new number.

Display system procedures

The procedures that are described next make up the Display system.

The DspBox_Change procedure sets the NewNum variable to True when the display text box is altered, this is the default action. The procedures that alter the display text box often reset the NewNum variable to False to override the action of procedure DspBox_Change.

The DspBtn_Click procedure invokes the InputBox$ function to prompt you for a new format string. The form-level variable Frmt maintains the current format string; the InputBox$ function uses this variable to display the current format string. If you accept the current or the edited format string, then Frmt is updated. The procedure also tests the format string. If the accepted format string generates an error, you are prompted to enter a new format string.

Functions system procedures

The form has the following procedures that are associated with the Functions system. All of these procedures push any pending number into the stack before proceeding.

The CosBtn_Click procedure handles the cosine, inverse cosine, hyperbolic cosine, and inverse hyperbolic cosine functions. The procedure examines the Boolean values of the PressHYP and PressINV variables to select the proper call to the function FunctionOp.

The CubeRootBtn_Click procedure handles the cube and cube root functions. The procedure examines the Boolean value of the variable PressINV to determine the proper call to FunctionOp.

The DegreesChk_Click procedure updates the angle conversion factor based on the current Value property of the DegreeChk check box.

The HypBtn_Click procedure assigns True to the variable PressHYP. This assignment turns on the hyperbolic mode.

The InvBtn_Click procedure assigns True to the variable PressINV. This assignment turns on the inverse mode.

The LnBtn_Click procedure handles the natural and exponential functions. The procedure examines the Boolean value of the variable PressINV to determine the proper call to the function FunctionOp.

The LogBtn_Click procedure handles the common logarithm and power of ten functions. The procedure examines the Boolean value of the variable PressINV to determine the proper call to FunctionOp.

The PiBtn_Click procedure pushes the value of Pi into the stack.

The ReciprocalBtn_Click procedure handles the reciprocal and the absolute value functions. The procedure examines the Boolean value of the variable PressINV to determine the proper call to FunctionOp.

The SinBtn_Click procedure handles the sine, inverse sine, hyperbolic sine, and inverse hyperbolic sine functions. The procedure examines the Boolean values of the PressHYP and PressINV variables to select the proper version of the FunctionOp call.

The SqrtBtn_Click procedure manages the square root and the square functions. The procedure examines the Boolean value of the variable PressINV to determine the proper call to FunctionOp.

The TanBtn_Click procedure handles the tangent, inverse tangent, hyperbolic tangent, and inverse hyperbolic tangent functions. The procedure examines the Boolean values of the PressHYP and PressINV variables to select the proper version of the FunctionOp call.

Memory Registers system procedures

The procedures described next implement the operations of the Memory Registers system.

The ClearAllBtn_Click procedure clears all of the memory registers by assigning them the string image of 0.

The ClrBtn_Click procedure clears the selected memory register by assigning it the string image of 0. The procedure performs no operation if there is no selected memory register.

The RclBtn_Click procedure pushes the selected memory register into the stack, with the first register as the default. If there is a new number pending, that number is first pushed into the stack. The procedure also copies the string of the selected memory register into the display text box.

The StoBtn_Click procedure copies the selected stack member into the selected memory register; again, the first memory register and the top stack member are the defaults. If there is a pending new number, that number is first pushed into the stack.

The StoPlusBtn_Click procedure is similar to StoBtn_Click, except that it adds the value of the selected stack member to the value of the selected memory register, and stores the result.

Operators system procedures

The form includes the following procedures that make up the Operators system.

The AddBtn_Click procedure simply invokes the BinaryOp function with the + argument to add the two top stack members. If there is a pending new number, that number is first pushed into the stack.

The DivBtn_Click procedure calls the BinaryOp function with the / argument to divide the two top stack members. Any pending new number is first pushed into the stack.

The MulBtn_Click procedure invokes the BinaryOp function with the * argument to multiply the two top stack members. Any pending new number is first pushed into the stack.

The PowerBtn_Click procedure invokes the BinaryOp function with the Y^X argument to take the power of the top stack members. Once again, if there is a pending new number, that number is first pushed into the stack.

The SubBtn_Click procedure invokes the BinaryOp function with the − argument to subtract the two top stack members; any pending new number is first pushed into the stack.

Processing system procedures

The form contains the following procedures that comprise the Processing system.

The BinaryOp procedure executes the binary operation specified by the argument for the OpStr parameter. The procedure invokes ProcessPendingNewNumber to push any new pending number into the stack, sets the PressINV and PressHYP variables to False, and examines whether the stack has at least two members. If not, the procedure displays a message box to that effect and then exits.

Next, the procedure pops the two top stack members by invoking the Pop procedure. The form-level variables X and Y are assigned the popped stack members. The procedure then turns on an error trap, which resumes at the BadBinaryOp label. There, the procedure pushes the operands back into the stack and then displays an error message. This single error trap efficiently deals with various operations that cause an overflow.

The procedure uses a Select Case statement to compare the expression UCase$(OpStr) with the various Case clauses; the matching Case clause invokes the proper operation. At this point, the procedure turns off the error trap, assigns the value of variable X (which represents the last top stack member) to the variable LastX, and writes the string image of the result to the display text box. It also pushes the number in the display text box into the RPN stack, and sets the NewNum variable to False before exiting.

The FunctionOp procedure is very similar to BinaryOp. It differs in that it handles the evaluation of mathematical functions, and it uses a nested Select Case statement to speed up selecting the proper function evaluation. The outer Select Case statement examines the length of the Function Name string, enabling the functions to be grouped by length of function names.

The Pop procedure pops off the two top stack members. The routine converts them into numbers and assigns them to the form-level variables X and Y. The procedure assumes that the stack has at least two members.
page 173

The PopX procedure pops off the top stack member. The procedure first converts the top stack member into a number and assigns it to the variable X, then removes the top stack member from the list box. The procedure assumes that the stack has at least one member.

The ProcessPendingNewNumber procedure pushes any pending new number into the stack and sets the NewNum variable to False.

The Push procedure pushes a new number into the stack. The routine first converts the string in the display text box into a double-typed number and then stores it in the variable X. Next, the procedure converts the contents of X back to a string and inserts that string in the stack. The procedure contains an error trap to guard against bad format strings, offering an additional check for the format strings.

Stack system procedures

The procedures that are described here comprise the Stack system.

The ClearBtn_Click procedure clears the RPN stack by removing all of its members. The routine also clears the display text box and assigns False to the NewNum variable.

The ClxBtn_Click procedure pops off the top stack member. If the updated stack is not empty, the new top member is copied into the display text box. This action keeps the top of the stack and the display text box in sync with each other.

The EnterBtn_Click procedure terminates the entry of a new number and pushes it into the RPN stack.

The LastXBtn_Click procedure pushes the value stored of the LastX variable into the RPN stack.

The RollDnBtn_Click procedure rolls down the stack. The old bottom stack member becomes the new top stack member, and every other stack member is moved downward. The procedure performs no action if the stack contains less than two elements.

The RollUpBtn_Click procedure rolls up the stack. The old top stack member becomes the new bottom stack member, and every other stack member is moved upward. No action is performed if the stack contains less than two elements.

The SwapBtn_Click procedure swaps the two topmost stack members. The procedure performs no action if the stack contains less than two elements.

Statistics system procedures

The procedures described in this section are associated with the Statistics system.

The ClrSumBtn_Click procedure assigns zeros to the statistical summations and disables the L.R., Mean, and Y^ buttons.

The LRBtn_Click procedure calculates the linear regression slope, intercept, and correlation coefficient, and pushes these statistics into the stack. The procedure also calculates the mean and standard deviations for the observations. These statistics are stored in the form-level variables MeanX, MeanY, SdevX, and SdevY.

The MeanBtn_Click procedure pushes the values for the means or the standard deviations into the stack. The routine examines the value of the PressINV variable to determine which statistics to push into the stack. If the variable PressINV is False, the routine pushes the string images of MeanY and MeanX into the stack. By contrast, if the variable PressINV is True, the routine pushes the string images of SdevY and SdevX into the stack.

The SumBtn_Click procedure adds or removes observations from the statistical summations. If the PressINV variable is False, the procedure calls the Pop procedure to obtain an observation (X,Y) from the stack. The procedure then adds this observation to the statistical summations. If the PressINV variable is True, the routine pops off an observation from the stack and subtracts it from the statistical summations.

The YhatBtn_Click procedure projects either X on Y or Y on X, depending on the Boolean value of variable PressINV. If PressINV is False, the routine pops off an X value from the stack and calculates the corresponding Y value based on the linear regression slope and intercept. If the variable PressINV is True, the routine pops off a Y value from the stack and calculates the corresponding X value based on the regression slope and intercept.

Part Three

The file and directory utilities

This part presents a series of modules and forms that are the building blocks for utilities used to manage files in various drives and directories. The design of these programming units involves the following levels:

- Low level modules, which support other modules and programming units.
- Auxiliary modules, which contain more general routines.
- Secondary forms, which work with "shell" application forms.
- "Shell" application forms, which are the front ends of Visual Basic applications.

13
The file and
directory modules

This chapter presents the low level and auxiliary modules used by the file and directory utilities. The GENERIC.BAS module, presented in chapter 2, is also part of this group of modules. This chapter presents the following modules:

- The STRLIB.BAS module is a small module that contains two string manipulation routines and a time-related procedure.
- The DIRLIB.BAS module contains the routines that map the directories of the current drive.
- The FILESLIB.BAS is a relatively large module that contains procedures to copy, move, print, view, and edit single and multiple files.

The STRLIB.BAS module

The STRLIB.BAS module, shown in Listing 13-1, contains a modest number of routines. It serves as a nucleus module, and it may include your own general string manipulation routines. The STRLIB.BAS module is independent of any other module and contains routines which follow.

The Boolean IsWord function returns True if the first character of its string argument is a letter.

The StringToWords procedure extracts the space-delimited words from the argument of the T$ parameter. The extracted words are returned through the W$( ) array parameter; the number of words extracted is reported by the parameter N%. The W$( ) parameter is not redimensioned inside the procedure; therefore, the caller should set the array W$( ) with a sufficient size (such as 80). If the number of words to be extracted is greater than the size of array W$( ), the extra words are discarded.

Listing 13-1 The code in the STRLIB.BAS module.

```
Const True = -1, False = 0

Function IsWord (S As String) As Integer
' Return True if the first character of string S is
' a letter.  Otherwise, the function returns False
  Dim C As String * 1
  C = UCase$(S)
  IsWord = (C >= "A") And (C <= "Z")
End Function

Sub StringToWords (ByVal T$, W$(), N%)
' Extract the space-delimited words from the string T$
' The procedure extracts N% words and places them in
' the array W$
  Dim InWord As Integer
  Dim I As Long
  Dim First As Long
  Dim SpaceStr As String * 2
  SpaceStr = " " + Chr$(8)
  ' trim both ends of the string T$
  T$ = RTrim$(LTrim$(T$))
  N% = 0 ' initialize number of extract words
  InWord = False
  ' scan the characters of the string T$
  For I = 1 To Len(T$)
    ' is character I a space or a tab character?
    If InStr(SpaceStr, Mid$(T$, I, 1)) > 0 Then
      ' is the procedure scanning a word
      If InWord Then
        ' found end of last word
        N% = N% + 1 ' increment the word counter
        If N% > UBound(W$) Then Exit Sub
        ' extract the last word
        W$(N%) = Mid$(T$, First, I - First)
        InWord = False ' set in-word flag to false
      End If
    Else
      ' is the procedure scanning spaces?
      If Not InWord Then
        InWord = True ' set in-word flag to true
        First = I ' mark the beginning of a word
      End If
    End If
  Next I
  ' extract last pending word?
  If InWord Then
    N% = N% + 1
    If N% > UBound(W$) Then Exit Sub
    W$(N%) = Mid$(T$, First, Len(T$) + 1 - First)
  End If
  ' are there vacant members in array W$?
  If N% < UBound(W$) Then
    ' assign empty strings to the remaining members of W$
    For I = N% + 1 To UBound(W$)
      W$(I) = ""
    Next I
  End If
End Sub

Sub Wait (ByVal Delay!)
' Wait for Delay& seconds
  Dim Start As Single
  ' read the number of seconds since midnight
  Start = Timer
```

Listing 13-1 Continued.

```
' loop until at least Delay! seconds have elapsed
Do
Loop Until (Timer - Start) >= Delay!
End Sub
```

The procedure employs a simple state engine while scanning the argument for T$. The procedure uses the local variable InWord to monitor the in-a-word scanning state. This state has two values: True (scanning a word) and False (scanning a space or a tab character).

The procedure initializes the local variable SpaceStr with characters that represent white space, which are the space and tab characters. It then trims the leading and trailing ends of the argument for T$, which should speed up scanning characters when leading and/or trailing spaces exist in T$. Next the procedure initializes the number of words, assigned to parameter N%, to 0. The procedure sets the scanning state, stored in the local variable InWord, to False. This assignment allows the procedure to correctly mark the position of the first nonwhite space character.

Next, StringToWords starts a loop to scan the characters of T$. The For Next loop contains an If-Then-Else statement that monitors the state of scanning and extracts the words. The If statement tests if the currently scanned character is a space or a tab character. If this condition is true, a nested If-Then statement examines the Boolean value of the variable InWord. If InWord is true, the loop has found the end of a word. The If-Then statement increments the number of extracted words, and exits the procedure if the number of words exceeds the upper bound of array W$( ). If not, the statement extracts the located word and assigns it to W$(N%), and also sets the InWord variable to False, since the loop is now scanning a white space.

When the currently scanned character is not a white space, the Else clause is executed. That clause also contains an If-Then statement that examines the expression Not InWord to determine if the loop was scanning a white space in the previous iteration. If the tested condition is true, then the loop has detected the beginning of a new word. Consequently, the Then clause sets the InWord variable to True and stores the location of the loop control variable I in the local variable First.

At this point, the StringToWords procedure extracts any pending word being scanned. The procedure examines the Boolean value of InWord; if that value is True, then the last word in T$ extends to the end of T$. The procedure then assigns empty strings to the unused elements of array W$( ). These elements have the index range of N% + 1 to UBound(W$( )).

The Wait procedure uses a Do-Loop-Until loop to wait for Delay! seconds. The procedure stores the current number of seconds since midnight into the local variable Start, and loops until the difference between the current number of seconds since midnight and Start is equal to or greater than the argument for Delay!.

The DIRLIB.BAS module

The DIRLIB.BAS module, shown in Listing 13-2, contains routines that build the directory tree map and extract information from that map. This module uses some of the routines in the GENERIC.BAS module; and has routines that do the following tasks:

- Build the tree directory map.
- Obtain the index for the parent directory of a specified non-root directory.
- Return the indices for the immediate children of a specified directory.
- Return the indices for all of the descendants of a specified directory.
- Return the indices of all sibling directories of a specified directory.
- Obtain the directory level of a specified directory.

Listing 13-2 The code in the DIRLIB.BAS module.

```
Const True = -1, False = 0

Sub BuildDirTree (D As Control, L As Control, Idx%())
' Build the directory tree map in list box L, using the
' directory list box D.  The array Idx%() contains the
' levels of each member of list box L.
'
' **** THIS PROCEDURE MUST BE CALLED BEFORE  ****
' **** ANY OTHER PROCEDURE IN THIS  LIBRARY  ****
'
  Dim I As Integer, J As Integer
  Dim OldPath As String
  MousePointer = 11 ' set the mouse to the hour-glass
  ' store the current path of the directory list box D in OldPath
  OldPath = D.Path
  ' reset the current path of the directory list box to the root
  ' of the current drive
  D.Path = "\"
  ' clear tree map list L
  ClearList L
  ' add the root of the directory list box in list box L
  L.AddItem D.List(-1)
  ' set the directory map tree index to first entry in list box L
  J = 0
  ' loop to build the directory tree map. Iterate until all of
  ' the members of list box L are visited.  This loop obtains
  ' the directory tree map in a breath-first scheme
  Do While J < L.ListCount
    ' set the current path of the directory list box to the
    ' current member of list box L.
    D.Path = L.List(J)
    ' obtain the subdirectories of the currently selected
    ' directory.  These subdirectories are in the directory
    ' list box, and are added to the list box L.
    For I = 0 To D.ListCount - 1
      L.AddItem D.List(I)
    Next I
    ' increment the index of the current member of list box L
    J = J + 1
  Loop
```

Listing 13-1 Continued.

```
      ' sort the members of the list box L.  This action yields a
      ' depth-first directory tree map.
      CombSort L, 1
      ' restore the original directory list box selection
      D.Path = OldPath
      ' obtain the levels of the directory tree map
      MapTreeDir L, Idx%()
      ' restore the mouse pointer
      MousePointer = 0
End Sub

Sub GetChildrenIdx (L As Control, Idx%(), ByVal Index%, ChildIdx%(),
Count%)
' Obtain the indices of the children subdirectories.  The list
' box L must contain the directory tree map.   The Idx%() array
' contains the levels of the directories.  The Index% parameter
' is the index of the client directory.  The procedure returns the
' indices of L.List(Index%)'s children in the ChildIdx% array.   The
' Count% parameter reports the actual number of children subdirectories
' found.
      Dim Level As Integer
      ' initialize the number of children subdirectories to 0
      Count% = 0
      ' is the argument for Index% valid?  Notice that the
      ' second Boolean term compares Index% with (L.ListCount-1).
      ' This comparison is valid since the children of L.List(Index%)
      ' are located at Index%+1 and beyond.
      If (Index% >= 0) And (Index% < (L.ListCount - 1)) Then
          ' redimension the ChildIdx%() array.  The upper limit is
          ' calculated based on the work case where L.List(Index+1) to
          ' L.List(ListCount-1) are all children of L.List(Index%).
          ReDim ChildIdx%(0 To L.ListCount - Index% - 1)
          ' is the L.List(Index%+1) list member a child subdirectory
          ' of L.List(Index%)?
          If Idx%(Index%) < Idx%(Index% + 1) Then
            ' Set the local variable Level to the level of the
            ' child subdirectory
            Level = Idx%(Index% + 1)
            Index% = Index% + 1
            ' Scan the rest of the list box members for children
            ' subdirectories.  Loop while the level of the
            ' member Index% is greater than or equal to Level
            Do While Level <= Idx%(Index%)
                ' does L.List(Index%) have the same level as
                ' the local variable Level
                If Level = Idx%(Index%) Then
                  ' store the index of the found child subdirectory
                  ChildIdx%(Count%) = Index%
                  ' increment the number of children subdirectories
                  Count% = Count% + 1
                End If
                ' increment the list box index
                Index% = Index% + 1
                ' exit the loop when the list box index has
                ' passed the last list box member
                If Index% = L.ListCount Then Exit Do
            Loop
          End If
      End If
End Sub

Sub GetDescIdx (L As Control, Idx%(), ByVal Index%, DescIdx%(), Count%)
' Obtain the array of indices that maps the descendants
' subdirectories, starting with L.List(Index%). The list
' box L must contain the directory tree map.  The Idx%() array
' contains the levels of the directories.  The Index% parameter
```

Listing 13-1 *Continued.*

```
' is the index of the client directory.  The procedure returns the
' indices of L.List(Index%)'s descendants in the DescIdx% array.
' The Count% parameter reports the actual number of descendent
' subdirectories found.  If argument for Index% is 0, then the
' DescIdx% array maps all of the directories of the disk, except
' the root.
  Dim Level As Integer
  ' initialize the number of children subdirectories to 0
  Count% = 0
  ' is the argument for Index% valid?  Notice that the
  ' second Boolean term compares Index% with (L.ListCount-1).
  ' This comparison is valid since the children of L.List(Index%)
  ' are located at Index%+1 and beyond.
  If (Index% >= 0) And (Index% < (L.ListCount - 1)) Then
      ' redimension the DescIdx%() array.  The upper limit is
      ' calculated based on the worst case where L.List(Index+1) to
      ' L.List(ListCount-1) are all descendants of L.List(Index%).
      ReDim DescIdx%(0 To L.ListCount - Index% - 1)
      ' is the L.List(Index%+1) list member a descendent
      ' subdirectory of L.List(Index%)?
      If Idx%(Index%) < Idx%(Index% + 1) Then
        ' Set the local variable Level to the level of the
        ' child subdirectory
        Level = Idx%(Index% + 1)
        Index% = Index% + 1
        ' loop while the level of member L.List(Index%) is
        ' greater or equal to the Level?
        Do While Level <= Idx%(Index%)
            ' store the index of the found descendent subdirectory
            DescIdx%(Count%) = Index%
            ' increment the number of descendent subdirectories
            Count% = Count% + 1
            ' increment the list box index
            Index% = Index% + 1
            ' exit the loop when the list box index has
            ' passed the last list box member
            If Index% = L.ListCount Then Exit Do
        Loop
      End If
  End If
End Sub

Function GetLevel (L As Control, ByVal Index%) As Integer
' Return the level of the directory L.List(Index%).  L is
' the list box that contains the directory tree map.  The
' function returns the level of L.List(Index%), or 0 if the
' argument for Index% is out of range.
  Dim N As Integer
  Dim I As Long
  ' is Index% within range?
  If (Index% >= 0) And (Index% < L.ListCount) Then
      ' is L.List(Index%) the root of the current directory?
      ' This condition is detected by comparing the last
      ' character of L.List(Index%) with "\".  This If
      ' statement is needed because subdirectories do not
      ' have a trailing "\" characters, but root directories
      ' do.  Therefore, the variable N must be correctly
      ' initialized, based on whether or not the examined
      ' directory is the root directory.
      If Right$(L.List(Index%), 1) = "\" Then
        N = 0
      Else
        N = 1
      End If
      ' find the location of the first "\" character
      I = InStr(L.List(Index), "\")
      ' loop to count the number of "\" in L.List(Index%)
```

Listing 13-1 Continued.

```
        Do While I > 0
            N = N + 1
            I = InStr(I + 1, L.List(Index), "\")
        Loop
        GetLevel = N ' return the function value
    Else
        GetLevel = 0 ' return an error value
    End If
End Function


Function GetParentIdx (L As Control, Idx%(), ByVal Index%) As Integer
' Return the index of the parent of L.List(Index%).  The Idx%() array
' contains the levels of the directories. The function returns the
' level of the parent directory, or -1 if Index% is either 0 or out
' of range.
    Dim I As Integer
    Dim CurrLevel As Integer
    ' is Index% an index of a valid subdirectory?
    If (Index% > 0) And (Index% < L.ListCount) Then
        ' set the value in I equal to the preceding
        ' list box member.
        I = Index% - 1
        ' store the level of L.List(Index%) in CurrLevel
        CurrLevel = Idx%(Index)
        ' loop while the level of the client list member is
        ' equal to or greater than the preceding list members.
        ' This loop searches for the parent directory, taking
        ' into consideration that there are sibling directories
        ' and their own descendants located before the client
        ' directory.  Notice the loop does not check I >= 0,
        ' since the parent directory must lie somewhere in
        ' the list.
        Do While (CurrLevel >= Idx%(I))
            I = I - 1
        Loop
        GetParentIdx = I ' return the function result
    Else
        GetParentIdx = -1 ' return an error code
    End If
End Function


Sub GetSiblingIdx (L As Control, Idx%(), ByVal Index%, SiblIdx%(), Count%)
' Obtain the indices of the sibling subdirectories.  The list
' box L must contain the directory tree map.  The Idx%() array
' contains the levels of the directories.  The Index% parameter
' is the index of the client directory.  The procedure returns the
' indices of L.List(Index%)'s siblings in the SiblIdx% array.   The
' Count% parameter reports the actual number of sibling subdirectories
' found.
    Dim ParentIdx As Integer
    Count% = 0
    ' is the value of Index% within range?
    If (Index% >= 0) And (Index% < L.ListCount) Then
        ParentIdx = GetParentIdx(L, Idx%(), Index%)
        ' call GetChildIdx to obtain the children of
        ' L.List(ParentIdx) which are also the siblings
        ' of L.List(Index%), including L.List(Index%) itself.
        GetChildrenIdx L, Idx%(), ParentIndex, SiblIdx%(), Count%
    End If
End Sub


Sub MapTreeDir (L As Control, Idx%())
' Obtain a map of directory tree levels.
    Dim I As Integer
    ' resize the Idx%() array
    ReDim Idx%(0 To L.ListCount - 1)
```

Listing 13-1 Continued.

```
' for every list member, call function GetLevel to
' obtain that member's level
For I = 0 To L.ListCount - 1
   Idx%(I) = GetLevel(L, I)
Next I
End Sub
```

The module routines use a directory list box to obtain the directory tree map for the currently selected drive. The map is stored in an invisible list box. In addition, the module establishes an array of indices that specify the directory levels. The root directory has a level of 1. Each directory attached to the root has an index of 2, and so on. Once the directories and their levels are known, other module routines can return information about the parent, children, descendant, and sibling directories of a specified directory. To reduce memory requirements, I chose to employ indices to specify those types of directories. These indices correspond to the members of the invisible list box control.

The DIRLIB.BAS module contains the routines described in the following paragraphs.

The BuildDirTree procedure must be called before any other routine in this module every time you scan a new drive. The procedure uses the directory list box control D to build a list of directories in the list box L. The array Idx%( ) returns the indices for the directories stored in the list box L. The procedure redimensions the array Idx%( ) with a lower bound of 0 and an upper bound of L.ListCount − 1.

☞ Before looking at the procedure's operation, I want to present the basic method used in scanning the directories using a directory list box D and an ordinary list box L. Figure 13-1 shows a sample directory tree. In

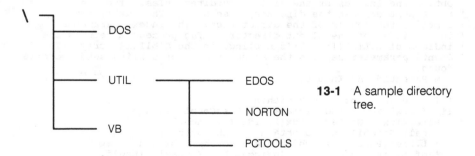

13-1 A sample directory tree.

this example, the path property of the directory list box is assigned the root directory \. The root directory becomes the currently selected directory in list box D, and that directory is added to list box L. The index J is assigned 0. The two list boxes have the following data:

Directory List Box D	List Box L	Index J
c:	c:\	0
dos		
util		
vb		

The Path property of list box D is assigned L.List(J). The directories attached to D.Path are added to the list box L:

Directory List Box D	List Box L	Index J
c:\	c:\	0
dos	c:\dos	
util	c:\util	
vb	c:\vb	

Next the index J is increased by 1. The Path property of list box D is assigned L.List(J), which is c:\dos. The list boxes have the following data:

Directory List Box D	List Box L	Index J
c:\	c:\	1
dos	c:\dos	
	c:\util	
	c:\vb	

Since the directory c:\dos has no subdirectories attached to it, no new members are added to the list box L.

The index J is increased by 1. The Path property of list box D is assigned L.List(J), which is c:\util. The list boxes have the following data:

Directory List Box D	List Box L	Index J
c:\	c:\	2
util	c:\dos	
edos	c:\util	
norton	c:\vb	
pctools		

The directories attached to D.Path are added to the list box L:

Directory List Box D	List Box L	Index J
c:\	c:\	3
util	c:\dos	
edos	c:\util	
norton	c:\vb	

Directory
List Box D   **List Box L**   **Index J**

   pctools   c: \ util \ edos

               c: \ util \ norton

               c: \ util \ pctools

The index J is increased by 1. The Path property of list box D is assigned L.List(J), which is c: \ vb. The list boxes have the following data:

Directory
List Box D   **List Box L**   **Index J**

c: \\
   vb   c: \\   3

               c: \ dos

               c: \ util

               c: \ vb

               c: \ util \ edos

               c: \ util \ norton

               c: \ util \ pctools

Since the c: \ vb has no subdirectories attached to it, no new members are added to list box L. The remaining steps increase the index J and assign L.List(J) to D.Path. The directories attached to the c: \ util descendants have no subdirectories of their own; again, no new members are added to the list box L. The building of the directory tree map ends when J reaches 7, which is equal to L.ListCount.

Sorting the members of the list box L yields the following:

List Box L

c: \\
c: \ util \ c: \ dos
c: \ util \ edos
c: \ util \ norton
c: \ util \ pctools
c: \ vb

Now we can resume the discussion of the procedure BuildDirTree. This procedure sets the mouse cursor to the hour-glass shape, stores the current path of the directory list box D in the local variable OldPath, and resets the path of the directory list box D to the root directory. It then clears the list box L by calling the ClearList routine in module GENERIC.BAS, and adds the root directory to the list box L. The root directory is accessed by the expression D.List(−1). The index −1 returns the currently selected directory, initially the root directory.

At this point, the procedure assigns 0 to the variable J, which is the current index to the members of the list box L, and uses a Do-While loop to build the directory tree map in list box L. The loop iterates while the value in variable J is less than the size of the list box L. Each iteration assigns the J member of list box L to the Path property of the directory list box D. This makes L.List(J) the current directory (same as D.List(– 1)). The D list members D.List(0) to D.List(D.ListCount – 1) represent the subdirectories that are connected to the directory L.List(J). These subdirectories are added to the list box L. The last statement inside the loop increments the variable J by 1. When the loop stops iterating, the list box L contains the directories scanned in a *breadth-first* fashion, or one level at a time.

Next, the procedure sorts the members of list box L, giving an ordered directory list that can alternately be obtained using *depth-first* search. Such a search, however, requires a more complex recursive procedure. Before exiting, the procedure restores the original Path setting of the directory list box D, invokes the routine MapTreeDir to obtain the directory levels in the array Idx%( ), and restores the mouse cursor.

The GetChildrenIdx procedure provides an array of indices, ChildIdx%( ), that indicates the children directories attached to a target directory. The parameter L is the list box containing the directory tree map; it is obtained by calling procedure BuildDirTree. The array Idx%( ) contains the directory levels in list box L. The argument for Index% points to the target directory L.List(Index%). The child subdirectories are indicated by the index array ChildIdx%( ); the reference parameter Count% reports their actual number.

This procedure begins by setting the argument for Count% to 0; it then checks if the argument for Index% is within range. The valid range is 0 to L.ListCount – 2. If Index% is equal to L.ListCount – 1, it points to a directory with no attached subdirectories. Thus the value L.ListCount – 1 is excluded from the valid range.

The procedure then redimensions the array ChildIdx%. The new dimension has a range of indices between 0 and L.ListCount – Index% – 1. This range represents the worst case where the members L.List(Index% + 1) to L.List(L.ListCount – 1) are children of L.List(Index%). The procedure checks if the level of the Index% list member is less than the level of the next list member; if it is, then L.List(Index%) has at least one child subdirectory. By contrast, if the tested condition is false, the program execution resumes at the latter part of the procedure.

Now the procedure assigns the level of the child subdirectory to the local variable Level, which is used to detect whether the subsequent list members are children or grandchildren of a target directory. It also increments the value of Index%, and uses a Do-While loop to iterate as long as the value in the variable Level is less than or equal to Idx%(Index%), the level of the currently scanned list member. The loop contains an If-Then statement that tests the equality of the variable Level with Idx%(Index%). If they are equal, then L.List(Index%) is a child of the target directory, and the current value of Index% is stored in ChildIdx%(Count%); also, the value of Count% is incremented. Otherwise, the list member is a grandchild of the target directory, and no data is stored in the ChildIdx%( ) array. After the If-Then statement, the procedure increments the value of Index% and tests if Index% has exceeded the upper limit of list box L. If it has, an Exit Do statement exits the Do-While loop.

The GetDescIdx procedure is very similar to the GetChildIdx procedure. The difference is that this routine returns the indices of all the descendant directories, both children and grandchildren, that are attached to the target directory. Only a few statements in the Do-While loop are different. In this procedure, the current value of the parameter Index% is automatically stored in DescIdx%(Count%), since the procedure is mapping all of the descendant directories.

The GetLevel function returns the directory level of a target directory. The parameter L is a list box control that contains the directory tree map, and the parameter Index% is the index to the target directory, as in L.List (Index%). The function returns 0 if the argument for Index% is outside the valid range of 0 to L.ListCount − 1. The function counts the number of \ characters in the target directory, and makes a correction for root directories in counting the number of \ characters. The function uses the local variable N to establish the directory level. It is initialized to 0 for a root directory and 1 for other directories. The function uses the built-in InStr function and a Do-While loop to find and count the \ characters in L.List (Index%).

The GetParentIdx function returns the index of the parent directory of the target directory. The parameter L is the list box that contains the directory tree map, obtained by calling procedure BuildDirTree. The array Idx%( ) contains the levels of the directories in list box L, and the argument for Index% points to the target directory L.List(Index%).

The function checks that the argument for Index% is within the valid range, 1 to L.ListCount − 1. If this condition is not true, the function returns − 1. If the argument is valid, the function assigns the index of the preceding list member, Index% − 1, to the local variable I, and stores the level of the target directory in the local variable CurrLevel. Then the function uses a Do-While loop to search for the parent directory. The loop condition iterates as long as the value stored in CurrLevel is greater than or equal to Idx%(I), the level of a preceding list member. This condition is true when scanning sibling directories and/or their descendants. The body of the loop decrements the value of the variable is a ; when the loop stops iterating, the value in variable I is the index of the parent directory. Then the function value is returned.

The GetSiblingIdx procedure returns the indices of the sibling directories. The parameter L is the list box that contains the directory tree map, obtained by calling procedure BuildDirTree. The array Idx%( ) contains the levels of the directories in the list box L. The argument for Index% points to the target directory L.List(Index%). The array SibIdx%( ) contains the indices of the sibling directories, and the parameter Count% reports their actual number.

When called, this procedure ensures that the argument for Index% is in the valid range of 0 to L.ListCount − 1, and obtains the index to the parent directory by invoking the GetParentIdx function. The value returned by that function is assigned to the local variable ParentIndex. Then the procedure obtains the indices for the sibling directories by calling GetChildrenIdx, using ParentIndex as an argument for parameter Index%, and SibIIdx%( ) as an argument for parameter ChildIdx%( ).

The MapTreeDir procedure is a short but important routine that is called by the BuildDirTree procedure. The parameter L is the list box that contains the directory tree map, and the array Idx%( ) contains the levels of the directories in the list box L. This procedure redimensions the array Idx%( ) to match the size and index range of the list box control L, and assigns the directory levels to each member of array Idx%( ) using a For-Next loop. Each loop iteration calls the function GetLevel with the arguments L and I. I is the loop control variable.

The FILESLIB.BAS module

The FILESLIB.BAS module, shown in Listing 13-3, is the biggest module and contains many file manipulating routines. This module performs the following jobs:

- Builds a list of files using multiple filename wildcards.
- Copies files.
- Deletes files.
- Moves files.
- Prints files.

Listing 13-3 The code in the FILESLIB.BAS module.

```
Const True = -1, False = 0

Function CopyFile (ByVal Source$, ByVal Target$) As Integer
' Copy file Source$ into file Target$.  The function returns
' True if the file copying was successful.  Otherwise, the
' function returns False.
  ' declare buffer size constant
  Const BUFFER_SIZE = 4096
  Dim Buffer As String ' declare buffer
  Dim InFileNum As Integer
  Dim OutFileNum As Integer
  Dim TheFileSize As Long
  ' are the source and target files the same?
  If LCase$(Source$) = LCase$(Target$) Then
    CopyFile = True
    Exit Function
  End If
  ' set the error trap
On Error GoTo BadCopyFile:
  ' get the input file handle
InFileNum = FreeFile
  ' open the source file as a binary file
Open Source$ For Binary As InFileNum
  ' get the output file handle
OutFileNum = FreeFile
  ' open the target file as a binary file
Open Target$ For Binary As OutFileNum
  ' store the size of the input file in TheFileSize
TheFileSize = LOF(InFileNum)
```

Listing 13-3 Continued.

```
' specify the buffer size
Buffer = Space$(BUFFER_SIZE)
' copy the contents of the source file into the target file
Do While Not EOF(InFileNum)
    ' are there fewer than BUFFER_SIZE bytes to copy?
    If TheFileSize < BUFFER_SIZE Then
        If TheFileSize < 1 Then Exit Do
        ' adjust the buffer size accordingly
        Buffer = Space$(TheFileSize)
    End If
    Get #InFileNum, , Buffer
    Put #OutFileNum, , Buffer
    ' decrement the remaining number of bytes to copy
    TheFileSize = TheFileSize - BUFFER_SIZE
Loop
On Error GoTo 0 ' turn off error trap
' close file buffers
Close #InFileNum
Close #OutFileNum
CopyFile = True ' return the function result
Exit Function
'********************** Error Handler **********************
BadCopyFile:
    CopyFile = False ' return the function result
    Close #InFileNum
    Close #OutFileNum
    Resume ExitCopyFile
ExitCopyFile:
End Function

Sub CopyFiles (L As Control, ByVal TargetDir$, T As Control)
' Copy the files specified in the list box L to the target
' directory TargetDir$.  The T parameter is a text box that
' is used to display the status of the copying process.
'
' The procedure removes the files, that were successfully copied,
' from the files list.  This enables you to use this routine to
' copy to multiple disks, by repeating to process after inserting
' new disks.
'
' !!!!!!!!!!!!!!!!!!!!!!!!!!!!!!!!!!!!!!!!!!!!!!!!!!!!!!!!!!!!!!!!!
' ! WARNING! If the files list contains files with duplicate names !
' ! that reside in different directories, then the last file copied !
' ! will overwrite all of the previous ones.                      !
' !!!!!!!!!!!!!!!!!!!!!!!!!!!!!!!!!!!!!!!!!!!!!!!!!!!!!!!!!!!!!!!!!
'
    Dim I As Integer
    Dim Source As String, Target As String
    ' append a trailing "\" to the target directory, if needed
    If Right$(TargetDir$, 1) <> "\" Then
        TargetDir$ = TargetDir$ + "\"
    End If
    ' copy the files in list box L, starting with the
    ' last member.
    For I = L.ListCount - 1 To 0 Step -1
        ' copy the list member I into the string variable Source
        Source = L.list(I)
        ' build the full target filename
        Target = TargetDir$ + GetFileName(Source)
        ' did the current file copy without error?
        If CopyFile(Source, Target) Then
            ' display a confirming message
            T.Text = "Copying " + Source + " to " + Target
            ' remove member I from the list
            L.RemoveItem I
        End If
```

Listing 13-3 *Continued.*

```
  Next I
  T.Text = ""
End Sub

Sub DeleteFiles (L As Control, T As Control)
' Delete the files in the list box L.  The parameter T is a
' text box that is used to display the confirming messages.
  ' set error handler
  On Error Resume Next
  ' delete the files in the list box
  Do While L.ListCount > 0
    ' display confirming message
    T.Text = "Deleting file " + L.list(0)
    Kill L.list(0) ' delete the file
    L.RemoveItem 0 ' remove the filename from the list
  Loop
  T.Text = "" ' clear the text box
  On Error GoTo 0 ' turn off the error trap
End Sub

Function GetFileName (ByVal FullFilename$) As String
' Obtain the filename from a given full filename.

  Dim Count As Integer
  Dim I As Integer

  Count = 0 ' set the size of the extracted filename to 0
  ' store the length of the full filename in variable I
  I = Len(FullFilename$)
  ' scan the string FullFilename backwards, until
  ' the first "\" is encountered.
  Do While (I > 0) And (Mid$(FullFilename, I, 1) <> "\")
    I = I - 1
    Count = Count + 1
  Loop
  ' return the extracted filename
  GetFileName = Right$(FullFilename, Count)
End Function

Sub MoveFiles (L As Control, ByVal TargetDir$, T As Control)
' Move the files specified in the list box L to the target
' directory TargetDir$.  The T parameter is a text box that
' is used to display the status of the moving process.
'
' The procedure removes the files, that were successfully moved,
' from the files list.  This enables you to use this routine to
' move to multiple disks, by repeating to process after inserting
' new disks.
'
' !!!!!!!!!!!!!!!!!!!!!!!!!!!!!!!!!!!!!!!!!!!!!!!!!!!!!!!!!!!!!!!!!!
' ! WARNING! If the files list contains files with duplicate names  !
' ! that reside in different directories, then the last file moved  !
' ! will overwrite all of the previous ones.                        !
' !!!!!!!!!!!!!!!!!!!!!!!!!!!!!!!!!!!!!!!!!!!!!!!!!!!!!!!!!!!!!!!!!!
'
  Dim I As Integer
  Dim Source As String, Target As String
  ' append a trailing "\" to the target directory, if needed
  If Right$(TargetDir$, 1) <> "\" Then
    TargetDir$ = TargetDir$ + "\"
  End If
  ' are the files moved in the same drive?
  If UCase$(Left$(L.list(0), 1)) = UCase$(Left$(TargetDir$, 1)) Then
    ' move the files in the list, starting with the last one
    For I = L.ListCount - 1 To 0 Step -1
      ' copy the list member I into the string variable Source
```

Listing 13-3 Continued.

```
            Source = L.list(I)
            ' build the full target filename
            Target = TargetDir$ + GetFileName(Source)
            ' set error trap
            On Error GoTo BadMoveFiles
            ' move the file by using the Name statement
            Name Source As Target
            ' turn off error trap
            On Error GoTo 0
            ' display a confirming message
            T.Text = "Moving " + Source + " to " + Target
            ' remove the moved file from the list box L
            L.RemoveItem I
ResumeMoveFiles:
        Next I
    Else
        For I = L.ListCount - 1 To 0 Step -1
            ' copy the list member I into the string variable Source
            Source = L.list(I)
            ' build the full target filename
            Target = TargetDir$ + GetFileName(Source)
            ' was the Source file copied without error?
            If CopyFile(Source, Target) Then
                ' display a confirming message
                T.Text = "Moving " + Source + " to " + Target
                Kill Source ' delete the source file
                ' remove the moved file from the list box L
                L.RemoveItem I
            End If
        Next I
    End If
    ' clear the text box
    T.Text = ""
    Exit Sub
    '****************** Error Handler ****************
BadMoveFiles:
    MsgBox "Cannot move file " + Source, 64, "Error"
    Resume ResumeMoveFiles
End Sub

Sub PrintFile (ByVal Filename$)
' Print the file Filename$.
    ' local constants
    Const MAX_LINES = 60 ' maximum number of lines per page
    Const TAB_SIZE = 65 ' heading tab size

    Dim TextLine As String
    Dim I As Integer
    Dim CurrentLineNumber As Integer
    ' exit sub if Filename is empty
    If Filename = "" Then Exit Sub
    On Error GoTo BadFile ' set error-handling trap
    Open Filename For Input As #1 ' open file for input
    On Error GoTo 0 ' disable error-handling trap
    ' print the heading of the first page
    GoSub PrintHeading
    ' read lines from the text file
    Do While Not EOF(1)
        Line Input #1, TextLine
        ' update line counter
        CurrentLineNumber = CurrentLineNumber + 1
        ' line counter exceed page size?
        If CurrentLineNumber > MAX_LINES Then
            Printer.NewPage ' print to a new page
            ' print page heading
            GoSub PrintHeading
```

Listing 13-3 Continued.

```
    End If
    Printer.Print TextLine ' print the current line
  Loop
  Printer.NewPage ' eject the last page
  Printer.EndDoc  ' release print device
  Close #1 ' close the file buffer
  Beep
  Exit Sub
'********************* Internal Subroutine ****************
PrintHeading:
  ' internal subroutine to print the heading
  Printer.Print Filename; Tab(TAB_SIZE);
  Printer.Print "Page "; Format$(Printer.Page, "###")
  Printer.Print Format$(Now, "hh:mm");
  Printer.Print Tab(TAB_SIZE);
  Printer.Print Format$(Now, "MM-DD-YYYY")
  Printer.Print
  Printer.Print
  CurrentLineNumber = 4
Return
'**************** Error-Handling Statements **************
BadFile:
  Beep
  MsgBox "Cannot open file " + Filename, 0, "File I/O Error"
  Resume ExitSub
ExitSub:
End Sub

Sub PrintFiles (L As Control, T As Control)
' Print the files in the list box L.  The parameter T is
' a text box that displays the name of the currently
' printed file .
  Dim I As Integer
  ' print the files in the list box L
  For I = 0 To L.ListCount - 1
    ' display a confirming message
    T.Text = "Printing file " + L.list(I)
    PrintFile L.list(I) ' print the file
  Next I
  ' clear the text box
  T.Text = ""
End Sub

Sub WhereIsEntireList (F As Control, L As Control, ByVal WildCards$)
' Search the entire current drive for the files that match the
' set of wildcards in WildCards$.  The WildCard$ parameter contains
' two sublists in the following format:
'
'          add_wildcards_list [EXCEPT prune_wildcards_list]
'
' The add_wildcards_list is a mandatory sublist that contains
' multiple, space-delimited, wildcards, such as "*.BAS *.FRM *.MAK".
' This sublist specifies the files to add to the list.
' The optional EXCEPT (which is not case-sensitive) keyword
' separates the two sublists.  The prune_wildcards_list contains
' multiple, space-delimited, wildcards that specify the files
' to remove from the list.

  Static Word(15) As String
  Dim NumWords As Integer
  Dim I As Integer, J As Integer, K As Integer
  Dim S As String, DirStr As String
  Dim AddFiles As Integer

  CLearList L ' clear target list box
  ' extract the words in the WildCard$ string
```

Listing 13-3 Continued.

```
        StringToWords WildCards$, Word(), NumWords
        AddFiles = True ' set adding-files mode to True
        ' loop to build the list containing the
        ' filenames
  For I = 1 To NumWords
      ' convert the element I of Word() into lower case
      Word(I) = LCase$(Word(I))
      ' is the element I of Word() the string "except"?
      If Word(I) = "except" Then
          AddFiles = False ' set adding-files mode to False
          I = I + 1 ' select the next member of Word()
          ' exit if I has exceeded NumWords
          If I > NumWords Then Exit Sub
          ' exit if the next element of Word() is an empty string
          If Word(I) = "" Then Exit Sub
      End If
      ' is adding-files mode True?
      If AddFiles Then
          ' add the members of the directory list box F to the
          ' list box L
          For J = 0 To F.ListCount - 1
              ' assign a new file pattern
              DirStr = F.list(J)
              ' append a "\" if needed
              If Right$(DirStr, 1) <> "\" Then
                  DirStr = DirStr + "\"
              End If
              ' find the first file that matches the wildcard
              ' (DirStr + Word(I))
              S = Dir$(DirStr + Word(I))
              ' loop for every file that matches the above wildcard
              Do While S <> ""
                  ' add (DirStr + S) to list box L
                  L.AddItem LCase$(DirStr + S)
                  ' find the next file that matches the current wildcard
                  S = Dir$
              Loop
          Next J
      Else
          ' remove the members of the directory list box F from the
          ' list box L
          For J = 0 To F.ListCount - 1
              ' assign a new file pattern
              DirStr = F.list(J)
              ' append a "\" if needed
              If Right$(DirStr, 1) <> "\" Then
                  DirStr = DirStr + "\"
              End If
              ' find the first file that matches the wildcard
              ' (DirStr + Word(I))
              S = Dir$(DirStr + Word(I))
              ' loop for every file that matches the above wildcard
              Do While S <> ""
                  ' find the index of the matching file in the list box L
                  K = LinSearch(L, LCase$(DirStr + S), False, 1, 1, 0)
                  If K > -1 Then L.RemoveItem K ' remove matching file
                  ' find the next file that matches the current wildcard
                  S = Dir$
              Loop
          Next J
      End If
  Next I
End Sub

Sub WhereIsFromCurList (F As Control, L As Control, ByVal StDir$, Idx%(),
ChildIdx%(), Count%, ByVal WildCards$)
```

Listing 13-3 Continued.

```
' Search from the current directory for the files that match the
' set of wildcards in WildCards$.  The WildCard$ parameter contains
' two sublists in the following format:
'
'          add_wildcards_list [EXCEPT prune_wildcards_list]
'
' The add_wildcards_list is a mandatory sublist that contains
' multiple, space-delimited, wildcards, such as "*.BAS *.FRM *.MAK".
' This sublists specifies the files to add to the list.
' The optional EXCEPT (which is not case-sensitive) keyword
' separates the two sublists.  The prune_wildcards_list contains
' multiple, space-delimited, wildcards that specify the files
' to remove from the list.

   Static Word(15) As String
   Dim NumWords As Integer
   Dim index As Integer
   Dim I As Integer, J As Integer, K As Integer
   Dim S As String, DirStr As String
   Dim AddFiles As Integer

   CLearList L ' clear target list box
   ' extract the words in the WildCard$ string
   StringToWords WildCards$, Word(), NumWords
   ' search for the index of F that matches StDir$.
   index = BinSearch(F, StDir$, 1, 1, 0)
   ' get the indices to the descendant subdirectories
   GetDescIdx F, Idx%(), index, ChildIdx%(), Count
   AddFiles = True ' set the adding-files mode to True
   ' loop to build the list containing the
   ' filenames
   For I = 1 To NumWords
      ' convert the element I of Word() into lowercase
      Word(I) = LCase$(Word(I))
      ' is the element I of Word() the string "except"?
      If Word(I) = "except" Then
        AddFiles = False ' set adding-files mode to False
        I = I + 1 ' select the next member of Word()
      ' exit if I has exceeded NumWords
      If I > NumWords Then Exit Sub
      ' exit if the next element of Word() is an empty string
      If Word(I) = "" Then Exit Sub
   End If
   ' is the adding-files mode True?
   If AddFiles Then
      DirStr = StDir$ ' start with the current directory
      ' append a "\" if needed
      If Right$(DirStr, 1) <> "\" Then
        DirStr = DirStr + "\"
      End If
      ' find the first file that matches the wildcard
      ' (DirStr + Word(I))
      S = Dir$(DirStr + Word(I))
      ' loop for every file that matches the above wildcard
      Do While S <> ""
         ' add (DirStr + S) to list box L
         L.AddItem LCase$(DirStr + S)
         ' find the next file that matches the current wildcard
         S = Dir$
      Loop
      ' are there any descendant subdirectories?
      If Count > 0 Then
         ' process each descendant subdirectory
         For J = 0 To Count - 1
            ' assign the descendant subdirectory to DirStr
            DirStr = F.list(ChildIdx(J))
```

Listing 13-3 Continued.

```
                   ' append a "\" if needed
                   If Right$(DirStr, 1) <> "\" Then
                      DirStr = DirStr + "\"
                   End If
                   ' find the first file that matches the wildcard
                   ' (DirStr + Word(I))
                   S = Dir$(DirStr + Word(I))
                   ' loop for every file that matches the above wildcard
                   Do While S <> ""
                      ' add (DirStr + S) to list box L
                      L.AddItem LCase$(DirStr + S)
                      ' find the next file that matches the current wildcard
                      S = Dir$
                   Loop
                 Next J
             End If
         Else
           ' delete files from the list
           DirStr = StDir$ ' start with the current directory
           ' append a "\" if needed
           If Right$(DirStr, 1) <> "\" Then
              DirStr = DirStr + "\"
           End If
           ' find the first file that matches the wildcard
           ' (DirStr + Word(I))
           S = Dir$(DirStr + Word(I))
           ' loop for every file that matches the above wildcard
           Do While S <> ""
              ' find the index of the matching file in the list box L
              K = LinSearch(L, LCase$(DirStr + S), False, 1, 1, 0)
              If K > -1 Then L.RemoveItem K ' remove the matching member
              ' find the next file that matches the current wildcard
              S = Dir$
           Loop
           ' are there any descendant subdirectories?
           If Count > 0 Then
              ' process each descendant subdirectory
              For J = 0 To Count - 1
                 ' assign the descendant subdirectory to DirStr
                 DirStr = F.list(ChildIdx(J))
                 ' append a "\" if needed
                 If Right$(DirStr, 1) <> "\" Then
                    DirStr = DirStr + "\"
                 End If
                 ' find the first file that matches the wildcard
                 ' (DirStr + Word(I))
                 S = Dir$(DirStr + Word(I))
                 ' loop for every file that matches the above wildcard
                 Do While S <> ""
                    ' find the index of the matching file in the list box L
                    K = LinSearch(L, LCase$(DirStr + S), False, 1, 1, 0)
                    ' remove the matching member
                    If K > -1 Then L.RemoveItem K
                    ' find the next file that matches the current wildcard
                    S = Dir$
                 Loop
              Next J
           End If
         End If
   Next I
End Sub

Sub WhereIsOnlyCurList (F As String, L As Control, ByVal WildCards$)
' Search only the current directory for the files that match the
' set of wildcards in WildCards$.  The WildCard$ parameter contains
```

Listing 13-3 Continued.

```
' two sublists in the following format:
'
'           add_wildcards_list [EXCEPT prune_wildcards_list]
'
' The add_wildcards_list is a mandatory sublist that contains
' multiple, space-delimited, wildcards, such as "*.BAS *.FRM *.MAK".
' This sublists specifies the files to add to the list.
' The optional EXCEPT (which is not case-sensitive) keyword
' separates the two sublists.  The prune_wildcards_list contains
' multiple, space-delimited, wildcards that specify the files
' to remove from the list.

    Static Word(15) As String
    Dim NumWords As Integer
    Dim I As Integer, K As Integer
    Dim S As String
    Dim AddFiles As Integer

    CLearList L ' clear target list box
    ' extract the words in the WildCard$ string
    StringToWords WildCards$, Word(), NumWords
    AddFiles = True ' set the adding-files mode to True
    ' loop to build the list containing the
    ' filenames
    For I = 1 To NumWords
        ' convert the element I of Word() into lowercase
        Word(I) = LCase$(Word(I))
        ' is the element I of Word() the string "except"?
        If Word(I) = "except" Then
            AddFiles = False ' set adding-files mode to False
            I = I + 1 ' select the next member of Word()
            ' exit if I has exceeded NumWords
            If I > NumWords Then Exit Sub
            ' exit if the next element of Word() is an empty string
            If Word(I) = "" Then Exit Sub
        End If
        ' is the adding-files mode True?
        If AddFiles Then
            ' append an "\" if needed
            If Right$(F, 1) <> "\" Then F = F + "\"
            ' find the first file that matches the wildcard
            ' (F + Word(I))
            S = Dir$(F + Word(I))
            ' loop for every file that matches the above wildcard
            Do While S <> ""
                ' add (F + S) to list box L
                L.AddItem LCase$(F + S)
                ' find the next file that matches the current wildcard
                S = Dir$
            Loop
        Else
            ' delete files from the list box L
            ' append an "\" if needed
            If Right$(F, 1) <> "\" Then F = F + "\"
            ' find the first file that matches the wildcard
            ' (F + Word(I))
            S = Dir$(F + Word(I))
            ' loop for every file that matches the above wildcard
        Do While S <> ""
            ' find the index of the matching file in the list box L
            K = LinSearch(L, LCase$(F + S), False, 1, 1, 0)
            ' remove the matching member
            If K > -1 Then L.RemoveItem K
            ' find the next file that matches the current wildcard
```

Listing 13-3 Continued.

```
        S = Dir$
      Loop
    End If
  Next I
End Sub
```

The FILESLIB.BAS module builds a list of files in various ways which share the same basic scheme. This scheme allows you to specify multiple filename wildcards that add and remove files from the final list. The general syntax of the wildcard string is:

add_wc1 [add_wc2..add_wcn] [EXCEPT *del_wc1 [del_wc2..del_wcn]*]

The wildcard string contains two sets of wildcards. The first mandatory set specifies at least one filename wildcard or exact filename. The option and case-insensitive EXCEPT keyword separates the two sets of wildcards. The second set specifies the files that should be removed from the list of files created using the first set of wildcards. I will call this kind of wildcard an *extended wildcard*.

Once a list of files is created, the other routines can perform their tasks on that list.

The module contains the routines that follow.

The Boolean CopyFile function copies a single file. The Source$ and Target$ parameters specify the source and target files, respectively. The function returns True if the copying process is carried out without any error, such as bad filenames, bad directory names, or disk full. Otherwise, the function returns False. The routine uses binary file modes to copy any type of file.

This function checks whether the source and target files are the same; if so, the function exits and returns a True value. If not, it sets the error trap for any file I/O error, obtains an input file handle, and uses that handle in opening the source file as a binary file. Then the function obtains an output file handle and uses that handle in opening the target file as a binary file. Next it assigns the size of the input file to the local variable TheFileSize.

☞ The CopyFile function establishes the size of the file I/O buffer by creating a string with 4096 bytes. You can alter the size of the buffer by changing the value of the local constant BUFFER_SIZE. Note that assigning large values may exhaust your system's memory.

Next, the function copies the contents of the source file into the target file using a Do-While loop. The Get and Put statements perform the required data transfer. Each loop iteration decrements the value in variable TheFileSize by BUFFER_SIZE. If the value in TheFileSize is less than the BUFFER_SIZE, the size of the I/O buffer is changed to TheFileSize. This protects the output file from receiving more bytes than there are in the input file.

After that, the function turns off the error trap, closes the source and target files, and assigns True to the function value before exiting.

When activated, the error handler assigns False to the function value and then exits.

The CopyFiles procedure copies the files in the list box L to the target directory TargetDir$. The procedure uses the text box parameter T to display the progress of copying the files. You may remove the parameter T and its related code without affecting the basic tasks of this procedure. The procedure removes the files that are successfully copied from the list box L, enabling your Visual Basic applications to invoke CopyFiles to copy files from a hard disk to multiple files.

The CopyFiles procedure appends a \ to the argument for TargetDir$ if it does not end with a \, then copies the files in the list box L, using a downward-counting For-Next loop. Such a loop enables the procedure to easily remove file number I from the list L only if it copied correctly. Each loop iteration assigns the full source and target filenames to the local variables Source and Target respectively. The function GetFileName extracts the filename from the variable Source. An If-Then statement tests the Boolean value of function CopyFile(Source, Target); if that value is true, the T text box displays a copy message and the copied file is removed from the list L. Finally, the procedure clears the text box T when the files are copied.

☠ **Warning!**   The CopyFiles routine will overwrite existing files in the target directory that have the same name as the files being copied. Moreover, the file selection scheme allows you to specify files from different directories. This feature makes it possible to copy files with the same names into the same target directory. **Only the last of these files will exist in the target directory!**

The DeleteFiles procedure deletes the files in the list box control L. The text box T is used to display messages regarding the progress of the deletion process. This procedure uses the Visual Basic Kill procedure to delete a file. It begins its operations by setting the error trap so that if the Kill statement fails, the program execution resumes at the next statement. Then the procedure deletes the files in the list L using a Do-While loop. The loop iterates as long as L.ListCount is positive (that is, the list L is not empty). Each loop iteration displays a progress message in the text box, deletes the file at list member 0, and then removes list member 0. Then the procedure clears the text box T and turns off the error trap.

The function GetFileName returns the name of a file with its extension from the argument FullFileName, which contains a full filename with drive and path.

The MoveFiles procedure moves files either in the same drive or across different drives. Each case utilizes a different basic method. Moving files to different directories on the same drive makes good use of the Visual Basic Name statement. This statement simply renames the file using a different path name; there is no actual transfer of bytes. This operation is quick.

Moving files across drives, on the other hand, requires copying the files to the target directory and then deleting them from the source directory. This is a slower and more error-prone process. The slowness results from the actual copying of files; also, the target drive may not be able to store the moved files.

The procedure appends a \ character to the argument for TargetDir$ if the latter lacks a trailing \ character. The routine then checks the first letters of L.List(0) and TargetDir$. If these letters are the same, then the files are moved in the same drive. In this case, the procedure starts a downward counting loop to process the files in list L, assigns the names of the source and target files to the local variables Source and Target, and sets the error trap so that the program resumes after the offending statement. In particular, the error trap is aimed at the Name statement that follows it. Then the procedure renames the source file into the target file. If the files are the same, the error handler resumes the execution to the next statement. Then the procedure turns off the error trap, displays a message about moving the file, and removes the member I from the list L.

In the case where the files are moved across drives, the procedure starts a downward counting loop to process the files in list L and assigns the names of the source and target files to the local variables Source and Target. Then it tests the Boolean value returned by the CopyFile function. If that value is True, the text box T first displays a message about the moved file; then the moved file is deleted from the source directory, and the list member I is removed.

Warning! When moving files across drives, the MoveFiles routine will overwrite existing files in the target directory that have the same name as the files being moved. Moreover, because the file selection scheme allows you to specify files from different directories, it is possible to move files with the same names (across drives) into the same target directory. **Only the last of these files will exist in the target directory!** The code will prevent moving files in the same drive.

The PrintFile procedure prints a file specified by the parameter Filename$. Each printed page contains a heading with the filename, page number, time, and date. The procedure contains the local subroutine, at label PrintHeading, that prints the heading on a page.

The procedure verifies that the argument for Filename$ is not an empty string; if it is, the procedure exits without any further action. If not, it sets the error trap for bad filenames, opens the file for input as a text file, and turns off the error trap. Then it calls the internal subroutine to print the heading of the first page.

At this point, the procedure reads the lines of the text file and prints them using a Do-While loop. As the procedure reads and prints each line, it increments the CurrentLineNumber variable and monitors if the value in that variable has exceeded the local constant MAX_LINES. If this condition is true, the procedure issues a new-page command and prints the heading on that page. When the last line of the file has been printed, the procedure terminates the printing by ejecting the last page, releasing the print device, and closing the printer file. It then beeps and exits.

The error handler, if activated, displays a message box informing you that the routine could not open the specified file.

The PrintFiles procedure prints the files in the list box control L. The text box parameter T refers to a text box that displays the printing progress messages. The routine uses a For-Next loop to print each file in the list box L, using the PrintFile procedure. The list of files is not cleared after this routine ends.

The WhereIsEntireList procedure searches all directories of the current drive for the files specified by the WildCards$ argument. Keep in mind that the WildCards$ is an extended wildcard, and may contain multiple wildcards that add and delete files from the list box L. The parameter F is a list box control that contains the directory tree map.

The procedure begins by clearing the list L. Then it extracts the words from the argument WildCards$. The NumWords words are stored in array Word( ). The procedure then sets the AddFiles mode to True, and begins to process the extracted words.

For each extracted word, the procedure converts Word(I) into lowercase. If Word(I) is EXCEPT, the procedure sets the AddFiles mode to False, increments the loop counter to select the next extracted word, and exits if the next word is an empty string. Note that AddFiles acts as a switch that determines how the matching files will be handled. This switch is "on" (files are being added) until EXCEPT is encountered; then the switch is "off" (files are being deleted).

As long as the AddFiles mode is True, the procedure processes each member of list box F. For each member, the procedure assigns a new single file pattern and finds the first file that matches that pattern. While there is a file that matches the current pattern, the procedure adds the matching file (including its path) to the list box L, and finds the next file that matches the current pattern.

If the AddFiles mode has been changed to False, indicating that EXCEPT has been encountered, the procedure processes each member of list box F. For each member, the procedure assigns a new single file pattern and finds the first file that matches that pattern. While there is a file that matches the current pattern, the procedure deletes the matching file from the list box L, if it exists in that list box, and finds the next file that matches the current pattern.

The WhereIsFromCurList procedure searches from the current directory for the files specified by the WildCards$ argument. This procedure is somewhat similar to WhereIsEntireList. The procedure begins by clearing the list L. It then extracts the words from the argument WildCards$. The NumWords words are stored in array Word( ). The procedure next obtains the indices for the descendant directories. The AddFiles mode is set to True. Again, this variable acts as a switch to indicate that EXCEPT has been encountered and, as a result, any additional wildcard matches are to be deleted rather than added.

At this point the procedure begins processing each extracted word. For each word, it converts Word(I) into lowercase; if Word(I) is EXCEPT, it sets the AddFiles mode to False, increments the loop counter to select the next extracted word, and exits if the next word is an empty string.

As long as the AddFiles mode is True, the procedure does the following actions for the current directory and for all of its descendant directories, if any. It assigns a new single file pattern, and finds the first file that matches that pattern. While there is a file that matches the current pattern, the procedure adds the matching file, including its path, to the list box L. It then finds the next file that matches the current pattern.

Once the AddFiles mode has been set to False, the procedure performs the following actions for the current directory and any descendant directories. It assigns a new single file pattern and finds the first file that matches that pattern. While there is a file that matches the current pattern, the procedure removes the matching file from the list box L and finds the next file that matches the current pattern.

The WhereIsOnlyCurList procedure searches only the current directory for the files specified by the WildCards$ argument. This procedure is similar to WhereIsEntireList. First the procedure clears the list L. Then it extracts the words from the argument WildCards$ and stores the NumWords words in array Word( ). Then the procedure sets the AddFiles mode to True and begins to process the extracted words. Once again, AddFiles acts as a switch indicating that EXCEPT has been encountered, and remaining wildcard matches are to be deleted from, rather than added to, list box L.

At this point, the procedure begins processing the extracted words. For each extracted word, the procedure first converts Word(I) into lowercase; if Word(I) is EXCEPT, the procedure sets the AddFiles mode to False, increments the loop counter to select the next extracted word, and exits if the next word is an empty string.

As long as the AddFiles mode is True, the procedure performs the following actions for the current directory. It assigns a new single file pattern and finds the first file that matches that pattern. While there is a file that matches the current pattern, the procedure adds the matching file, including its path, to the list box L, and finds the next file that matches the current pattern.

When the AddFiles mode has been set to False, the procedure does the following actions for the current directory. It assign a new single file pattern, and finds the first file that matches that pattern. While there is a file that matches the pattern, the procedure removes the matching file from the list box L and finds the next file that matches the pattern.

14
File selection forms

The first step in processing a set of files is selecting the files themselves. This chapter presents two forms that assist you in the file selection process. The first form is more simple, and works faster by selecting files from the current directory. The second form is more complex, and is slower because it scans the various directories of the current drive.

The SelFiles form

The first form is stored in file SELFILES.FRM and is shown in FIG. 14-1. The SelFiles form contains the following controls:

- A drive list box that enables you to select the current drive.
- A directory list box that allows you to navigate in the directories of the current drive.
- A text box that permits you to enter multiple filename wildcards, such as *.doc *.txt.
- A list box that shows the currently selected files.
- A Get Files command button that triggers the search for the files that match the wildcards specified in the text box. The search is limited to the currently selected directory. Consequently, the search is relatively quick.
- A Delete Selected File button that removes the currently selected file from the list box. This button allows you to manually prune the list of selected files.
- A Return button that saves the selected files list to a data file, unloads the SelFiles form, and returns to the caller form.

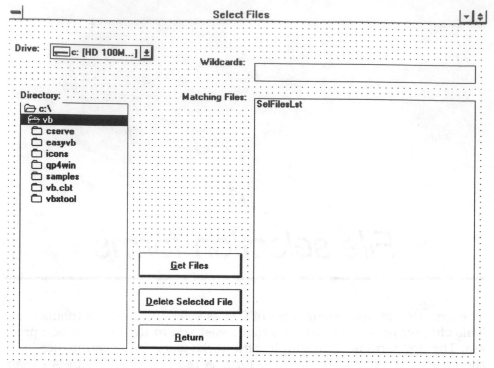

14-1 The SELFILES.FRM at design time.

When SelFiles is loaded, the Wildcards text box contains *.*, the default wildcard. In addition, the drive and directory list boxes show the current drive and directory. You can select other drives or directories, or type in other wildcards. When you have finalized the selection of the drive, directory, and wildcards, click on the Get Files button to view the matching files in the list box. To delete one or more files from the selection, click on the target files and then click on the Delete Selected File button. When you are satisfied with the current file selection, click on the Return button.

Figures 14-2 and 14-3 list the form controls and their custom settings, respectively. Figure 14-4 shows a sample session with the SELFILES.FRM form.

Listing 14-1 contains the code attached to the SELFILES.FRM form. The form contains the event-handling procedures which are described next.

The CurrentDrv_Change procedure handles selecting another drive. The procedure simply updates the Path setting of the TreeDir directory list box.

The DelSelFileBtn_Click procedure removes the currently selected file from SelFilesList list box. The routine then selects the next file as either the previous or last list member, depending on the position of selected file that was removed.

Form # 1   Form filename: SELFILES.FRM
Version: 1.0   Date: September 4, 1991

Control object type	Default CtlName	Purpose
Command button	Command1	Obtains the selected files and inserts them in List1
	Command2	Deletes the currently selected file in List1
	Command3	Return to the calling form
Text box	Text1	Wildcards input box
List box	List1	Contains the list of selected files
Directory list box	Dir1	Selects the current directory
Drive list box	Drive1	Selects the current drive
Label	Label1	Label for Drive list box
	Label2	Label for Directory list box
	Label3	Label for Selected Files list box
	Label4	Label for Wildcards text box

14-2 The list of controls in the SELFILES.FRM form file.

Form # 1
Version: 1.0   Date: September 4, 1991

Original control name	Property	New setting
Form	Caption	Select Files
	FormName	SelFiles
Command1	CtlName	GetFilesBtn
	Caption	&Get Files
Command2	CtlName	DelSelFileBtn
	Caption	&Delete Selected File
Command3	CtlName	ReturnBtn
	Caption	&Return
Text1	CtlName	WildCardsBox
	Text	(empty string)
List1	CtlName	SelFilesLst
Dir1	CtlName	TreeDir
Drive1	CtlName	CurrentDrv
Label1	CtlName	DriveLbl
	Caption	Drive:
Label2	CtlName	DirLbl
	Caption	Directory:

14-3 The customized settings for the SELFILES.FRM form.

Original control name	Property	New setting
Label3	CtlName	SelFilesLbl
	Caption	Matching Files:
Label4	CtlName	WildcardsLbl
	Caption	Wildcards:

14-3 Continued.

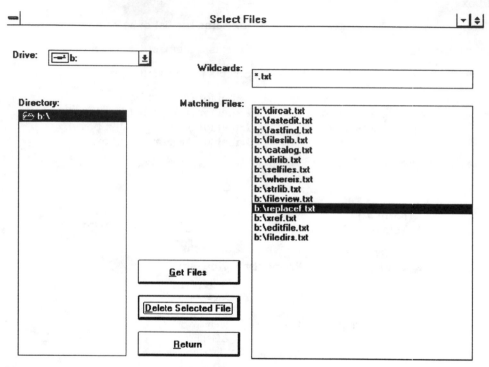

14-4 A sample session with the SELFILES.FRM form.

Listing 14-1 The code attached to the SELFILES.FRM form.

```
Const True = -1, False = 0

Sub CurrentDrv_Change ()
' Handle the change in the current drive
  ' update the directory list box Path property
  TreeDir.Path = CurrentDrv.Drive
End Sub

Sub DelSelFileBtn_Click ()
' Remove the currently selected file from SelFilesLst.
  Dim I As Integer
  ' get the index of the selected list member
  I = SelFilesLst.ListIndex
  ' is there a current selection?
  If I > -1 Then
    ' remove the selected file
```

Listing 14-1 Continued.

```
    SelFilesLst.RemoveItem I
    ' update the index for the selected list member
    If I >= SelFilesLst.ListCount Then
       I = SelFilesLst.ListCount - 1
    ElseIf I > 0 Then
       I = I - 1
    End If
    ' select another list member
    SelFilesLst.ListIndex = I
  End If
End Sub

Sub Form_Load ()
' Initialize the form.
  WindowState = 2 ' set the window to maximum
  WildcardsBox.Text = "*.*" ' set the wildcard text box to *.*
End Sub

Sub GetFilesBtn_Click ()
' Obtain the file selection according to the specified wildcards
  Dim I As Integer
  Dim Count As Integer
  Dim F As String
  Dim WildCards As String
  MousePointer = 11 ' set the mouse cursor to the hour-glass
  ' assign the string of the wildcard text box to the
  ' variable Wildcards
  WildCards = WildcardsBox.Text
  ' assign the current directory to the variable F
  F = TreeDir.List(-1)
  ' select the files in the current directory
  WhereIsOnlyCurList F, SelFilesLst, WildCards
  ' restore the mouse cursor
  MousePointer = 0
End Sub

Sub ReturnBtn_Click ()
' Write the members of the SelFilesLst to the WHEREIS_DATA file
' and then return to the calling form.
  Dim S As String
  ' assign the data file name to the local string variable S
  S = WHEREIS_DATA
  ' is the SelFilesLst not empty?
  If SelFilesLst.ListCount > 0 Then
     ' was there an error in  writing the data to the file
     If Not WriteList(SelFilesLst, S) Then
        ' display error message box
        MsgBox "Error in writing files list", 64, "I/O Error"
     End If
  Else
     ' set error handler
     On Error Resume Next
     ' delete the data file
     Kill S
     On Error GoTo 0 ' turn off error handler
  End If
  ' unload the SelFiles form
  Unload SelFiles
End Sub
```

The Form_Load procedure initializes the SelFiles form by maximizing the window and setting the string of the text box to *.*.

The GetFilesBtn_Click procedure obtains the file selection according to the wildcards specified in the text box. The procedure changes the mouse cursor to the hour-glass icon, assigns the string in the text box to the local variable WildCards, and assigns the current directory (obtained by the expression TreeDir.List(– 1)) to the local variable F. Then it selects the files in the current directory by calling the procedure WhereIsOnlyCurList (exported by module FILESLIB.BAS) with the arguments F, SelfilesLst, and WildCards. Finally the procedure restores the mouse cursor to its default shape.

The ReturnBtn_Click procedure writes the members of the SelFilesLst to the WHEREIS_DATA data file and then returns to the calling form. The WHEREIS_DATA is a global constant declared in the global module FILE-DIRS.GLB as C: ∖ VB ∖ VBXTOOL ∖ WHEREIS.DAT. The procedure assigns the constant WHEREIS_DATA to the local string variable S. If the SelFilesLst list box is not empty, the procedure writes the members of that list box to the data file. If SelFilesLst is empty the procedure tries to erase the previous version of the data file. This attempt is supported by an error handler in case the sought data file does not exist. Erasing the data file ensures that there is no mix-up between previous and current selections. Finally, the procedure unloads the SelFiles form.

The WhereIs form

The second form is stored in file WHEREIS.FRM and is shown in FIG. 14-5. This form is able to search files in multiple directories. The WhereIs form contains the following controls:

- A drive list box that enables you to select the current drive.
- A directory list box that allows you to navigate in the directories of the current drive.
- A text box that permits you to enter multiple wildcards.
- A list box that shows the currently selected files.
- An invisible list box that stores the directory tree map.

☞ • A frame that contains three option buttons, which direct the search for the matching files to one of three possible targets: the entire directory tree of the current drive, the current directory and all of its descendant subdirectories, or the current directory only. The last option makes the WhereIs form work like the SelFiles form. The difference is still in the search speed, since the WhereIs form needs to scan the entire directory tree of the current drive.

- A Get Files command button, which triggers the search for files which match the wildcards specified in the text box. The scope of the search is specified by the option buttons.
- A Delete Selected File button, which removes the selected file from the list box, allowing you to manually prune the list of selected files.
- A Return button, which saves the selected files list to a data file, unloads the WhereIs form, and returns to the caller form.

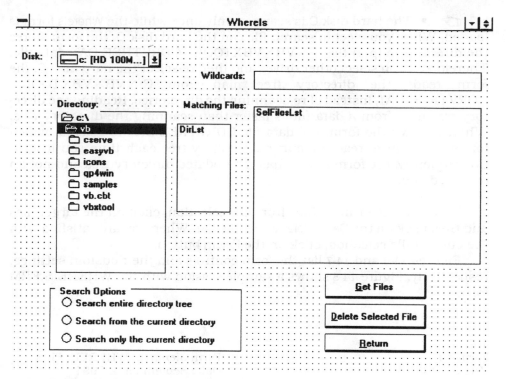

14-5 The WHEREIS.FRM at design time.

When WhereIs is loaded, the wildcards text box contains *.*, the default wildcard, and the drive and directory list boxes show the current drive and directory. You can select other drives or directories, or type in other wildcards. You can also choose the option button that specifies how to search for the files. When you have selected the various options, drive, directory, and wildcards, click on the Get Files button to view the matching files in the list box. The search process also involves scanning the directory tree of the current drive.

The WhereIs form uses the following rules in scanning the directories of a drive:

- A drive (floppy or fixed) is scanned at least once when it is selected. This includes the currently selected drive just after the WhereIs form is loaded. The directory tree of that drive is stored in an invisible list box.
- Subsequent searches in the same drive do not require re-scanning the directory tree.
- If you re-select a floppy drive as the current drive, the directory tree is re-scanned.

☞ • The hard disk C is scanned only once while the Wherels form is loaded. When you elect to search files on the hard disk C, the form stores the directory map in the C: \ VB \ VBXTOOL \ CDRVTREE.DAT data file. Therefore, if you select other drives and then re-select the hard disk C, the form reads the directory tree map from C: \ VB \ VBXTOOL \ CDRVTREE.DAT, instead of re-scanning the directories. Reading the directory tree map from a data file is faster than scanning the directory tree. When you exit the form, the data file CDRVTREE.DAT is deleted, which forces the form to read the current directory tree each time you load it. Consequently, the form always has the updated directory tree and not an outdated one.

To delete one or more files from the selection, click on the target files and then click on the Delete Selected File button. When you are satisfied with the current file selection, click on the Return button.

Figures 14-6 and 14-7 list the form controls and their custom settings, respectively. Figure 14-8 shows a sample session with the WHEREIS.FRM form.

Form # 1   Form filename: WHEREIS.FRM
Version: 1.0   Date: September 4, 1991

Control object type	Default CtlName	Purpose
Command button	Command1	Obtains the selected files and inserts them in List1
	Command2	Deletes the currently selected file in List1
	Command3	Return to the calling form
Text box	Text1	Wildcards input box
List box	List1	Contains the list of selected files
	List2	Invisible control used in obtaining files
Directory list box	Dir1	Selects the current directory
Drive list box	Drive1	Selects the current drive
Frame	Frame1	Contains the search option buttons
Option button	Option1	Searches the entire directories
	Option2	Searches from the current directory
	Option3	Searches only the current directory
Label	Label1	Label for Drive list box
	Label2	Label for Directory list box
	Label3	Label for Selected Files list box
	Label4	Label for Wildcards text box

14-6   The list of controls in the WHEREIS.FRM form file.

Form # 1
Version: 1.0   Date: September 4, 1991

Original control name	Property	New setting
Form	Caption	Select Files
	FormName	SelFiles
Command1	CtlName	GetFilesBtn
	Caption	&Get Files
Command2	CtlName	DelSelFileBtn
	Caption	&Delete Selected File
Command3	CtlName	ReturnBtn
	Caption	&Return
Text1	CtlName	WildcardsBox
	Text	(empty string)
List1	CtlName	SelFilesLst
List2	CtlName	DirLst
	Visible	False
Dir1	CtlName	TreeDir
Drive1	CtlName	CurrentDrv
Frame1	CtlName	SearchFrm
	Caption	Search Options
Option1	CtlName	AllOpt
	Caption	Search entire directory tree
Option2	CtlName	FromCurrentOpt
	Caption	Search from the current directory
Option3	CtlName	OnlyCurrentOpt
	Caption	Search only the current directory
Label1	CtlName	DriveLbl
	Caption	Drive:
Label2	CtlName	DirLbl
	Caption	Directory:
Label3	CtlName	SelFilesLbl
	Caption	Matching Files:
Label4	CtlName	WildcardsLbl
	Caption	Wildcards:

14-7 The customized settings for the WHEREIS.FRM form.

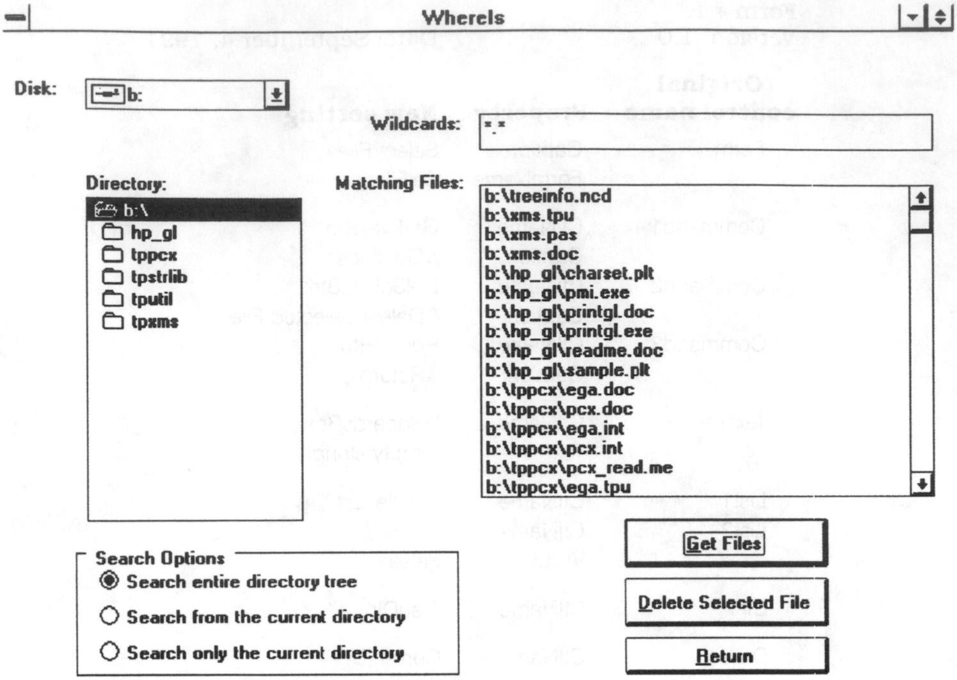
WhereIs
Disk:
b:
Wildcards:
.
Directory:
b:\
hp_gl
tppcx
tpstrlib
tputil
tpxms
Matching Files:
b:\treeinfo.ncd
b:\xms.tpu
b:\xms.pas
b:\xms.doc
b:\hp_gl\charset.plt
b:\hp_gl\pmi.exe
b:\hp_gl\printgl.doc
b:\hp_gl\printgl.exe
b:\hp_gl\readme.doc
b:\hp_gl\sample.plt
b:\tppcx\ega.doc
b:\tppcx\pcx.doc
b:\tppcx\ega.int
b:\tppcx\pcx.int
b:\tppcx\pcx_read.me
b:\tppcx\ega.tpu
Get Files
Delete Selected File
Return
Search Options
Search entire directory tree
Search from the current directory
Search only the current directory

14-8 A sample session with the WHEREIS.FRM form.

Listing 14-2 contains the code attached to the WHEREIS.FRM form. The form declares the following variables:

- The dynamic array Idx%( ) contains the levels of the directories.
- The dynamic array ChildIdx%( ) stores the indices to the children and descendants subdirectories.
- The Boolean DriveFlag variable serves as the scanned-drive flag. When the form is loaded it sets this variable to False to indicate that the directory tree of the current drive has not been mapped yet.

The form contains the event-handling procedures described here.

The CurrentDrv_Change procedure handles the process of selecting another drive. The procedure updates the Path setting of the TreeDir directory list box and sets the scanned-drive flag to False.

The DelSelFileBtn_Click procedure removes the currently selected file from SelFilesLst list box. The routine then selects the next file as either the previous or last list member, depending on the position of the selected file that was removed.

The Form_Load procedure initializes the SelFiles form. The procedure maximizes the form's window, sets the string of the text box to *.*, and selects the option button to search all the directories. The procedure then assigns False to the scanned-drive flag, stored in the variable DriveFlag.

Listing 14-2   The code attached to the WHEREIS.FRM form.

```
Const True = -1, False = 0

' declare dynamic array of file indices
Dim Idx%()
Dim ChildIdx%()
Dim DriveFlag As Integer

Sub CurrentDrv_Change ()
' Flag the change in the current drive
  ' update the directory list box
  TreeDir.Path = CurrentDrv.Drive
  ' set the scanned-drive flag to False
  DriveFlag = False
End Sub

Sub DelSelFileBtn_Click ()
' Remove the currently selected file from SelFilesLst.
  Dim I As Integer
  ' get the index of the selected list member
  I = SelFilesLst.ListIndex
  ' is there a current selection?
  If I > -1 Then
    ' remove the selected file
    SelFilesLst.RemoveItem I
    ' update the index for the selected list member
    If I >= SelFilesLst.ListCount Then
      I = SelFilesLst.ListCount - 1
    ElseIf I > 0 Then
      I = I - 1
    End If
    ' select another list member
    SelFilesLst.ListIndex = I
  End If
End Sub

Sub Form_Load ()
' Initialize the form.
  WindowState = 2 ' set the window to maximum
  WildcardsBox.Text = "*.*" ' set the wildcard text box to *.*
  AllOpt.Value = True ' select the first option button
  DriveFlag = False ' set the scanned-drive flag to False
End Sub

Sub GetFilesBtn_Click ()
' Obtain the file selection according to the specified wildcards and
' the current selection option button.
  Dim I As Integer
  Dim Count As Integer
  Dim F As String
  Dim WildCards As String
  Dim LastListIndex As Integer
  MousePointer = 11 ' set the mouse cursor to the hour-glass
  ' store the current selection of the directory list box in
  ' the local variable LastListIndex
  LastListIndex = TreeDir.ListIndex
  ' assign the string of the wildcard text box to the
  ' variable WildCards
  WildCards = WildCardsBox.Text
  ' is this a new drive, or is this the first time
  ' a file selection is made?
  If Not DriveFlag Then
    ' is the current drive the hard disk C:?
    If Left$(CurrentDrv.Drive, 1) = "c" Then
      ' is the C-drive data disk nonexistent?
      If Dir$(C_DRIVE_TREE) = "" Then
```

Listing 14-2 Continued.

```
            ' hide the directory list box
            TreeDir.Visible = False
            ' build the directory tree map
            BuildDirTree TreeDir, DirLst, Idx%()
            ' write the members of the DirLst list box to the
            ' C-drive data file
            I = WriteList(DirLst, C_DRIVE_TREE)
        Else
            ' read the directory tree map from the C-drive data file
            I = ReadList(DirLst, C_DRIVE_TREE, False)
        End If
    Else
        ' the drive is not C:
        ' hide the directory list box
        TreeDir.Visible = False
        ' build the directory tree map
        BuildDirTree TreeDir, DirLst, Idx%()
    End If
    ' set the scanned-drive flag to False
    DriveFlag = True
End If
' scanning the entire directory map?
If AllOpt.Value Then
    WhereIsEntireList DirLst, SelFilesLst, WildCards
' scanning from the current directory map?
ElseIf FromCurrentOpt.Value Then
    F = TreeDir.List(-1)
    WhereIsFromCurList DirLst, SelFilesLst, F, Idx%(), ChildIdx%(), Count,
WildCards
' scanning only the current directory?
ElseIf OnlyCurrentOpt.Value Then
    F = TreeDir.List(-1)

    WhereIsOnlyCurList F, SelFilesLst, WildCards
End If
' make the directory tree list box visible
TreeDir.Visible = True
' restore the original directory tree list box selection
TreeDir.ListIndex = LastListIndex
' restore the mouse cursor
MousePointer = 0
End Sub


Sub ReturnBtn_Click ()
' Write the members of the SelFilesLst to the WHEREIS_DATA file
' and then return to the calling form.
    Dim S As String
    ' assign the data file name to the local string variable S
    S = WHEREIS_DATA
    ' is the SelFilesLst not empty?
    If SelFilesLst.ListCount > 0 Then
        ' was there an error in  writing the data to the file
        If Not WriteList(SelFilesLst, S) Then
            ' display error message box
            MsgBox "Error in writing files list", 64, "I/O Error"
        End If
    Else
        ' set error handler
        On Error Resume Next
        ' delete the data file
        Kill S
        On Error Goto 0 ' turn off error handler
    End If
    ' unload the WhereIs form
    Unload WhereIs
End Sub
```

The GetFilesBtn_Click procedure obtains the file selection according to the selected search option button. The procedure sets the mouse cursor to the hour-glass icon, stores the current selection of the directory list box in the local variable LastListIndex, and assigns the string of the wild-card text box to the variable WildCards. Next it checks the scanned-drive flag to determine whether the directory tree of the drive has not yet been mapped. If the DriveFlag variable is False, the procedure needs to obtain the directory map. If the drive is not C:, the procedure calls BuildDirTree to obtain the needed directory map. If the drive is C:, however, the routine tries to locate and then read the CDRVTREE.DAT data file in directory C:\VB\VBXTOOL. If that data file is nonexistent, the routine calls Build-DirTree to scan the directories of the hard disk C: and then writes the tree map to the CDRVTREE.DAT data file.

Once the directory tree map is obtained, the procedure sets the DriveFlag variable to True. During the scanning of the directories, the procedure hides the directory list box to avoid its unpleasant visual appearance, which results from constantly changing the current directory.

Having obtained the tree map, the procedure determines if the Search entire directory tree option is selected; if so, the procedure invokes the routine WhereIsEntireList with the arguments DirLst, SelFilesLst, and WildCards.

If the Search from the current directory option is selected, the procedure invokes the routine WhereIsFromCurList with the arguments DirLst, SelFilesLst, F, Idx%( ), ChildIdx%, Count, and WildCards. The variable F is assigned the current directory.

If the Search only current directory option is selected, the procedure invokes the routine WhereIsOnlyCurList with the arguments F, SelFilesLst, and WildCards. The variable F is assigned the current directory.

Before exiting, the procedure makes the directory list box visible again, restores the original directory tree list box selection, and restores the mouse cursor to its default shape.

The ReturnBtn_Click procedure writes the members of the SelFilesLst to the WHEREIS_DATA data file and then returns to the calling form. The WHEREIS_DATA is a global constant declared in the global module FILE-DIRS.GLB as C:\VB\VBXTOOL\WHEREIS.DAT. The procedure assigns the constant WHEREIS_DATA to the local string variable S. If the SelFilesLst list box is not empty, the procedure writes the members of that list box to the data file; if it is empty, the procedure tries to erase the previous version of the data file. This attempt is supported by an error handler, in case the sought data file is nonexistent. Erasing the data file ensures that there is no mix-up between the previous and current selections. Finally, the procedure unloads the SelFiles form.

Both SelFiles and WhereIs forms use the C:\VB\VBXTOOL\WHEREIS .DAT data file, since it makes no difference to the calling program which form actually obtained the selected files. This scheme also allows the selected files to be supplied by customized versions of either form, or by entirely new forms that you develop.

15

The View File form

This chapter and the next three chapters present secondary forms that are used in processing the list of files obtained by using the SELFILES.FRM or WHEREIS.FRM forms. This chapter presents the file view form, VIEW FILE.FRM. Figure 15-1 shows a sample session with the file view form; the FormName property is set to ViewFile. The ViewFile form contains the following controls:

- A menu with two selections, File and Search. The File selection has the Read Next, Read Previous, and Quit options. The accelerator keys for these options are Ctrl – N, Ctrl – P, and Ctrl – Q, respectively. The Search menu selection has a single option, Find, with an accelerator key of Ctrl – F. You can add more options to the Search menu, thus expanding its range of options.
- A filename text box that displays the name of the file currently being viewed. The code attached to the text box prevents you from typing any text in the text box.
- A find text box that allows you to key in a string that you want to search in the currently viewed file.
- A multiline scrollable text box that displays the text lines of the viewed file.

When the ViewFile form is loaded it reads the list of filenames from the WHE-REIS.DAT data file in the C: \ VB \ VBXTOOL directory, and stores them in an invisible list box. The form also loads the first file in the list. You can view the next or previous files by pressing the Ctrl – N and Ctrl – P keys, respectively. The ViewFile form treats the list of files as a circular list. You can search for a string by typing that string in the Find Text box and press-

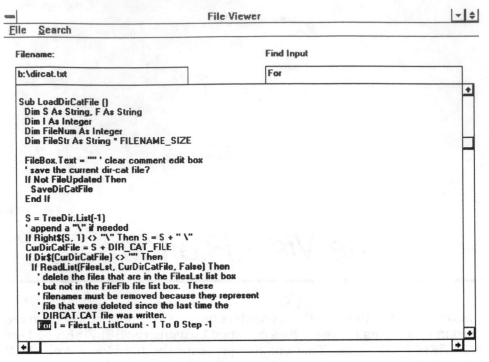

15-1 A sample session with the VIEWFILE.FRM form.

ing the Ctrl – F keys. When you want to exit the ViewFile form, select the Quit option from the File selection, or press the Ctrl – Q keys.

Figures 15-2 to 15-4 contain the documentation for the ViewFile form. Listing 15-1 contains the code for the various event-handling procedures of the form FILEWVIEW.FRM. The form declares the CurFileIndex variable to maintain the index of the currently selected file. The procedures in the ViewFile form are described next.

| Form # 1 | | Form filename: VIEWFILE.FRM |
| Version: 1.0 | | Date: July 2, 1991 |

Control object type	Default CtlName	Purpose
Text box	Text1	Contains the filename to read
	Text2	Contains the test search string
	Text3	Displays the text lines of a file
List box	List1	Stores the files list
Label	Label1	Label of Text1
	Label2	Label of Text2

15-2 List of control objects for the VIEWFILE.FRM form.

Application (code) name: VIEWFILE
Form # 1
Version: 1.0   Date: September 2, 1991

Original control name	Property	New setting
Form	Caption	File Viewer
	FormName	ViewFile
Text1	CtlName	FilenameBox
	Text	(empty string)
Text2	CtlName	FindBox
	Text	(empty string)
Text3	CtlName	TextBox
	Text	(empty string)
	MultiLine	True
	ScrollBars	3 - both
List1	CtlName	FilesLst
	Visible	False
Label1	CtlName	FilenameLbl
	Caption	Filename Input
Label2	CtlName	FindLbl
	Caption	Find Input

15-3 The modified control settings for the VIEWFILE.FRM form.

Form # 1   Form filename: VIEWFILE.FRM
Version: 1.0   Date: September 2, 1991

Caption	Property	Setting	Purpose
&File	CtlName	FileCom	
Read Next	CtlName	ReadNextCom	Reads the next file
	Accelerator	CTRL + N	
	Indented	Once	
Read Previous	CtlName	ReadPreviousCom	Reads the previous file
	Accelerator	CTRL + P	
	Indented	Once	
–	CtlName	Sep1	
	Indented	Once	
Quit	CtlName	QuitCom	Exits the application
	Accelerator	CTRL + Q	
	Indented	Once	
&Search	CtlName	SearchCom	
Find	CtlName	FindCom	Finds text in Text1
	Accelerator	CTRL + F	
	Indented	Once	

15-4 The menu structure for VIEWFILE.

Listing 15-1 The code attached to the FILEWVIEW.FRM form.

```
Const True = -1, False = 0

Dim CurFileIndex As Integer

Sub FilenameBox_Change ()
  FilenameBox.Text = FilesLst.List(CurFileIndex)
End Sub

Sub FilenameBox_KeyPress (KeyAScii As Integer)
  KeyAScii = 0
End Sub

Sub FindBox_Change ()
  FindCom.Checked = False
End Sub

Sub FindCom_Click ()
  Static CurIndex As Long
  Dim Find As String
  ' update the index to the current character
  CurIndex = TextBox.SelStart + 1
  ' store the text of the Find box in the variable Find
  Find = FindBox.Text
  ' is variable Find empty?
  If Find = "" Then Exit Sub ' nothing to find
  ' locate the index of the next substring Find in the
  ' text box
  CurIndex = InStr(CurIndex + 1, TextBox.Text, Find)
  ' found a match?
  If CurIndex > 0 Then
    ' Yes! Display the matching text as selected text
    TextBox.SelStart = CurIndex - 1
    TextBox.SelLength = Len(Find)
    TextBox.SetFocus
    FindCom.Checked = True
  Else
    ' No! Clear any selected text
    TextBox.SelStart = 0
    TextBox.SelLength = 0
    FindCom.Checked = False
  End If
End Sub

Sub FindLbl_Change ()
  FindCom.Checked = False
End Sub

Sub Form_Load ()
' Initialize the form.
  Dim S As String
  WindowState = 2  ' set the window to maximum
  ' read the WHEREIS_DATA file.  If the file input is not
  ' successfull, then unload the form
  S = WHEREIS_DATA
  If Not ReadList(FilesLst, S, False) Then
    MsgBox "Cannot find file " + S, 64, "File I/O Error"
    Unload ViewFile
  End If
  ' set the current file index to -1
  CurFileIndex = -1
  ' read the first file in the list
  ReadNextCom_Click
End Sub

Sub QuitCom_Click ()
' Unload the ViewFile form
```

Listing 15-1 Continued.

```
    Unload ViewFile
End Sub

Sub ReadFile ()
' Reads and displays the file Filename.
    Dim F As String
    Dim L As String
    Dim NL As String * 2
    Dim FileNum As Integer
    MousePointer = 11 ' set mouse cursor to the hour-glass
    ' obtain filename from the FilesLst list box
    F = FilesLst.List(CurFileIndex)
    ' write filename to the filename text box
    FilenameBox.Text = F
    NL = Chr$(13) + Chr$(10)
    FileNum = FreeFile
    ' open the file
    Open F For Input As #FileNum
    F = "" ' clear string variable and reuse it
    ' loop to read the text lines from the ASCII file
    Do While Not EOF(FileNum)
        Line Input #FileNum, L
        F = F + L + NL ' append a new line
    Loop
    TextBox.Text = F ' copy F into text box
    ' close the file
    Close #FileNum
    MousePointer = 0 ' restore default mouse cursor
End Sub

Sub ReadNextCom_Click ()
' Read the next file on the FilesLst list box.  The procedure
' treats the files list as a circular list.
    ' update the current dile index
    CurFileIndex = (CurFileIndex + 1) Mod FilesLst.ListCount
    ReadFile
End Sub

Sub ReadPreviousCom_Click ()
' Read the previous file in the FilesLst list box.  The procedure
' treats the files list as a circular list.
    ' update the current dile index
    CurFileIndex = (CurFileIndex - 1)
    If CurFileIndex < 0 Then CurFileIndex = FilesLst.ListCount - 1
    ReadFile
End Sub
```

The FilenameBox_Change procedure ensures that the name of the currently edited file remains displayed in the filename text box.

The FilenameBox_KeyPress procedure prevents you from keying in any text in the filename text box.

The FindBox_Change procedure clears the Checked property associated with the Find menu option.

The FindCom_Click procedure performs a simple case-sensitive text search. The procedure employs the local static variable CurIndex to maintain the character index of the last matching text. The procedure begins by assigning the value of TextBox.SelStart + 1 to the static variable CurIndex. The value of TextBox.SelStart is the index to the current cursor location when there is no selected text, or 0 when the last search found no match. Non-zero values for SelStart may result from the presence of selected text from the last matching text or from user-defined selected text. The offset 1 is added to SelStart to prevent the search process from being stuck in the same location of a previous match. Moreover, if SelStart is 0, adding 1 makes the CurIndex variable point to the first character in TextBox.

Next, the procedure assigns the string in the FindBox to the local string variable Find. The procedure exits if the variable Find contains an empty string. If it doesn't, the procedure locates the occurrence of the next matching text using the built-in InStr function. The call to InStr includes the CurIndex argument to start the search at the CurIndex character of TextBox. Omitting the CurIndex argument results in the search always being conducted from the beginning of the file. The result of the InStr function is reassigned to the CurIndex variable.

Then the procedure examines if the new value of CurIndex is positive; if so, there is a matching string found at character CurIndex. The first two statements in the Then clause make the matching text the new selected text. The last statement in the Then clause sets the focus to TextBox to make the selected text visible. If the CurIndex is zero, there is no matching text and the statements in the Else clause are executed to turn off any existing selected text. This action visually signals the absence of any matching text. The Find menu option is checked if the last text search found a match.

The Form_Load procedure initializes the form. The procedure maximizes the form's window, then reads the WHEREIS.DAT data file. If this task is not successful, an error message box appears and the form is unloaded. If it is successful, the list of files is read into the invisible FilesLst list box. Then the procedure assigns – 1 to the index of the currently viewed file, stored in the variable CurFileIndex, and invokes the ReadNextCom_Click procedure to load and view the first file in the FilesLst list box.

The QuitCom_Click procedure unloads and exits the ViewFile form.

The ReadFile procedure reads and displays the file which corresponds to the list member FilesLst.List(CurFileIndex). This procedure sets the mouse cursor to the hour-glass icon, assigns the list member FilesLst.List(CurFile Index) to the local string variable F, and copies the contents of variable F into the filename text box. The procedure then assigns the sequence of Chr$(13) and Chr$(10) to the local variable NL and opens the file F for input. Then it assigns an empty string to the variable F. This variable is reused in storing the lines of the text files.

Next, the procedure reads the text lines using the Do-While loop. Each line read is stored in the local variable L. The variable F is appended to the L + NL string expression, ensuring that each line is followed by a set of carriage return/line feed characters. Then the procedure assigns the variable F, which now stores all of the text lines, to the Text property of TextBox. Finally , it closes the file buffer and restores the mouse cursor to its default value.

The ReadNextCom_Click procedure reads the next file in the FilesLst list box. The procedure treats the files list as a circular list. The routine updates the value stored in the CurFileIndex variable and then calls procedure ReadFile.

The ReadPreviousCom_Click procedure reads the previous file on the FilesLst list box. This procedure also treats the files list as a circular list; the routine simply updates the CurFileIndex value, then calls procedure ReadFile.

16
The file editing forms

This chapter presents the file editing forms and their accompanying global module. The file editing forms are made up of two forms: the editor form and the replace text form. These two forms implement a simple yet very usable text editor. The editing forms process the files in the list obtained by the SELFILES.FRM and WHEREIS.FRM forms. By using the editing forms, you can perform the *normal* editing of multiple files, one after the other. I use the word normal because chapter 18 presents the FASTEDIT.FRM, which enables you to do a *fast* editing of a group of files—that is, you can rapidly change the same string throughout a group of files. For example, you can quickly and efficiently update the copyright year in your own listings by using such a utility.

The global module FILEDIRS.GLB

The global module FILEDIRS.GLB, shown in Listing 16-1, contains a minimum number of global constants and variables that are used by the file editing and viewing forms.

There are two global constants. The WHEREIS_DATA constant is assigned the full name for the data file that stores the list of files obtained in the SELFILES.FRM or WHEREIS.FRM forms. The C_DRIVE_TREE constant represents the name of the data file that contains the directory tree map for the hard disk C. If you have a hard disk that is D: or E:, or any other name, you can create additional constants that are similar to C_DRIVE_TREE. For example, if you have a hard disk C: and D:, you can declare the D_DRIVE_TREE constant as follows:

```
Global Const D_DRIVE_TREE = "C:\VB\VBXTOOL\DDRVTREE.DAT"
```

225

Listing 16-1 The code attached to the global module FILEDIRS.GLB.

```
' declares the constant for the name of the file that
' stores the list of selected files
Global Const WHEREIS_DATA = "C:\VB\VBXTOOL\WHEREIS.DAT"
' declares the constant for the name of the file that
' stores the list of directories for drive C:
Global Const C_DRIVE_TREE = "C:\VB\VBXTOOL\CDIRTREE.DAT"

' Constants used by the FastFind, FastEdit, and FileEdit forms
Global FindString As String
Global ReplaceString As String
Global Val As Integer
Global WholeWordVal As Integer
Global PromptVal As Integer
Global GlobalVal As Integer
```

☞ These two global constants assume that the directory C:\VB\ VBXTOOL contains the files related to this book's forms, modules, and data files. If you are using another directory, please alter these constants to reflect these directories.

The global module declares the following set of global variables that are used by the file editing forms EDITFILE.FRM and FASTEDIT.FRM:

- The FindString variable, which stores the string of the Find Input text box.
- The ReplaceString variable, which stores the string of the Replace text box.
- The CaseSenseVal variable, which stores the Value setting of the Case SenseChk check box.
- The WholeWordVal variable, which stores the Value setting of the WholeWordChk check box.
- The PromptVal variable, which stores the Value setting of the PromptChk check box.
- The GlobalVal variable, which stores the Value setting of the GlobalChk check box.

These constants enable the replace form to preserve the strings of the Find and Replace text boxes and the check box settings between subsequent calls to the form.

The EditFile form

The EDITFILE.FRM, which has the FormName setting EditFile, is a simple menu-driven text editor form. When the EditFile form is loaded, it reads the WHEREIS.DAT data file to obtain the current list of selected files, and stores the list in an invisible list box. The files in the list are sequentially edited by the EditFile form. You need not edit every file in the list; you can simply browse through files and edit the ones you wish. You may exit the form at any time. A sample session with the EditFile form is shown in FIG. 16-1. The EditFile form controls are made up of menu selections and options, as well as form controls. The menu items are described next, along with a presentation of their options.

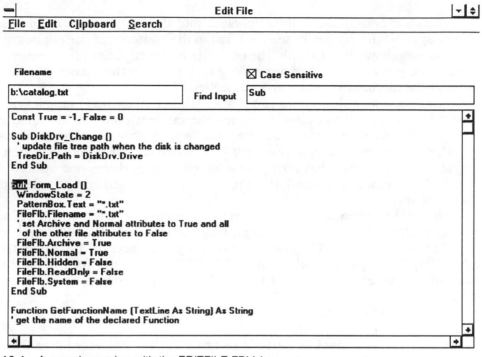

16-1 A sample session with the EDITFILE.FRM form.

The File selection has three options. The Load Next File option loads the next file in the files list. The form treats that list as a circular list; once you have finished editing the last file in the list, the next file you edit is the first one in the list. Before you load a new file, the form prompts you to save the current file if it has been edited but not yet saved.

The Save This File option saves the file you are currently editing, and the Quit option allows you to end the file editing and exit the form. The form prompts you to save the current file if it has been edited but not yet saved.

The Edit selection allows you to manipulate the selected text using its three menu options. The Cut option deletes the selected text and stores that text in the clipboard; the Copy option copies the selected text in the clipboard, the Paste option copies the contents of the clipboard into the current cursor location.

The clipboard selection enables you to manipulate the contents of the clipboard using the menu options that follow. The View Clipboard option displays a copy of the clipboard in the scrollable text box. The contents of the edited file are stored in a variable. When the clipboard is displayed, the caption of this form changes to View File, and the other options in the same menu selections are disabled; also the Filename text box displays Clipboard instead of the name of the currently edited file. While the clipboard is in the scrollable text box, you can edit its contents. When you select to view the edited file, the edited copy of the clipboard is stored in the clipboard itself.

The Clear option clears the clipboard, and the Append option enables you to append the currently selected text to the contents of the clipboard. This option allows you to build the contents of the clipboard from several files. Once you have finished appending text, you can then paste the contents of the clipboard to the currently edited file.

The Search selection allows you to search and replace text using its various options. The find option searches the currently edited file for the string in the Find Input text box. The Case Sensitive check box determines whether or not the search is case-sensitive. When the form finds a matching string, it displays that string as selected text, and the Find option is checked. If no match is found, the check mark is removed and no selected text appears.

The Find Selected Text option searches the currently edited file for a string that matches the selected text; this text is automatically copied to the Find Input text box. The Replace option replaces text in the currently edited file. This option invokes the REPLACEF.FRM to prompt you for the find and replace strings. The REPLACEF.FRM is described in the next section.

The EditFile form has the following form controls:

- The invisible list box is used in storing the list of selected files. This list is read from the WHEREIS.DAT data file.
- The Filename text box displays the name of the currently edited file, or displays Clipboard if you are viewing the clipboard. Because you should not type any text in this text box, the event-handling procedures disable user input.
- The Find Input text box contains the text search string. You may type in the search string.
- The multi-line scrollable text box contains the text of the edited file.
- The Case Sensitive check box allows you to specify whether or not the text search is case-sensitive.

Figures 16-2 to 16-5 contain the specifications for the edit file forms and the list of controls for the EDITFILE.FRM form.

Listing 16-2 contains the code attached to the EDITFILE.FRM form. The form declares the True, False, BUFFER_SIZE, and C_TEXT constants. The BUFFER_SIZE constant specifies the size of the file I/O buffer. Experiment with larger values to determine the upper limit for the constants before the Visual Basic run-time system warns of insufficient memory. When I first

Application name: N/A
Application code name: N/A

Version: 1.0   Date created: September 4, 1991
Programmer(s): Namir Clement Shammas

16-2 The basic
specifications for the
edit file forms.

List of filenames

Storage path: \ VB \ VBXTOOL
Project   N/A
Global   FILEDIRS.GLB
Form 1   EDITFILE.FRM
Form 2   REPLACEF.FRM
Module 1   GENERIC.BAS

Form # 1   Form filename: EDITFILE.FRM
Version: 1.0   Date: September 4, 1991

Control object type	Default CtlName	Purpose
Text box	Text1	Contains the filename to read
	Text2	Contains the text search string
	Text3	Displays the text lines of a file
List box	List1	Stores the list of selected files
Label	Label1	Label of Text1
	Label2	Label of Text2
Check box	Check1	Specifies case-sensitive search

16-3 List of control objects for the EDITFILE.FRM form.

Form # 1
Version: 1.0   Date: September 4, 1991

Original control name	Property	New setting
Form	Caption	Edit File
	FormName	EditFile
Text1	CtlName	FilenameBox
	Text	(empty string)
Text2	CtlName	FindBox
	Text	(empty string)
Text3	CtlName	TextBox
	Text	(empty string)
	MultiLine	True
	ScrollBars	3 - both
List1	CtlName	FilesIst
	Visible	False
Label1	CtlName	FilenameLbl
	Caption	Filename

16-4 The modified control settings for the EDITFILE project.

Original control name	Property	New setting
Label2	CtlName	FindLbl
	Caption	Find Input
Check1	CtlName	CaseSenseChk
	Caption	Case Sensitive

16-4 Continued.

Form # 1   Form filename: WINDEDIT1.FRM
Version: 1.0   Date: September 4, 1991

Caption	Property	Setting	Purpose
&File	CtlName	FileCom	
Load Next File	CtlName	LoadCom	Reads the next file in the files list
	Accelerator	CTRL + N	
	Indented	Once	
Save This File	CtlName	SaveCom	Saves the current file
	Accelerator	CTRL + W	
	Indented	Once	
–	CtlName	Sep1	
	Indented	Once	
Quit	CtlName	QuitCom	Exits the application
	Accelerator	CTRL-Q	
	Indented	Once	
&Edit	CtlName	EditCom	Copies, cuts, and pastes menu
Cut	CtlName	CutCom	Cuts the selected text
	Accelerator	CTRL-X	
	Indented	Once	
Copy	CtlName	CopyCom	Copies the selected text into the Clipboard
	Accelerator	CTRL-C	
	Indented	Once	
Paste	CtlName	PasteCom	Pastes the text from the clipboard
	Accelerator	CTRL-V	
	Indented	Once	
C&lipboard	CtlName	ClipboardCom	Clipboard menu
View Clipboard	CtlName	ViewCom	Views the Clipboard
	Indented	Once	
Clear	CtlName	ClearCom	Clears the Clipboard
	Indented	Once	
Append	CtlName	AppendCom	Appends selected text to the Clipboard
	Indented	Once	

16-5 The menu structure for the EDITFILE.FRM form.

Caption	Property	Setting	Purpose
&Search	CtlName	SearchCom	
Find	CtlName	FindCom	Finds text in Text1
	Accelerator	CTRL-F	
	Indented	Once	
Find Selected	CtlName	FindSelTextCom	Finds selected text
Text	Accelerator	CTRL-S	
	Indented	Once	
Replace	CtlName	ReplaceCom	Replaces text
	Accelerator	CTRL + R	
	Indented	Once	

16-5 Continued.

Listing 16-2 The code attached to the EDITFILE.FRM form.

```
Const True = -1, False = 0
Const BUFFER_SIZE = 4096
Const C_TEXT = 1

Dim CurFileIndex As Integer
Dim FileWasChanged As Integer
Dim Buffer As String ' file I/O buffer
Dim ViewClipboard As Integer

Sub AppendCom_Click ()
' Append the selected text to the clipboard
  Dim S As String
  If TextBox.SelText = "" Then Exit Sub
  S = Clipboard.GetText()
  S = S + Chr$(13) + Chr$(10) + TextBox.SelText
  Clipboard.SetText S, C_TEXT
End Sub

Sub ClearCom_Click ()
' Clear the clipboard.
  Clipboard.Clear
End Sub

Sub CopyCom_Click ()
' Copy selected text to the clipboard
  If Screen.ActiveControl.SelText <> "" Then
    Clipboard.SetText Screen.ActiveControl.SelText, C_TEXT
  End If
End Sub

Sub CutCom_Click ()
' Cut selected text.
  Clipboard.SetText Screen.ActiveControl.SelText
  Screen.ActiveControl.SelText = ""
End Sub

Sub FilenameBox_Change ()
  If ViewClipboard Then
    FilenameBox.Text = "Clipboard"
  Else
    FilenameBox.Text = FilesLst.List(CurFileIndex)
  End If
End Sub

Sub FilenameBox_KeyPress (KeyAscii As Integer)
```

Listing 16-2 Continued.

```
  KeyAscii = 0
End Sub

Sub FindBox_Change ()
  FindCom.Checked = 0
End Sub

Sub FindCom_Click ()
' Search for text.
  Static CurIndex As Long
  Dim Find As String
  ' update the index to the current character
  CurIndex = TextBox.SelStart + 1
  ' store the text of the Find box in the variable Find
  Find = FindBox.Text
  ' is variable Find empty?
  If Find = "" Then Exit Sub ' nothing to find
  ' locate the index of the next substring Find in the
  ' text box
  If CaseSenseChk.Value = 1 Then
    CurIndex = InStr(CurIndex + 1, TextBox.Text, Find)
  Else
    CurIndex = InStr(CurIndex + 1, UCase$(TextBox.Text), UCase$(Find))
  End If
  ' found a match?
  If CurIndex > 0 Then
    ' Yes! Display the matching text as selected text
    TextBox.SelStart = CurIndex - 1
    TextBox.SelLength = Len(Find)
    TextBox.SetFocus
    FindCom.Checked = True
  Else
    ' No! Clear any selected text
    TextBox.SelStart = 0
    TextBox.SelLength = 0
    FindCom.Checked = False
  End If
End Sub

Sub FindSelTextCom_Click ()
  If TextBox.SelText <> "" Then
    FindBox.Text = TextBox.SelText
  End If
  FindCom_Click
End Sub

Sub Form_Load ()
' Initialize the form.
  Dim S As String
  WindowState = 2 ' set the window to maximum
  ' set view clipboard flag to False
  ViewClipboard = False
  ' read the list from data file WHEREIS_DATA
  S = WHEREIS_DATA
  If ReadList(FilesLst, S, False) Then
    ' set the curren file index to -1
    CurFileIndex = -1
    ' set the file changed flag to False
    FileWasChanged = False
    ' load the first file
    LoadCom_Click
  Else
    MsgBox "Cannot find file " + S, 64, "File I/I Error"
    ' unload the form
    Unload EditFile
  End If
End Sub
```

Listing 16-2 Continued.

```
Sub LoadCom_Click ()
' Load a file for viewing and editing.  The procedure treats the
' list of files as a circular list.
  Dim F As String
  Dim BufNum As Integer
  ' was the previous file changed?
  If FileWasChanged Then
      ' prompt user to choose whether or not to save the
      ' updated contents of the edited file
      If MsgBox("Save edited file?", 32 + 4, "Warning!") = 6 Then
        ' save the file
        SaveCom_Click
      End If
  End If
  MousePointer = 11 ' hour-glass
  ' update the current file index.
  CurFileIndex = (CurFileIndex + 1) Mod FilesLst.ListCount
  ' obtain filename from the filename text box
  F = FilesLst.List(CurFileIndex)
  ' display the filename in the Filename text box
  FilenameBox.Text = F
  ' set error-handler
  On Error GoTo BadLoadCom
  BufNum = FreeFile ' get next free buffer number
  ' open the file
  Open F For Binary As #BufNum
  F = ""
  Do While Not EOF(BufNum)
      Buffer = Space$(BUFFER_SIZE)
      Get #1, , Buffer
      F = F + Buffer
  Loop
  TextBox.Text = F
  ' close the file
  Close #BufNum
  TextBox.Text = RTrim$(TextBox.Text) ' trim trailing spaces
  FileWasChanged = False
  MousePointer = 0 ' restore the mouse cursor
  ' exit procedure
  Exit Sub
' ********** Error-handler **********
BadLoadCom:
  Beep
  MsgBox "Cannot open file " + F, 64, "File I/O Error"
  On Error GoTo 0
  MousePointer = 0 ' restore the mouse cursor
  Resume ExitLoadCom
ExitLoadCom:
End Sub

Sub PasteCom_Click ()
' Paste from the clipboard
  Screen.ActiveControl.SelText = Clipboard.GetText()
End Sub

Sub QuitCom_Click ()
' Exit the form
  ' was the file changed?
  If FileWasChanged Then
      ' prompt user to choose whether or not to save the
      ' updated contents of the edited file
      If MsgBox("Save edited file?", 32 + 4, "Warning!") = 6 Then
        ' save the file
        SaveCom_Click
      End If
  End If
```

Listing 16-2 Continued.

```
    ' unload the form
    Unload EditFile
End Sub

Sub ReplaceCom_Click ()
' Replace text by invoking the ReplaceForm.
    ReplaceForm.Show 1
End Sub

Sub SaveCom_Click ()
' Save the text lines of the currently edited file.
    Dim FileNum As Integer
    Dim I As Long
    If (FilenameBox.Text <> "") And (TextBox.Text <> "") Then
        MousePointer = 11 ' hour-glass
        ' set error trap
        On Error GoTo BadSaveCom
        FileNum = FreeFile ' get next free buffer number
        ' open file in binary mode
        Open FilesLst.List(CurFileIndex) For Output As #FileNum
        ' write the contents of the lines text box to the file
        Print #FileNum, TextBox.Text
        Close #FileNum ' close output file
        On Error GoTo 0 ' clear error trap
    End If
    ' clear the file-was-changed flag
    FileWasChanged = False
    MousePointer = 0 ' restore the mouse cursor
    Exit Sub
    ' **************** Error-Handler **************
BadSaveCom:
    MsgBox "Cannot write to file " + FilenameBox.Text, 64, "File I/O Error"
    MousePointer = 0 ' restore the mouse cursor
    Resume ExitSaveCom
ExitSaveCom:
End Sub

Sub TextBox_Change ()
    ' set the file-was-changed flag to True
    FileWasChanged = True
End Sub

Sub ViewCom_Click ()
' View the clipboard
    Static theFilename As String
    Static theFileText As String
    ' toggle view clipboard flag
    ViewClipboard = Not ViewClipboard
    ' view the clipboard
    If ViewClipboard Then
        ViewCom.Caption = "View File"
        ClearCom.Enabled = False
        AppendCom.Enabled = False
        theFilename = FilenameBox.Text
        theFileText = TextBox.Text
        FilenameBox.Text = "Clipboard"
        TextBox.Text = Clipboard.GetText()
    Else
        ViewCom.Caption = "View Clipboard"
        ClearCom.Enabled = True
        AppendCom.Enabled = True
        FilenameBox.Text = theFilename
        Clipboard.SetText TextBox.Text, C_TEXT
```

Listing 16-2 Continued.
```
   TextBox.Text = theFileText
   theFileText = ""

  End If
End Sub
```

wrote the code for the EDITFILE.FRM form I made the buffer size 16384. This 16K buffer size turned out to be more than my system could handle! The C_TEXT constant specifies the text format of the clipboard.

The form also declares the following variables:

- The CurFileIndex variable maintains the index of the currently edited file. The index points to the member of the invisible list box that contains the selected list of files.
- The Boolean FileWasChanged variable indicates whether or not a file was changed. This variable is used to prompt you for saving an altered file before you either exit the form or load another file.
- The Buffer string variable is file I/O buffer.
- The Boolean ViewClipboard variable stores the view-clipboard state. When this variable is True, the scrollable text box is showing the clipboard.

The EditFile form contains the procedures that are described in the following paragraphs.

The AppendCom_Click procedure appends the selected text to the clipboard. The procedure copies the contents of the clipboard to the local string variable S, appends the contents of the scrollable text box to variable S, and then writes the contents of variable S to the clipboard.

The ClearCom_Click procedure clears the clipboard by using the Clear method with the Clipboard object.

The CopyCom_Click procedure copies the nonempty string of the selected text to the clipboard. The Screen.ActiveControl is able to specify any one of the three text boxes.

The CutCom_Click procedure allows you to copy the contents of the clipboard into the selected text box, which is usually the scrollable text box.

The FilenameBox_Change procedure guards the contents of the Filename text box against any changes. If the ViewClipBoard variable is True, the procedure maintains the string Clipboard in the text box. Otherwise, the procedure maintains the name of the currently edited file, obtained from the expression FilesLst.List(CurFileIndex).

The FilenameBox_KeyPress procedure prevents you from keying in any text in the Filename text box. The routine replaces the ASCII code of each entered key with zero.

The FindBox_Change procedure removes the check mark from the Find option when the text in the Find Input text box is altered.

The FindCom_Click procedure searches for text in the currently edited file. The procedure updates the index of the last match, which is stored in the static variable CurIndex; the TextBox.SelStart indicates the cursor location. Then the contents of the Find Input text box are assigned to the local string variable Find. If Find contains an empty string, the procedure exits without performing any text search. If not, the procedure locates the index of the next matching string. The procedures uses an If-Then-Else statement to perform either case-sensitive or case-insensitive searches based on Value setting of the Case Sensitive check box. If a matching text is found, the value of CurIndex is positive, and the procedure displays the matching text as selected text and sets the Checked property of the Find menu option to True. If no matching text is found, the procedure does not display any selected text and turns off the check mark from the Find menu option.

The FindBox_Change procedure sets the Checked property of the Find menu option to False if Find Input is changed.

The FindSelTextCom_Click procedure copies the selected text of the scrollable text box to the Find Input text box and then calls the FindCom_Click procedure to search for the selected text.

The Form_Load procedure initializes the EditFile form. First, the procedure maximizes the form's window; then it sets the ViewClipboard variable to False. It assigns the constant WHEREIS_DATA, which contains the full path and name of the WHEREIS.DAT data file to the local string variable S. Then the procedure reads the WHEREIS.DAT data file. If the file is successfully read, the procedure sets the CurFileIndex variable to −1, sets the File-WasChanged flag to False, and then calls the LoadCom_Click procedure to load the file in the FilesLst list box. If the procedure fails to find or read the data file, it displays an error message and then unloads the EditFile form.

The LoadCom_Click loads the next file in the file list. If the current file was changed the FileWasChanged variable is True. The procedure examines the Boolean value of variable FileWasChanged to determine if the file should be saved. If this is the case, the procedure prompts you to save the file, so you have the final say on whether or not the currently edited file should be saved. The procedure then reads the next file, obtained using the expression FilesLst.List(CurFileIndex). While the procedure is reading the next file, the mouse cursor is changed to the hourglass. The variable CurFileIndex is incremented in an expression that uses the Mod operator: this expression results in treating the FilesLst list box as a circular list. The routine reads the text lines of the next edited file and stores them in the scrollable text box. The Boolean variable FileWasChanged is reset to False. The procedure uses an error trap and handler to handle file I/O errors.

The PasteCom_Click procedure inserts the contents of the clipboard at the current cursor location of the selected text box.

The QuitCom_Click procedure exits the form. The procedure first examines the Boolean value of variable FileWasChanged; if that value is True, the procedure prompts you to save the currently edited file. The routine then unloads the EditFile form and returns program execution to the caller.

The ReplaceCom_Click procedure loads the REPLACEF.FRM to perform text replacement. The REPLACEF.FRM form is loaded as a modal form and prompts you for text replacement input as well as the actual text replacement.

The SaveCom_Click procedure saves the contents of the scrollable text box to the currently edited file. The procedure changes the mouse cursor to the hourglass. The routine opens the target file as a text file and writes the contents of the scrollable text box in one step. The routine assigns False to the variable FileWasChanged.

The TextBox_Change procedure sets FileWasChanged to True. This action is primarily meant to detect editing changes; however, there is a side effect that is created by viewing the clipboard. If you view the clipboard and do not edit the current file, the form still prompts you to save that file.

The ViewCom_Click procedure toggles between viewing and editing the currently edited file and the clipboard. When a copy of the clipboard's contents is in the scrollable text box, the procedure sets the ViewCom caption to View File and disables the Clear and Append options. The routine uses the local static string variables theFilename and theFileText to store the name and contents of the edited file. When you toggle back to viewing and editing the current file, the procedure restores the file's text and the View option's normal caption. In addition, the routine enables the Clear and Append menu options.

The Replace form

The EditFile form contains its own controls for searching for text. However, when it comes to replacing text, there are more options to consider. These options require additional controls, and therefore warrant the use of a separate form, the REPLACEF.FRM form. This form has the form name ReplaceForm. Figure 16-6 shows a sample session with ReplaceForm. This form combines the visual interface and engine for replacing text. The form contains the following controls:

- The Find text box, which stores the search text. When this text box gets the focus it selects the entire text. This enables you to overwrite the old text by merely typing in the new text.
- The Replace text box, which contains the replacement text. This text box works similarly to the Find text box.
- The Case sensitive check box, which allows you to toggle between case-sensitive and case-insensitive text search.
- The Prompt before replacing check box, which enables you to specify whether or not you should be asked for each text replacement.
- The Whole word check box, which indicates whether or not the matching text should be an entire word or possibly part of a longer word.

- The Global check box, which indicates whether or not the text replacement starts from the beginning of the file, or starts from the current cursor position.
- The OK button, which triggers the text replacement.
- The Cancel button, which unloads the ReplaceForm form.

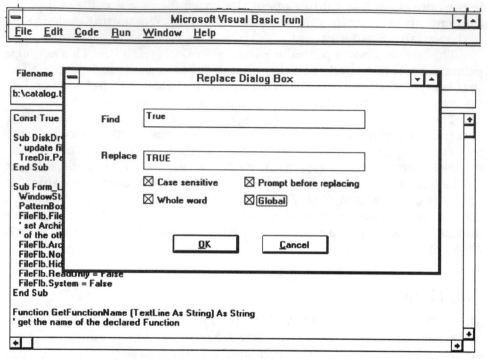

16-6 A sample session with the REPLACEF.FRM form.

Once you click on the OK button, its associated event-handling procedure hides the ReplaceForm form but does not unload it. This enables you to see the changes to the scrollable text box in the EditFile form. The actual editing and prompting is performed by the ReplaceForm form. The form is unloaded either when the text replacement is terminated or when you click on the Cancel button. The ReplaceForm form uses the global variables in Listing 16-1 to store the values of its controls between form invocations. This allows ReplaceForm to maintain your preferred settings during a program session.

Figures 16-7 and 16-8 show the controls and customized settings for the REPLACEF.FRM.

Listing 16-3 contains the procedures attached to the REPLACEF.FRM form. The relevant procedures are described in the following paragraphs.

The CancelBtn_Click procedure stores the values of the form's controls and then unloads the form.

Form # 2   Form filename: REPLACEF.FRM
Version: 1.0   Date: September 4, 1991

Control object type	Default CtlName	Purpose
Command button	Command1	Starts the text replacement
	Command2	Exits the ReplaceForm form
Text box	Text1	The Find text box
	Text2	The Replace text box
Check box	Check1	Case-sensitive option
	Check2	Prompt before replacing option
	Check3	Whole word option
	Check4	Global replacement option
Label	Label1	Label for Find text box
	Label2	Label for Replace text box

16-7   The list of controls in the REPLACEF.FRM form file.

Form # 2
Version: 1.0   Date: September 4, 1991

Original control name	Property	New setting
Form	FormName	ReplaceForm
	Caption	Replace
Command1	CtlName	OKBtn
	Caption	&OK
Command2	CtlName	CancelBtn
	Caption	&Cancel
Text1	CtlName	FindBox
	Text	(empty string)
Text2	CtlName	ReplaceBox
	Text	(empty string)
Check1	CtlName	CaseSenseChk
	Caption	Case sensitive
Check2	CtlName	PromptChk
	Caption	Prompt
Check3	CtlName	WholeWordChk
	Caption	Whole word
Check4	CtlName	GlobalChk
	Caption	Global
Label1	CtlName	FindLbl
	Caption	Find
Label2	CtlName	ReplaceLbl
	Caption	Replace

16-8   The customized settings for the REPLACEF.FRM form.

Listing 16-3 The code attached to the REPLACEF.FRM form.

```
Const True = -1, False = 0

Sub CancelBtn_Click ()
' Store the current status and unload the form
  StoreStatus
  Unload ReplaceForm
End Sub

Sub FindBox_GotFocus ()
  HighlightTextBox FindBox
End Sub

Sub Form_Load ()
' Initialize the form by assigning the global variables to the
' corresponding control properties.
  FindBox.Text = FindString
  ReplaceBox.Text = ReplaceString
  CaseSenseChk.Value = CaseSenseVal
  WholeWordChk.Value = WholeWordVal
  PromptChk.Value = PromptVal
  GlobalChk.Value = GlobalVal
End Sub

Sub OKBtn_Click ()
' Start the text search and replace process.
  Dim CurIndex As Long
  Dim FindCount As Integer
  Dim FoundMatch As Integer ' found a match
  Dim OK As Integer ' replace flag
  Dim Find As String, Replace As String
  ' store the status of the control properties
  StoreStatus
  ReplaceForm.Hide ' hide the ReplaceForm
  ' update the index to the current character
  If GlobalChk.Value = 1 Then
    CurIndex = 0
  Else
    CurIndex = EditFile.TextBox.SelStart + 1
  End If
  ' store the text of the Find box in the variable Find
  Find = FindBox.Text
  ' store the text of the Replace box in the variable Replace
  Replace = ReplaceBox.Text
  ' is variable Find empty?
  If Find = "" Then
    ReplaceForm.Show 1 ' nothing to find
    Exit Sub
  End If
  FindCount = 0
  Do
    ' locate the index of the next substring Find in the
    ' text box
    If CaseSenseChk.Value = 1 Then
      CurIndex = InStr(CurIndex + 1, EditFile.TextBox.Text, Find)
    Else
      CurIndex = InStr(CurIndex + 1, UCase$(EditFile.TextBox.Text),
UCase$(Find))
    End If
    FoundMatch = CurIndex > 0
    If FoundMatch Then FindCount = FindCount + 1
    OK = FoundMatch
    ' are we looking for a whole word?
    If OK And (WholeWordChk.Value = 1) Then
      If CurIndex > 1 Then
        OK = OK Xor IsWord(Mid$(EditFile.TextBox.Text, CurIndex - 1, 1))
```

Listing 16-3 Continued.

```
           End If
           If OK And ((CurIndex + Len(Find)) < Len(EditFile.TextBox.Text)) Then
               OK = OK Xor IsWord(Mid$(EditFile.TextBox.Text, CurIndex +
Len(Find), 1))
           End If
       End If
     ' found a match?
       If OK Then
     ' Yes! Display the matching text as selected text
           EditFile.TextBox.SelStart = CurIndex - 1
           EditFile.TextBox.SelLength = Len(Find)
           EditFile.TextBox.SetFocus
           Wait 1#
           If PromptChk.Value = 1 Then
               Select Case MsgBox("Replace '" + Find + "' ?", 35, "")
                   Case 2 ' Cancel
                       ReplaceForm.Show 1
                       Exit Sub
                   Case 6 ' Yes
                       OK = True
                   Case 7 ' No
                       OK = False
               End Select
           End If
           If OK Then
               EditFile.TextBox.SelText = Replace
               EditFile.TextBox.SelLength = Len(Replace)
               EditFile.TextBox.SetFocus
           Else
               EditFile.TextBox.SelLength = Len(Find)
               EditFile.TextBox.SetFocus
           End If
       End If
       If FoundMatch Then
         ' advance CurIndex
         CurIndex = CurIndex + Len(Replace) - Len(Find) + 1
       End If
   Loop While FoundMatch
   If FindCount > 0 Then
     MsgBox "No more matching strings", 64, "Information"
   Else
     MsgBox "No match was found", 64, "Information"
   End If
   ' now unload the dialog box
   Unload ReplaceForm
End Sub

Sub ReplaceBox_GotFocus ()
   HighlightTextBox ReplaceBox
End Sub

Sub StoreStatus ()
' Store the properties of the various controls in the
' corresponding global variables
   FindString = FindBox.Text
   ReplaceString = ReplaceBox.Text
   CaseSenseVal = CaseSenseChk.Value
   WholeWordVal = WholeWordChk.Value
   PromptVal = PromptChk.Value
   GlobalVal = GlobalChk.Value
End Sub
```

The Form_Load procedure initializes the form by recalling the previous control settings from the global variables.

The OKBtn_Click procedure searches for the specified text and replaces it with the string in the Replace text box. The search is influenced by the various check boxes. The procedure stores the controls' settings by calling the StoreStatus procedure, hides the ReplaceForm form, and updates the current character index, based on the Global check box setting. If that check box is marked, the CurIndex variable is assigned 0 to force the text search to start at the beginning of the file. Then the procedure stores the contents of the Find and Replace text boxes in the variables Find and Replace, respectively, and shows the form; the procedure exits the subroutine if the variable Find contains an empty string.

Next, the procedure sets the variable FindCount to 0. This variable stores the number of times a matching string is found. Then the procedure loops until there is no matching text. The numerous statements in the loop perform the search according to the Case sensitive and Whole word check boxes. If a matching string is found, the procedure prompts you to replace it, not to replace it, or to stop the text replacement. If you select the latter option, you exit the procedure but remain in the form; you can then exit the form by clicking the Cancel button. When the procedure finds a matching string, it displays that string as a selected text and waits for about a second before prompting you to replace the text.

When the loop stops iterating, the procedure displays a message indicating either that no matching string was found or that there are no more matching strings. The procedure uses the local variable FindCount to determine whether or not the search found any match. Finally, the procedure unloads the form and returns to the EditFile form.

The StoreStatus procedure stores the controls' settings in the global variables.

17
The Fast Find form

The ViewFile form presented in chapter 15 allows you to view a set of selected files and search for various strings. This chapter discusses the FASTFIND.FRM form, which has the FormName setting of FastFind. It allows you to quickly search for the same string in a set of files; you need not specify the search string and trigger the search every time you load a file.

Figure 17-1 shows a sample session with the FastFind form. The code of the form reads the WHEREIS.DAT data file to obtain the list of selected files. If the form is unable to find or read the data file, it unloads itself. The form is made up of the following controls:

- The Find text box contains the search string that you key in.
- The Case sensitive check box allows you to toggle between case-sensitive and case-insensitive text search.
- The Whole word check box permits you to toggle between searching for whole words and plain text.
- The OK button triggers a new search for the specified text in the selected files.
- The Cancel button allows you to end the text search and unload the FastFind form.
- An invisible list box contains the list of selected files read from the WHEREIS.DAT data file.
- The Filename text box displays the name of the file that is currently being searched.
- A multiline scrollable text box contains the lines of the currently searched file.

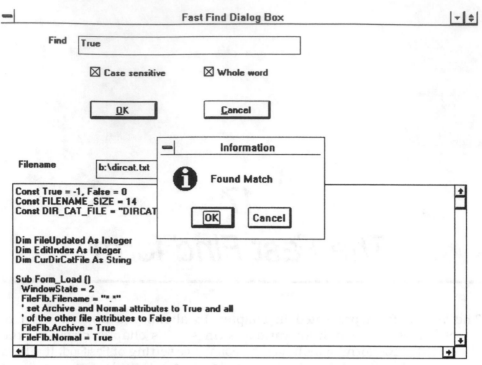

17-1 A sample session with the FASTFIND.FRM form.

Using the FastFind form is very easy. You type the search text in the Find text box and optionally toggle the two check boxes to fine-tune the text search. Once you are ready to start searching, you click on the OK button. The search process examines the files in the invisible list box. If no match is found in a file, the next file is automatically loaded and searched. When the form finds a match, it displays that match as selected text and waits for about one second before prompting you to either search for the next occurrence or stop searching. The form uses a message box with OK and Cancel buttons. If you click on the OK button or press Enter, the form looks for the next occurrence of the search text. If you click on the Cancel button, you stop the search but remain in the form. The next time you click on the form's own OK button, you start searching for text beginning with the first file in the set of selected files. To end the text search, click on the form's Cancel button.

Figures 17-2 and 17-3 contain the controls and their custom settings for the FASTFIND.FRM form.

Listing 17-1 shows the code attached to the FASTFIND.FRM form. The form declares the CurFilename variable that stores the name of the currently viewed file. The procedures attached to the form are very similar to the procedures attached to the VIEWFILE.FRM form.

The CancelBtn_Click procedure stores the string of the Find text box and

Form # 1
Version: 1.0

Form filename: FASTFIND.FRM
Date: September 7, 1991

Control object type	Default CtlName	Purpose
Command button	Command1	Searches for the specified text in the selected files
	Command2	Unloads the form
Text box	Text1	The Find text box
	Text2	Displays the name of the current file
	Text3	Displays the lines of a file
List box	List1	Stores the list of selected files
Check box	Check1	Toggles case-sensitive search
	Check2	Toggles whole word search
Label	Label1	Label for the Find text box
	Label2	Label for the Filename text box

17-2   The list of controls in the FASTFIND.FRM form file.

Form # 1
Version: 1.0

Date: September 7, 1991

Original control name	Property	New setting
Form	FormName	FastFind
	Caption	Fast Find Dialog Box
Command1	CtlName	OKBtn
	Caption	&OK
Command2	CtlName	CancelBtn
	Caption	&Cancel
Text1	CtlName	FindBox
	Text	(empty string)
Text2	CtlName	FilenameBox
	Text	(empty string)
Text3	CtlName	TextBox
	Text	(empty string)
List1	CtlName	FilesLst
	Visible	False
Check1	CtlName	CaseSenseChk
	Caption	Case sensitive
Check2	CtlName	WholeWordChk
	Caption	Whole word
Label1	CtlName	FindLbl
	Caption	Find
Label2	CtlName	FilenameLbl
	Caption	Filename

17-3   The customized settings for the FASTFIND.FRM form.

Listing 17-1   The code attached to the FASTFIND.FRM form.

```
Const True = -1, False = 0

' stores the name of the currently viewed file
Dim CurFilename As String

Sub CancelBtn_Click ()
' Exit the form
  ' store the status of the form controls
  StoreStatus
  ' unload the form
  Unload FastFind
End Sub

Sub FindBox_GotFocus ()
  HighlightTextBox FindBox
End Sub

Sub Form_Load ()
' Initialize the form
  Dim S As String
  ' read the WHEREIS_DATA file.  If there is an error, unload
  ' the form.
  S = WHEREIS_DATA
  If ReadList(FilesLst, S, False) Then
    WindowState = 2 ' set window to maximum
    ' restore the properties of the form controls using
    ' the corresponding global variables
    FindBox.text = FindString
    CaseSenseChk.Value = CaseSenseVal
    WholeWordChk.Value = WholeWordVal
  Else
    MsgBox "Cannot find file " + S, 65, "File I/O Error"
    Unload FastFind
  End If
End Sub

Sub OKBtn_Click ()
' Start the multi-file text search.
  Const BUFFER_SIZE = 4096
  Dim I As Integer
  Dim FileNum As Integer
  Dim CurIndex As Long
  Dim FindCount As Integer
  Dim FoundMatch As Integer ' found a match
  Dim Find As String
  ' store the status of the form controls
  StoreStatus
' exit the procedure if the string of the Find text box is empty
If FindBox.text = "" Then
  Exit Sub
End If
' process the files in the FilesLst list box
For I = 0 To FilesLst.ListCount - 1
  MousePointer = 11 ' hour-glass
  ' assign the file name to variable Filename
  CurFilename = FilesLst.List(I)
  ' show the name of the scanned file in the Filename text box
  FilenameBox.text = CurFilename
  ' get the input file handle
  FileNum = FreeFile
  ' open the viewed file as a binary file
  Open CurFilename For Binary As #FileNum
  TextBox.text = "" ' clear the lines text box
  Do While Not EOF(FileNum)
    ' size up the input buffer, using string variable Find
```

Listing 17-1 Continued.

```
              ' as the input buffer.
          Find = Space$(BUFFER_SIZE)
              ' read from the input file
          Get #FileNum, , Find
              ' append the input to the text box
          TextBox.text = TextBox.text + Find
      Loop
      ' close the input file
      Close #FileNum
      MousePointer = 0 ' restore default mouse pointer
      CurIndex = 0 ' initialize the current matching string index
      ' store the text of the Find in the variable Find
      Find = FindBox.text
      FindCount = 0
      Do
          ' locate the index of the next substring Find in the
          ' text box
          If CaseSenseChk.Value = 1 Then
            CurIndex = InStr(CurIndex + 1, TextBox.text, Find)
          Else
            CurIndex = InStr(CurIndex + 1, UCase$(TextBox.text), UCase$(Find))
          End If
          FoundMatch = CurIndex > 0
          If FoundMatch Then FindCount = FindCount + 1
          OK = FoundMatch
          ' are we looking for a whole word?
          If OK And (WholeWordChk.Value = 1) Then
            If CurIndex > 1 Then
              OK = OK Xor IsWord(Mid$(TextBox.text, CurIndex - 1, 1))
            End If
            If OK And ((CurIndex + Len(Find)) < Len(TextBox.text)) Then
              OK = OK Xor IsWord(Mid$(TextBox.text, CurIndex + Len(Find), 1))
            End If
          End If
          ' found a match?
          If OK Then
            ' Yes! Display the matching text as selected text
            TextBox.SelStart = CurIndex - 1
            TextBox.SelLength = Len(Find)
            TextBox.SetFocus
            Wait 1# ' wait for 1 second
            If MsgBox("Found Match", 65, "Information") = 2 Then
              Exit Sub
            End If
          Else
            TextBox.SelLength = Len(Find)
            TextBox.SetFocus
          End If
          If FoundMatch Then
            ' advance CurIndex
            CurIndex = CurIndex + 1
          End If
      Loop While FoundMatch
    Next I
End Sub

Sub StoreStatus ()
' Store the status of the form controls in their corresponding
' global variables.
    FindString = FindBox.text
    CaseSenseVal = CaseSenseChk.Value
    WholeWordVal = WholeWordChk.Value
End Sub

Sub FilenameBox_Change ()
' Maintain the name of current file in the
```

Listing 17-1 Continued.

```
' Filename text box
  FilenameBox.text = CurFilename
End Sub
```

the check box settings in their corresponding global variables, then unloads the the FastFind form.

The FilenameBox_Change procedure guards the name of the currently loaded file. If you edit the string in the Filename text box, this procedure restores the filename.

The Form_Load procedure is similar to the Form_Load procedure in the EditFile form. It reads the list of selected files into the invisible list box, maximizes the form's window, and restores the control settings stored in the global variables. If the file input fails, the form unloads itself.

☞ The EditFile, FastFind, and FastEdit (presented in the next chapter) all share the same set of global variables to store the settings of their controls. This means that the settings of one form will appear in the other forms. This feature allows you to retain the same preferences in these three forms.

The OKBtn_Click procedure processes the list of files, searching each file for the text specified in the Find text box. The routine uses a For-Next loop to read a file and then examines it for the occurrences of the search text. When the procedure finds a matching string, it displays that string as a selected text and waits for about one second before prompting you to continue searching or to stop.

18
The Fast Edit form

The previous chapter presented a form that quickly searches for the same text in a set of selected files. This chapter presents FASTEDIT.FRM, a similar form that performs the same text replacement in a set of files.

Figure 18-1 shows a sample session with the FASTEDIT.FRM form, which has its FormName set to FastEdit. The code of the form reads the WHEREIS.DAT data file to obtain the list of selected files. If the form is unable to find or read the data file, it unloads itself. The form consists of the following controls:

- The Find text box contains the search string that you key in.
- The Replace text box stores the replacement string that you also enter.
- The Case sensitive check box allows you to toggle between case-sensitive and case-insensitive text search.
- The Whole word check box permits you to toggle between searching for whole words.
- The Prompt before replacing check box allows you to verify each text replacement.
- The OK button triggers a new search and replace process in the selected files.
- The Cancel button allows you to end the text replacement and unload the FastEdit form.
- An invisible list box contains the list of selected files read from the WHEREIS.DAT data file.
- The Filename text box displays the name of the file that is currently being searched.
- A multiline scrollable text box contains the lines of the currently edited file.

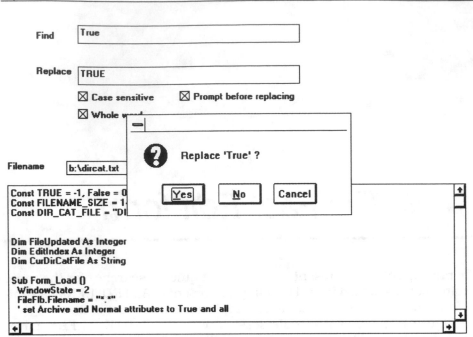

18-1   A sample session with the FASTEDIT.FRM form.

Using the FastEdit form is very simple. You key in the search and replace text in the Find and Replace text boxes, respectively. You can optionally toggle either check box to fine-tune the search and replace process. When you are ready to replace text, you click on the OK button. The process searches through the files in the invisible list box. If no match is found in a file, the next file is automatically loaded and searched. When the form finds a matching text, it replaces it without asking you if the Prompt check box is not checked; otherwise, the form displays the matching string as a selected text, waits for about one second, and then displays a message box with the buttons Yes, No, and Cancel. Clicking on the Yes button gives your approval to replace the text. Clicking on the No button prevents the current instance of the matching text from being replaced, and clicking on the Cancel button results in storing the currently edited file and halting further text replacement. You still remain in the FastEdit form. You can then either trigger other text replacements or exit the form by clicking on the form's Cancel button.

Figures 18-2 and 18-3 contain the controls and their custom settings for the FASTEDIT.FRM form.

Listing 18-1 shows the code attached to the FASTEDIT.FRM form. The form declares the CurFilename variable that stores the name of the currently viewed file. The procedures attached to this form are very similar to the procedures attached to the VIEWFILE.FRM form.

Form # 1   Form filename: FASTEDIT.FRM
Version: 1.0   Date: September 7, 1991

Control object type	Default CtlName	Purpose
Command button	Command1	Searches for the specified text in the selected files
	Command2	Unloads the form
Text box	Text1	The Find text box
	Text2	The Replace text box
	Text3	Displays the name of the current file
	Text4	Displays the lines of a file
List box	List1	Stores the list of selected files
Check box	Check1	Toggles case-sensitive search
	Check2	Toggles whole word search
	Check3	Toggles replacement prompt
Label	Label1	Label for the Find text box
	Label2	Label for the Replace text box
	Label3	Label for the Filename text box

18-2 The list of controls in the FASTEDIT.FRM form file.

Form # 1
Version: 1.0   Date: September 7, 1991

Original control name	Property	New setting
Form	FormName	FastEdit
	Caption	Fast Edit Dialog Box
Command1	CtlName	OKBtn
	Caption	&OK
Command2	CtlName	CancelBtn
	Caption	&Cancel
Text1	CtlName	FindBox
	Text	(empty string)
Text2	CtlName	FilenameBox
	Text	(empty string)
Text3	CtlName	ReplaceBox
	Text	(empty string)
Text4	CtlName	TextBox
	Text	(empty string)
List1	CtlName	FilesLst
	Visible	False
Check1	CtlName	CaseSenseChk
	Caption	Case sensitive
Check2	CtlName	WholeWordChk
	Caption	Whole word

18-3 The customized settings for the FASTEDIT.FRM form.

Original control name	Property	New setting
Check3	CtlName	PromptChk
	Caption	Prompt before replacing
Label1	CtlName	FindLbl
	Caption	Find
Label2	CtlName	ReplaceLbl
	Caption	Replace
Label3	CtlName	FilenameLbl
	Caption	Filename

18-3 Continued.

Listing 18-1 The code attached to the FASTEDIT.FRM form.

```
Const True = -1, False = 0

' stores the currently edited filename
Dim CurFilename As String

Sub CancelBtn_Click ()
' Exit the form
  ' store the status of the form controls
  StoreStatus
  ' unload the form
  Unload FastEdit
End Sub

Sub FilenameBox_KeyPress (KeyAscii As Integer)
  KeyAscii = 0
End Sub

Sub FindBox_GotFocus ()
  HighlightTextBox FindBox
End Sub

Sub Form_Load ()
' Initialize the form
  Dim S As String
  ' read the WHEREIS_DATA file.  If there is an error, unload
  ' the form.
  S = WHEREIS_DATA
  If ReadList(FilesLst, S, False) Then
    WindowState = 2 ' set window to maximum
    ' restore the properties of the form controls using
    ' the corresponding global variables
    FindBox.Text = FindString
    ReplaceBox.Text = ReplaceString
    CaseSenseChk.Value = CaseSenseVal
    WholeWordChk.Value = WholeWordVal
    PromptChk.Value = PromptVal
  Else
    MsgBox "Cannot find file " + S, 65, "File I/O Error"
    Unload FastEdit
  End If
End Sub

Sub OKBtn_Click ()
' Start the multi-file edit.
  Const BUFFER_SIZE = 4096

  Dim I As Integer
```

Listing 18-1 Continued.

```
Dim FileNum As Integer
Dim CurIndex As Long
Dim WasFileChanged As Integer
Dim FoundMatch As Integer ' found a match
Dim OK As Integer ' replace flag
Dim Find As String, Replace As String
' store the status of the form controls
StoreStatus
' process the files in the FilesLst list box
For I = 0 To FilesLst.ListCount - 1
  ReadFile I ' read file FilesLst.List(I)
  CurIndex = 0 ' initialize the current matching string index
  ' store the text of the Find box in the variable Find
  Find = FindBox.Text
  ' store the text of the Replace box in the variable Replace
  Replace = ReplaceBox.Text
  ' is variable Find empty?
  If Find = "" Then Exit Sub ' nothing to find
  WasFileChanged = False
  Do
    ' locate the index of the next substring Find in the
    ' text box
    If CaseSenseChk.Value = 1 Then
     CurIndex = InStr(CurIndex + 1, TextBox.Text, Find)
    Else
     CurIndex = InStr(CurIndex + 1, UCase$(TextBox.Text), UCase$(Find))
    End If
    FoundMatch = CurIndex > 0
    OK = FoundMatch
    ' are we looking for a whole word?
    If OK And (WholeWordChk.Value = 1) Then
      If CurIndex > 1 Then
       OK = OK Xor IsWord(Mid$(TextBox.Text, CurIndex - 1, 1))
      End If
      If OK And ((CurIndex + Len(Find)) < Len(TextBox.Text)) Then
       OK = OK Xor IsWord(Mid$(TextBox.Text, CurIndex + Len(Find), 1))
      End If
    End If
    ' found a match?
    If OK Then
      ' Yes! Display the matching text as selected text
      TextBox.SelStart = CurIndex - 1
      TextBox.SelLength = Len(Find)
      TextBox.SetFocus
      If PromptChk.Value = 1 Then
        Wait 1# ' wait for about 1 second
        Select Case MsgBox("Replace '" + Find + "' ?", 35, "")
          Case 2 ' Cancel
            ' save current file if it was changed
            If WasFileChanged Then SaveFile
            Exit Sub
          Case 6 ' Yes
            OK = True
          Case 7 ' No
            OK = False
        End Select
      End If
      If OK Then
        WasFileChanged = True
        TextBox.SelText = Replace
        TextBox.SelLength = Len(Replace)
        TextBox.SetFocus
      Else
        TextBox.SelLength = Len(Find)
        TextBox.SetFocus
      End If
    End If
```

Listing 18-1 Continued.

```
      If FoundMatch Then
         ' advance CurIndex
         CurIndex = CurIndex + Len(Replace) - Len(Find) + 1
      End If
   Loop While FoundMatch
   ' save file if it was changed?
   If WasFileChanged Then SaveFile
   Next I
End Sub

Sub ReadFile (ByVal I%)
' Read the the member I% in the lis box FilesLst.
   Const BUFFER_SIZE = 4096

   Dim FileNum As Integer
   Dim S As String

   MousePointer = 11 ' house-glass
   ' assign the file name to variable CurFilename
   CurFilename = FilesLst.List(I%)
   ' show the name of the scanned file in the Filename text box
   FilenameBox.Text = CurFilename
   ' get the input file handle
   FileNum = FreeFile
   ' open the edited file as a binary file
   Open CurFilename For Binary As #FileNum
   TextBox.Text = "" ' clear the lines text box
   Do While Not EOF(FileNum)
      ' size up the input buffer, using string variable Find
      ' as the input buffer.
      S = Space$(BUFFER_SIZE)
      ' read from the input file
      Get #FileNum, , S
      ' append the input to the text box
      TextBox.Text = TextBox.Text + S
   Loop
   ' close the input file
   Close #FileNum
   MousePointer = 0 ' restore default mouse cursor
End Sub

Sub ReplaceBox_GotFocus ()
   HighlightTextBox ReplaceBox
End Sub

Sub SaveFile ()
' Save the currently edited file.
   Dim FileNum As Integer
   MousePointer = 11 ' hour-glass
   FileNum = FreeFile ' get the input file handle
   ' open output file as a binary file
   Open CurFilename For Output As #FileNum
   ' write the contents of TextBox to the output file in one swoop
   Print #FileNum, TextBox.Text
   Close #FileNum ' close the file
   MousePointer = 0 ' restore the default mouse cursor
End Sub

Sub StoreStatus ()
' Store the status of the form controls in their corresponding
' global variables.
   FindString = FindBox.Text
   ReplaceString = ReplaceBox.Text
   CaseSenseVal = CaseSenseChk.Value
   WholeWordVal = WholeWordChk.Value
   PromptVal = PromptChk.Value
End Sub
```

Listing 18-1 Continued.

```
Sub FilenameBox_Change ()
  FilenameBox.Text = CurFilename
End Sub
```

The CancelBtn_Click procedure stores the string of the Find text box and the check box settings in their corresponding global variables, and then unloads the FastEdit form.

The FilenameBox_Click procedure guards the name of the currently loaded file. If you edit the string in the Filename text box, this procedure restores the filename.

The Form_Load procedure is similar to that of the EditFile form. It reads the list of selected files into the invisible list box, maximizes the form's window, and restores the control settings stored in the global variables. If the file input fails, the form unloads itself.

☞ The EditFile, FastFind, and FastEdit share the same set of global variables to store the settings of their controls. This means that the settings of one form will appear in the other forms. This feature allows you to retain the same preferences in these three forms.

The OKBtn_Click procedure processes the list of files, searching and replacing text in each file that matches the settings of the Find text box, Replace text box, and the check boxes. The routine uses a For-Next loop to process the files in the invisible list box FilesLst. In each iteration, the procedure calls the ReadFile procedure to read the next file, processes the text of that file, and writes the contents of the altered file. When you decide to stop editing, the procedure saves the currently loaded file if it was changed. The procedure uses the local variable WasFileChanged to detect whether or not text was replaced in a file.

The ReadFile procedure reads the file in FilesLst member I% into the scrollable text box. The routine also stores the name of the file in the form-level variable CurFilename.

The SaveFile procedure writes the contents of the scrollable text box to the file CurFilename.

19
The General Shell
Application form

This chapter concludes the third part of the book. After presenting the various modules and secondary forms, I offer the GENSHELL.MAK project file and the GENSHELL.FRM form file. You may regard this form as a custom application form that invokes the other forms that I presented earlier in this part of the book.

The GENSHELL.FRM is a form that has both a menu and a number of control objects. Figure 19-1 shows a sample session with the GENSHELL.FRM form. The form contains the following menu items:

- The Quit selection allows you to exit the application.
- The Select menu selection has two options which allow you to select files. The From Current Directory option invokes the SELFILES.FRM form, whereas the From Any Directory option invokes the WHEREIS.FRM form. Both options place the files you select in the FilesLst list box.
- The Delete selection lets you delete the files in the FilesLst list box.
- The Copy selection allows you to copy the list of files to the target path. The form deletes the files that are successfully copied from the list of selected files. This feature enables you to copy a set of files with a large total byte size to multiple disks.
- The Move selection permits you to move the list of files to the target path. Like the Copy selection, Move deletes the files that are successfully moved from the list of selected files.
- The View menu selection loads the VIEWFILE.FRM form and allows you to view the files in the FilesLst list box.
- The Edit menu selection contains three options. The Single File option loads the EDITFILE.FRM form that allows you to edit vari-

ous parts of each selected file. The Fast Find option loads the FAST-FIND.FRM form, permitting you to quickly locate the same text in the selected files. The Fast Edit option loads the FASTEDIT.FRM form and permits you to rapidly replace the same text in the selected files.

- The Print menu selection prints the files in the FilesLst list box. Each printed page includes the filename, page number, time, and date.

19-1 A sample session with the GENSHELL.FRM form.

The GENSHELL.FRM form has the following control objects drawn on the form:

- The visible FilesLst list box displays the current selection of files. This selection is obtained by using either the SELFILES.FRM form or the WHEREIS.FRM form.
- The Delete Selected File button allows you to delete one or more selected files. The presence of this button in the GENSHELL.FRM form allows you an additional opportunity to delete files after your initial selection. Such a feature is desirable in certain conditions. For example, suppose you have selected a large group of files to print. Before you print these files, you might want to view them to make sure that they contain the text you want printed. After view-

ing these files, you can use the Delete Selected File button to remove files that you do not want to print.

- The message text box displays progress messages for the file deletion, copy, and movement operations.
- The Drive and Target Directory list boxes allow you to select the target path for such operations as copying and moving files.

Figures 19-2 to 19-5 contain the specifications for the GENSHELL.MAK project file and the GENSHELL.FRM form file. The GENSHELL.MAK file contains a long list of modules and forms, since the program acts as both a test program and a utility.

Application name: General Shell Application
Application code name: GENSHELL

Version: 1.0   Date created: September 7, 1991
Programmer(s): Namir Clement Shammas

List of filenames

19-2 The basic specifications for the GENSHELL.MAK project file.

Storage path: \VB\VBXTOOL

Project	GENSHELL.MAK
Global	FILEDIRS.GLB
Form 1	GENSHELL.FRM
Form 2	SELFILES.FRM
Form 3	WHEREIS.FRM
Form 4	VIEWFILE.FRM
Form 5	EDITFILE.FRM
Form 6	REPLACEF.FRM
Form 7	FASTFIND.FRM
Form 8	FASTEDIT.FRM
Module 1	GENERIC.BAS
Module 2	STRLIB.BAS
Module 3	FILESLIB.BAS
Module 4	DIRLIB.BAS

Form # 1   Form filename: GENSHELL.FRM
Version: 1.0   Date: September 7, 1991

Control object type	Default CtlName	Purpose
Command button	Command1	Deletes the selected file from List1
Text box	Text1	Displays progress messages
List box	List1	Contains the selected files
Directory list box	Dir1	The target directory
Drive list box	Drive1	The target drive
Label	Label1	Label for Text1 text box
	Label2	Label for List1 list box
	Label3	Label for Directory list box
	Label4	Label for Drive list box

19-3 The list of controls in the GENSHELL.FRM form file.

Application (code) name: GENSHELL
Form # 1
Version: 1.0   Date: September 7, 1991

Original control name	Property	New setting
Form	Caption	General Shell
Command1	CtlName	DelelFileBtn
	Caption	&Delete Selected File
Text1	CtlName	MessageBox
	Text	(empty string)
List1	CtlName	FilesLst
Dir1	CtlName	TreeDir
Drive1	CtlName	DriveDrv
Label1	CtlName	MessageLbl
	Caption	Message:
Label2	CtlName	FilesLbl
	Caption	Files List:
Label3	CtlName	DirectoryLbl
	Caption	Target Directory:
Label4	CtlName	DriveLbl
	Caption	Target Drive:

19-4 The customized settings for the GENSHELL.FRM form.

Form # 1   Form filename: GENSHELL.FRM
Version: 1.0   Date: September 7, 1991

Caption	Property	Setting	Purpose
&Quit	CtlName	QuitCom	Exits the application
&Select			
From Current Directory	CtlName	FromCurDirCom	Selects files from the
	Accelerator	CTRL + C	current directory
	Indented	Once	
From Any Directory	CtlName	FromAnyDirCom	Selects files from any
	Accelerator	CTRL + A	directory
	Indented	Once	
&Delete	CtlName	DeleteCom	Deletes selected files
&Copy	CtlName	CopyCom	Copies selected file to specified target path
&Move	CtlName	MoveCom	Moves selected file to specified target path

19-5 The menu structure for the GENSHELL.FRM form.

Caption	Property	Setting	Purpose
&View	CtlName	ViewCom	Views selected file to specified target path
&Edit	CtlName	EditCom	
Single File	CtlName	EditSingleCom	Invokes the EditFile form
	Accelerator	CTRL + S	
	Indented	Once	
Fast Edit	CtlName	FastEditCom	Invokes the FastEdit form
	Accelerator	CTRL + E	
	Indented	Once	
Fast Find	CtlName	FastFindCom	Invokes the FastFind form
	Accelerator	CTRL + F	
	Indented	Once	
&Print	CtlName	PrintCom	Prints the selected files

19-5 Continued.

Listing 19-1 contains the code attached to the GENSHELL.FRM. The form declares the constants True, False, and UpdateList. The latter constant signals that the FilesLst list box was updated by removing one or more files.

A description of the form's relevant procedures follows. Most of these procedures start by invoking the UpdateListProc to update the list of selected files in the WHEREIS.DAT file.

Listing 19-1 The code attached to the GENSHELL.FRM application form.

```
Const True = -1, False = 0

' Flag for updating the files list
Dim UpdateList As Integer

Sub CopyCom_Click ()
  ' update the files-list data file
  UpdateListProc
  ' copy the files in the FilesLst list box
  CopyFiles FilesLst, TreeDir.List(-1), MessageBox
  UpdateList = True ' set the update-files-list flag
End Sub

Sub DeleteCom_Click ()
  ' update the files-list data file
  UpdateListProc
  ' delete the files in the FilesLst list box
  DeleteFiles FilesLst, MessageBox
  UpdateList = True
End Sub

Sub DelSelFileBtn_Click ()
' Remove the selected file
  Dim I As Integer
  ' update the files-list data file
  UpdateListProc
  ' get the index of the selected list member
  I = FilesLst.ListIndex
  ' is there a current selection?
```

Listing 19-1 Continued.

```
  If I > -1 Then
    ' remove the selected file
    FilesLst.RemoveItem I
    UpdateList = True ' set the update-files-list flag
    ' update the index for the selected list member
    If I >= FilesLst.ListCount Then
      I = FilesLst.ListCount - 1
    ElseIf I > 0 Then
      I = I - 1
    End If
    ' select another list member
    FilesLst.ListIndex = I
  End If
End Sub

Sub DriveDrv_Change ()
' Update the target directory list box
  TreeDir.Path = DriveDrv.Drive
End Sub

Sub FastEditCom_Click ()
  ' update the files-list data file
  UpdateListProc
  ' invoke the FastEdit form as a modal form to quickly edit
  ' the selected files (in WHEREIS_DATA)
  FastEdit.Show 1
End Sub

Sub FastFindCom_Click ()
  ' update the files-list data file
  UpdateListProc
  ' invoke the fastFind form as a modal form to quickly find
  ' text in the selected files (in WHEREIS_DATA)
  FastFind.Show 1
End Sub

Sub Form_Load ()
  WindowState = 2
  ' update the files-list data file
  UpdateList = False
  ' delete existing directory tree mapa data file
  On Error Resume Next
  Kill C_DRIVE_TREE
  On Error GoTo 0
End Sub

Sub FromAnyDirCom_Click ()
' Search for files from the any directory
  Dim Dummy As Integer
  Dim S As String
  ' update the files-list data file
  UpdateListProc
  ' invoke the Whereis form as a modal form
  Whereis.Show 1
  ' read the files-list data file
  S = WHEREIS_DATA
  Dummy = ReadList(FilesLst, S, False)
End Sub

Sub FromCurDirCom_Click ()
' Search for files from the current directory
  Dim Dummy As Integer
  Dim S As String
  ' update the files-list data file
  UpdateListProc
  ' invoke the SelFiles form as a modal form
```

Listing 19-1 Continued.

```
    SelFiles.Show 1
    ' read the files-list data file
    S = WHEREIS_DATA
    Dummy = ReadList(FilesLst, S, False)
End Sub

Sub MoveCom_Click ()
    ' update the files-list data file
    UpdateListProc
    ' move the files in the FilesLst list box
    MoveFiles FilesLst, TreeDir.List(-1), MessageBox
    UpdateList = True ' set the update-files-list flag
End Sub

Sub PrintCom_Click ()
    ' update the files-list data file
    UpdateListProc
    ' print the files in the FilesLst list box
    PrintFiles FilesLst, MessageBox
End Sub

Sub QuitCom_Click ()
' Exit the application
    End
End Sub

Sub UpdateListProc ()
' Update the files-list data file
    Dim Dummy As Integer
    ' is the update-files-list flag set?
    If UpdateList Then
        ' write the FilesLst list box to file WHEREIS_DATA
        Dummy = WriteList(FilesLst, WHEREIS_DATA)
        ' clear the update-files-list flag
        UpdateList = False
    End If
End Sub

Sub ViewCom_Click ()
    ' update the files-list data file
    UpdateListProc
    ' invoke the FilewView form as a modal form to view
    ' the selected files (in WHEREIS_DATA)
    ViewFile.Show 1
End Sub

Sub EditSingleCom_Click ()
    ' update the files-list data file
    UpdateListProc
    ' invoke the EditFile form as a modal form to edit
    ' the selected files (in WHEREIS_DATA)
    EditFile.Show 1
End Sub
```

The CopyCom_Click procedure copies the files in the selected list to the target path determined by the Target Directory and Drive list boxes. The routine calls the CopyFiles procedure found in the FILESLIB.BAS module.

The DeleteCom_Click procedure deletes the selected files by invoking the procedure DeleteFiles, found in the FILESLIB.BAS module.

The DelSelFileBtn_Click procedure removes the currently selected file from the FilesLst list box. The code of this routine is very similar to that of the Delete Select File button in the SELFILES.FRM and WHEREIS.FRM forms.

The DriveDrv_Change procedure updates the target directory when you select a new target drive.

The EditSingleCom_Click procedure loads and shows the EditFile form as a modal form.

The FastEditCom_Click procedure loads and shows the FastEdit form as a modal form.

The FastFindCom_Click procedure loads and shows the FastFind form as a modal form.

The Form_Load procedure initializes the form. It maximizes the application window, assigns False to the UpdateList variable, and deletes the CDRVTREE.DAT data file if present. This step forces the WhereIs form to scan the hard disk C: and obtain the current directory tree map.

The FromAnyDirCom_Click procedure invokes the WhereIs form as a modal form, reads the data file WHEREIS.DAT, and stores the list of selected files in the FilesLst list box.

The FromCurDirCom_Click procedure invokes the SelFiles form as a modal form, reads the data file WHEREIS.DAT, and stores the list of selected files in the FilesLst list box.

The MoveCom_Click procedure moves the selected files to the target path by calling the MoveFiles procedure, found in module FILESLIB.BAS.

The PrintCom_Click procedure prints the selected files by calling the PrintFiles procedure, found in module FILESLIB.BAS.

The QuitCom_Click procedure exits the application.

The UpdateList procedure updates the selected files stored in the WHEREIS.DAT file.

The ViewCom_Click procedure views the selected file by loading the View-File form as a modal form.

Part Four

Text processing utilities

This part of the book presents a collection of utilities that perform various types of text processing. The next few chapters introduce the following utilities:

- The CATALOG.MAK project, which sorts the procedures of Visual Basic .TXT listing files by procedure name.
- The DIRCAT.MAK project, which allows you to attach comments to files.
- The XREF.MAK project, which yields a cross reference file for a Visual Basic .TXT file.
- The STRIPREM.MAK project, which removes single-quote remarks from Visual Basic .TXT files.

The last chapter discusses the *QuickPak Professional for Windows* package, a Visual Basic library of routines produced by Crescent Software. That chapter also includes the BackUp and SDIR utilities, which perform tasks not possible with the current version of Visual Basic.

20
The Listing Sort utility

Visual Basic offers the Save Text option in the Code menu to save the code attached to a form or a module in a text file with the default file extension .TXT. However, the procedures in the output text files appear in the order in which you typed them rather than alphabetically. This disorder makes it difficult to locate a particular procedure in a long listing with many procedures. This chapter presents a utility that solves this problem. The program, stored in project CATALOG.MAK, reads the text file produced by Visual Basic and rewrites it so that the procedures are listed alphabetically.

The visual interface of the program contains various types of list boxes, command buttons, and a text box. These controls include the Drive, Directory, and Files list boxes that enable you to locate and select the file you want to process. The command buttons allow you to exit the program, sort the listing file, view a text file, and print a text file. The multiline scrollable text box facilitates viewing text files. I have included viewing and printing options for added convenience.

When you click on the Sort listing file button, the current selection in the Files list box is processed. The program reads through the source listing file and scans for Sub and Function declarations; the text lines are stored in a list box. The utility stores the name of each Sub or Function procedure along with the declaration line numbers and the number of lines they occupy. Then the program sorts the data related to procedures, using the procedure name as the sort key. Finally, it writes the .TXT file with the general declarations written first, followed by the various procedures in name order.

Figures 20-1 to 20-3 contain the specifications for the CATALOG.MAK project file and the CATALOG.FRM form file. Figure 20-4 shows a sample session with the program.

Application name: Listing Sort Utility
Application code name: CATALOG

Version: 1.1   Date created: September 6, 1991   **20-1** The basic
Programmer(s): Namir Clement Shammas   specifications for the
Lists of filenames   CATALOG.MAK project
                                                              file.
Storage path: \ VB \ VBXTOOL
Project   CATALOG.MAK
Global   GLOBAL.BAS (not used)
Form 1   CATALOG.FRM

Form # 1   Form filename: CATALOG.FRM
Version: 1.1   Date: September 6, 1991

Control object type	Default CtlName	Purpose
Drive list box	Drive1	Shows and selects the current drive
Directory list	Dir1	Shows and selects the current directory
File list box	File1	Shows a group of files
List box	List1	Stores the text lines of the sorted .TXT file
Text box	Text1	Specifies the filename pattern
	Text2	Views a text file
Command box	Command1	Exits the program
	Command2	Sorts the procedures of a listing file
	Command3	Loads a text file for viewing
	Command4	Prints a text file
Label	Label1	Label for filename pattern
	Label2	Label for Drive list box
	Label3	Label for Directory list box
	Label4	Label for File list box

20-2 The list of controls in the CATALOG.FRM form file.

Application (code) name: CATALOG
Form # 1
Version: 1.1   Date: September 7, 1991

Original control name	Property	New setting
Form	Caption	Program to Sort VB Procedures in .TXT files
Drive1	CtlName	DiskDrv
Dir1	CtlName	TreeDir

20-3 The customized settings for the CATALOG.FRM form.

Original control name	Property	New setting
File1	CtlName	FileFlb
List1	CtlName	LinesLst
	Visible	False
Text1	CtlName	PatternBox
	Text	(empty string)
Text2	CtlName	TextBox
	Text	(empty string)
	MultiLine	True
	ScrollBars	3 - Both
Command1	CtlName	QuitBtn
	Caption	&Quit
	Cancel	True
Command2	CtlName	SortVBfileBtn
	Caption	&Sort VB .TXT file
Command3	CtlName	ViewFileBtn
	Caption	&View File
Command4	CtlName	PrintBtn
	Caption	&Print File
Label1	CtlName	PatternLbl
	Caption	Filename:
Label2	CtlName	DriveLbl
	Caption	Drive:
Label3	CtlName	DirectoryLbl
	Caption	Directory:
Label4	CtlName	FilesLbl
	Caption	Files:

20-3 Continued.

Listing 20-1 shows the code attached to the CATALOG.FRM form. You should note that Listing 20-1 was obtained by using the Listing Sort Utility program itself. The procedures that are relevant to the sorting process are presented next.

The Form_Load procedure sets the WindowState property to 2 (maximized), the file pattern to *.TXT, and the Archive and Normal file attribute properties to True. The rest of the file attribute properties are set to False.

☞ The GetFunctionName function extracts the name of the function from a text line. It assumes that the function declarations appear in the following general format; leading spaces or tab characters are not allowed:

Function *functionName* (...

The dots mean that what comes after the open parenthesis is not relevant to the GetFunctionName function. This format is generated by Visual Basic; the Listing Sort utility assumes that you do not change the format. The

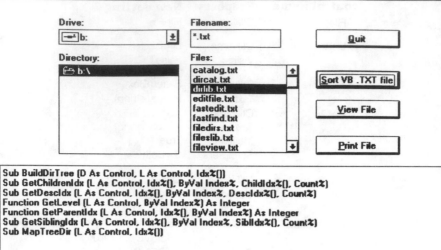

Drive:
`📀 b:`

Filename:
`*.txt`

Directory:
`📂 b:\`

Files:
```
catalog.txt
dircat.txt
dirlib.txt
editfile.txt
fastedit.txt
fastfind.txt
filedirs.txt
fileslib.txt
fileview.txt
```

Quit

Sort VB .TXT file

View File

Print File

```
Sub BuildDirTree (D As Control, L As Control, Idx%())
Sub GetChildrenIdx (L As Control, Idx%(), ByVal Index%, ChildIdx%(), Count%)
Sub GetDescIdx (L As Control, Idx%(), ByVal Index%, DescIdx%(), Count%)
Function GetLevel (L As Control, ByVal Index%) As Integer
Function GetParentIdx (L As Control, Idx%(), ByVal Index%) As Integer
Sub GetSiblingIdx (L As Control, Idx%(), ByVal Index%, SiblIdx%(), Count%)
Sub MapTreeDir (L As Control, Idx%())
```

20-4   A sample session with the Listing Sort Utility.

Listing 20-1   The code attached to the CATALOG.FRM form.

```
Const True = -1, False = 0

Sub DiskDrv_Change ()
  ' update file tree path when the disk is changed
  TreeDir.Path = DiskDrv.Drive
End Sub

Sub Form_Load ()
  WindowState = 2
  PatternBox.Text = "*.txt"
  FileFlb.Filename = "*.txt"
  ' set Archive and Normal attributes to True and all
  ' of the other file attributes to False
  FileFlb.Archive = True
  FileFlb.Normal = True
  FileFlb.Hidden = False
  FileFlb.ReadOnly = False
  FileFlb.System = False
End Sub

Function GetFunctionName (TextLine As String) As String
' get the name of the declared Function
  Dim I As Integer, L As Integer
  ' locate the open parenthesis
  I = InStr(TextLine, " (") - 1
  L = Len("Function ")
  ' extract the name of the function
  GetFunctionName = UCase$(Mid$(TextLine, L + 1, I - L))
End Function
```

Listing 20-1 Continued.

```
Function GetSubName (TextLine As String) As String
' get the name of the procedure
  Dim I As Integer, L As Integer
  ' locate the open parenthesis
  I = InStr(TextLine, " (") - 1
  L = Len("Sub ")
  ' extract the file name
  GetSubName = UCase$(Mid$(TextLine, L + 1, I - L))
End Function

Function Max (I As Integer, J As Integer) As Integer
' return the larger value of I or J
  If I > J Then
    Max = I
  Else
    Max = J
  End If
End Function

Sub PatternBox_KeyPress (KeyAScii As Integer)
  KeyAScii = Asc(LCase$(Chr$(KeyAScii)))
End Sub

Sub PatternBox_LostFocus ()
  Dim I As Integer
  If PatternBox.Text = "" Then PatternBox.Text = "*.*"
  ' locate and remove multiple wildcards
  I = InStr(PatternBox.Text, " ") ' find first space
  If I > 0 Then
    PatternBox.Text = Mid$(PatternBox.Text, 1, I - 1)
  End If
  FileFlb.Filename = PatternBox.Text
End Sub

Sub PrintFileCom_Click ()
' performs a simple print task
  Dim F As String, TextLine As String
  Dim LineNum As Integer
  If FileFlb.Filename <> "" Then
    Form1.MousePointer = 11 ' hourglass
    LineNum = FreeFile ' get the next file buffer
    ' obtain the full filename
    F = TreeDir.Path
    If Right$(F, 1) <> "\" Then F = F + "\"
    F = F + FileFlb.Filename
    Open F For Input As #LineNum ' open file
    ' read each line and print it
    Do While Not EOF(LineNum)
      Line Input #LineNum, TextLine
      Printer.Print TextLine
    Loop
    Printer.EndDoc ' close printer buffer
    Close #LineNum ' close file buffer
    Form1.MousePointer = 0 ' restore mouse pointer
  End If
End Sub

Sub QuitBtn_Click ()
  End
End Sub

Sub SortProcedureData (ProcName$(), LineNum%(), LineCount%(), N%)
' perform a Combsort on the arrays ProcName, LineNum, and LineCount.
' The arrays are sorted by using the data in ProcName.
  Dim Skip As Integer, InOrder As Integer
  Dim I As Integer, J As Integer
  Dim T As Integer
```

Listing 20-1 Continued.

```
    Skip = N%
    Do
       Skip = Max(Int(Skip / 1.3), 1)
       InOrder = True
       For I = 1 To N% - Skip
          J = I + Skip
          If ProcName$(I) > ProcName$(J) Then
             ' swap array members
             InOrder = False
             ProcName$(0) = ProcName$(I)
             ProcName$(I) = ProcName$(J)
             ProcName$(J) = ProcName$(0)
             T = LineNum%(I)
             LineNum%(I) = LineNum%(J)
             LineNum%(J) = T
             T = LineCount%(I)
             LineCount%(I) = LineCount%(J)
             LineCount%(J) = T
          End If
       Next I
    Loop Until InOrder And (Skip = 1)
End Sub

Sub SortVBfileBtn_Click ()
    Dim NL As String * 2
    Dim F As String
    Dim TextLine As String
    Dim MainFilename As String ' main filename
    Dim ExtFilename As String  ' extension name
    ' declare file I/O channel variables
    Dim FileNum As Integer
    ' declare the procedure counter
    Dim CountProc As Integer
    Dim I As Integer, J As Integer, K As Integer
    ' declare dynamic arrays for procedure names
    Dim ProcName() As String ' name
    Dim LineNum() As Integer ' line number
    Dim LineCount() As Integer ' line count
    '--------------------------------
    If FileFlb.Filename = "" Then Exit Sub
    NL = Chr$(13) + Chr$(10)
    MousePointer = 11 ' hour-glass
    ' obtain the full filename
    F = TreeDir.Path
    If Right$(F, 1) <> "\" Then F = F + "\"
    F = F + FileFlb.Filename
    TextBox.Text = "" ' clear text box
    ' clear the LinesLst list box
    Do While LinesLst.ListCount
       LinesLst.RemoveItem 0
    Loop
    FileNum = FreeFile ' get the next file buffer
    Open F For Input As #FileNum
    I = 0 ' initialize the number of lines
    CountProc = 0 ' initialize procedure counter
    ' loop to read each line
    Do While Not EOF(FileNum)
       Line Input #FileNum, TextLine
       ' does the line read contain the declaration of a Sub or Function?
       If (InStr(TextLine,"Sub ")=1) Or (InStr(TextLine,"Function "))=1) Then
          CountProc = CountProc + 1 ' increment the procedure counter
       End If
       LinesLst.AddItem TextLine, I
       I = I + 1
    Loop
    Close #FileNum ' close file buffer
    ' redimension the arrays
```

Listing 20-1 Continued.

```
ReDim ProcName(0 To CountProc)
ReDim LineNum(0 To CountProc)
ReDim LineCount(0 To CountProc)
CountProc = 0 ' reset the procedure counter
' set the index to the general declarations section to 0
LineNum(0) = 0
' examine the lines in the LinesLst list box
For I = 0 To LinesLst.ListCount - 1
  ' copy the current line into TextLine
  TextLine = LinesLst.List(I)
  ' is there a Sub declaration in the current text line?
  If InStr(TextLine, "Sub ") = 1 Then
    LineCount(CountProc) = I - LineNum(CountProc)
    CountProc = CountProc + 1
    ProcName(CountProc) = GetSubName(TextLine) ' get procedure name
    LineNum(CountProc) = I
    ' insert procedure heading in the text box
    TextBox.Text = TextBox.Text + TextLine + NL
  ' is there a Function declaration in the current text line?
  ElseIf InStr(TextLine, "Function ") = 1 Then
    LineCount(CountProc) = I - LineNum(CountProc)
    CountProc = CountProc + 1
    ProcName(CountProc) = GetFunctionName(TextLine) ' get function name
    LineNum(CountProc) = I
    ' insert procedure heading in the text box
    TextBox.Text = TextBox.Text + TextLine + NL
  End If
Next I
LineCount(CountProc) = LinesLst.ListCount - LineNum(CountProc)
If CountProc = 0 Then ' found no procedures
  MsgBox "No Sub or Function were found", 0, "Information"
  Form1.MousePointer = 0 ' restore mouse pointer
  Exit Sub
  End If
  ' sort the data
  SortProcedureData ProcName(), LineNum(), LineCount(), CountProc
  FileNum = FreeFile ' get the next file buffer
  ' open the file for output
  Open F For Output As #FileNum
  For I = 0 To CountProc
    K = LineNum(I)
    For J = 0 To LineCount(I) - 1
      Print #FileNum, LinesLst.List(K + J)
    Next J
  Next I
  Close #FileNum ' close output buffer
  MousePointer = 0 ' restore mouse cursor
End Sub

Sub TextBox_KeyPress (KeyAScii As Integer)
  KeyAScii = 0
End Sub

Sub TreeDir_Change ()
  FileFlb.Path = TreeDir.Path
End Sub

Sub ViewFileBtn_Click ()
' view the target file in TextBox
  Dim F As String, TextLine As String
  Dim LineNum As Integer
  Dim NL As String * 2
  If FileFlb.Filename <> "" Then
    NL = Chr$(13) + Chr$(10)
    LineNum = FreeFile ' get the next file buffer
    F = TreeDir.Path
    If Right$(F, 1) <> "\" Then F = F + "\"
```

Listing 20-1 Continued.

```
      F = F + FileFlb.Filename
      Open F For Input As #LineNum
      F = ""
      Do While Not EOF(LineNum)
        Line Input #LineNum, TextLine
        F = F + TextLine + NL
      Loop
      Close #LineNum
      TextBox.Text = F
  End If
End Sub
```

Function keyword must appear in this form and there must be a single space before and after the function name.

☞ The GetSubName function extracts the name of the Sub procedure from a text line. The GetSubName procedure assumes that the procedure declaration appears in the following general format; leading spaces or tab characters are not allowed:

Sub *procedureName* (...

The dots mean that what comes after the open parenthesis is not relevant to the GetSubName procedure. This format is generated by Visual Basic; the Listing Sort Utility assumes that you do not change it. The Sub keyword must appear in this form and there must be a single space before and after the procedure name.

The Max function returns the larger value of argument I or J.

The SortProcedureData sorts the arrays that store the names of the procedures and their sequence in the original text file. The SortProcedureData uses the new Combsort method that was developed by Richard Box and Stephen Lacey (see their article in the April 1991 issue of *BYTE* magazine). The algorithm of this method resembles that of the Shell-Metzner sort. However, the Combsort method is two to three times faster than the Shell-Metzner method if the original array is not sorted. By contrast, if the original array is in reverse order, the Combsort is hardly faster.

The SortVBfileBtn_Click procedure is the workhorse of the program. This procedure declares a number of variables. The arrays ProcName, LineNum, and LineCount are declared as dynamic. The ProcName array stores the name of the procedures; the LineNum array stores the line number in which the procedures appear in the source listing file; and the LineCount array contains the number of lines that a procedure occupies.

The procedure changes the mouse cursor to the hourglass, obtains the full name of the listing file being processed, and stores it in the variable F. This process may involve appending a \ character to the directory name. Then the procedure sets the procedure counter variable Countproc to 0, clears the scrollable text box and the list box LinesLst, and opens the source file for input.

Next, the procedure reads the text lines of the source listing file, and counts the total number of lines and total number of routines, which is stored in the variable CountProc. The text lines are stored in the invisible list box LinesLst, with each text line stored as a separate member. At this point source listing file is closed.

The procedure now redimensions the dynamic arrays ProcName, LineNum, and LineCount to have a range of indices from 0 to CountProc; it also resets the value of variable CountProc to 0, and scans the members of the list box LinesLst for the declarations of procedures. As each declaration is detected, its name and line number are stored in the arrays ProcName and LineNum. At the same time, the LineCount array stores the size of the previous procedure. When the For-Next loop used for these subtasks ends, the LineCount element for the last procedure is calculated. The declarations of the procedures are also displayed in the scrollable text box.

The procedure's next operation is to examine the value of the CountProc variable. If it is zero, the source file has no procedures; a message box appears to tell you this. If not, the procedure sorts the arrays Proc Name, LineNum, and LineCount by calling procedure SortProcedureData. The elements of ProcName are used in ordering both arrays. The target listing file is opened for output, and a For-Next loop is used to copy the lines from the LinesLst list box into the target listing file. The element LineNum(I) supplies the line number where the procedure is declared. A nested For-Next loop copies LineCount(I) number of lines to the target listing file.

Before exiting, the procedure closes the target listing file and restores the mouse cursor to its default setting.

21
The Directory Catalog utility

Have you ever looked at a set of old files and wondered what these files did? This is a very common problem that most of us experience. There are a number of DOS utilities that allow you to attach one line comments to a file. This chapter presents a similar utility that works under Windows. I will discuss the basic idea for crafting such a utility and then present some modifications.

The basic idea

The approach for implementing the Directory Catalog utility is to "divide and conquer." Rather than storing all of the comments for all of the files in one data file, each directory will have a catalog data file that contains the notes and comments for the files in that directory. The filename DIR CAT.CAT is a suitable name for the catalog data file; if you want to use another filename, be sure to change the filename in the code *before* you start using the utility.

The next steps in developing the design for the utility determine how the information is read, edited, and written. First, let's focus on the format of the information handled by the utility. This format maintains the name of the files in the current directory and their accompanying comments. A list box will serve to store each filename and its comment. To handle the varying filename length, there should be a fixed number of characters reserved for the filename, regardless of its length. Sorted filenames are padded with spaces. This approach guarantees that the attached comment starts at a fixed character in a list box member.

What about entering and editing the comments? A text box can be used for entering new comments and editing existing ones. The Edit text box should contain a copy of the comments attached to a file. When writing or editing a comment is finished, the new comment is copied back into the selected file, overwriting the previous comment.

Writing the member of the list box to the catalog data file is a straightforward file output process. By contrast, reading the catalog data file is a more complex matter. First, consider the case when you attach comments to the files of a directory for the first time. Initially, there are no comments present. Another possibility is that the existing catalog data file might not contain current information on the files in the current directory; this condition would exist if you added new files or deleted old ones after the last time you recorded the comments for that directory. The following rules are used to handle these problems:

- If the catalog data file does not exist, the list box is supplied the names of the files that are in the current directory.
- If the catalog data file exists, it is read and then checked against a current list of files in the current directory. This involves adding new files to the list box and removing deleted files. When these steps are done, the list box contains an accurate list of files.

Losing the comment attached to a deleted file will upset very few of us; however, when renaming a file, the utility should be able to preserve the comments attached to the file. This feature requires controls that enable you to rename a file and retain its comment. Of course, you can rename a file outside the utility and end up losing the attached comment. There is no remedy for that problem; after all, this is Visual Basic programming—not magic!

The catalog utility

Now that we have discussed the general design of the directory catalog utility, let's focus on more specific areas. Figure 21-1 shows a sample session with the DIRCAT.FRM form. The form contains the following controls:

- The Drive list box, which allows you to select a new drive.
- The Directory list box, which permits you to choose a new directory.
- An invisible file list box, which is used by the utility to obtain the current list of files in the current drive and directory.
- The Comment Edit text box, which allows you to enter new comments and edit current ones.
- The list box that displays the filenames with their attached comments.
- The Edit Comment button, which begins editing the comment of the selected list box member.
- The Save Comment button, which saves the comment in the selected list box member.

- The Save Comment File button, which enables you to explicitly save the filenames and comments found in the list box.
- The Rename File button, which enables you to rename the file in the selected list box member, and retain its comments.

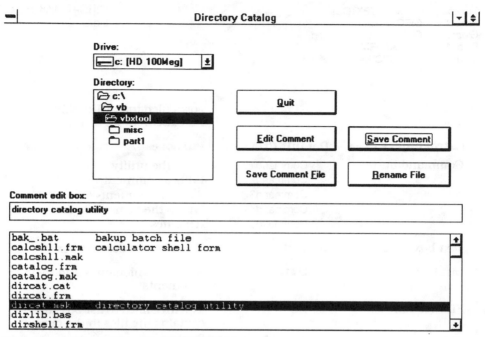

21-1 A sample session with DIRCAT.FRM form.

Using the Directory Catalog utility is fairly easy. When you begin to use the utility, the list of files that appears in the list box contains no comments. To add or edit a comment, you can click or double click on the selected list member, or click on the Edit Comment button. This copies any comment into the comment edit text box. You can then type in a new comment or edit the current one. The edited comment is placed back in the list box when the text box loses its focus; this can be done by clicking on another list member or other buttons.

Using the Drive and Directory list boxes, you can navigate to other directories. When you leave the current directory, the utility stores the catalog data file in that directory. Then, the program attempts to read the catalog data file in the new directory. The utility automatically saves the catalog data file; using the Save Comment File button is optional.

You can experiment with the utility before you read more about it. This should give you a good idea of what the utility does.

Figures 21-2 to 21-4 contain the specifications of the DIRCAT.MAK project file and the DIRCAT.FRM form file. Notice that the list box uses the fixed-pitch Courier font, which causes the comments to appear aligned.

Application name: Directory catalog utility
Application code name: DIRCAT

Version: 1.0   Date created: September 8, 1991
Programmer(s): Namir Clement Shammas

List of filenames

Storage path: \ VB \ VBXTOOL
Project   DIRCAT.MAK
Global   GLOBAL.BAS (not used)
Form 1   DIRCAT.FRM
Module 1   GENERIC.BAS

21-2 The basic specifications for the DIRCAT.MAK project file.

Form # 1
Version: 1.0

Form filename: DIRCAT.FRM
Date: September 8, 1991

Control object type	Default CtlName	Purpose
Command button	Command1	Exits the utility
	Command2	Edits a comment
	Command3	Saves a comment
	Command4	Writes the comments to file
	Command5	Renames a file
Text box	Text1	The Comment Edit text box
List box	List1	Stores the filenames and their comments
File list box	File1	The invisible File list box that contains the files in the current path
Directory list box	Dir1	The Directory list box
Drive list box	Drive1	The Drive list box
Label	Label1	Label for the Comment Edit text box
	Label2	Label for the Directory list box
	Label3	Label for the Drive list box

21-3 The list of controls in the DIRCAT.FRM form file.

Listing 21-1 contains the code attached to the form DIRCAT.FRM. The form declares the following constants:

- The True and False constants.
- The FILENAME_SIZE constant, which specifies the number of characters reserved for the filename. Setting this to 14 ensures that there is at least one space character between the filename and its accompanying comment.
- The DIR_CAT_FILE constant, which specifies the name of the catalog data file.

Application (code) name: DIRCAT
Form # 1
Version: 1.0   Date: September 8, 1991

Original control name	Property	New setting
Form	Caption	Directory Catalog
Command1	CtlName	QuitBtn
	Caption	&Quit
Command2	CtlName	EditCommentBtn
	Caption	&Edit Comment
Command3	CtlName	SaveCommentBtn
	Caption	&Save Comment
Command4	CtlName	SaveCommentFileBtn
	Caption	Save Comment &File
Command5	CtlName	RenameFileBtn
	Caption	&Rename File
Text1	CtlName	EditBox
	Text	(empty text)
List1	CtlName	FilesLst
	Sorted	True
	FontName	Courier
	FontSize	9.75
	FontBold	False
File1	CtlName	FileFlb
	Visible	False
Dir1	CtlName	TreeDir
Drive1	CtlName	DiskDrv
Label1	CtlName	EditLbl
	Caption	Comment edit box:
Label2	CtlName	DirectoryLbl
	Caption	Directory:
Label3	CtlName	DriveLbl
	Caption	Drive:

21-4 The customized settings for the DIRCAT.FRM form.

The form also declares a number of form-level variables:

- The Boolean FileUpdated variable, which determines whether or not the catalog data file was updated.
- The EditIndex variable, which stores the index of the selected list box member.
- The CurDirCatFile variable, which stores the full path and name of the current catalog data file.

Listing 21-1   The code attached to the form DIRCAT.FRM.

```
Const True = -1, False = 0
Const FILENAME_SIZE = 14
' declare the constant for the name of the
' directory catalog data file
Const DIR_CAT_FILE = "DIRCAT.CAT"


Dim FileUpdated As Integer ' file update flag
Dim EditIndex As Integer
Dim CurDirCatFile As String

Sub DiskDrv_Change ()
   ' update file tree path when the disk is changed
   TreeDir.Path = DiskDrv.Drive
End Sub

Sub EditCommentBtn_Click ()
' Edit the comment attached to the currently selected
' member of the list box FilesLst.
   ' is there is selected item?
   If FilesLst.ListIndex > -1 Then
      ' extract the comment part of the list member, starting
      ' at character FILENAME_SIZE + 1.
      EditBox.Text = Mid$(FilesLst.Text, FILENAME_SIZE + 1)
      ' store the index of the selected list member in
      ' the variable EditIndex
      EditIndex = FilesLst.ListIndex
   End If
End Sub

Sub FilesLst_Click ()
' Treat a click event by invoking the procedure EditCommentBtn_Click
   EditCommentBtn_Click
End Sub

Sub FilesLst_DblClick ()
' Treat a double click event by invoking the
' procedure EditCommentBtn_Click
   EditCommentBtn_Click
End Sub

Sub Form_Load ()
' Load the form.
   WindowState = 2 ' maximize the application window
   FileFlb.Filename = "*.*" ' set the filename pattern
   ' set Archive and Normal attributes to True and all
   ' of the other file attributes to False
   FileFlb.Archive = True
   FileFlb.Normal = True
   FileFlb.Hidden = False
   FileFlb.ReadOnly = False
   FileFlb.System = False
   ' clear the file updated flag
   FileUpdated = True
   ' load the directory catalog file, if exists
   LoadDirCatFile
   ' set the index of the edited list member as -1 (no selection)
   EditIndex = -1
End Sub

Function GetExtname (ByVal S$) As String
' Extract the extended filename.
   Dim I As Integer
   ' find the location of the dot in the filename S$
   I = InStr(S$, ".")
```

Listing 21-1 Continued.

```
    ' is there a dot in the filename S$?
    If I > 0 Then
      ' extract the characters that are past the dot
      GetExtname = Mid$(S$, I + 1)
    Else
      ' return an empty string
      GetExtname = ""
    End If
End Function

Function GetFilename (ByVal S$) As String
' Extract the primary or main filename.
    Dim I As Integer
    ' find the location of the dot in the filename S$
    I = InStr(S$, ".")
    ' is there a dot in the filename S$?
    If I > 0 Then
      ' return the first I-1 character as the primary filename
      GetFilename = Left$(S$, I - 1)
    Else
      ' return the entire string S$ as the primary filename
      GetFilename = S$
    End If
End Function


Sub LoadDirCatFile ()
' Load the directory catalog file from the current directory.
    Dim S As String, F As String
    Dim I As Integer
    Dim FileNum As Integer
    Dim FileStr As String * FILENAME_SIZE
EditBox.Text = "" ' clear comment edit box
' save the current dir-cat file?
If Not FileUpdated Then SaveDirCatFile
' get the current path
S = TreeDir.List(-1)
' append a "\" if needed
If Right$(S, 1) <> "\" Then S = S + " \"
' assign the full filename of the directory catalog data file
' to the variable CurDirCatFile
CurDirCatFile = S + DIR_CAT_FILE
' does the CurDirCatFile file exist?
If Dir$(CurDirCatFile) <> "" Then
    ' read the file and store the lines in the
    ' list box FilesLst
    If ReadList(FilesLst, CurDirCatFile, False) Then
        ' delete the files that are in the FilesLst list box
        ' but not in the FileFlb file list box.  These
        ' filenames must be removed because they represent
        ' file that were deleted since the last time the
        ' DIRCAT.CAT file was written.
        For I = FilesLst.ListCount - 1 To 0 Step -1
            ' get the member I of the FilesLst
            F = RTrim$(Mid$(FilesLst.List(I), 1, FILENAME_SIZE))
            ' is that member NOT in the files list box?
            If BinSearch(FileFlb, F, 1, 1, 0) = -1 Then
                ' remove it
                FilesLst.RemoveItem I
            End If
        Next I
    End If
    ' insert new files in the FilesLst list box.  These
    ' files were created after the last time the DIRCAT.CAT
    ' data file was written.
    For I = 0 To FileFlb.ListCount - 1
      ' get file member I
      FileStr = FileFlb.List(I)
```

Listing 21-1 Continued.

```
                  ' is that file NOT in the FilesLst list box?
                  If BinSearch(FilesLst, FileStr, 1, 1, FILENAME_SIZE) = -1 Then
                     ' add that file
                     FilesLst.AddItem FileStr
                  End If
               Next I
            Else
               ' clear the FilesLst list box
               CLearList FilesLst
               ' add the files of the FileFlb file list box to
               ' the FilesLst list box.  There is no need for
               ' an index with the AddItem method, since the
               ' FilesLst control has its Sorted property set to
               ' True.
               For I = 0 To FileFlb.ListCount - 1
                  FileStr = FileFlb.List(I)
                  FilesLst.AddItem FileStr
               Next I
            End If
         End Sub

         Sub QuitBtn_Click ()
         ' Exit the application
            ' save the current dir-cat file?
            If Not Updated Then SaveDirCatFile
            End
         End Sub

         Sub RenameFileBtn_Click ()
         ' Rename a file while preserving the comments associated
         ' with that file.
            Dim OldFilename As String
            Dim NewFilename As String
            Dim DirStr As String
            Dim S1 As String, S2 As String
            Dim I As Integer, J As Integer
            ' get the index of the selected FilesLst list member
            I = FilesLst.ListIndex
            ' is there a selected member?
            If I > -1 Then
               ' extract the old filename from the selected list member
               OldFilename = RTrim$(Mid$(FilesLst.Text, 1, FILENAME_SIZE))
               ' obtain the current path
               DirStr = TreeDir.List(-1)
               ' append a "\" character to DirStr, if needed
               If Right$(DirStr, 1) <> "\" Then DirStr = DirStr + "\"
               ' get the new filename by prompting the user
               NewFilename = InputBox$("Enter new filename", "Input", OldFilename)
               ' is the new filename not an empty string
               If NewFilename <> "" Then
                  ' convert the new filename into lowercase characters
                  NewFilename = LCase$(NewFilename)
                  ' set the error trap
                  On Error GoTo BadRenameFile
                  ' rename the file
                  Name DirStr + OldFilename As DirStr + NewFilename
                  ' turn off the error trap
                  On Error GoTo 0
                  ' S1 is the string of padded spaces that are appended
                  ' later to the new filename
                  S1 = Space$(FILENAME_SIZE - Len(NewFilename))
                  ' S2 stores the comment associated with the
                  ' selected FilesLst list member
                  S2 = Mid$(FilesLst.List(I), FILENAME_SIZE + 1)
               ' remove the currently selected FilesLst list member
               FilesLst.RemoveItem I
               ' insert the new filename with the old comment
```

Listing 21-1 Continued.

```
        FilesLst.AddItem NewFilename + S1 + S2
        ' clear the file update flag
        FileUpdated = False
    End If
  End If
  Exit Sub
  '******************* Error Handler **************
BadRenameFile:
  MsgBox "Error in renaming File " + OldFilename, 64, "Error"
  Resume ExitRenameFile
ExitRenameFile:
End Sub

Sub SaveCommentBtn_Click ()
' Save currently edited comment by
' calling the procedure FileBox_LostFocus
  EditBox_LostFocus
End Sub

Sub SaveCommentFileBtn_Click ()
' Save the directory catalog file.
  SaveDirCatFile
End Sub

Sub SaveDirCatFile ()
' Save the directory catalog file.
  ' was there an error while saving the data file?
  If Not WriteList(FilesLst, CurDirCatFile) Then
    MsgBox "Error in writing file " + CurDirCatFile, 64, "File I/O Error"
  End If
End Sub

Sub TreeDir_Change ()
' Handle the change in directory.
  ' update path
  FileFlb.Path = TreeDir.Path
  ' load the catalog directory file from the current directory
  LoadDirCatFile
End Sub

Sub EditBox_LostFocus ()
  If EditIndex > -1 Then
    FilesLst.List(EditIndex) = Mid$(FilesLst.List(EditIndex), 1,
FILENAME_SIZE) + EditBox.Text
    EditIndex = -1
    FileUpdated = False
  End If
End Sub
```

The form's procedures are described in the paragraphs that follow.

The DiskDrv_Change procedure updates the file tree path when the disk is changed.

The EditBox_LostFocus procedure places the string of the edit text box back in the selected list box member. In addition, the routine sets the EditIndex variable to −1, and assigns False to the Boolean variable FileUp dated; this ensures the prompt update of the comments.

The EditCommentBtn_Click procedure copies the comment attached to the selected member of the list box FilesLst to the comment edit text box. It also stores the index of the selected list member in the variable EditIndex.

The FilesLst_Click procedure handles a click event by invoking the procedure EditCommentBtn_Click. Thus, clicking on a list member copies the comment in that member to the comment edit text box.

The FilesLst_DblClick procedure handles a double click event by invoking the procedure EditCommentBtn_Click.

The Form_Load procedure initializes the form. The procedure maximizes the application's window, sets the filename pattern *.*, sets the Archive and Normal attributes to True, and sets all other file attributes to False. Then it clears the FileUpdated flag, and loads the catalog data file from the current directory, if the data file exists. Then the procedure sets the index of the edited list member to −1 (no selection).

The GetExtname function extracts the extended filename from a given filename.

The GetFilename function extracts the primary filename.

The LoadDirCatFile procedure loads the directory catalog file from the current directory. The procedure clears the Comment Edit text box, then saves the current catalog data file to update it, if the FileUpdate variable is False. Then the procedure obtains the current path and stores it in the local string variable S, appending a \ character if the last character in S is not a \. Next, the full filename of the directory catalog data file is assigned to the form-level variable CurDirCatFile, and the catalog data file is read if it exists in the current directory. The text lines are stored in the FilesLst list box. The routine then deletes the names of the files in FilesLst that are not found in the FilesFlb file list box, which has the actual files in the current directory.

Next, the procedure inserts the new files in the FilesLst list box. These files were created after the last time the DIRCAT.CAT data file was written. Initially, the new files exist in the FileFlb file list box and not in the FilesLst list box.

If the catalog data file does not exist, the procedure clears the FilesLst box and adds the files of the FileFlb file list box to the FilesLst list box. There is no need for an index with the AddItem method, because the FilesLst control has its Sorted property set to True.

The QuitBtn_Click procedure updates the catalog data file (if needed) and exits the application.

The RenameFileBtn_Click procedure renames a file and preserves the comments associated with that file. The procedure obtains the index of the selected FilesLst member and stores it in the local variable I. If there is a selected file, the procedure performs the subsequent tasks; otherwise, it takes no further action. The procedure extracts the old filename from the selected list member, and obtains the current directory and stores it in the variable DirStr, appending a \ character if the string in DirStr does not end with one.

The procedure obtains the new filename by prompting the user. If the new filename differs from the old filename, the routine continues; otherwise, it takes no further action. Assuming the filename differs, the procedure converts the new filename into lowercase characters, and then sets an error trap for the renaming process. The procedure uses the Visual Basic Name statement to rename the client file. It stores the string of padded spaces in the local variable S1; this string is later appended to the new filename.

At this point, the procedure stores in variable S2 the comment associated with the selected FilesLst member. Then it removes the currently selected FilesLst member and inserts the new filename with the old comment into the FilesLst list box. Since the Sorted property of the list box is True, the new string is inserted in the proper location. Finally, the procedure assigns False to the UpdateList variable. If there is an error while renaming the file, the error-handling code displays an error message.

The SaveCommentBtn_Click procedure saves the currently edited comment by calling the procedure FileBox_LostFocus.

The SaveCommentFileBtn_Click procedure saves the catalog data file by invoking the procedure SaveDirCatFile.

The SaveDirCatFile procedure saves the directory catalog file using the WriteList procedure from module GENERIC.BAS.

The TreeDir_Change handles the change in directory by updating the path and then loading the catalog data file from the new directory.

22
The XREF utility

You can ask Visual Basic to save the declarations and procedures of a form or module in text files, which can then be used to study and manipulate the copy of the Visual Basic code. Chapter 20 presented a utility that sorts the procedures in such text files; this chapter presents another utility that generates a cross-reference file for a Visual Basic text file. In this chapter you will learn about the basics of scanning identifiers and building a list of line numbers. The later sections of this chapter present the various aspects of the cross-referencing process, which is rather complex.

The XREF basics

The purpose of the cross-referencing utilities in general, and the XREF utility in particular, is to create a list of the identifiers that appear in a code text file; an example is the *.TXT files produced by Visual Basic. Each identifier is accompanied by a list of line numbers where the identifier appears in the text file. Notice that the word *identifier* is used to indicate that the generated cross-reference list can include constants, variables, functions, procedures, and even language keywords.

A full or *maximum* cross-reference list contains every single identifier in the code file, and includes the language keywords. By contrast, a *minimum* cross-reference list contains only the names of the identifiers that you declare and create in the code file. In practice, you may want to use a "middle ground" between these two extreme cases. You might want to exclude some keywords and allow others, in addition to the nonkeyword identifiers. In the case of the maximum cross-reference list, the identifiers found in the listing are simply added to the list of identifiers. On the other hand, if you exclude any keyword, you must first read the list of excluded keywords, and test whether or not the extracted identifiers are members of the keyword list.

☞ The Visual Basic identifiers start with a letter and may contain other letters, digits, and the underscore character. The dot is a special access operator that is used in associating data fields, properties, and methods with other variables and objects. Normally, you exclude the dot from the characters that define an identifier; this causes the variables and objects to be cross-referenced separately from their accompanying data fields, properties, and methods. However, if you allow the dot operator to be considered as part of an identifier's name, then both identifiers are considered as one and appear as such in the cross-reference list. I prefer including the dot as part of the identifier, to obtain a clearer cross-reference list; you can alter the code according to your own preference.

To implement a flexible scheme for determining the set of identifier characters and the list of keywords, you might want to use a special text file, which can be called the keyword data file. The first line of text in this data file is the string that specifies the identifiers. Subsequent text lines contain the keywords and any other identifiers that you wish to exclude from the cross-reference list. Using alternate keyword data files, you can select different levels of cross-referencing your code.

Scanning identifiers

Scanning identifiers in a string of characters is slightly complicated by the presence of comments and string literals. For example, consider the following line of Visual Basic code:

```
Print #1, "Can't find file" + Filename ' print error message
```

The line contains the keyword Print, the user-defined variable Filename, the string literal "Can't find file" and a trailing remark. Notice that the string literal contains a single-quote character which is also used in commenting code. This example shows that scanning a string can be tricky business. You need to exclude the contents of string literal and comments; also, you should exclude numbers—while digits are a legitimate part of an identifier, such as L10, numbers themselves are not identifiers.

The technique involved in correctly scanning identifiers involves what is known as a state engine. This method scans a line of code, one character at a time. At any given moment, the scanner is at a specific state. This state changes depending on the current state and on the scanned character. The scanner presented here has three scanning states: code-mode, comment-mode, and string-mode. These states correspond to the types of text in a listing.

In code-mode, the scanner is looking either at an identifier or at a white space character, such as a space or a punctuation character. Also keep in mind that Visual Basic supports both the single quote comment and the Rem comment. The Rem comment appears on a separate line with Rem keyword as the first word. The scanning process is made easier when the Rem keyword is replaced by single-quote comments.

The initial state of the scanner is the code-mode. While in the code-mode, the following actions occur:

- If the current character is a double-quote, indicating the beginning of a string literal, the scanner state changes to string-mode. If the scanner was looking at an identifier, that identifier is extracted and catalogued.
- If the current character is a single-quote character signaling that the rest of the string is a comment, the scanner switches to the comment-mode, and scanning is terminated. If the scanner was looking at an identifier, it is extracted and catalogued.
- For any other character, the scanner state remains the code-mode, and the scanner examines the current character to determine if a new identifier is detected, the end of the current identifier has been reached, the end of the current identifier has not been reached, or the current character is another white space character (same as the previous one).

While in string-mode, the scanner watches for the closing double-quote character of a string literal. When that character is found, the scanner switches to the code-mode state; it also clears the identifier scanning flag, because the next character might be a white space or the beginning of a comment.

As stated previously, when the scanner reaches the comment-mode, it stops scanning the remaining string characters. This action is typical for languages such as Visual Basic, where comments are assumed to extend to the end of the line. In other languages, such as Pascal and C, comments may be surrounded by code, making the scanner for such languages a bit more complex.

The XREF utility

Now that you have seen the basics of generating a Visual Basic cross-reference list, let's take a look at the XREF utility. Figure 22-1 shows a sample session with that utility. The XREF.FRM contains the following controls:

- The Drive list box enables you to select files on a different drive.
- The Directory list box permits you to change directories.
- The Filename text box allows you to specify the pattern for the Visual Basic text listings. This text box is assigned *.txt, the pattern for the default Visual Basic text files.
- The Files list box permits you to select a listing file to cross-reference.

- A multiline scrollable text box displays the cross-reference list and also allows you to view a text file.
- The Quit button ends the utility.
- The Xref VB .TXT file button generates the cross-reference list. The button displays that list in the scrollable text box and also writes it to an .XRF file that has the same main filename as the selected file.
- The View File button allows you to view the selected text file.
- The Print File button generates a simple printout of the selected file.
- An invisible list box that contains the keywords are excluded from the cross-reference list.
- An invisible cross-reference identifier list.
- An invisible list contains the comma-delimited lists of line numbers associated with the various identifiers.

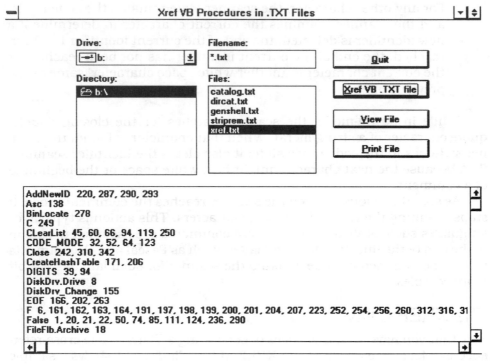

22-1 A sample session with the XREF utility.

Using the XREF utility is fairly straightforward. Select the drive and directory that contains the files you want to cross-reference. You can alter the file pattern if you have stored the Visual Basic listings under a file extension other than .TXT. Next, select a file for processing and click the Xref button. The mouse cursor changes to the hourglass while the utility is generating the cross-reference list; the list appears in the scrollable text box and is also stored in an .XRF file. You can use the View File and Print File buttons to view and print text files. To exit the utility, click on the Quit button, or press ALT + Q.

Figures 22-2 to 22-4 show the specifications for the XREF.MAK project file and the XREF.FRM form file.

Application name: Listings cross-reference utility
Application code name: XREF

Version: 1.0   Date created: September 6, 1991
Programmer(s): Namir Clement Shammas

22-2 The basic specifications for the XREF.MAK project file.

List of filenames

Storage path: ＼VB＼VBXTOOL
Project   XREF.MAX
Global   GLOBAL.BAS (not used)
Form 1   XREF.FRM
Module 1   GENERIC.BAS
Module 2   HASHTABL.BAS

Form # 1   Form filename: XREF.FRM
Version: 1.0   Date: September 6, 1991

Control object type	Default CtlName	Purpose
Drive list box	Drive1	Shows and selects the current drive
Directory list	Dir1	Shows and selects the current directory
File list box	File1	Shows a group of files
List box	List1	Stores reserved keywords
	List2	Stores the cross-referenced identifiers
	List3	Stores the lists of line numbers
Text box	Text1	Specifies the filename pattern
	Text2	Views a text file
Command box	Command1	Exits the program
	Command2	Obtains a cross-reference for the selected file
	Command3	Loads a text file for viewing
	Command4	Prints a text file
Label	Label1	Label for filename pattern
	Label2	Label for Drive list box
	Label3	Label for Directory list box

22-3 The list of controls in the XREF.FRM form file.

Listing 22-1 contains the code attached to the XREF.FRM form. Before discussing these procedures, let me first clarify the roles of the invisible list boxes. The KeyWordLst list box contains the list of keywords. This list is read from the keyword data file and is maintained as a hash table, which enables the program to quickly determine whether or not an identifier is also a keyword. The XrefLst list box stores the cross-referenced identifiers.

Application (code) name: XREF
Form # 1
Version: 1.0   Date: September 7, 1991

Original control name	Property	New setting
Form	Caption	Xref VB Procedures in .TXT Files
Drive1	CtlName	DiskDrv
Dir1	CtlName	TreeDir
File1	CtlName	FileFlb
List1	CtlName	KeyWordLst
	Visible	False
List2	CtlName	XrefLst
	Visible	False
List1	CtlName	LinesLst
	Visible	False
Text1	CtlName	PatternBox
	Text	(empty string)
Text2	CtlName	TextBox
	Text	(empty string)
	MultiLine	True
	ScrollBars	3 - Both
Command1	CtlName	QuitBtn
	Caption	&Quit
	Cancel	True
Command2	CtlName	XrefVBFileBtn
	Caption	&Xref VB .TXT File
Command3	CtlName	ViewFileBtn
	Caption	&View File
Command4	CtlName	PrintBtn
	Caption	&Print File
Label1	CtlName	PatternLbl
	Caption	Filename:
Label2	CtlName	DriveLbl
	Caption	Drive:
Label3	CtlName	DirectoryLbl
	Caption	Directory:

22-4   The customized settings for the XREF.FRM form.

The corresponding list of line numbers is stored in the LinesLst list box. I chose to separate the identifiers from the line number lists to make it easier to search for and insert an identifier; moreover, this approach makes it easier to frequently update the lists of line numbers.

The form declares the True, False, and KEYWORDS_FILE constants. The

Listing 22-1 The code attached to the XREF.FRM form.

```
Const True = -1, False = 0
' Declare constant that specifies the name of the
' keywords data file
Const KEYWORDS_FILE = "C:\VB\VBXTOOL\KEY.DAT"

Sub DiskDrv_Change ()
  ' update file tree path when the disk is changed
  TreeDir.Path = DiskDrv.Drive
End Sub

Sub Form_Load ()
  WindowState = 2 ' maximize window
  ' set initial file pattern
  PatternBox.Text = "*.txt"
  FileFlb.Filename = "*.txt"
  ' set Archive and Normal attributes to True and all
  ' of the other file attributes to False
  FileFlb.Archive = True
  FileFlb.Normal = True
  FileFlb.Hidden = False
  FileFlb.ReadOnly = False
  FileFlb.System = False
End Sub

Sub ParseLine (ByVal S$, ByVal Idchars$, ID$(), IDcount%)
' Parse the parameter S$ into an array of identifiers ID$().
' The Idchars$ parameter specifies the characters that are
' part of an identifier.  The IDcount% parameter returns the
' actual number of identifiers parsed.

  ' declare the constants for the scanning modes
  Const CODE_MODE = 1
  Const REM_MODE = 2
  Const STR_MODE = 3
  ' specify the set of characters that do not make up
  ' an identifier, if these characters are the leading
  ' characters in an identifier's name.  For example,
  ' the number 10 is not an identifier, but L10 is.
  Const DIGITS = "0123456789_."

  Dim Status As Integer
  Dim InWord As Integer
  Dim I As Integer
  Dim Q As String * 1
  Dim C As String * 1

  ' assign the double quote character to the
  ' single-character string variable Q
  Q = Chr$(34)
  InWord = False ' initialize in-word flag
  ' set status to code mode
  Status = CODE_MODE
  ' initialize the identifier count
  IDcount% = 0
  ' Replace REMs with single-quote comments
  ReplaceRem S$
  ' examine every string character
  For I = 1 To Len(S$)
    ' copy the I'th character to C
    C = Mid$(S$, I, 1)
    ' main Select-Case statement
    Select Case Status
      ' scanning code?
      Case CODE_MODE
        ' examine the character in C
```

Listing 22-1 Continued.

```
Select Case C
  ' shift to string mode?
  Case Q
    ' was scanning an identifier?
    If InWord Then
      ' store last identifier
      IDcount% = IDcount% + 1
      ID$(IDcount%) = Mid$(S$, First, I - First)
      InWord = False
    End If
    ' set status to string mode
    Status = STR_MODE
  ' shift to remark?
  Case "'"
    ' was scanning an identifier?
    If InWord Then
      ' store last identifier
      IDcount% = IDcount% + 1
      ID$(IDcount%) = Mid$(S$, First, I - First)
      InWord = False
    End If
    ' exit, since the rest of the string is a remark
    Exit Sub
  ' code mode
  Case Else
    ' is the scanned character in string Idchars$?
    If (InStr(Idchars$, Mid$(S$, I, 1)) > 0) Then
      ' make sure that the identifier starts with a letter
      If (Not InWord) And (InStr(DIGITS, C) = 0) Then
        ' yes, it is.  Mark the first character of the
        ' identifier
        First = I
            ' set InWord to True, since we started scanning
            ' an identifier.
            InWord = True
        End If
      Else
        If InWord Then
          ' increment the identifier count
          IDcount% = IDcount% + 1
          ' extract another identifier and store it in
          ' the array ID$()
          ID$(IDcount%) = Mid$(S$, First, I - First)
          ' set InWord to False, since we finished scanning
          ' an identifier.
          InWord = False
        End If
      End If
    End Select
  ' Scanning a string?
  Case STR_MODE
    ' did the scanner encounter the closing double quote
    ' character of a string literal?
    If C = Q Then
      ' we're back scanning code, but we're not sure if the
      ' next character is actually part of the code.  It
      ' might be a white space or a remark!
      Status = CODE_MODE
      InWord = False
    End If
End Select
Next I
' was scanning an identifier?
If InWord Then
  ' store last identifier
  IDcount% = IDcount% + 1
  ' extract the last identifier
```

Listing 22-1 Continued.

```
        ID$(IDcount%) = Mid$(S$, First, Len(S$) + 1 - First)
   End If
End Sub

Sub PatternBox_KeyPress (KeyAScii As Integer)
  KeyAScii = Asc(LCase$(Chr$(KeyAScii)))
End Sub

Sub PatternBox_LostFocus ()
' Handle change in the filename pattern.
  Dim I As Integer
  If PatternBox.Text = "" Then PatternBox.Text = "*.*"
  ' locate and remove multiple wildcards
  I = InStr(PatternBox.Text, " ") ' find first space
  If I > 0 Then
    PatternBox.Text = Mid$(PatternBox.Text, 1, I - 1)
  End If
  FileFlb.Filename = PatternBox.Text
End Sub

Sub PrintFileCom_Click ()
' Perform a simple print task
  Dim F As String, TextLine As String
  Dim LineNum As Integer
  If FileFlb.Filename <> "" Then
    Form1.MousePointer = 11 ' hour-glass
    LineNum = FreeFile ' get the next file buffer
    ' obtain the full filename
    F = TreeDir.Path
    If Right$(F, 1) <> "\" Then F = F + "\"
    F = F + FileFlb.Filename
    Open F For Input As #LineNum ' open file
    ' read each line and print it
    Do While Not EOF(LineNum)
       Line Input #LineNum, TextLine
       Printer.Print TextLine
    Loop
    Printer.EndDoc ' close printer buffer
    Close #LineNum ' close file buffer
    Form1.MousePointer = 0 ' restore mouse pointer
  End If
End Sub

Sub QuitBtn_Click ()
' Exit the application.
   End
End Sub

Sub TextBox_KeyPress (KeyAScii As Integer)
  KeyAScii = 0
End Sub

Sub TreeDir_Change ()
   FileFlb.Path = TreeDir.Path
End Sub

Sub ViewFileBtn_Click ()
' View the target file in TextBox.
  Dim F As String, TextLine As String
  Dim FileNum As Integer
  Dim NL As String * 2
  If FileFlb.Filename <> "" Then
    NL = Chr$(13) + Chr$(10)
    FileNum = FreeFile ' get the next file buffer
    F = TreeDir.Path
  If Right$(F, 1) <> "\" Then F = F + "\"
```

Listing 22-1 Continued.

```
    F = F + FileFlb.Filename
    Open F For Input As #FileNum
    F = ""
    Do While Not EOF(FileNum)
      Line Input #FileNum, TextLine
      F = F + TextLine + NL
    Loop
    Close #FileNum
    TextBox.Text = F
  End If
End Sub

Sub XrefVBFileBtn_Click ()
' Build the cross-reference list.
  ' declare the maximum number of identifiers per line.  You may
  ' increase this number if you are scanning lines with a lot of
  ' single or double-character identifiers.
  Const MAX_ID_COUNT = 50
  Dim FileNum As Integer
  Dim IDcount As Integer
  Dim LineNum As Integer
  Dim AddNewID As Integer
  Dim LineNumStr As String
  Static Idchars As String
  Dim F As String
  Dim TextLine As String
  Dim NL As String * 2
  ' declare the array of identifiers
  Static ID(1 To MAX_ID_COUNT) As String
  Dim I As Integer, J As Integer
  ' exit if there is no filename pattern
  If FileFlb.Filename = "" Then Exit Sub
  NL = Chr$(13) + Chr$(10)
  MousePointer = 11 ' set the mouse cursor to the hour-glass
  ' is the keyword list empty?
  If KeyWordLst.ListCount = 0 Then
    ' was the list read from the file without error?
    If ReadList(XrefLst, KEYWORDS_FILE, False) Then
      ' read the string containing the set of characters
      ' that make up valid identifiers
      Idchars = XrefLst.List(0)
      XrefLst.RemoveItem 0
      ' create the hash table using list box KeyWordLst
      CreateHashTable KeyWordLst, XrefLst.ListCount
      For I = XrefLst.ListCount - 1 To 0 Step -1
        J = InsertInHashTable(KeyWordLst, XrefLst.List(I), "")
      Next I
    End If
  End If
  ' clear the XrefLst and LinesLst list boxes
  CLearList XrefLst
  CLearList LinesLst
  ' get the current path
  F = TreeDir.Path
  ' append a "\", if needed
  If Right$(F, 1) <> "\" Then F = F + "\"
  ' obtain the full filename
  F = F + FileFlb.Filename
  ' get the next file handle
  FileNum = FreeFile
  ' open the selected file for input
  Open F For Input As #FileNum
  LineNum = 0 ' reset the line number counter
  ' read and process every line in the selected file
  Do While Not EOF(FileNum)
    ' read the next line
    Line Input #FileNum, TextLine
```

Listing 22-1 Continued.

```
LineNum = LineNum + 1 ' increment the line number counter
' obtain a string image of the current line number
LineNumStr = Format$(LineNum)
' parse the current line
ParseLine TextLine, Idchars, ID(), IDcount
' for each identifier extracted from TextLine
For I = 1 To IDcount
  ' is the ID(I) identifier not a keyword?
  If Not IsInHashTable(KeyWordLst, ID(I)) Then
    ' is the XrefLst list box not empty?
    If XrefLst.ListCount > 0 Then
      ' is the identifier already in the XrefLst list?
      J = BinLocate(XrefLst, ID(I), 1, 0)
      If ID(I) <> XrefLst.List(J) Then
        ' add identifier to the XrefLst list
        If ID(I) <= XrefLst.List(J) Then
          XrefLst.AddItem ID(I), J
        Else
          XrefLst.AddItem ID(I), J + 1
        End If
        ' set the new identifier flag
        AddNewID = True
      Else
        ' clear the new identifier flag
        AddNewID = False
      End If
      ' is the new identifier flag set?
      If AddNewID Then
        ' insert new line number in LinesLst
        LinesLst.AddItem ", " + LineNumStr + ", ", J
      Else
        ' is the line number not already in the list?
        If InStr(LinesLst.List(J), ", " + LineNumStr + ", ") = 0 Then
          LinesLst.List(J) = LinesLst.List(J) + LineNumStr + ", "
        End If
      End If
    Else
      ' add the first keyword
      XrefLst.AddItem ID(I), 0
      LinesLst.AddItem ", " + LineNumStr + ", ", 0
    End If
  End If
Next I
Loop
Close #FileNum ' close the input file
' locate the dot in the name of the selected file
I = InStr(F, ".")
If I > 0 Then
  ' set the output filename by replacing the extension name
  ' of the selected file with XRF.
  F = Left$(F, I) + "xrf"
Else
  ' append .XRF to the name of the selected file
  F = F + ".xrf"
End If
' get the next available file handle
FileNum = FreeFile
' open the cross-reference file for output
Open F For Output As #FileNum
F = "" ' clear variable F for reuse
' for each member of the XrefLst list box
For I = 0 To XrefLst.ListCount - 1
  ' build the output text line by appending the identifier name
  ' with the line that contains the comma-delimited list of
  ' line numbers where the identifier appears.
  TextLine = XrefLst.List(I) + LinesLst.List(I)
  ' delete trailing ", "
```

Listing 22-1 Continued.

```
        TextLine = Left$(TextLine, Len(TextLine) - 2)
        J = InStr(TextLine, ", ")
        Mid$(TextLine, J, 2) = "  "
        Print #FileNum, TextLine   ' write line to file
        F = F + TextLine + NL
      Next I
      ' show output in the text box
      TextBox.Text = F
      ' close the output cross-reference file
      Close #FileNum
      ' restore the mouse cursor to its default value
      MousePointer = 0
    End Sub

    Sub ReplaceRem (S$)
    ' Replace the Rem keyword with a single-quote
      S$ = LTrim$(S$)
      ' does the trimmed line start with Rem?
      If Mid$(S$, 1, 4) = "Rem " Then
        ' make the first character a single-quote
        ' comment
        Mid$(S$, 1, 1) = "'"
      End If
    End Sub
```

latter constant defines the full path and name of the keyword data file. If you want to select a different filename, you need to alter the KEYWORDS _FILE constant. If you use multiple keyword data files, you can select the one to use by copying or renaming that file to KEY.DAT.

A description of the procedures used to generate the cross-reference lists follows.

The ParseLine procedure extracts the identifiers from the argument of S$. The parameter IDchars$ contains the set of characters that make up an identifier's name. The array ID$( ) returns the set of extracted identifiers, and the parameter IDcount% reports the actual number of identifiers extracted from S$. The procedure declares the CODE_MODE, REM_MODE, and STR_MODE constants to represent the code-mode, comment-mode, and string-mode states of the scanner. The procedure also declares the constant DIGITS to specify the characters that cannot be the first character in an identifier's name. The procedure uses the DIGITS constant to distinguish between numbers and identifiers. The routine also uses the local variable InWord to determine whether or not the current character is part of an identifier. The procedure performs the following tasks:

In operation, the procedure initializes a number of variables, including the State variable that represents the state of the scanner. Then it invokes the ReplaceRem routine to replace the keyword Rem with a single-quote remark character, and proceeds to examine every character in S$ using a For-Next loop. The procedure scans the characters using the method described earlier in this chapter, extracting any pending identifiers.

The ReplaceRem procedure is a short procedure that replaces the first letter of the keyword Rem with the single-quote character. The routine first trims the leading spaces of its argument S$, then determines whether the string S$ starts with the substring Rem. If so, the procedure assigns the single-quote character to the first character of string S$.

The XrefVBFileBtn_Click procedure builds the cross-reference list. The routine declares the constant MAX_ID_COUNT to specify the size of the string array ID( ). The procedure changes the mouse cursor to the hourglass icon; then, if the KeyWordLst list box is empty, it reads the lines of the KEY.DAT data file into the XrefLst list box. The procedure stores the first member of XrefLst in the Idchars variable before removing that member. The procedure then creates a hash table using the KeyWordLst; the XrefLst list members are inserted in the KeyWordLst list box. Then the XrefLst and LinesLst list boxes are cleared.

Next, the procedure obtains the current path and full name of the selected file, opens the selected file for input as a text file, and resets the line number variable LineNum. Then it reads each line of the selected file, incrementing the LineNum variable and storing its string image in the variable LineNumStr. The procedure then calls ParseLine with the arguments Text Line, Idchars, ID( ), and IDCount.

Next, the procedure uses a For-Next Loop to process each identifier. Each loop iteration performs several subtasks. First, it checks to see if the element ID(I) is a member of the KeyWordLst list box. If not, the element ID(I) is inserted in the cross-reference list. Also, the loop checks to see if element ID(I) is already in the XrefLst list box. If so, the string LineNumStr is appended to the appropriate list of line numbers; if not, the element is inserted in the XrefLst list box and the contents of variable LineNumStr are inserted in the corresponding member of LinesLst list box.

After all identifiers have been processed, the procedure closes the input file, obtains the name of the output .XRF file using the main name of the selected file, and opens the file for output. It then writes the cross-reference list to the output file, and displays the cross-reference list in the scrollable text box. Before exiting, the procedure closes the output file and restores the mouse cursor to its default shape.

23
The Comments Stripping utility

Did you know that the comments in Visual Basic program somehow add to the size of the .EXE file produced by the Visual Basic compiler? Did you also know that as you edit and recompile your Visual Basic program, the size of the .EXE file increases? The explanation for these rather surprising features of Visual Basic is that the product lacks what is called *garbage collection*—the ability to remove unwanted code. While commenting your code adds clarity, it also adds to the size of the .EXE file. The solution is to remove these comments. This chapter presents a utility that removes comments from .TXT listing files written by Visual Basic. The processed files can be reloaded into the Visual Basic forms and modules just before you create the compiled .EXE file.

The basic idea

The last chapter presented a cross-reference utility that uses a state engine to scan the various identifiers in the lines of listings. The same principles can be applied to design a utility that removes comments from listing files. In fact, the work done by the comments stripping utility is a lot less, since there is no need to store and manage keywords, identifiers, and their list of line numbers. The utility simply deletes the remark. A state engine is still needed to determine if the single quote character happens to be part of a string literal. Deleting a literal single-quote might very well result in a mess.

The comments stripping utility uses a scanner that is similar to the XREF scanner, but simpler. The scanner uses the same three states: code-mode, comments-mode, and string-mode. When the scanner state is in code-mode and the scanner encounters a comment, the comment characters are deleted. Other than that, the scanner shifts between code-mode and string-mode without doing much work.

Introducing the Comments Stripping utility

Figure 23-1 shows a sample session with the Comments Stripping utility. The interface greatly resembles that of the XREF utility. The STRIPREM .FRM form contains the following controls:

- The Drive list box enables you to select files on a different drive.
- The Directory list box permits you to change directories.
- The Filename text box allows you to specify the pattern for the Visual Basic text listings. This text box is assigned *.txt, the pattern for the default Visual Basic text files.
- The File list box permits you to select a listing file to process.
- A multiline scrollable text box that displays the uncommented listing and also allows you to view a text file.
- The Quit button ends the utility.
- The Strip Comments button strips comments from the selected file. The button displays the processed listing in the scrollable text box and also writes the listing to the selected file. The original file is renamed with the .DOC extension. If there already is a file with that name, the utility prompts you to either delete it or select a different name.
- The View File button allows you to view the selected text file.
- The Print File button generates a simple printout of the selected file.

Working with the Comments Stripping utility is simple. Select the drive and directory by manipulating the Drive and Directory list boxes. You may key in a new filename pattern if you save your Visual Basic listings in files that do not have the .TXT extension. Once you reach the desired directory, select the file from the file list box and click on the Strip Comments button. The processed file appears in the scrollable text box and is written back to the source file. The utility removes blank lines and inserts its own blank lines between procedures. Also, the program renames the original source file using the .DOC extension, if the renamed file matches the name of an existing file, the utility prompts you to delete the existing file or to enter a new name. You can view a file before or after processing, using the View File button; you can also print any text file using the Print File button. When you are done using the utility, click on the Quit button to exit.

Figures 23-2 to 23-4 contain the specifications for the STRIPREM.MAK project file and the STRIPREM.FRM form file.

Listing 23-1 contains the code attached to the STRIPREM.FRM form. The form contains the following procedures that are used to strip the comments.

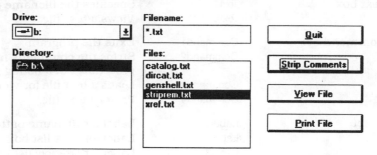

Drive:
b:

Filename:
*.txt

Quit

Directory:
b:\

Files:
catalog.txt
dircat.txt
genshell.txt
striprem.txt
xref.txt

Strip Comments

View File

Print File

```
Const True = -1, False = 0

Sub DeleteStr (S$, ByVal St&, ByVal Count&)
  Dim StrLen As Long
  StrLen = Len(S$)
  If (St& < 0) Or (St& > StrLen) Then Exit Sub
  If (Count& < 1) Then Exit Sub
  If (St& = 1) And (Count& >= StrLen) Then
    S$ = ""
  ElseIf (St& = 1) And (Count& < StrLen) Then
    S$ = Right$(S$, StrLen - Count&)
  ElseIf (St& > 1) And ((St& + Count&) > StrLen) Then
    S$ = Left$(S$, St& - 1)
  Else
    S$ = Mid$(S$, 1, St& - 1) + Mid$(S$, St& + Count&)
```

23-1 A sample session with the STRIPREM.FRM form.

Application name: Comment stripping utility
Application code name: STRIPREM

23-2 The basic
specifications for the
STRIPREM.MAK
project file.

Version: 1.0   Date created: September 6, 1991
Programmer(s): Namir Clement Shammas

List of filenames

Storage path: \VB\VBXTOOL
Project   STRIPREM.MAK
Global   GLOBAL.BAS (not used)
Form 1   STRIPREM.FRM

Form # 1   Form filename: STRIPREM.FRM
Version: 1.0   Date: September 6, 1991

Control object type	Default CtlName	Purpose
Drive list box	Drive1	Shows and selects the current drive
Directory list	Dir1	Shows and selects the current directory
File list box	File1	Shows a group of files

23-3 The list of controls in the STRIPREM.FRM form file.

Control object type	Default CtlName	Purpose
Text box	Text1	Specifies the filename pattern
	Text2	Views a text file
Command box	Command1	Exits the program
	Command2	Strips the comments from the procedures of a listing file
	Command3	Loads a text file for viewing
	Command4	Prints a text file
Label	Label1	Label for filename pattern
	Label2	Label for Drive list box
	Label3	Label for Directory list box

23-3 Continued.

Application (code) name: STRIPREM
Form # 1
Version: 1.0 Date: September 7, 1991

Original control name	Property	New setting
Form	Caption	Strip Comments From VB *.TXT Files
Drive1	CtlName	DiskDrv
Dir1	CtlName	TreeDir
File1	CtlName	FileFlb
Text1	CtlName	PatternBox
	Text	(empty string)
Text2	CtlName	TextBox
	Text	(empty string)
	MultiLine	True
	ScrollBars	3 - Both
Command1	CtlName	QuitBtn
	Caption	&Quit
	Cancel	True
Command2	CtlName	StripCommentsBtn
	Caption	&Strip Comments
Command3	CtlName	ViewFileBtn
	Caption	&View File
Command4	CtlName	PrintBtn
	Caption	&Print File
Label1	CtlName	PatternLbl
	Caption	Filename:
Label2	CtlName	DriveLbl
	Caption	Drive:
Label3	CtlName	DirectoryLbl
	Caption	Directory:

23-4 The customized settings for the STRIPREM.FRM form.

Listing 23-1 The code attached to the STRIPREM.FRM form.

```
Const True = -1, False = 0

Sub DeleteStr (S$, ByVal St&, ByVal Count&)
' Delete Count& characters from the string S$, starting at
' the index St&.
  Dim StrLen As Long

   StrLen = Len(S$)
  If (St& < 0) Or (St& > StrLen) Then Exit Sub
  If (Count& < 1) Then Exit Sub

  ' delete from first to the last (or beyond the last)
  ' character?  Then, string S$ returns an empty
  ' string.
  If (St& = 1) And (Count& >= StrLen) Then
    S$ = ""
  ' delete leading substring?
  ElseIf (St& = 1) And (Count& < StrLen) Then
    ' extract the trailing substring
    S$ = Right$(S$, StrLen - Count&)
  ' delete the trailing part of the string?
  ElseIf (St& > 1) And ((St& + Count&) > StrLen) Then
    ' extract the leading substring
    S$ = Left$(S$, St& - 1)
  Else
    ' extract the leading and trailing undeleted substrings
    S$ = Mid$(S$, 1, St& - 1) + Mid$(S$, St& + Count&)
  End If
End Sub

Sub DiskDrv_Change ()
  ' update file tree path when the disk is changed
  TreeDir.Path = DiskDrv.Drive
End Sub

Sub Form_Load ()
' Initialize the form  .
  WindowState = 2 ' maximize the window
  ' set the default filename pattern
  PatternBox.Text = "*.txt"
  FileFlb.Filename = "*.txt"
  ' set Archive and Normal attributes to True and all
  ' of the other file attributes to False
  FileFlb.Archive = True
  FileFlb.Normal = True
  FileFlb.Hidden = False
  FileFlb.ReadOnly = False
  FileFlb.System = False
End Sub

Sub PatternBox_KeyPress (KeyAScii As Integer)
  KeyAScii = Asc(LCase$(Chr$(KeyAScii)))
End Sub

Sub PatternBox_LostFocus ()
  Dim I As Integer
  If PatternBox.Text = "" Then PatternBox.Text = "*.*"
  ' locate and remove multiple wildcards
  I = InStr(PatternBox.Text, " ") ' find first space
  If I > 0 Then
    PatternBox.Text = Mid$(PatternBox.Text, 1, I - 1)
  End If
  FileFlb.Filename = PatternBox.Text
End Sub

Sub PrintFileCom_Click ()
```

```
' Perform a simple print task.
  Dim F As String, TextLine As String
  Dim LineNum As Integer
  If FileFlb.Filename <> "" Then
    Form1.MousePointer = 11 ' hourglass
    LineNum = FreeFile ' get the next file buffer
    ' obtain the full filename
    F = TreeDir.Path
    If Right$(F, 1) <> "\" Then F = F + "\"
    F = F + FileFlb.Filename
    Open F For Input As #LineNum ' open file
    ' read each line and print it
    Do While Not EOF(LineNum)
      Line Input #LineNum, TextLine
      Printer.Print TextLine
    Loop
    Printer.EndDoc ' close printer buffer
    Close #LineNum ' close file buffer
    Form1.MousePointer = 0 ' restore mouse pointer
  End If
End Sub

Sub QuitBtn_Click ()
' Exit the application.
    End
End Sub

Sub ReplaceRem (S$)
' Replace the Rem keyword with a single-quote
  Dim S2 As String
  Dim I As Integer
  S2$ = LTrim$(S$)
  ' does the trimmed line start with Rem?
  If Mid$(S2$, 1, 4) = "Rem " Then
    ' make the first character a single-quote
    ' comment
    I = InStr(S$, "Rem ")
    Mid$(S$, I, 1) = "'"
  End If
End Sub

Sub RemoveComments (S$)
' Remove single-quote comments from the line S$.
  Const CODE_MODE = 1
  Const REM_MODE = 2
  Const STR_MODE = 3

  Dim Status As Integer
  Dim I As Integer
  Dim Q As String * 1
  Dim C As String * 1

  Q = Chr$(34)
  InWord = False ' initialize in-word flag
  ' set status to code mode
  Status = CODE_MODE
  ' initialize the identifier count
  IDcount% = 0
  ' replace the Rem keyword with the single-quote character
  ReplaceRem S$
  ' examine every string character
  For I = 1 To Len(S$)
    ' copy the I'th character to C
    C = Mid$(S$, I, 1)
    ' main Select-Case statement
    Select Case Status
      ' scanning code?
```

```
       Case CODE_MODE
          ' examine the character in C
          Select Case C
            ' shift to string mode?
            Case Q
              ' set status to string mode
              Status = STR_MODE
            ' shift to remark?
            Case "'"
              ' remove remark
              DeleteStr S$, I, Len(S$)
              Exit Sub
          End Select
       Case STR_MODE
          If C = Q Then Status = CODE_MODE
       End Select
   Next I
End Sub

Sub StripCommentsBtn_Click ()
' Strip the comments out of a VB text file.
   Const YES = 6
   Dim Filename As String
   Dim NewFilename As String
   Dim TextLine As String
   Dim S As String
   Dim InputStr As String
   Dim NL As String * 2
   Dim I As Integer
   Dim FileNum As Integer
   ' exit if there is no selected file
   If FileFlb.ListIndex = -1 Then Exit Sub
   NL = Chr$(13) + Chr$(10)
   ' get the current directory
   Filename = TreeDir.List(-1)
   ' append a "\", if needed
   If Right$(Filename, 1) <> "\" Then
     Filename = Filename + "\"
   End If
   ' get the full name of the selected file
   Filename = Filename + FileFlb.List(FileFlb.ListIndex)
   ' copy filename to the new filename
   NewFilename = Filename
   ' obtain the new filename for the source file
   I = InStr(NewFilename, ".")
   If I > 0 Then
     NewFilename = Mid$(NewFilename, 1, I) + "DOC"
   Else
     NewFilename = NewFilename + ".DOC"
   End If
   ' get the next available file handle
   FileNum = FreeFile
   ' open the selected file for input
   Open Filename For Input As #FileNum
   S = ""
   ' read every line in the selected file
   Do While Not EOF(FileNum)
      ' read the next line
      Line Input #FileNum, TextLine
      ' remove the comments from TextLine
      RemoveComments TextLine
      ' is TextLine not an empty string?
      If RTrim$(LTrim$(TextLine)) <> "" Then
        ' does TextLine contain a Sub declaration?
        If InStr(TextLine, "Sub ") = 1 Then
          S = S + NL ' insert a blank line
          ' does TextLine contain a Function declaration?
```

```
        ElseIf InStr(TextLine, "Function ") = 1 Then
          S = S + NL ' insert a blank line
        End If
        ' append TextLine to variable S
        S = S + TextLine + NL
      End If
  Loop
  Close #FileNum ' close the input file
  ' does the NewFilename exist?
  Do While Dir$(NewFilename) <> ""
    ' prompt the user to delete NewFilename
    I = MsgBox("Delete file " + NewFilename, 68, "Input")
    If I = YES Then
      ' delete existing NewFilename
      Kill NewFilename
    Else
      ' prompt the user for another filename
      InputStr = InputBox$("Enter new filename", "Input", NewFilename)
      If InputStr <> "" Then NewFilename = InputStr
    End If
  Loop
  ' rename input file as NewFilename
  Name Filename As NewFilename
  ' display the processed filename
  TextBox.Text = S
  S = "" ' clear the variable S
  ' set the error trap
  On Error GoTo BadFileSave
  ' get the next available file handle
  FileNum = FreeFile
  ' open the selected file for output
  Open Filename For Output As #FileNum
  ' write TextBox.Text to the selected file
  Print #FileNum, TextBox.Text
  ' close the output file
  Close #FileNum
  ' turn off the error trap
  On Error GoTo 0
  Exit Sub
  '****************** Error Handler ****************
BadFileSave:
  MsgBox "Error in writing to file " + Filename, 64, "File I/O Error"
  Resume ExitFileSave
ExitFileSave:
  On Error GoTo 0
  On Error Resume Next
  ' delete the partially written file (??)
  Kill Filename
  ' restore the old filename
  Name NewFilename As Filename
End Sub

Sub TextBox_KeyPress (KeyAScii As Integer)
  KeyAScii = 0
End Sub

Sub TreeDir_Change ()
  FileFlb.Path = TreeDir.Path
End Sub

Sub ViewFileBtn_Click ()
' View the target file in TextBox.
  Dim F As String, TextLine As String
  Dim FileNum As Integer
  Dim NL As String * 2
  If FileFlb.Filename <> "" Then
    NL = Chr$(13) + Chr$(10)
```

```
    FileNum = FreeFile ' get the next file buffer
    F = TreeDir.Path
    If Right$(F, 1) <> "\" Then F = F + "\"
    F = F + FileFlb.Filename
    Open F For Input As #FileNum
    F = ""
    Do While Not EOF(FileNum)
      Line Input #FileNum, TextLine
      F = F + TextLine + NL
    Loop
    Close #FileNum
    TextBox.Text = F
  End If
End Sub
```

The DeleteStr procedure deletes Count& characters from the S$ parameter, starting with character St&. This procedure can also be used as a general-purpose string deletion procedure. The routine performs one of the following mutually exclusive tasks:

- Exits if the argument for St& is out of range.
- Exits if the argument for Count& is not a positive integer.
- Deletes the entire string if St& is 1 and Count& is equal to or greater than the length of S$. This deletion is done by assigning an empty string to the parameter S$.
- Removes the leading Count& characters if St& is 1 and the argument for Count& is less than the length of S$.
- Deletes the trailing characters of S$ if St& is greater than 1 and the expression St& + Count& exceeds the length of S$.
- Removes an internal substring by extracting the undeleted leading and trailing portions of S$.

The ReplaceRem procedure replaces the first character of the Rem keyword with the single-quote character, which maintains the comment but changes its form. The procedure copies the left-trimmed value of parameter S$ into the local string variable S2. S2 is used as a copy to avoid stripping the argument of S$ from leading spaces. Then the procedure tests whether the first four characters of S2 are Rem. If so, the routine locates the occurrence of Rem in the parameter S$ and replaces the first character of the Rem keyword with the single-quote character.

The RemoveComments procedure removes comments from its parameter S$. The procedure uses a scanner to detect and delete comments found in a text line. The procedure calls on ReplaceRem to modify Rem comments into single-quote comments, and calls DeleteStr to remove the comments.

The StripCommentsBtn_Click procedure starts the process of stripping comments from the selected file. The routine declares the YES constant to use with a Yes/No prompt. The procedure exits immediately if there is no selected file; otherwise, it obtains the currently selected directory and appends a \ if needed. Then it obtains the full path and name of the selected file, and determines the name of the file that will store the original listings, using a .DOC extension.

Next, the procedure opens the selected file for input as a text file, and reads and processes the lines of the selected file using a Do-While loop. Each iteration reads a text line, calls procedure RemoveComments, and inserts the processed line in the local string variable S. If the processed line contains a Sub or Function declaration, a new line is inserted in the variable S. Then the input file is closed.

At this point, the procedure determines whether there is a file with the name stored in variable NewFilename. While this condition is true, the program prompts you to either delete the file or supply a new filename. When the filename is satisfactory, the input file is renamed using the string in variable NewFilename. The name of the originally selected file is now used to write the uncommented listing.

To write the file, the procedure copies the contents of variable S to the scrollable text box, opens the output file as a text file, and then writes Text Box.Text to the output file. Finally, the procedure closes the output file and exits to avoid running into the local error handler.

24
QuickPak Professional for Windows

Earlier chapters of this book presented libraries and form tools developed using only Visual Basic. As you have seen, the implementation is quite flexible. However, like many other implementations, the more you use Visual Basic, the more you realize its limitations. There are a number of third-party products that extend the capabilities of Visual Basic programming and enhance the speed of Visual Basic programs. One such product is QuickPak Professional for Windows, a product of Crescent Software. This company has been in the BASIC tools business for a number of years. The president of Crescent Software is Ethan Winer, considered among the most knowledgeable BASIC programmers outside Microsoft. Winer is a fellow author and writes in various publications. His company developed the QuickPak Professional package for QuickBasic, and also offers a Windows version of this package for the Visual Basic programmer. Both versions of QuickPak Professional offer practical and quick assembly-coded routines. Appendix A contains information supplied by Crescent Software about their QuickPak Professional for Windows product.

This chapter briefly presents the routines offered by QuickPak Professional for Windows. In addition, it presents utilities that use the QuickPak routines. These utilities illustrate the ability to implement operations not possible using only Visual Basic, and also demonstrate the enhanced speed of routines coded in assembly language. A number of these routines have similar Visual Basic statements, the difference is that the QuickPak routines are considerably faster.

☞ This chapter was written with a beta copy of QuickPak Professional for Windows. The documentation was primarily that of the most recent QuickBasic versions; as a result, there might be some minor changes and additions in the routines shown in the next few listings.

A QuickPak tour

The QuickPak Professional for Windows groups its routines by the following categories: Arrays, DOS, Windows API, Strings, Time/Date, Keyboard, and Miscellaneous. The next subsections discuss each category of routines.

The Arrays routines

QuickPak offers a rich set of fast and flexible routines to manipulate arrays. Such manipulation includes sorting (both indexed and nonindexed), searching, finding the smallest or largest array element, and inserting and deleting elements. The QuickPak library includes multiple versions of these routines to handle arrays of the various types: integer, long integer, single, double, currency, fixed-length string, and variable-length string. Moreover, some string manipulating routines, such as the sort and search routines, have both case-sensitive and case-insensitive versions. In addition, QuickPak offers search routines that scan either forward or backward. Listing 24-1 contains a portion of the PRODECL.BAS module to which I have added comments that describe the various array-manipulating routines.

Listing 24-1 The declarations of the array routines.

```
'================================================================
'  ProDecl.BAS for QuickPak Professional for Windows
'  Copyright (c) 1991 Crescent Software
'================================================================

'-------------------- Array Routines --------------------
Declare Sub AddInt Lib "QPro.DLL" (IntArray%, ByVal Num2Add%, ByVal
NumEls%)
' adds a constant value, Num2Add%, to NumEls% elements of an integer
' array.
Declare Sub DeleteStr Lib "QPro.DLL" (Array$, ByVal NumEls%)
' remove NumEls% elements from a variable-length string array.
Declare Sub DeleteT Lib "QPro.DLL" (Array As Any, ByVal ElSize%, ByVal
NumEls%)
' removes NumEls% elements from a fixed-string array.
Declare Sub Fill2 Lib "QPro.DLL" (Array%, ByVal Value%, ByVal NumEls%)
' Assigns all of the elements in a designated part of an integer array
' to any value.
Declare Sub Fill4 Lib "QPro.DLL" (Array As Any, Value As Any, ByVal
NumEls%)
' Assigns all of the elements in a designated part of an single-precision
' array to any value.
Declare Sub Fill8 Lib "QPro.DLL" (Array As Any, Value As Any, ByVal
NumEls%)
' Assigns all of the elements in a designated part of an double-precision
' array to any value.
Declare Sub Find Lib "QPro.DLL" (Array$, NumEls%, Search$)
' searches the elements of a variable-length string array for the first
' occurrence of a string or a substring.
Declare Sub Find2 Lib "QPro.DLL" (Array$, NumEls%, Search$)
' a version of Find that is case-sensitive.
```

Listing 24-1 Continued.

```
Declare Sub FindB Lib "QPro.DLL" (Array$, NumEls%, Search$)
' a version of Find that searches backwards.
Declare Sub FindB2 Lib "QPro.DLL" (Array$, NumEls%, Search$)
' a version of FindB that searches backward
Declare Function FindLast% Lib "QPro.DLL" (Array$, ByVal NumEls%)
' finds the last non-empty string in an array of variable-length strings.
Declare Sub FindT Lib "QPro.DLL" (Array As Any, ByVal ElSize%, NumEls%,
ByVal Search$)
' searches all or part of a fixed-length string array for a string or a
' substring.
Declare Sub FindT2 Lib "QPro.DLL" (Array As Any, ByVal ElSize%, NumEls%,
ByVal Search$)
' a version of FindT that is case-sensitive.
Declare Sub FindTB Lib "QPro.DLL" (Array As Any, ByVal ElSize%, NumEls%,
ByVal Search$)
' a version of FindT that searches backward.
Declare Sub FindTB2 Lib "QPro.DLL" (Array As Any, ByVal ElSize%, NumEls%,
ByVal Search$)
' a version of FindB that searches backward.
Declare Sub FindExact Lib "QPro.DLL" (Array$, NumEls%, Search$)
' searches for an exact string or substring in a variable-length string
' array.
Declare Function GetBit% Lib "QPro.DLL" (Array$, ByVal Element%)
' returns the on/off status of a bit in a QuickPak bit array.
Declare Function IMinI% Lib "QPro.DLL" (Array As Any, ByVal NumEls%)
' searches an entire integer array and returns the index of the element
' that contains the smallest value.
Declare Function IMinL% Lib "QPro.DLL" (Array As Any, ByVal NumEls%)
' searches an entire long integer array and returns the index of the
' element that contains the smallest value.
Declare Function IMinS% Lib "QPro.DLL" (Array As Any, ByVal NumEls%)
' searches an entire single-precision array and returns the index of the
' element that contains the smallest value.
Declare Function IMinD% Lib "QPro.DLL" (Array As Any, ByVal NumEls%)
' searches an entire double-precision array and returns the index of the
' element that contains the smallest value.
Declare Function IMinC% Lib "QPro.DLL" (Array As Any, ByVal NumEls%)
' searches an entire currency array and returns the index of the
' element that contains the smallest value.
Declare Function IMaxI% Lib "QPro.DLL" (Array As Any, ByVal NumEls%)
' searches an entire integer array and returns the index of the element
' that contains the largest value.
Declare Function IMaxL% Lib "QPro.DLL" (Array As Any, ByVal NumEls%)
' searches an entire long integer array and returns the index of the
' element that contains the largest value.
Declare Function IMaxS% Lib "QPro.DLL" (Array As Any, ByVal NumEls%)
' searches an entire single-precision array and returns the index of the
' element that contains the largest value.
Declare Function IMaxD% Lib "QPro.DLL" (Array As Any, ByVal NumEls%)
' searches an entire double-precision array and returns the index of the
' element that contains the largest value.
Declare Function IMaxC% Lib "QPro.DLL" (Array As Any, ByVal NumEls%)
' searches an entire currency array and returns the index of the
' element that contains the largest value.
Declare Sub InsertStr Lib "QPro.DLL" (Array$, NewItem$, ByVal NumEls%)
' inserts an element in a variable-length string array.
Declare Sub InsertT Lib "QPro.DLL" (Array As Any, ByVal ElSize%, ByVal
NumEls%)
' inserts an element in a fixed-length string array.
Declare Sub InitInt Lib "QPro.DLL" (Array%, ByVal StartValue%, ByVal
NumEls%)
' initializes all or part of an integer array with a sequence of increasing
' values.
Declare Sub ISortC Lib "QPro.DLL" (Array@, Index%, ByVal NumEls%, ByVal
Direct%)
' performs an indexed sorting on part or all of a currency array.
```

Listing 24-1 Continued.

```
Declare Sub ISortD Lib "QPro.DLL" (Array#, Index%, ByVal NumEls%, ByVal
Direct%)
' performs an indexed sorting on part or all of a double-precision array.
Declare Sub ISortI Lib "QPro.DLL" (Array%, Index%, ByVal NumEls%, ByVal
Direct%)
' performs an indexed sorting on part or all of a integer array.
Declare Sub ISortL Lib "QPro.DLL" (Array&, Index%, ByVal NumEls%, ByVal
Direct%)
' performs an indexed sorting on part or all of a long integer array.
Declare Sub ISortS Lib "QPro.DLL" (Array!, Index%, ByVal NumEls%, ByVal
Direct%)
' performs an indexed sorting on part or all of a single-precision array.
Declare Sub ISortStr Lib "QPro.DLL" (Array$, Index%, ByVal NumEls%, ByVal
Direct%)
' performs an indexed sorting on part or all of a variable-length string
' array.
Declare Sub ISortStr2 Lib "QPro.DLL" (Array$, Index%, ByVal NumEls%, ByVal
Direct%)
' a version of ISortStr that performs case-insensitive sorting.
Declare Sub ISortT Lib "QPro.DLL" (Array As Any, Index%, ByVal NumEls%,
ByVal Direct%, ByVal ElSize%, ByVal MemberOffset%, ByVal MemberSize%)
' performs an indexed sorting on part or all of a fixed-length string
' array.
Declare Sub ISortT2 Lib "QPro.DLL" (Array As Any, Index%, ByVal NumEls%,
ByVal Direct%, ByVal ElSize%, ByVal MemberOffset%, ByVal MemberSize%)
' a version of ISortT that performs case-insensitive sorting.
Declare Sub KeySort Lib "QPro.DLL" (Array As Any, ByVal ElSize%, ByVal
NumEls%, Table%, ByVal NumKeys%)
' sorts a user-defined TYPE on any number of keys.
Declare Function MaxD# Lib "QPro.DLL" (Array As Any, ByVal NumEls%)
' returns the largest value in part of all of a double-precision array.
Declare Function MinD# Lib "QPro.DLL" (Array As Any, ByVal NumEls%)
' returns the smallest value in part of all of a double-precision
array.Declare Function MaxS! Lib "QPro.DLL" (Array As Any, ByVal NumEls%)
' returns the largest value in part of all of a single-precision array.
Declare Function MinS! Lib "QPro.DLL" (Array As Any, ByVal NumEls%)
' returns the smallest value in part of all of a single-precision array.
Declare Function MaxL& Lib "QPro.DLL" (Array As Any, ByVal NumEls%)
' returns the largest value in part of all of a long integer array.
Declare Function MinL& Lib "QPro.DLL" (Array As Any, ByVal NumEls%)
' returns the smallest value in part of all of a long integer array.
Declare Function MaxI% Lib "QPro.DLL" (Array As Any, ByVal NumEls%)
' returns the largest value in part of all of an integer array.
Declare Function MinI% Lib "QPro.DLL" (Array As Any, ByVal NumEls%)
' returns the smallest value in part of all of an integer array.
Declare Function MaxC@ Lib "QPro.DLL" (Array As Any, ByVal NumEls%)
' returns the largest value in part of all of a currency array.
Declare Function MinC@ Lib "QPro.DLL" (Array As Any, ByVal NumEls%)
' returns the smallest value in part of all of a currency array.
Declare Sub Search Lib "QPro.DLL" (Array As Any, ByVal NumEls%, Match As
Any, Found%, ByVal Direc%, ByVal Code%, ByVal VarType%)
' an advances search routine that scans all or portion of a numeric array.
Declare Function SearchT% Lib "QPro.DLL" (Array As Any, ByVal NumEls%,
Match As Any, ByVal Direc%, ByVal Code%, ByVal Strsize%, ByVal MemOf%,
ByVal Memsize%)
' scans a user-defined TYPE array.
Declare Function SearchT2% Lib "QPro.DLL" (Array As Any, ByVal NumEls%,
Match As Any, ByVal Direc%, ByVal Code%, ByVal Strsize%, ByVal MemOf%,
ByVal Memsize%)
' a case-insensitive version of function SearchT.
Declare Sub SetBit Lib "QPro.DLL" (Array$, ByVal Element%, ByVal Bit)
' sets a bit in a QuickPak bit array.
Declare Sub SortC Lib "QPro.DLL" (Array@, ByVal NumEls%, ByVal Direct%)
' sorts a currency array.
Declare Sub SortD Lib "QPro.DLL" (Array#, ByVal NumEls%, ByVal Direct%)
' sorts a double-precision array.
```

Listing 24-1 Continued.

```
Declare Sub SortI Lib "QPro.DLL" (Array%, ByVal NumEls%, ByVal Direct%)
' sorts an integer array.
Declare Sub SortL Lib "QPro.DLL" (Array&, ByVal NumEls%, ByVal Direct%)
' sorts a long integer array.
Declare Sub SortS Lib "QPro.DLL" (Array!, ByVal NumEls%, ByVal Direct%)
' sorts a single-precision array.
Declare Sub SortStr Lib "QPro.DLL" (Array$, ByVal NumEls%, ByVal Direct%)
' sorts a variable-length string array.
Declare Sub SortStr2 Lib "QPro.DLL" (Array$, ByVal NumEls%, ByVal Direct%)
' a case-insensitive version of procedure SortStr.
Declare Sub SortT Lib "QPro.DLL" (Array As Any, ByVal NumEls%, ByVal
Direct%, ByVal ElSize%, ByVal MemberOffset%, ByVal MemberSize%)
' sorts a fixed-length string array.
Declare Sub SortT2 Lib "QPro.DLL" (Array As Any, ByVal NumEls%, ByVal
Direct%, ByVal ElSize%, ByVal MemberOffset%, ByVal MemberSize%)
' a case-insensitive version of procedure SortT.
```

The SortStr routine sorts either all or part of an array. The declaration of the SortStr procedure is:

```
Sub SortStr (Array$, ByVal NumEls%, ByVal Direct%)
```

The Array$ parameter is a reference parameter that allows you to specify the first array element involved in the sort. The NumEls% parameter designates the number of array elements to sort. The Direct% parameter specifies the ascending (when set to 0) or descending (when set to a non-zero value) sort order. Using the Array$ parameter implements a clever programming trick that, in effect, kills two birds with one stone. It replaces two parameters: one for the array itself, and the other for the index of the first sortable element, as shown:

```
' Visual Basic coded version
Sub VBSortStr (Array$( ), ByVal First%, ByVal NumElms%, ByVal Direct%)
```

A short example of using the SortStr is shown below:

```
Dim A(0 To 100) As String
First% = 1
Num% = 50
GetStringData A, First%, Num%
SortStr A(First%), Num%, 0 ' QuickPak routine
ShowStringArray A, First%, Num%
```

The above example shows that you can sort any portion of a string array with SortStr. This observation can be generalized to other arrays of predefined data types. This feature proves to be very useful in special applications where arrays are used as buffers. The QuickPak package also offers indexed sorting routines. The ISortStr routine, for example, offers an indexed sort routine for variable-length strings:

```
Sub ISortStr (Array$, Index%, ByVal NumElms%, ByVal Direct%)
```

The Index% parameter passes the first element of the index array. Quick-Pak also offers case-insensitive versions of SortStr and ISortStr routines.

The routines that complement the string-array sorting routines are those that search for strings and substring in string arrays. The Find routine is such a routine and is declared as follows:

Declare Sub Find Lib "QPro.DLL" *(Array$, NumElms%, Search$)*

The Array$ parameter passes the first element of the array to be searched. The NumElms% parameter supplies the index of successive elements to search. The same parameter also reports back to the caller the *offset index* (that is, an index relative to first searched array element) of the matching element, or – 1 if no match is found. There are versions of the routine Find that perform case-insensitive search, backward search, and exact search. The QuickPak library also contains a parallel set of routines that handle fixed-length string arrays.

The DOS routines

The DOS routines enable you to obtain information not easily available (if available at all) from Visual Basic. For example, you cannot obtain the date/time file stamp and file attributes from any Visual Basic statement. Such information is commonly used by a variety of DOS utilities and should be made available for the Windows versions of similar utilities.

Listing 24-2 contains the declarations of the DOS services routines found in the PRODECL.BAS module, with comments that briefly explain what the routines do. If you examine the routines in Listing 24-2, you will notice that that there are a number of file and directory manipulating routines that resemble existing Visual Basic functions and statements. What's the difference, you might ask? The QuickPak versions allow you to perform file I/O and manipulate directories without using the On Error traps. For example, the FOpen routine opens a file by associating the name of the file with a file handle number. If the filename is invalid, the Quick-Pak DOSerror and WhichError functions return the error status of the last file manipulating QuickPak routine. This approach greatly resembles that of C, and is more efficient. The increased efficiency is due to avoiding the On Error trap. Such a trap adds error-checking code to the .EXE file.

The library of DOS services routines presents a valuable programming tool for the Visual Basic programmer. Personally, I would buy the QuickPak package just for the DOS library alone.

The following paragraphs describe some of the interesting and valuable DOS routines available with QuickPak.

The ClipFile procedure enables you to truncate a file and reduce its size. Consequently, this routine enables you to reduce the number of records in a random-access file. Under Visual Basic, you can only increase the size of a random-access file; this feature poses a problem when you want to delete records. The current practice is to copy the undeleted records of a file into a new file. This is time consuming, especially if you maintain a large number of records in a database file.

The FCount% function returns the number of files that match a speci-

Listing 24-2 The declarations of the DOS services routines.

```
' --------------------- Dos Services ---------------------
Declare Sub CDir Lib "QPro.DLL" (ByVal Path$)
' changes the directory.
Declare Sub ClipFile Lib "QPro.DLL" (ByVal FileName$, NewLen&)
' truncates a file.
Declare Function DCount% Lib "QPro.DLL" (ByVal FileName$)
' returns the number of subdirectories attached to the current
' directory.
Declare Sub DiskInfo Lib "QPro.DLL" (Drive$, Bytes%, Sectors%,
FreeClusters%, TotalClusters%)
' reports the sector and cluster makeup of a disk.
Declare Function DiskRoom& Lib "QPro.DLL" (ByVal Drive$)
' returns the available bytes on a disk.
Declare Function DiskSize& Lib "QPro.DLL" (ByVal Drive$)
' returns the total disk space, in bytes.
Declare Function DOSError% Lib "QPro.DLL" ()
' reports if an error has occurred during the last call to a QuickPak
' routine.
Declare Function DosVer% Lib "QPro.DLL" ()
' reports the DOS version under which Windows is loaded.
Declare Function ErrorMsg$ Lib "QPro.DLL" (ByVal ErrorNum%)
' reports the error message for a Visual Basic error.
Declare Function ExeName$ Lib "QPro.DLL" ()
' returns the full name of the currently running program.
Declare Function Exist% Lib "QPro.DLL" (ByVal FileName$)
' returns a Boolean value to indicate whether or not file Filename$ exists.
Declare Sub FClose Lib "QPro.DLL" (ByVal Handle%)
' closes a file opened with procedure FOpen.
Declare Sub FCopy Lib "QPro.DLL" (ByVal Source$, ByVal Dest$, Buffer$,
ErrCode%)
' copies a file without using any shell.
Declare Function FCount% Lib "QPro.DLL" (ByVal FileName$)
' counts the number of files in the specified filename pattern.  The
' pattern may include a drive and path.
Declare Sub FCreate Lib "QPro.DLL" (ByVal FileName$)
' creates a new file.
Declare Function FEof% Lib "QPro.DLL" (ByVal Handle%)
' similar to Visual Basic Eof function.
Declare Sub FFlush Lib "QPro.DLL" (ByVal Handle%)
' flushes the file buffer to disk.
Declare Sub FGet Lib "QPro.DLL" (ByVal Handle%, Text$)
' similar to Visual Basic Get statement.  The data is read into the
' string Text$.
Declare Sub FGetA Lib "QPro.DLL" (ByVal Handle%, Array As Any, NumBytes&)
' similar to FGet.  Reads from a file into an array.
Declare Sub FGetAH Lib "QPro.DLL" (ByVal FileName$, Array As Any, ByVal
ElSize%, ByVal NumEls%)
' reads an entire huge array from a file.
Declare Sub FGetR Lib "QPro.DLL" (ByVal Handle%, Text$, RecNum&)
' reads data from a random-access file.
Declare Sub FGetRT Lib "QPro.DLL" (ByVal Handle%, Array As Any, RecNum&,
ByVal RecSize%)
' reads data from a random-access file into a user-defined TYPE variable.
Declare Sub FGetRTA Lib "QPro.DLL" (ByVal Handle%, Array As Any, RecNum&,
ByVal RecSize%)
' reads data from a random-access file into an array of a
' user-defined TYPE.
Declare Sub FGetT Lib "QPro.DLL" (ByVal Handle%, ByVal Text$, NumBytes&)
' reads from a binary file to a user-defined TYPE variable.
Declare Sub FileInfo Lib "QPro.DLL" (ByVal FileName$, Array As Any)
' returns all of the size, date/time stamp, and attributes of a file.
Declare Function FileSize& Lib "QPro.DLL" (ByVal Drive$)
; returns the size of the specified file.
Declare Function FLInput$ Lib "QPro.DLL" (ByVal Handle, Buffer$)
```

Listing 24-2 Continued.

```
' reads a line of data from a file opened with FOpen.
Declare Function Floc& Lib "QPro.DLL" (ByVal Handle%)
' similar to the Visual Basic Loc function.
Declare Function FLof& Lib "QPro.DLL" (ByVal Handle%)
' similar to the Visual Basic  Lof function.
Declare Sub FOpen Lib "QPro.DLL" (ByVal FileName$, Handle%)
' opens a disk for input or output.
Declare Sub FOpenS Lib "QPro.DLL" (ByVal FileName$, Handle%)
' a version of FOpen aimed for networks.
Declare Sub FOpenAll Lib "QPro.DLL" (ByVal FileName$, ByVal AccessMode%,
ByVal Share%, Handle%)
' open a file for all access modes.
Declare Sub FPut Lib "QPro.DLL" (ByVal Handle%, Text$)
' writes the contents of a string to a file.
Declare Sub FPutA Lib "QPro.DLL" (ByVal Handle%, Array As Any, NumBytes&)
' writes an array to a file.
Declare Sub FPutAH Lib "QPro.DLL" (ByVal FileName$, Array As Any, ByVal
ElSize%, ByVal NumEls%)
' writes a huge array to a file.
Declare Sub FputR Lib "QPro.DLL" (ByVal Handle%, Text$, RecNum&)
' writes data to a random-access file.
Declare Sub FPutRT Lib "QPro.DLL" (ByVal Handle%, Array As Any, RecNum&,
ByVal RecSize%)
' writes user-defined TYPE data to a random-access file.
Declare Sub FputRTA Lib "QPro.DLL" (ByVal Handle%, Array As Any, RecNum&,
ByVal RecSize%)
' writes an array of user-defined TYPE data to a random-access file.
Declare Sub FputT Lib "QPro.DLL" (ByVal Handle%, ByVal Text$, NumBytes&)
' writes user-defined TYPE data to file.
Declare Function Fre& Lib "QPro.DLL" (ByVal Number%)
' returns the amount of free EMS memory, or the total amount of
' real and disk-based protected mode memory.
Declare Sub FSeek Lib "QPro.DLL" (ByVal Handle%, NewLocation&)
' similar to the Visual Basic Seek statement.
Declare Sub FStamp Lib "QPro.DLL" (ByVal FileName$, ByVal NewTime$, ByVal
NewDate$)
' creates a new date and time stamps for a file.
Declare Function GetAttr% Lib "QPro.DLL" (ByVal FileName$)
' returns the attribute byte of file.
Declare Function GetDir$ Lib "QPro.DLL" (Drive$)
' obtains the current directory of the specified drive.
Declare Function GetDrive% Lib "QPro.DLL" ()
' returns the currently selected drive.
Declare Function GetVol$ Lib "QPro.DLL" (ByVal Drive$)
' obtains the volume label of the specified drive.
Declare Function GoodDrive% Lib "QPro.DLL" (ByVal Drive$)
' Ascertains whether or not a specified drive is a valid one.
Declare Sub KillDir Lib "QPro.DLL" (ByVal DirName$)
' removes a directory DirName$.
Declare Sub KillFile Lib "QPro.DLL" (ByVal DirName$)
' similar to the Visual Basic Kill statement.
Declare Function LastDrive% Lib "QPro.DLL" ()
' returns the last consecutively drive available on the PC system.
Declare Function LineCount& Lib "QPro.DLL" (ByVal FileName$, ByVal Buffer$)
' counts the number of lines in a file.
Declare Sub LockFile Lib "QPro.DLL" (ByVal Handle%, Offset&, Length&)
' locks all or part of a network file.
Declare Sub MakeDir Lib "QPro.DLL" (ByVal FileName$)
' similar to the Visual Basic MKDir statement.
Declare Sub NameDir Lib "QPro.DLL" (ByVal OldName$, ByVal NewName$)
' renames a directory.
Declare Function ModeInfo$ Lib "QPro.DLL" ()
' returns a string that defines the current Windows operating mode
' (that is, "Standard mode" or "Enhanced mode").
Declare Sub NameFile Lib "QPro.DLL" (ByVal OldName$, ByVal NewName$)
' similar to the Visual Basic Name statement.
Declare Sub PutVol Lib "QPro.DLL" (ByVal Drive$, ByVal NewName$)
```

Listing 24-2 Continued.

```
' writes a new volume label to the specified drive.
Declare Sub QBLoad Lib "QPro.DLL" (ByVal FileName$, Array%)
' emulates to the QuickBasic BLoad statement.
Declare Sub QBSave Lib "QPro.DLL" (ByVal FileName$, Array%, ASize&)
' emulates the QuickBasic BSave statement.
Declare Sub ReadDir Lib "QPro.DLL" (DirArray$)
' obtains a list of directory names from disk and loads them in a
' variable-length string array.
Declare Sub ReadDirT Lib "QPro.DLL" (ByVal Spec$, DirArray As Any)
' obtains a list of directory names from disk and loads them in a
' fixed-length string array.
Declare Sub ReadFile Lib "QPro.DLL" (FileArray$)
' obtains a list of files from disk and loads them in a
' variable-length string array.
Declare Sub ReadFileI Lib "QPro.DLL" (FileArray$)
' retrieves a list of file names, size, dates, and times from disk and
' loads them in a variable-length string array.
Declare Sub ReadFileT Lib "QPro.DLL" (ByVal Spec$, FileArray As Any)
' retrieves a list of file names, size, dates, and times from disk and
' loads them in a fixed-length string array.
Declare Sub ReadFileX Lib "QPro.DLL" (ByVal Spec$, DirSize&, FullInfo As
Any)
' retrieves a list of file names, size, dates, and times from disk and
' loads them in a special data TYPE array.
Declare Function ReadTest% Lib "QPro.DLL" (ByVal Drive$)
' reports whether or not the specified drive is ready for reading.
Declare Sub SetAttr Lib "QPro.DLL" (ByVal FileName$, ByVal Attr%)
' sets the attribute byte of a file.
Declare Sub SetDrive Lib "QPro.DLL" (ByVal Drive$)
' changes the current drive.
Declare Sub SetError Lib "QPro.DLL" (ByVal ErrNum%)
' sets or clears a DOSerror and WhichError functions.
Declare Function SysDir$ Lib "QPro.DLL" ()
' returns the Windows drive and the System directory name.
Declare Sub UnLockFile Lib "QPro.DLL" (ByVal Handle%, Offset&, Length&)
' unlocks part or all of a network file.
Declare Function Valid% Lib "QPro.DLL" (ByVal FileName$)
' examines the string in FileName$ for a valid DOS filename.
Declare Function WinVer% Lib "QPro.DLL" ()
' returns the Windows version.
Declare Function WhichError% Lib "QPro.DLL" ()
' reports which error occurred during the last call to a QuickPak routine.
Declare Function WinDir$ Lib "QPro.DLL" ()
' returns the Windows drive and directory name
Declare Function WriteTest% Lib "QPro.DLL" (ByVal Drive$)
' determines whether or not the specified drive is ready for writing.
```

fied filename wildcard. The FCount% is equivalent to the following Visual Basic function:

```
Function VB_FCount (ByVal Spec$)
Dim Count As Integer
Count = 0
If Dir$(Spec$) < > "" Then
    Count = 1
    Do While Dir$ < > ""
    Count = Count + 1
    Loop
End If
VB_FCount = Count
End Function
```

The assembly-coded FCount% function is, of course, much faster than the Visual Basic VB_FCount function.

The ReadFilel routine obtains a list of file names, sizes, and date/time stamps that match a specified filename wildcard. The ReadFilel procedure is declared in Listing 24-2 as follows:

Declare Sub ReadFilel Lib "QPro.DLL" *(FileArray$)*

The FileArray$ parameter passes the first element of a string array whose first element contains the filename wildcard; the second and subsequent elements of this array receive the information on the matching files.

By using the FCount% function and the ReadFilel you can display the file names, sizes, and date/time stamps in a text box or list box. An example using the ReadFilel routine is shown below:

```
Dim FileInfo(0 To 100) As String
FileInfo(0) = "*.*"
Count% = FCount%(FileInfo(0))
ReadFilel FileInfo(0)
For I% = 1 To Count%
   AListBox.AddItem FileInfo(I%), I% – 1
Next I%
```

The ReadFileX routine is an extended version of ReadFilel that returns the name, size, data stamp, time stamp, and attribute byte of one or more files that match the specified filename wildcard. ReadFileX is declared as follows (I have omitted the Lib "QPro.DLL" to shorten the declaration):

Declare Sub ReadFileX (ByVal *Spec$*, *DirSize&*, FullInfo As Any)

The Spec$ specifies the filename wildcard. The DirSize& parameter reports the total size of the matching files. The FullInfo parameter is a user-defined array TYPE that contains the required structure. Listing 24-3 contains the declaration of the FullInfo TYPE. The BackUp Utility presented later in this chapter illustrates the use of the ReadFileX routine.

Listing 24-3   The declaration for the FullInfo user-defined data type.

```
' Type for ReadFileX routine

Type FullInfo
   BaseName As String * 8
   ExtName As String * 3
   FileSize As Long
   FileDate As String * 8
   FileTime As String * 6
   Attrib As String * 1
End Type
```

The FStamp routine enables you to assign a new date and/or time stamp to a file. The FStamp procedure is declared as follows:

Declare Sub FStamp (ByVal *Filename$*, ByVal *NewTime$*, ByVal *NewDate$*)

If the argument for NewTime$ or NewDate$ is an empty string, the corresponding file stamp is unaltered. If either argument is *, the current system time or date is used as the new file stamp. The argument for NewTime$ is normally the string image of a 24-hour time.

☞ The LinCount function quickly counts the number of lines in the specified file by counting the number of carriage return characters. Some files do not end the last line with a carriage return; however, the LinCount function also counts that line. Therefore, you should use a Do While Not Eof ( ) loop to read the lines of a file, since the LineCount result might be one line off.

The Keyboard routines

The QuickPak package includes a number of routines that set and query the keyboard. Listing 24-4 contains the declarations of these routines which allow you to determine whether or not the ALT, SHIFT, and CTRL keys are pressed. In addition, these routines allow you to query and toggle the Caps-Lock, Num-Lock, and Scroll-Lock keys. The keyboard routines help you fine-tune your Visual Basic applications and offer a nice professional touch.

Listing 24-4 The declarations of the keyboard routines.

```
'---------------------- Keyboard routines ----------------------

Declare Function AltKey% Lib "QPro.DLL" ()
' reports whether the ALT key is pressed.
Declare Function CapsLock% Lib "QPro.DLL" ()
' reports whether the Caps-Lock key is pressed.
Declare Sub CapsOff Lib "QPro.DLL" ()
' turns off the Caps-Lock key.
Declare Sub CapsOn Lib "QPro.DLL" ()
' turns on the Caps-Lock key.
Declare Function CtrlKey% Lib "QPro.DLL" ()
' reports if the CTRL key is pressed.
Declare Function NumLock% Lib "QPro.DLL" ()
' reports if the NumLock key is pressed.
Declare Sub NumOff Lib "QPro.DLL" ()
' turns off the NumLock key.
Declare Sub NumOn Lib "QPro.DLL" ()
' turns on the NumLock key.
Declare Function ScrolLock% Lib "QPro.DLL" ()
' reports if the Scoll-Lock key is pressed.
Declare Sub ScrollOn Lib "QPro.DLL" ()
' turns on the Scroll Lock key.
Declare Sub ScrollOff Lib "QPro.DLL" ()
' turns off the Scroll Lock key.
Declare Function ShiftKey% Lib "QPro.DLL" ()
' reports if the Shift key is pressed.
```

The String routines

Another area where the QuickPak routines excel is string manipulation. These assembly-coded routines add much-welcomed speed and flexibility to string manipulation. While some routines, like QPLen%( ), Lower, and Upper, have equivalent Visual Basic functions, the difference is again in speed. Other routines enhance existing Visual Basic functions. For example, consider the QInStr function, which is similar to the Visual Basic InStr function. The differences are speed and the ability to include one or more ? wildcard characters in the search string. In addition, the QuickPak library offers other versions of QInstr that perform case-insensitive and backward search. The versatility of the family of QInstr functions is demonstrated in the file viewer form that I present later in this chapter.

The QuickPak library also contains many string-manipulating routines not available in Visual Basic. Some examples are:

- The Encrypt procedure, which enables you to encrypt a string.
- The InCount function, which counts the number of times a substring occurs in a string. The InCount2 function is a case-insensitive version of InCount.
- A number of functions that return the index of the first character that is or is not in a set of characters.

The declarations for the string routines are shown in Listing 24-5.

Listing 24-5 The declarations of the string routines.

```
'---------------------- String Manipulation routines ----------------------

Declare Function Ascii% Lib "QPro.DLL" (ByVal Character$)
' a more tolerant version of the Visual Basic Asc() function.
Declare Function Blanks% Lib "QPro.DLL" (CharString$)
' counts the number of leading blanks in a string.
Declare Function CheckSum% Lib "QPro.DLL" (CharString$)
Declare Sub Encrypt Lib "QPro.DLL" (X$, Password$)
' encrypts the string X$ using a password.
Declare Sub Encrypt2 Lib "QPro.DLL" (X$, Password$)
' a more secure encrypting routine.
Declare Function Far2Str$ Lib "QPro.DLL" (ByVal Segment%, ByVal Address%)
' obtains an ASCIIZ string from any memory location and converts it into
' a variable-length Visual Basic string.
Declare Function FUsing$ Lib "QPro.DLL" (Number$, Image$)
' similar to the Visual Basic Format$ function
Declare Function InCount% Lib "QPro.DLL" (ByVal Source$, ByVal Search$)
' counts the number of times substring Search$ occurs in string Source$
Declare Function InCount2% Lib "QPro.DLL" (ByVal Source$, ByVal Search$)
' a case-insensitive version of function InCount%.
Declare Function IncountTbl% Lib "QPro.DLL" (ByVal Work$, ByVal Table$)
' returns the number of characters in string Work$ that match any character
' in the Table$ string.
Declare Function InstrTbl% Lib "QPro.DLL" (ByVal Start%, ByVal Source$,
ByVal Table$)
' returns the index of the first occurrence of any Table$ character in
' string Source$.
Declare Function InstrTbl2% Lib "QPro.DLL" (ByVal Start%, ByVal Source$,
ByVal Table$)
' a case-sensitive version of function InstrTbl%.
Declare Function InstrTblB% Lib "QPro.DLL" (ByVal Start%, ByVal Source$,
ByVal Table$)
' a version of InstrTbl that searches the string Source$ backwards.
```

Listing 24-5 Continued.

```
Declare Function InstrTblB2% Lib "QPro.DLL" (ByVal Start%, ByVal Source$,
ByVal Table$)
' a version of InstrTbl2 that searches the string Source$ backwards.
Declare Function LongestStr% Lib "QPro.DLL" (Array$, ByVal NumEls%)
Declare Sub LowASCII Lib "QPro.DLL" (Text$)
' strips the high bit from the characters of string Text$.
Declare Sub Lower Lib "QPro.DLL" (XString$)
' converts the characters of XString$ to lowercase.
Declare Sub LowerTbl Lib "QPro.DLL" (XString$, ByVal Table$)
' converts the characters of XString$ to lowercase and then uses string
' Table$ to handle foreign characters.
Declare Function NotInstr% Lib "QPro.DLL" (ByVal Start%, Source$, Table$)
' returns the index to the first character in Source$ that does not match
' any character in string Table$.
Declare Function Null% Lib "QPro.DLL" (Work$)
' reports if the string Work$ is either null or is filled with either
' spaces or Chr$(0) characters.
Declare Sub ProperName Lib "QPro.DLL" (PName$)
' converts the first letter of each word in PName$ to uppercase.
Declare Function QInstr% Lib "QPro.DLL" (ByVal Start%, ByVal Source$, ByVal
Search$)
' a faster version of the Visual Basic InStr function.
Declare Function QInstr2% Lib "QPro.DLL" (ByVal Start%, ByVal Source$,
ByVal Search$)
' a case-insensitive version of QInstr.
Declare Function QInstrB% Lib "QPro.DLL" (ByVal Start%, ByVal Source$,
ByVal Search$)
' a version of QInstr that scans string Source$ backwards.
Declare Function QInstrB2% Lib "QPro.DLL" (ByVal Start%, ByVal Source$,
ByVal Search$)
' a case-insensitive version of QInstrB.
Declare Function QPLen% Lib "QPro.DLL" (A$)
' a faster version of the Visual Basic Len function.
Declare Sub RemCtrl Lib "QPro.DLL" (X$, Replace$)
' replaces all the control characters in string X$ with the
' character in Replace$
Declare Sub ReplaceChar Lib "QPro.DLL" (Work$, Old$, New$)
' replaces the Old$ character in string X$ with the New$ character.
Declare Sub Sequence Lib "QPro.DLL" (Sequence$)
' Increments the characters in a string.
Declare Sub Upper Lib "QPro.DLL" (XString$)
' converts the characters of XString$ to uppercase.
Declare Sub UpperTbl Lib "QPro.DLL" (ByVal XString$, ByVal Table$)
' converts the characters of XString$ to uppercase and then use string
' Table$ to handle the foreign characters.
```

The QPro functions

The QuickPak package contains a set of base conversion functions, whose declarations are shown in Listing 24-6. These routines are very useful if you are performing bit manipulation of your data.

The miscellaneous routines

The QuickPak package contains a rich set of miscellaneous routines, shown in Listing 24-7, which includes functions Microsoft omitted from the QuickBasic engine when Visual Basic was developed. These functions and routines include Peek, Poke, Inp, Out, CVI, CVS, CVD, CVL, MKI, MKL, MKS,

Listing 24-6 The declarations of QPro functions.

```
'-------------------- QPro Functions --------------------
Declare Function Bin2Num% Lib "QPro.DLL" (ByVal Bin$)
' converts a string containing the image of a binary number into an
' integer.
Declare Function Num2Bin$ Lib "QPro.DLL" (ByVal Value%)
' converts an integer into a string that contains the image of the
' equivalent binary number.
Declare Function Num2Bin2$ Lib "QPro.DLL" (ByVal Value%)
' similar to Num2Bin except it returns as many digits as required to
' represent the converted number.
Declare Function QPHex$ Lib "QPro.DLL" (Number As Any, ByVal Digits%)
' returns a hexadecimal string image of a number.
```

Listing 24-7 The declarations of the miscellaneous routines.

```
'--------------------- Miscellaneous routines -----------------------
Declare Function AddUsi% Lib "QPro.DLL" (ByVal Int1%, ByVal Int2%)
' add two unsigned integers.
Declare Sub BCopy Lib "QPro.DLL" (Array1 As Any, Array2 As Any, ByVal
NumBytes%, ByVal Direction%)
' copies a block of memory.
Declare Sub BCopyT Lib "QPro.DLL" (Array1%, Array2%, ByVal ElSize%, ByVal
NumEls%)
' copies user-defined TYPE elements.
Declare Function Compact$ Lib "QPro.DLL" (Old$)
' removes all imbedded blanks from a string.
Declare Function Compare% Lib "QPro.DLL" (ByVal Segment1%, ByVal Address1%,
ByVal Segment2%, ByVal Address2%, ByVal NumBytes%)
' determines if two blocks of memory contain the same data.
Declare Function CompareT% Lib "QPro.DLL" (Type1 As Any, Type2 As Any,
ByVal NumBytes%)
' determines if two user-defined TYPE variables contain the same data.
Declare Function ControlHWnd% Lib "QPro.DLL" (Ctrl As Control)
' returns the Windows handle of a given control.
Declare Function CVI% Lib "QPro.DLL" (Number$)
' emulates the QuickBasic CVI function.
Declare Function CVL& Lib "QPro.DLL" (Number$)
' emulates the QuickBasic CVL function.
Declare Function CVS! Lib "QPro.DLL" (Number$)
' emulates the QuickBasic CVS function.
Declare Function CVD# Lib "QPro.DLL" (Number$)
' emulates the QuickBasic CVD function.
Declare Function CVC@ Lib "QPro.DLL" (Number$)
' emulates a CVD function.
Declare Function Date2Num% Lib "QPro.DLL" (ByVal Dat$)
' converts a date string into a number.
Declare Function DayName$ Lib "QPro.DLL" (ByVal Number%)
' returns the name of the weekday for a give date number.
Declare Sub DosCall Lib "QPro.DLL" (Reg As Any)
' offers the interface to the Windows API Dos3Call routine.  The Dos3Call
' routine does not support FCB operations.
Declare Function EDate2Num% Lib "QPro.DLL" (ByVal Dat$)
' converts a string with a European date format into a date number.
Declare Function ENum2Date$ Lib "QPro.DLL" (ByVal X%)
' converts a date number to a European date string.
Declare Function Factorial# Lib "QPro.DLL" (ByVal Number%)
' returns a factorial.
Declare Function FindLastSM& Lib "QPro.DLL" (Array As Any, ByVal NumBytes%)
' finds the last non-empty string in a string array.  The scanning is
' performed backward.
Declare Sub FloppyType Lib "QPro.DLL" (DriveA%, DriveB%)
```

Listing 24-7 Continued.

```
' returns the type of floppy drives for drives A: and B:.
Declare Function GetCPU% Lib "QPro.DLL" ()
' returns an integer value that represents the type of CPU in a PC.
Declare Sub GetEquip Lib "QPro.DLL" (Flopps%, Parallel%, Serial%)
' returns the number of floppy disks, parallel ports, and serial port,
' as indicated by the BIOS.
Declare Function GetSystemResources% Lib "QPro.DLL" ()
' returns the percentage of free Windows system resources.
Declare Function Inp% Lib "QPro.DLL" (ByVal Port%)
' emulates the QuickBasic Inp function that reads directly
' from a machine port.
Declare Function LpStr& Lib "QPro.DLL" (A$)
' returns the long integer far pointer to a Visual Basic High
' Level Language string.
Declare Function MathChip% Lib "QPro.DLL" ()
' determines if a PC has a math co-processor installed.
Declare Function MaxLong& Lib "QPro.DLL" (ByVal value1&, ByVal value2&)
' returns the larger of two long integers.
Declare Function MaxInt% Lib "QPro.DLL" (ByVal value1%, ByVal value2%)
' returns the large of two integers.
Declare Function MinInt% Lib "QPro.DLL" (ByVal value1%, ByVal value2%)
' returns the smaller of two integers.
Declare Function MinLong& Lib "QPro.DLL" (ByVal value1&, ByVal value2&)
' returns the smaller of two long integers.
Declare Function MKI$ Lib "QPro.DLL" (ByVal Number%)
' emulates the QuickBasic MKI$ function.
Declare Function MKL$ Lib "QPro.DLL" (ByVal Number&)
' emulates the QuickBasic MKL$ function.
Declare Function MKS$ Lib "QPro.DLL" (ByVal Number!)
' emulates the QuickBasic MKS$ function.
Declare Function MKD$ Lib "QPro.DLL" (ByVal Number#)
' emulates the QuickBasic MKD$ function.
Declare Function MKC$ Lib "QPro.DLL" (ByVal Number@)
' emulates the QuickBasic MKC$ function.
Declare Sub MonoPrint Lib "QPro.DLL" (Text$, ByVal Row%, ByVal Col%, ByVal
Attr%)
' permits printing debug or other data to a second monochrome monitor.
Declare Function MonthName$ Lib "QPro.DLL" (ByVal Number%)
' returns the name of the month for the specified date number.
Declare Function NetName$ Lib "QPro.DLL" ()
' returns the name of the active network connected to a PC.
Declare Function Num2Date$ Lib "QPro.DLL" (ByVal X%)
' converts a date code into a string image.
Declare Function Num2Day% Lib "QPro.DLL" (ByVal X%)
' converts a date code into a day number.
Declare Function Num2Time$ Lib "QPro.DLL" (X&)
' converts the number of seconds since the last midnight into a
' string image of the time.
Declare Function Num2Time2$ Lib "QPro.DLL" (X&)
Declare Sub Out Lib "QPro.DLL" (ByVal Port%, ByVal bData%)
' emulates the QuickBasic Out routine that directly writes to a port.
Declare Function Peek1% Lib "QPro.DLL" (ByVal Segment%, ByVal Address%)
' emulates a QuickBasic Peek.
Declare Function Peek2% Lib "QPro.DLL" (ByVal Segment%, ByVal Address%)
' reads a 2-byte word.
Declare Function PMatch% Lib "QPro.DLL" (Work$)
Declare Sub Poke1 Lib "QPro.DLL" (ByVal Segment%, ByVal Address%, ByVal
Byte%)
' emulates a QuickBasic Poke.
Declare Sub Poke2 Lib "QPro.DLL" (ByVal Segment%, ByVal Address%, ByVal
Word%)
' pokes a word.
Declare Function Power% Lib "QPro.DLL" (ByVal Mantissa%, ByVal Exponent%)
' returns the value of Mantissa% ^ Exponent%
Declare Function Power2% Lib "QPro.DLL" (ByVal Exponent%)
' returns 2 ^ Exponent%
Declare Function QPSegAddr& Lib "QPro.DLL" (Array As Any)
```

Listing 24-7 Continued.

```
' emulates
Declare Function QPUSI% Lib "QPro.DLL" (ByVal LongInt&)
Declare Function QPWeekDay% Lib "QPro.DLL" (D$)
Declare Function ShiftLL& Lib "QPro.DLL" (ByVal NumberLong&, ByVal
Numbits%)
Declare Function ShiftLR& Lib "QPro.DLL" (ByVal NumberLong&, ByVal
Numbits%)
Declare Function ShiftIL% Lib "QPro.DLL" (ByVal Number%, ByVal Numbits%)
Declare Function ShiftIR% Lib "QPro.DLL" (ByVal Number%, ByVal Numbits%)
Declare Function Soundex$ Lib "QPro.DLL" (Work$)
' returns the sound-like code that enables you to compare two words that
' differ in their vowels.
Declare Sub SplitColor Lib "QPro.DLL" (Red%, Green%, Blue%, OrigColr&)
' splits the Windows long integer color code into its red, green, and blue
' component values.
Declare Sub SysTime Lib "QPro.DLL" (t$)
Declare Function Times2% Lib "QPro.DLL" (ByVal NumberX%)
Declare Function Time2Num& Lib "QPro.DLL" (ByVal Tim$)
Declare Function TrapInt% Lib "QPro.DLL" (ByVal Value, ByVal LoLimit%,
ByVal HiLimit%)
Declare Function VarSeg% Lib "QPro.DLL" (Variable As Any)
' returns the segment portion of a non-string variable's far address.
Declare Function VarPtr% Lib "QPro.DLL" (Variable As Any)
' returns the near address of a non-string variable's far address.
Declare Function Sadd% Lib "QPro.DLL" (ByVal A$)
' returns the near address of the data associated with
' a variable-length string
Declare Function SSeg% Lib "QPro.DLL" (ByVal A$)
' returns the segment portion of a variable-length string.
Declare Function XTwp2Pixel% Lib "QPro.DLL" (xTwip&)
' returns the number of pixels (logical units) contained in a given
' number of horizontal twips.
Declare Function XPixel2Twp& Lib "QPro.DLL" (ByVal xPixel%)
' returns the number of twips contained in a given
' number of horizontal pixels.
Declare Function YPixel2Twp& Lib "QPro.DLL" (ByVal yPixel%)
' returns the number of twips contained in a given
' number of vertical pixels.
Declare Function YTwp2Pixel% Lib "QPro.DLL" (yTwip&)
' returns the number of pixels (logical units) contained in a given
' number of vertical twips.
Declare Function EnumWins% Lib "QPro.DLL" (ByVal EnumFlag%, Array As
Integer)
' returns the number of all top windows, children under a given window, all
' tasks, or all parent tasks.
```

MKD, and the string address functions. The set of CVx and MKx functions enable you to efficiently store and quickly recall numeric data in strings, text boxes, and list box members.

The miscellaneous routines also include members that query the equipment, the presence of a math co-processor, the type of floppy drives. In addition, there are date and time functions. One very interesting function is Soundex$, which converts a string into a four-character sounds-like string. This function empowers you to add a sounds-like search feature in a file viewer or text editor.

The Windows API routines

The QuickPak package includes a number of Windows API declarations, shown in Listing 24-8. These declarations tap into the Windows services and enable you to draw lines and write text on form or in a picture. In addition, the QuickPak package offers two new controls, QPHScroll and QPVScroll. While these controls resemble the Visual Basic horizontal and vertical scrolls, they offer constant feedback regarding the movement of the scroll bar.

Listing 24-8 The declarations of the Windows API routines.

```
'---------------------- Windows API routines ----------------------

Declare Function CreateBrushIndirect% Lib "GDI" (Strct As Any)
' creates a logical brush tht has a style, color, and pattern specified
' by the data structure Strct.
Declare Function FloodFill% Lib "GDI" (ByVal h%, ByVal X%, ByVal Y%, ByVal
BoundColor&)
' fills the area of the display surface with the current brush.
Declare Function SelectObject% Lib "GDI" (ByVal h%, ByVal nIndex%)
' selects the object nIndex% as the selected object of the specified
' devide context h%.
Declare Function CreatePen% Lib "gdi" (ByVal nPenStyle%, ByVal nWidth%,
ByVal crColor&)
' creates a logical pen with a style, width, and color.
Declare Function DeleteObject% Lib "gdi" (ByVal hObject%)
' deletes a logical pen, brush, font, bitmpa, region, or
' palette from memory.
Declare Function Polyline% Lib "gdi" (ByVal hDC%, lpPoints As tagPOINT,
ByVal nCount%)
' draws a set of lines segments.
Declare Function GetTextMetrics% Lib "gdi" (ByVal hDC%, lpMetric As
tagTEXTMETRIC)
' fills the buffer pointed by tagTEXTMETRIC with the metrics
' for the selected font.
Declare Function DestroyWindow% Lib "user" (ByVal hWnd%)
' destroys the window accessed by handle hWnd%.
Declare Function GetDC% Lib "user" (ByVal hWnd%)
' retrieves a handle to a display context.
Declare Function ReleaseDC% Lib "user" (ByVal hWnd%, ByVal hDC%)
' realses the device context hDC% freeing it for use by other applications.
Declare Function GetWindowText% Lib "user" (ByVal hWnd%, ByVal Title$,
ByVal MaxChars%)
' returns the title of a window.
Declare Function GetWindowTextLength% Lib "user" (ByVal hWnd%)
' returns the length of a window's caption title.
Declare Sub BringWindowToTop Lib "user" (ByVal hWnd%)
' pops a window to the top, overlapping any other windows.
Declare Function SendMessage& Lib "user" (ByVal hWnd%, ByVal wMsg%, ByVal
wParam%, ByVal lParam&)
' sends a message to one or more windows.
```

The BackUp utility

The first program presented is a backup utility. The utility is aimed at making a backup of a directory to a single disk. The files on the backup disks are normal files (that is, you can readily use them) and have the same date and time file stamps as the original files in the source path. You can use higher density disks to back up a large number of files that you create with various other applications. For example, I keep the word processing files for each book project in a separate directory. The total size of such files normally fits on a 1.2 or 1.4Mb disk, making the BackUp utility practical.

The BackUp utility has several backup options. You can delete the files of the target directory that are not in the source directory; when you turn off this option, you can back up the files from different directories to the same disk, assuming there is enough disk space to store all of these files. You can also update the files of the target directory with more recent source directory files, and add new files from the source directory to the target directory.

These tasks are enabled or disabled using check box controls. This feature enables you to fine-tune the BackUp utility according to your own preferences. Figure 24-1 shows a sample session with the BackUp utility.

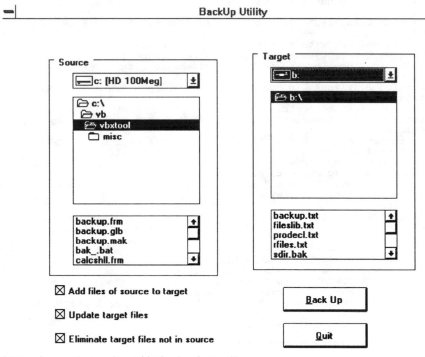

24-1 A sample session with the backup utility.

The BackUp utility contains the following controls:

- A frame control for the source directory, which contains a Drive list box, a Directory list box, and a File list box.
- A frame control for the target directory, which also contains Drive, Directory, and File list boxes.

- Three check boxes that allow you to fine-tune the backup operations of the utility. By default, all three check boxes are checked.
- A Backup command button, which triggers the backup operation.
- A command button that exits the application.

You can add and eliminate files without using the QuickPak Professional package, however, updating existing files does require QuickPak routines that obtain the date and time stamps of files to decide if the source directory files are more recent. You might suppose that the file size, available through the Visual Basic Lof function, could be used instead of the date/time stamp. However, this would not be as reliable as the date/time file stamp, because you can update a file by, for example, replacing text, which yields the same file size but a different date/time stamp.

Adding new files to the target directory is done by determining which files in the Source list box are not in the Target list box. These files are then copied to the target directory.

Eliminating files from the target directory involves just the opposite: determining which files in the Target list box are not in the Source list box. These files are then removed from the target directory.

Updating the target directory files involves the following process, which is repeated for each file in the source directory. First, the file with the same name as the source file is located in the target directory. Then the date and time stamps of both files are obtained and compared. If the source file is more recent, the file is copied from the source directory to the target directory. In the rare case that the file in the target directory is more recent, the user is prompted if he wants to copy the file from the target directory to the source directory. This type of prompt is a good, safe practice.

Handling the date and time stamps of a file is not limited to determining if a file is a more recent version of another. Backing up files by copying has one bad side effect: the target files are assigned the date/time stamp of when the copy is actually made, not the date/time stamp of the source file. To correct this, the BackUp utility has to read the date/time stamp of the source file and write it to the date/time stamp of the target file. This task requires routines from the QuickPak package.

Figures 24-2 to 24-4 contain the specifications for the BACKUP.MAK project file and the BACKUP.FRM form file. Figure 24-2 indicates that the global VBXVB.BAS module is used. This module contains the declarations of sample QuickPak routines, included in the companion disk. This allows you to customize the BackUp utility and compile it.

Listing 24-9 contains the code attached to the BACKUP.FRM form. The form declares two dynamic arrays of the FullInfo type. The declaration of the FullInfo type appears in Listing 24-7. The two dynamic arrays store the files of the source and target directories to compare their date/time stamps.

Application name: Single-disk backup utility
Application code name: BACKUP

Version: 1.0   Date created: September 14, 1991
Programmer(s): Namir Clement Shammas

List of filenames

Storage path: \ VB \ VBXTOOL
Project   BACKUP.MAK
Global   VBXVB.BAS
Form 1   BACKUP.FRM
Module 1   GENERIC.BAS

24-2 The basic specifications for the BACKUP.MAK project file.

Form # 1   Form filename: BACKUP.FRM
Version: 1.0   Date: September 14, 1991

Control object type	Default CtlName	Purpose
Frame	Frame1	Frame for source path list boxes
	Frame2	Frame for target path list boxes
Drive list box	Drive1	Source drive list box
	Drive2	Target drive list box
Directory list box	Dir1	Source directory list box
	Dir2	Target directory list box
File list box	File1	Source file list box
	File2	Target file list box
Command button	Command1	Backs up files
	Command2	Exits the application
Check box	Check1	Adds files of source path to target path
	Check2	Updates files in target path
	Check3	Eliminates target path files that are not in the source path

24-3 The list of controls in the BACKUP.FRM form file.

Application (code) name: BACKUP
Form # 1
Version: 1.0   Date: September 14, 1991

Original control name	Property	New setting
Form	Caption	BackUp Utility
Frame1	CtlName	SourceFrm
	Caption	Source
Frame2	CtlName	TargetFrm
	Caption	Target
Drive1	CtlName	SourceDrv

24-4 The customized settings for the BACKUP.FRM form.

Original control name	Property	New setting
Drive2	CtlName	TargetDrv
Dir1	CtlName	SourceDir
Dir2	CtlName	TargetDir
File1	CtlName	SourceFlb
File2	CtlName	TargetFlb
Command1	CtlName	BackUpBtn
	Caption	&Back Up
Command2	CtlName	QuitBtn
	Caption	&Quit
Check1	CtlName	AddChk
	Caption	Add files of source to target
Check2	CtlName	UpdateChk
	Caption	Update target files
Check3	CtlName	ElimChk
	Caption	Eliminate target files not in source

24-4 Continued.

Listing 24-9 The code attached to the BACKUP.FRM form.

```
' declare dynamic arrays for source and target files
Dim SourceFiles() As FullInfo
Dim TargetFiles() As FullInfo

Sub AdjustTimeStr (T$)
' Adjust the time string.
  Dim X As Integer
  Dim I As Integer
  Dim StrLen As Integer
  ' store the length of string T$ in StrLen
  StrLen = Len(T$)
  ' is the last character in T$ a "p" (that is,
  ' does T$ refer to a p.m. time?
  If Right$(T$, 1) = "p" Then
    ' find the location of the colon character
    I = InStr(T$, ":")
    ' extract the hours from T$
    X = Val(Mid$(T$, 1, I - 1))
    X = X + 12 ' add 12 hours
    ' rebuild the time string
    T$ = Format$(X, "##") + Mid$(T$, I)
  End If
  T$ = Left$(T$, StrLen - 1)
End Sub

Sub AppendBackSlash (S$)
' Append a backlash character to path S$ if needed
  If Right$(S$, 1) <> "\" Then S$ = S$ + "\"
End Sub

Sub BackUpBtn_Click ()
' Backup files.
  Const YES = 6
  Dim I As Integer
```

Listing 24-9 Continued.

```
Dim J As Integer
Dim K As Integer
Dim L As Integer
Dim Dummy As Integer
Dim SourceCount As Integer
Dim TargetCount As Integer
Dim LongDummy As Long
Dim SFile As String
Dim TFile As String
Dim SourceDirStr As String
Dim TargetDirStr As String
Dim Message As String
' build the message
Message = " in the target directory is more recent. "
Message = Message + "Update file in source directory?"
MousePointer = 11 ' hour-glass
' get the source directory
SourceDirStr = SourceDir.List(-1)
' get the target directory
TargetDirStr = TargetDir.List(-1)
' append a "\" to the source directory, if needed
AppendBackSlash SourceDirStr
' append a "\" to the target directory, if needed
AppendBackSlash TargetDirStr

' eliminate Files that are in the target path but
' not in the source path
If ElimChk.Value = 1 Then
  ' for every file in the target directory
  For I = 0 To TargetFlb.ListCount - 1
    ' get the file from TargetFlb file list box member I
    SFile = TargetFlb.List(I)
    ' if the file in variable SFile is not in the SourceFlb
    ' file list box, delete the file in the target directory
    If BinSearch(SourceFlb, SFile, 1, 1, 0) = -1 Then
      Kill TargetDirStr + SFile
    End If
  Next I
  TargetFlb.Refresh ' update TargetFlb file list box
End If
' update files in the target directory if the corresponding files
' in the source directory as more recent?
If UpdateChk.Value = 1 Then
  ' get the number of files in the source directory
  SourceCount = SourceFlb.ListCount
  ' get the number of files in the target directory
  TargetCount = TargetFlb.ListCount
  ' are there files in both directories?
  If (SourceCount > 0) And (TargetCount > 0) Then
    ' redimension the SourceFiles dynamic array
    ReDim SourceFiles(0 To SourceCount)
    ' read the data for the SourceFiles array
    ReadFileX SourceDirStr + "*.*", LongDummy, SourceFiles(1)
    ' redimension the TargetFiles dynamic array
    ReDim TargetFiles(0 To TargetCount)
    ' read the data for the TargetFiles array
    ReadFileX TargetDirStr + "*.*", LongDummy, TargetFiles(1)
    ' for each file in the source directory
    For I = 1 To SourceCount
      ' get file from element I of the SourceFiles array
      SFile = SourceFiles(I).BaseName + "." + SourceFiles(I).ExtName
      ' obtain the location of file SFile in TargetFiles() array
      J = LinearSearch(SFile, TargetFiles())
' does the file exist in the TargetFIles() array?
If J > 0 Then
  ' compare the file in the source and target directory
```

Listing 24-9 Continued.

```
        K = CompareStamps(SourceFiles(I), TargetFiles(J))
        ' obtain source filename (without any internal spaces)
        SFile = SourceDirStr + GetFilename(SourceFiles(I))
        ' obtain target filename (without any internal spaces)
        TFile = TargetDirStr + GetFilename(TargetFiles(J))
        ' is the file in the source directory more recent that the
        ' same file in the target directory?
        If K > 0 Then
          ' copy files
          If CopyFile(SFile, TFile) Then
            ' also update date/time stamps
            MatchDateTimeStamps SFile, TFile
          End If
        ' is the file in the source directory older
        ' than the one in the target directory
        ElseIf K < 0 Then
          L = MsgBox("File " + TFile + Message, 68, "Warning!")
          If L = YES Then
            If CopyFile(TFile, SFile) Then
              ' also update date/time stamps
              MatchDateTimeStamps TFile, SFile
            End If
          End If ' L = YES
        End If ' K > 0
      End If ' J > 0
    Next I
  End If
  TargetFlb.Refresh ' update TargetFlb file list box
End If
' add files that are in the source directory, but not in the
' target directory?
If AddChk.Value = 1 Then
  ' for each file in the source directory
  For I = 0 To SourceFlb.ListCount - 1
    ' get the file from member I of SourceFlb
    SFile = SourceFlb.List(I)
    ' is SFile not in TargetFlb file list box?
    If BinSearch(TargetFlb, SFile, 1, 1, 0) = -1 Then
      ' copy file to target directory
      If CopyFile(SourceDirStr + SFile, TargetDirStr + SFile) Then
        ' update the date/time stamps
        MatchDateTimeStamps SourceDirStr + SFile, TargetDirStr + SFile
      End If
    End If
  Next I
  TargetFlb.Refresh ' update TargetFlb file list box
End If
  MousePointer = 0 ' restore mouse cursor
End Sub

Function CompareStamps (F1 As FullInfo, F2 As FullInfo) As Integer
' Compare the file date and time stamps of files F1 and F2.  The
' function returns the following results:
'
'   +1 when file F1 is has a more recent date/time stamp than F2
'
'    0 when files F1 and F2 have the exact date/time stamp
'
'   -1 when file F2 is has a more recent date/time stamp than F1
'
  Dim FileDate1 As Long
  Dim FileDate2 As Long
  Dim FileTime1 As Long
  Dim FileTime2 As Long
  ' get the file date stamp of file F1
  FileDate1 = GetFileDate(F1.FileDate)
```

Listing 24-9 Continued.

```
    ' get the file date stamp of file F2
    FileDate2 = GetFileDate(F2.FileDate)
    ' get the file time stamp of file F1
    FileTime1 = GetFileTime(F1.FileTime)
    ' get the file time stamp of file F2
    FileTime2 = GetFileTime(F2.FileTime)

    ' first compare the date stamps
    ' is the date stamp of F1 more recent than that of F2
    If FileDate1 > FileDate2 Then
      CompareStamps = 1
    ' is the date stamp of F2 more recent than that of F1
    ElseIf FileDate1 < FileDate2 Then
      CompareStamps = -1
    ' now compare the time stamps
    ' is the time stamp of F1 more recent than that of F2
    ElseIf FileTime1 > FileTime2 Then
      CompareStamps = 1
    ' is the time stamp of F2 more recent than that of F1
    ElseIf FileTime1 < FileTime2 Then
      CompareStamps = -1
    ' the files F1 and F2 have the same date and time stamps
    Else
      CompareStamps = 0
    End If
End Function

Function CopyFile (ByVal Source$, ByVal Target$) As Integer
' Copy file Source$ into file Target$.  The function returns
' True if the file copying was successful.  Otherwise, the
' function returns False.
    ' declare buffer size constant
    Const BUFFER_SIZE = 16384
    Dim Buffer As String ' declare buffer
    Dim InFileNum As Integer
    Dim OutFileNum As Integer
    Dim TheFileSize As Long
    ' are the source and target files the same?
    If LCase$(Source$) = LCase$(Target$) Then
      CopyFile = True
      Exit Function
    End If
    ' set the error trap
    On Error GoTo BadCopyFile:
    ' get the input file handle
    InFileNum = FreeFile
    ' open the source file as a binary file
    Open Source$ For Binary As InFileNum
    ' get the output file handle
    OutFileNum = FreeFile
    ' open the target file as a binary file
    Open Target$ For Binary As OutFileNum
    ' store the size of the input file in TheFileSize
    TheFileSize = LOF(InFileNum)
    ' specify the buffer size
    Buffer = Space$(BUFFER_SIZE)
    ' copy the contents of the source file into the target file
    Do While Not EOF(InFileNum)
      ' are there fewer than BUFFER_SIZE bytes to copy?
      If TheFileSize < BUFFER_SIZE Then
        If TheFileSize < 1 Then Exit Do
        ' adjust the buffer size accordingly
        Buffer = Space$(TheFileSize)
      End If
      Get #InFileNum, , Buffer
      Put #OutFileNum, , Buffer
```

Listing 24-9 Continued.

```
       ' decrement the remaining number of bytes to copy
         TheFileSize = TheFileSize - BUFFER_SIZE
     Loop
     On Error GoTo 0 ' turn off error trap
     ' close file buffers
     Close #InFileNum
     Close #OutFileNum
     CopyFile = True ' return the function result
     Exit Function
     '********************* Error Handler *********************
BadCopyFile:
     CopyFile = False ' return the function result
     Close #InFileNum
     Close #OutFileNum
     Resume ExitCopyFile
ExitCopyFile:
End Function

Sub Form_Load ()
' Initialize the form.
     WindowState = 2 ' maximize the window
     ' select all of the files in the source and target directory
     SourceFlb.Filename = "*.*"
     TargetFlb.Filename = "*.*"
     ' select all of the check boxes
     AddChk.Value = 1
     UpdateChk.Value = 1
     ElimChk.Value = 1
End Sub

Function GetFileDate (ByVal D$) As Long
' Obtain the file date stamp as a long integer.  The parameter
' D$ supplies the function with a string image of the date in
' the following format mm-dd-yy.
     Dim X As Long
     X = 10000 * Val(Mid$(D$, 7, 2))
     X = X + 100 * Val(Mid$(D$, 1, 2))
     X = X + Val(Mid$(D$, 4, 2))
     GetFileDate = X
End Function

Function GetFilename (F As FullInfo) As String
' Return the filename without internal spaces
     GetFilename = RTrim$(F.BaseName) + "." + RTrim$(F.ExtName)
End Function

Function GetFileTime (ByVal T$) As Long
' Obtain the file time stamp as a long integer.  The parameter
' T$ supplies the function with a string image of the time in
' the following format:
'
'          hh:mma    (example 10:30a)
' or
'
'          hh:mmp    (example 10:30p)
'
' where the letters a and p indicate a.m. or p.m.
     Dim X As Long
     X = 60 * Val(Mid$(T$, 1, 2)) + Val(Mid$(T$, 4, 2))
     If Right$(T$, 1) = "p" Then
       X = 12 * 60 + X
     End If
     GetFileTime = X
End Function

Function LinearSearch (ByVal F$, A() As FullInfo) As Integer
' Performs a linear search to find the location of F$ in the
```

Listing 24-9 Continued.

```
' array A().  The function returns the index of the matching
' element, or returns 0 when no match is found.
  Dim I As Integer
  Dim Hi As Integer
  Dim NotFound As Integer

  NotFound = True
  I = 1
  Hi = UBound(A)
  ' loop until there is a match for F$ or until
  ' the entire array is examined.
  Do While NotFound And (I <= Hi)
    If F$ <> (A(I).BaseName + "." + A(I).ExtName) Then
      I = I + 1
    Else
      NotFound = False
    End If
  Loop
  ' if there is no match
  If NotFound Then
    LinearSearch = 0
  Else
    LinearSearch = I
  End If
End Function

Sub MatchDateTimeStamps (ByVal Source$, ByVal Target$)
' Make the date/time stamp of file Target$ the same as
' that of file Source$.

  Dim LongDummy As Long
  Static SourceFileInfo(0 To 1)  As FullInfo
  Dim DateStr As String
  Dim TimeStr As String
  ' read the source file information that includes
  ' the date/time stamp.
  ReadFileX Source$, LongDummy, SourceFileInfo(1)
  DateStr = RTrim$(SourceFileInfo(1).FileDate)
  TimeStr = RTrim$(SourceFileInfo(1).FileTime)
  AdjustTimeStr TimeStr
  ' write the date/time stamp to the target file
  FStamp Target$, TimeStr, DateStr
End Sub

Sub QuitBtn_Click ()
  End
End Sub

Sub SourceDir_Change ()
  SourceFlb.Path = SourceDir.Path
End Sub

Sub SourceDrv_Change ()
  SourceDir.Path = SourceDrv.Drive
  SourceFlb.Filename = "*.*"
End Sub

Sub TargetDir_Change ()
  TargetFlb.Path = TargetDir.Path
End Sub

Sub TargetDrv_Change ()
  TargetDir.Path = TargetDrv.Drive
End Sub
```

The procedures of Listing 24-9 are described briefly in the paragraphs that follow.

The AdjustTimeStr procedure converts a 12-hour format string into a 24-hour format string, which is required by the FStamp procedure in the QuickPak library.

The BackUpBtn_Click procedure is the workhorse of the BackUp utility. The procedure first obtains the source directory from the Source directory list box, and the the target directory from the Target directory list box. Then it eliminates target directory files that are not in the source directory. The routine examines the files in target file list box, and uses the BinSearch function implemented in module GENERIC.BAS, to determine whether or not a target directory file is in the source directory. The procedure uses the Visual Basic Kill statement to remove the old target files.

Then the procedure updates the target directory files. It obtains the number of files in both the source and the target directories, and bypasses the remaining subtasks if the source or target directories are empty. If not, the procedure invokes the ReadFileX procedure from the QuickPak library to read the data into the FullInfo-typed SourceFiles array, and to read the data into the FullInfo-typed TargetFiles array.

For each source directory file, the procedure finds the target directory file with the same name and compares the date/file stamps of the two files by calling the CompareStamps function. If the source file is more recent, the routine copies it to the target directory; if the target file is more recent, the procedure prompts you whether or not to copy that file to the source directory.

Finally, the procedure adds the new source directory files to the target directory, by searching the source file list box for files that are not in the target file list box and copying them to the target directory.

Notice that after every call to function CopyFile, the procedure issues a MatchDateTimeStamps call to equalize the date/time stamp of the target file with that of the source file.

The CompareStamps function compares the date/time file stamps of two files F1 and F2 supplied as FullInfo-typed parameters, and returns 1 if F1 is more recent, −1 if F2 is more recent, and 0 if both files have the same date/time stamps. The function first compares the date stamps of the two files; if these stamps are equal, it compares the time stamps to determine which file is more recent.

The Boolean CopyFile function is almost identical to the version in the module FILESLIB.BAS, except this version uses a 16K buffer (rather than 4K) to copy files. I have included this special version to avoid dragging the entire code of the FILESLIB.BAS into the .EXE file of the BackUp utility.

The Form_Load procedure initializes the form. First, it maximizes the application's window, and then assigns the *.* filename pattern to both the source and target file list boxes, which selects all of the files in both source and target directories. Then, it selects all of the check boxes.

The GetFileDate function returns the date stamp of a file as a long integer. The function converts the string mm – dd – yy into the long integer yymmdd. For example, the string 10 – 15 – 91 yields the number 911015.

The GetFilename function removes the internal spaces from a filename. Such internal spaces appear when using the fixed-length fields BaseName and ExtName that are part of the FullInfo data type.

The GetFileTime function converts the string image of a 12-hour time format into the number of minutes.

The LinSearch function returns the index of the FullInfo-typed array A( ) that matches the filename of parameter F$. The function returns 0 if no match is found.

The MatchDateTimeStamps procedure equalizes the date/time file stamp of the target file Target$ with that of the source file Source$. The routine calls the QuickPak procedure ReadFileX to obtain the full source file information and stores it in the local static array SourceFileInfo. Then it reads the date and time stamps into the local variables DateStr and TimeStr, and calls Adjust TimeStr to convert the 12-hour time format in TimeStr into the 24-hour time format required by the FStamp routine. Then the FStamp routine is called to supply the target file with new date and time stamps.

The SDIR utility

The Visual Basic file list box control enables you to view the files in a selected path. The control displays only the file names; the file sizes, date/time stamps, and attributes are not included. This information is valuable, as demonstrated by the BackUp utility. This section presents the SDIR utility, a small shell utility that displays a list of files with their sizes and date/time stamps, using the ReadFileI QuickPak procedure. In addition, SDIR has menu selections that view, print, sort, and delete the selected file. Figure 24-5 shows a sample session with the SDIR utility, which contains the following controls:

- The Drive list box, which enables you to specify a new drive.
- The Directory list box, which enables you to specify a new directory.
- The Filename Pattern text box, which allows you to specify the files you want to appear in the list box.
- A list box that displays the sorted files in the selected path that match the specified filename pattern. The files are sorted in an ascending order.
- A check box that enables and disables the display of files in the list box.

When you first run the application, the list box contains all of the files in the current directory. You can use the Drive and Directory list boxes to select a different path. You can also type in a new filename pattern in the text box. All of these changes are immediately reflected by updating the files in

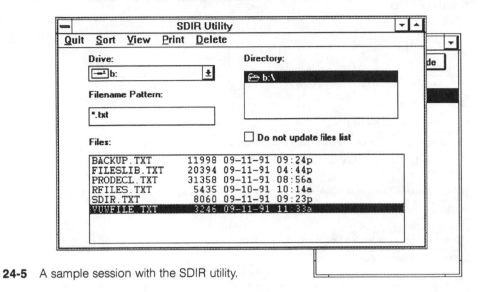

SDIR Utility

Quit   Sort   View   Print   Delete

Drive:

b:

Directory:

b:\

Filename Pattern:

*.txt

☐ **Do not update files list**

Files:

```
BACKUP.TXT      11998  09-11-91  09:24p
FILESLIB.TXT    20394  09-11-91  04:44p
PRODECL.TXT     31358  09-11-91  08:56a
RFILES.TXT       5435  09-10-91  10:14a
SDIR.TXT         8060  09-11-91  09:23p
VUWFILE.TXT      3246  09-11-91  11:33a
```

24-5   A sample session with the SDIR utility.

the list box, unless you check the check box. When you check that control, you can alter the drive, directory, and filename pattern, while maintaining an empty list box. This feature enables you specifically to navigate through the directory tree until you reach a desired directory; you can then uncheck the check box and view the files of that directory.

The SDIR utility has a simple one-level menu that offers the following options:

- The Quit selection exits the application.
- The Sort selection reads the selected file (assumed to be a text file), sorts it, prompts you for an output filename, and then saves the sorted lines to the output file. The default output filename is the selected file. You can enter another filename to preserve the original file.
- The View selection loads and displays the ViewFile form, which will be discussed later in this section.
- The Print selection provides a paginated hard copy of the selected file.
- The Delete section deletes the selected file. The utility prompts you to confirm the deletion, which guards against the accidental erasure of important files.

When you select the View menu selection, the SDIR utility loads the VUW-FILE.FRM form (which has the FormName setting ViewFile). Figure 24-6

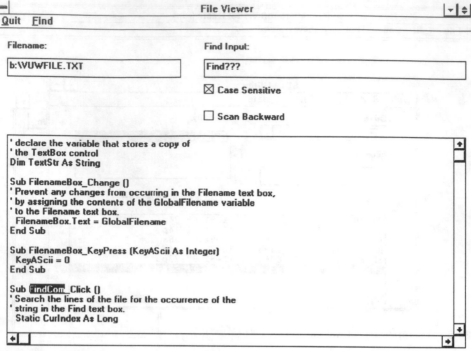

Code shown in the multiline text box:

```
' declare the variable that stores a copy of
' the TextBox control
Dim TextStr As String

Sub FilenameBox_Change ()
' Prevent any changes from occurring in the Filename text box,
' by assigning the contents of the GlobalFilename variable
' to the Filename text box.
  FilenameBox.Text = GlobalFilename
End Sub

Sub FilenameBox_KeyPress (KeyAScii As Integer)
  KeyAScii = 0
End Sub

Sub FindCom_Click ()
' Search the lines of the file for the occurrence of the
' string in the Find text box.
  Static CurIndex As Long
```

24-6 A sample session with the ViewFile form.

shows a sample session with the ViewFile form. The form contains the following controls:

- The Filename text box, which displays the name of the currently viewed file. The text box accepts no keyboard input.
- A multiline scrollable text box that displays the lines of the selected file.
- The Find text box, which allows you to key in the text you want to search in the currently viewed file.
- The Case Sensitive check box, which toggles case-sensitive search. By default, the search is case-insensitive.
- The Scan Backward check box, which toggles backward search. The default search direction is forward.

Unlike the ViewFile and EditFile forms presented in earlier chapters, this version uses the QInstr, QInstr2, QInstrB, and QInstr2B routines in the QuickPak library to perform a text search that may include one or more ? wildcards. Thus, for example, the search text F?r can match any For keyword in a Visual Basic listing text file.

The ViewFile form has Quit and Find menu selections that allow you to exit the form and perform a text search, respectively. The Find selection uses the string in the Find text box and the check box settings to perform a text search. If the file viewer finds a match, it displays the matching text as selected text.

Figures 24-7 to 24-13 show the specifications for the project file SDIR .MAK, the SDIR.FRM form file, and the VUWFILE.FRM form file. The SDIR.GLB is a global module created by adding the following declaration to the Crescent Software PRODECL.BAS global module:

```
Global GlobalFilename As String
```

Application name: Sorted directory shell utility
Application code name: SDIR

Version: 1.0   Date created: September 14, 1991
Programmer(s): Namir Clement Shammas

24-7 The basic specifications for the SDIR.MAK project file.

List of filenames

Storage path: \ VB \ VBXTOOL
Project   SDIR.MAK
Global   SDIR.GLB
Form 1   SDIR.FRM
Form 2   VUWFILE.FRM

Form # 1   Form filename: SDIR.FRM
Version: 1.0   Date: September 14, 1991

Control object type	Default CtlName	Purpose
Drive list box	Drive1	Selects the current drive
Directory list box	Dir1	Selects the current directory
List box	List1	Displays the matching files
Text box	Text1	Filename pattern
Label	Label1	Label for Drive
	Label2	Label for Directory list box
	Label3	Label for text box
	Label4	Label for list box

24-8 The list of controls in the SDIR.FRM form file.

Application (code) name: SDIR
Form # 1
Version: 1.0   Date: September 14, 1991

Original control name	Property	New setting
Form	Caption	SDIR Utility
Drive1	CtlName	DiskDrv
Dir1	CtlName	TreeDir

24-9 The customized settings for the SDIR.FRM form.

Original control name	Property	New setting
List1	CtlName	FilesLst
	FontBold	False
	FontName	Courier
	FontSize	9.75
Text1	CtlName	TextBox
	Text	(empty text)
Label1	CtlName	DriveLbl
	Caption	Drive:
Label2	CtlName	DirectoryLbl
	Caption	Directory:
Label3	CtlName	FilenameLbl
	Caption	Filename Pattern:
Label4	CtlName	FilesLbl
	Caption	Files:

24-9 Continued.

Form # 1
Version:
1.0   Date: September 14, 1991

Caption	Property	Setting	Purpose
&Quit	CtlName	QuitCom	Exits the application
&Sort	CtlName	SortCom	Sorts the selected file
&View	CtlName	ViewCom	Views the selected file
&Print	CtlName	PrintCom	Prints the selected file
&Delete	CtlName	DeleteCom	Deletes the selected file

24-10 The menu structure for the SDIR.FRM form.

Form # 2   Form filename: VUWFILE.FRM
Version: 1.0   Date: September 14, 1991

Control object type	Default CtlName	Purpose
Text box	Text1	Displays the name of the viewed file
	Text2	Views the lines of the file
	Text3	The text search text box
Check box	Check1	Case-sensitive check box
	Check2	Backward search check box
Label	Label1	Label of Filename text box
	Label2	Label of Search text box

24-11 The list of controls in the VUWFILE.FRM form file.

Application (code) name: SDIR
Form # 2
Version: 1.0   Date: September 14, 1991

Original control name	Property	New setting
Form	FormName	ViewFile
	Caption	File Viewer
Text1	CtlName	FilenameBox
	Text	(empty string)
Text2	CtlName	TextBox
	Text	(empty string)
	Multiline	True
	Scrollable	3 - both
Text3	CtlName	FindBox
	Text	(empty string)
Check1	CtlName	CaseSenseChk
	Caption	Case Sensitive
Check2	CtlName	ScanBackwardChk
	Caption	Scan Backward
Label1	CtlName	FilenameLbl
	Caption	Filename:
Label2	CtlName	FindLbl
	Caption	Find Input:

24-12 The customized settings for the VUWFILE.FRM form.

Form # 2   Form filename: VUWFILE.FRM
Version:
1.0   Date: September 14, 1991

Caption	Property	Setting	Purpose
&Quit	CtlName	QuitCom	Exits the form
&Find	CtlName	FindCom	Searches for text

24-13 The menu structure for the VUWFILE.FRM form.

The SDIR.FRM uses this global variable to convey the name of the viewed file to the VUWFILE.FRM form.

☞ The compiled SDIR.EXE program is included in the companion disk. Because the QuickPak routines used in the SDIR utility are *not* included in the companion disk, you cannot compile the utility.

Listing 24-10 contains the code attached to the SDIR.FRM form file. The form declares two dynamic arrays, FilesArray( ) and TextLines( ). The Files

Listing 24-10 The code attached to the SDIR.FRM form.

```
' declare dynamic array of files
Dim FilesArray() As String
' declare dynamic arrays of file text lines
Dim TextLines() As String

Sub DeleteCom_Click ()
' Delete the selected file.
  Const YES = 6
  Dim F As String
  Dim Answer As Integer
  F = GetFilename()
  If F = "" Then Exit Sub
  Answer = MsgBox("Are you sure you want to delete file " + F, 68, "Input")
  If Answer = YES Then
    On Error Resume Next
    Kill F
    UpdateFilesLst
  End If
End Sub

Sub DiskDrv_Change ()
' Update the directory file list box when the
' drive list box changes.
  Treedir.Path = DiskDrv.Drive
End Sub

Sub Form_Load ()
' Initialize the form.
  ' assign the default filename pattern
  TextBox.Text = "*.*"
  ' show the files in the current path
  UpdateFilesLst
End Sub

Function GetFilename () As String
' Return the complete selected filename
  Dim S As String
  Dim DirStr As String
  Dim I As Integer
  ' is there a selected file?
  If FilesLst.ListIndex > -1 Then
    ' get the directory of the selected file
    DirStr = Treedir.List(-1)
    ' append a trailing "\" if one does not already exist
    If Right$(DirStr, 1) <> "\" Then
      DirStr = DirStr + "\"
    End If
    ' copy the selected list member into variable S
    S = FilesLst.Text
    ' locate the first space inside S
    I = InStr(S, " ")
    ' return the leading characters of S, up to the space (excluded).
    GetFilename = DirStr + Left$(S, I - 1)
  Else
    GetFilename = ""
  End If
End Function

Sub PrintCom_Click ()
' Print the selected file.
  PrintFile GetFilename()
End Sub

Sub PrintFile (ByVal Filename$)
' Print the file Filename$.
```

Listing 24-10 Continued.

```
' local constants
Const MAX_LINES = 60 ' maximum number of lines per page
Const TAB_SIZE = 65 ' heading tab size

Dim TextLine As String
Dim I As Integer
Dim CurrentLineNumber As Integer
' exit sub if Filename is empty
If Filename = "" Then Exit Sub
On Error GoTo BadFile ' set error-handling trap
Open Filename For Input As #1 ' open file for input
On Error GoTo 0 ' disable error-handling trap
' print the heading of the first page
GoSub PrintHeading
' read lines from the text file
Do While Not EOF(1)
   Line Input #1, TextLine
   ' update line counter
   CurrentLineNumber = CurrentLineNumber + 1
   ' line counter exceed page size?
   If CurrentLineNumber > MAX_LINES Then
     Printer.NewPage ' print to a new page
      ' print page heading
     GoSub PrintHeading
   End If
   Printer.Print TextLine ' print the current line
Loop
Printer.NewPage ' eject the last page
Printer.EndDoc  ' release print device
Close #1 ' close the file buffer
Beep
Exit Sub
   '********************** Internal Subroutine ***************
PrintHeading:
   ' internal subroutine to print the heading
   Printer.Print Filename; Tab(TAB_SIZE);
   Printer.Print "Page "; Format$(Printer.Page, "###")
   Printer.Print Format$(Now, "hh:mm");
   Printer.Print Tab(TAB_SIZE);
   Printer.Print Format$(Now, "MM-DD-YYYY")
   Printer.Print
   Printer.Print
   CurrentLineNumber = 4
Return
'***************** Error-Handling Statements **************
BadFile:
   Beep
   MsgBox "Cannot open file " + Filename, 0, "File I/O Error"
   Resume ExitSub
ExitSub:
End Sub

Sub QuitCom_Click ()
' Exit the application.
   End
End Sub

Sub SortCom_Click ()
' Sort the selected file.
   Const IO_ER = "File I/O Error"
   Dim InFilename As String
   Dim OutFilename As String
   Dim NumLines As Long
   Dim I As Integer
   Dim FileNum As Integer
   ' store the selected file in the variable InFilename
   InFilename = GetFilename()
```

Listing 24-10 Continued.

```
' if the selected filename is an empty string, exit
If InFilename = "" Then Exit Sub
MousePointer = 11 ' set the mouse cursor to the hour-glass
' count the number of lines in the selected files
'*** invoke the QuickPak routine LineCount&
NumLines = LineCount&(InFilename, Space$(4096))
' resize the dynamic array TextLines according to NumLines
ReDim TextLines(1 To NumLines)
' open the selected file for input
FileNum = FreeFile
' set the error trap
On Error GoTo BadInputFile
Open InFilename For Input As FileNum
I = 1
Do While Not EOF(FileNum)
  Line Input #FileNum, TextLines(I)
  I = I + 1
Loop
NumLines = I ' adjust NumLines
Close #FileNum ' close the input file
On Error GoTo 0 ' turn off error trap
SortStr TextLines(1), NumLines, 0
BadFilename:
' copy the contents of variable InFilename to
' variable OutFilename
' prompt the user until an non-empty string is entered
Do
  OutFilename = InputBox$("Enter output filename", "Input", InFilename)
Loop Until OutFilename <> ""
' set error trap for file output
On Error GoTo BadOutputFile
' open output file
FileNum = FreeFile
Open OutFilename For Output As FileNum
' write the elements of array TextLines to the output file
For I = 1 To NumLines - 1
  Print #FileNum, TextLines(I)
Next I
' close the output file
Close #FileNum
' turn off the error trap
On Error GoTo 0
ExitSortCom:
  MousePointer = 0 ' restore the mouse cursor
  ' update the list of files
  UpdateFilesLst
  Exit Sub
'***************** Error Handlers ***************
BadInputFile:
  MsgBox "Error in reading file " + InFilename, 64, IO_ER
  Resume ExitSortCom
BadOutputFile:
  MsgBox "Error in writing to file " + OutFilename, 64, IO_ER
  Close #FileNum
  Resume BadFilename
End Sub

Sub TextBox_LostFocus ()
' Maintain the filename pattern and update the list of
' selected files that are in the selected path.
  Dim I As Integer
  ' remove extra wildcards
  I = InStr(TextBox.Text, " ")
  If I > 0 Then
    TextBox.Text = Left$(TextBox.Text, I - 1)
  End If
```

Listing 24-10 Continued.

```
  ' update the selected files
  UpdateFilesLst
End Sub

Sub TreeDir_Change ()
' Update the FilesLst box when the directory list box changes.
  UpdateFilesLst
End Sub

Sub UpdateChk_Click ()
' Toggle the files list update
  ' is the check box checked?
  If UpdateChk.Value = 1 Then
    ' clear the FilesLSt list box
    Do While FilesLst.ListCount
      FilesLst.RemoveItem 0
    Loop
  Else
    ' show the files in the selected path
    UpdateFilesLst
  End If
End Sub

Sub UpdateFilesLst ()
' Update the FilesLst box that contains the names, sizes,
' date stamps, and time stamps of the selected files in the
' specified directory
  Const ASCENDING_ORDER = 0
  Dim Count As Integer
  Dim I As Integer
  Dim DirStr As String
  ' if the check box is marked, exit
  If UpdateChk.Value = 1 Then Exit Sub
  ' obtain the selected directory
  DirStr = Treedir.List(-1)
  ' append a "\" if needed
  If Right$(DirStr, 1) <> "\" Then DirStr = DirStr + "\"
  ' obtain the filename pattern
  DirStr = DirStr + TextBox.Text
  ' count the number of files in the pattern stored
  ' in the variable DirStr
  '*** invoke the QuickPak routine FCount%
  Count = FCount%(DirStr)
  ' clear the FilesLst list box
  Do While FilesLst.ListCount
    FilesLst.RemoveItem 0
  Loop
  ' are there files that match the specified pattern?
  If Count > 0 Then
    ' resize the dynamic array FilesArray to match the
    ' number of files that match the specified pattern
    ReDim FilesArray(0 To Count)
    ' assign the file pattern to element 0 of FilesArray
    FilesArray(0) = DirStr
    '*** invoke the QuickPak routine ReadFileI to obtain
    ' the array of filenames, sizes, dates, and times.
    ReadFileI FilesArray(0)
    ' sort the FilesArray
    '*** invoke the QuickPak routine SortStr
    SortStr FilesArray(1), Count, ASCENDING_ORDER
    ' insert the elements of FilesArray in the FilesLst list box
    For I = 1 To Count
      FilesLst.AddItem FilesArray(I), I - 1
    Next I
  End If
End Sub
```

Listing 24-10 Continued.

```
Sub ViewCom_Click ()
' View the selected file.
  ' assign the name of the selected file to the global
  ' variable GlobalFilename.
  GlobalFilename = GetFilename()
  ' if GlobalFilename contains an empty string, exit
  If GlobalFilename = "" Then Exit Sub
  ' load and show the ViewFile form
  ViewFile.Show 1
End Sub
```

Array( ) stores the names of the files in the currently selected directory, and TextLines( ) stores the lines of a file for sorting.

The relevant procedures of the SDIR form are described in the paragraphs that follow.

The DeleteCom_Click procedure deletes the selected file. If there is no selected file, the routine exits. The procedure also prompts you to confirm the deletion using a message box with Yes and No buttons.

The Form_Load procedure assigns the wildcard *.* as the initial filename pattern and invokes the UpdateFilesLst procedure to display the files in the current directory.

The GetFilename function extracts the filename of the selected FilesLst list box member. If there is no selected member, the function returns an empty string. Other procedures compare the function's result with a literal empty string to determine whether or not there is a selected file.

The PrintCom__Click procedure prints the selected file by invoking the PrintFile routine with a GetFilename( ) argument, which is the name of the currently selected file.

The PrintFile procedure is an exact copy of the routine found in the FILESLIB.BAS module. It is used here to avoid dragging the entire code of the FILESLIB.BAS module when creating the SDIR.EXE file.

The SortCom_Click procedure sorts the selected file. The routine obtains the name of the selected file using the GetFilename( ) function, exiting if the result is an empty string, and changes the mouse cursor to the hourglass icon.

☞ SortCom_Click invokes the QuickPak routine LineCount& to quickly count the number of lines in file InFilename, the number is stored in the local variable NumLines. The number in NumLines may exceed the actual number of lines by one. This enables you to read files that do not have carriage return and line feed characters on the last text line.

After determining the line count, SortCom_Click resizes the dynamic array TextLines( ) according to value of variable NumLines, sets the error trap for bad file input, and opens the selected file for input. It then reads the text lines of the selected files into the array TextLines( ), and counts the number of lines read. This number is assigned to the variable NumLines, and the input file is closed.

Next, the procedure turns off the error trap and calls the QuickPak routine SortStr to quickly sort the elements of the array TextLine( ). The arguments specify that sorting begins with the first array element and includes the first NumLines elements. Then the user is prompted for an output filename, using the input filename as a default.

When the filename has been specified, the procedure sets an error trap for bad file output, opens the output file, and writes the elements of array TextLines( ) to that file. Then it closes the output file. Finally, the procedure turns off the error trap, restores the mouse cursor to its default shape, and updates the list of files in the FilesLst control.

The TextBox_LostFocus procedure handles the loss of text box focus. It retains only the first set of filename patterns, in case you type multiple patterns, and updates the list of files in the FilesLst control.

The TreeDir_Change procedure handles the change in the selected directory by invoking the routine UpdateFilesLst. This action updates the list of files in the FilesLst control.

The UpdateChk_Click procedure toggles the updating of the files in the FilesLst list box. If the Value setting of the check box is 1, the procedure clears the FilesLst list box, preventing the user from assuming that the files in the FilesLst control are in the currently selected directory. If the Value setting of the check box is 0, the routine calls UpdateFilesLst to show the matching files of the current directory.

The UpdateFilesLst procedure plays an important role in displaying an updated list of files in the FilesLst control. The procedure exits if the Value of the UpdateChk check box is 1; if not, it obtains the selected directory, obtains the filename pattern that includes the selected directory, and invokes the QuickPak function FCount% to count the number of files that match the specified pattern. Then it clears the FilesLst list box. The procedure performs no further action if there are no matching files in the specified path and pattern.

Assuming that there are matching files, the procedure resizes the dynamic array FilesArray( ) to match the number of files that correspond to the specified pattern. The lower and upper indices of the array FilesArray( ) are 0 and Count, respectively. Then the file pattern is assigned to element FilesArray(0) as required by the QuickPak ReadFileI procedure, which is called next.

ReadFileI obtains the array of filenames, sizes, dates, and times. The array FilesArray( ) now contains the above information in a format suitable for display. To properly display such information, I chose to use the proportional Courier font for the FilesLst control.

Next, the QuickPak SortStr routine is called to sort FilesArray( ) in as cending order. The arguments for SortStr specify that Count members of the array be sorted, starting with element FilesArray(1). This excludes the unwanted FilesArray(0) element, which does not contain a file information string. Finally, the elements of FilesArray( ) are displayed in the FilesLst list box.

The ViewCom_Click procedure views the selected file by loading and showing the ViewFile form. The procedure assigns the name of the selected file to the global variable GlobalFilename, and exits if it contains an empty string. Otherwise, the procedure loads and shows the ViewFile form as a modal form.

Listing 24-11 contains the code attached to the VUWFILE.FRM form, which declares two variables: TextStr and LockTextBox. These variables are used to protect the contents of the scrollable text box from any change.

The form's relevant procedures are described in the next several paragraphs.

Listing 24-11 The code attached to the VUWFILE.FRM form.

```
' declare the variable that stores a copy of
' the TextBox control
Dim TextStr As String
' declare the flag for "locking" the TextBox control
Dim LockTextBox As Integer

Sub FilenameBox_Change ()
' Prevent any changes from occurring in the Filename text box,
' by assigning the contents of the GlobalFilename variable
' to the Filename text box.
  FilenameBox.Text = GlobalFilename
End Sub

Sub FilenameBox_KeyPress (KeyAScii As Integer)
' Prevent the user from typing anything in the control.
  KeyAScii = 0
End Sub

Sub FindCom_Click ()
' Search the lines of the file for the occurrence of the
' string in the Find text box.
  Static CurIndex As Long
  Dim Find As String
  ' store the text of the Find box in the variable Find
  Find = FindBox.Text
  ' is variable Find empty?
  If Find = "" Then Exit Sub ' nothing to find
  ' is the search case-sensitive?
  If CaseSenseChk.Value = 1 Then
    ' scanning forward?
    If Not (ScanBackwardChk.Value = 1) Then
      ' update the index to the current character
      CurIndex = TextBox.SelStart + 1
      '** use the QuickPak routine QInstr
      CurIndex = QInstr(CurIndex + 1, TextStr, Find)
    Else
      ' update the index to the current character
      CurIndex = TextBox.SelStart - 1
      If CurIndex < 1 Then CurIndex = Len(TextStr)
      '** use the QuickPak routine QInstrB
      CurIndex = QInstrB(CurIndex, TextStr, Find)
    End If
  Else
    ' scanning forward?
    If Not (ScanBackwardChk.Value = 1) Then
      ' update the index to the current character
      CurIndex = TextBox.SelStart + 1
      '** use the QuickPak routine QInstr2
```

Listing 24-11 Continued.

```
        CurIndex = QInstr2(CurIndex + 1, TextStr, Find)
      Else
        ' update the index to the current character
        CurIndex = TextBox.SelStart - 1
        If CurIndex < 1 Then CurIndex = Len(TextStr)
        '** use the QuickPak routine QInstrB2
        CurIndex = QInstrB2(CurIndex, TextStr, Find)
      End If
    End If
    ' found a match?
    If CurIndex > 0 Then
      ' Yes! Display the matching text as selected text
      TextBox.SelStart = CurIndex - 1
      TextBox.SelLength = Len(Find)
      TextBox.SetFocus
    Else
      ' No! Clear any selected text
      TextBox.SelStart = 0
      TextBox.SelLength = 0
    End If
End Sub

Sub Form_Load ()
' Initialize the form.
  WindowState = 2  ' set the window to maximum
  LockTextBox = False
  ' read the selected file
  ReadFile GlobalFilename
  LockTextBox = True
  ' copy the contents of the TextBox control into the
  ' form-level string TextStr
  TextStr = TextBox.Text
End Sub

Sub QuitCom_Click ()
' Unload the ViewFile form
  Unload ViewFile
End Sub

Sub ReadFile (ByVal Filename$)
' Reads and displays the file Filename.
  Dim F As String
  Dim L As String
  Dim NL As String * 2
  Dim FileNum As Integer
  MousePointer = 11 ' set mouse cursor to the hour-glass
  ' write filename to the filename text box
  FilenameBox.Text = GlobalFilename
  NL = Chr$(13) + Chr$(10)
  FileNum = FreeFile
  ' open the file
  Open GlobalFilename For Input As #FileNum
  F = "" ' clear string variable
  ' loop to read the text lines from the ASCII file
  Do While Not EOF(FileNum)
    Line Input #FileNum, L
    F = F + L + NL ' append a new line
  Loop
  TextBox.Text = F ' copy F into text box
  ' close the file
  Close #FileNum
  MousePointer = 0 ' restore default mouse cursor
End Sub

Sub TextBox_Change ()
  If LockTextBox Then
```

Listing 24-11 Continued.

```
    TextBox.Text = TextStr
  End If
End Sub

Sub TextBox_KeyPress (KeyAScii As Integer)
' Prevent the user from typing anything in the control.
  KeyAScii = 0
End Sub
```

The FilenameBox_Change procedure prevents any changes from occurring in the Filename text box, by assigning the contents of the GlobalFilename variable to the Filename text box.

The FilenameBox_KeyPress procedure prevents the user from typing anything in the control.

The FindCom_Click procedure searches the lines of the file for the occurrence of the string in the Find text box. The routine is similar to the Find Com_Click routine in the VIEWFILE.FRM form. This version, however, examines the check boxes to determine whether or not to conduct case-sensitive search, and whether to search forward or backward. These four possibilities translate in calling one of the QuickPak routines QInstr, QInstr2, QInstrB, and QInstr2B. This version also permits the use of one or more ? wildcard characters, making it more flexible in searching for text. Also, the QuickPak search routines use the TextStr variable and not the TextBox .Text property.

The Form_Load procedure initializes the form. First, it maximizes the application's window, then assigns False to the variable LockTextBox to allow the form to load text in the control. Then the procedure reads the selected file, and assigns True to LockTextBox to prevent user input to the control. Finally, the string of the TextBox control is copied to the the variable TextStr.

The ReadFile procedure reads and displays the file Filename.

The TextBox_Change procedure assigns the contents of variable TextStr to TextBox.Text if the variable LockTextBox is True.

The TextBox_KeyPress procedure prevents the user from typing anything in the control.

Appendices

Appendices

A
About QuickPak Professional for Windows

This appendix contains general information about QuickPak Professional for Windows which has been supplied by Crescent Software.

QuickPak Professional is the most complete collection of subroutines, functions, and custom controls for Visual Basic ever produced. It includes more than 300 services that help you improve the quality of your programs, and complete them faster. All of the low-level routines are written in pure assembly language for the fastest speed and smallest code size possible. The remainder are high-level services written in Visual Basic.

Low-level routines for high-level performance

Because Visual Basic creates programs that are interpreted at run time, assembly language routines are essential for attaining acceptable speed in many programming situations. Routines are provided for searching and sorting all data types including floating point and currency arrays. A special multikey recursive Type sort lets you sort on any number of keys—both in memory and on disk. Other important low-level assembler routines include loading and saving entire arrays in one operation, simplified access to the Windows API services, direct access to hardware ports, extremely fast date and time arithmetic, and much more.

Many Visual Basic custom controls are provided:

- A unique time display with adjustable offset for different time zones.
- An enhanced text box control features masked input that lets you specify allowable characters for each position in a field. This control also features changeable tab stops, overstrike mode, enforcing a maximum field length, and definable data types.

- Enhanced scroll bars that provide instant updating as the sliders are moved.
- Enhanced list boxes offering multiple columns and multiple selections.
- Keyboard and mouse controls that let you intercept those events before they are passed on to your program or other Windows applications. With these controls you can pop up a program on a hot key, or examine and filter keyboard and mouse events destined for *other* Windows programs that are currently running.

All of the low-level routines are very easy to use, and employ sensible names and a simple, intuitive calling syntax. You do not have to know anything about assembly language to use QuickPak Professional for Windows. Simply specify the supplied DLL library in your Declare statements, and QuickPak does the rest.

Don't reinvent the wheel

Many high-level subroutines and functions are provided, including BASIC equivalents of every financial and statistical function in Lotus 1-2-3. High-level file services include file searching and encryption, and copying multiple files based on wildcard specifications. A full-featured expression evaluator accepts formulas even with nested parentheses, and computes the result. There's also a pop-up ASCII chart that you can add to your programs.

Special enhanced dialog boxes are supplied for File Open, File Save, Search, and Search and Replace.

Contouring routines create an attractive sculpted look on your Visual Basic forms. Painting routines fill irregularly shaped areas are also provided. All of the high-level routines are easily loaded as modules, then you can call the routines as needed.

Spectacular demonstration programs

Numerous demonstration programs are provided that show many of the routines in context, and also serve as excellent examples of professional programming using Visual Basic. Further, QuickPak Professional for Windows includes all of the source code—both BASIC and assembler—so you can see how the routines really work, and learn from them.

Many of the demonstration programs are complete applications in their own right. For example, the ReadDirs program shows how to search all directory levels for a given file or group of files. The SysInfo demo is a complete utility program that reports all of the system resources such as installed memory, CPU type, number and type of disk drives, and so forth. The file encryption demonstration accepts a filename and password, and actually encrypts the file.

Routines by category

The section that follows lists all of the features in QuickPak Professional for Windows by category. It isn't possible to describe every routine in detail; however, each category header lists the highlights, and describes those routines that have proven most popular in the QuickBasic version of QuickPak Professional. Note that all of these routines are written in pure assembly language, except for the financial and scientific functions.

Array processing

Sort routines are provided to sort any type of array including string and floating point in either ascending or descending order. A Type array sort lets you sort elements based on any component in the Type, regardless of the data type. A multikey Type array sort accommodates any number of keys, including mixed data types. Indexed versions of all sort routines are also provided (except multikey), so you can access your arrays in both the original and sorted order simultaneously.

Complementing the array sorts is an additional family of routines for searching any type of data. Besides recognizing all data types, the Type array search can examine all elements, but consider only one component in the comparisons. When searching string arrays or the string portion of a Type array, searching can either honor or ignore capitalization.

Routines are included to quickly determine the minimum and maximum values in numeric arrays, and the number of active elements in a string array. Additional subroutines let you initialize arrays with fixed or ascending values, and perform simple matrix operations such as adding and subtracting a constant value from each element. You can also insert and delete elements, and even create bit arrays to hold many true/false values in as little memory as possible.

DOS services

A complete set of file access routines are included that use a sensible system of error codes, to avoid Basic's clumsy On Error and Resume. You can also test if a given drive is ready for reading or writing directly.

The file and directory name services let you quickly load an entire string or Type array with the names of all files or directories that match a given wildcard specification. Full information about each file is optionally returned, including its date, time, size, and attributes. You can even change file attributes to mark them as read-only or hidden.

Full information can be retrieved for any floppy or hard disk, such as its type, size, available space, and sector and cluster size. A unique ClipFile routine lets you change a file's size, making it either longer or shorter. A special message function is also included that returns the appropriate text for any BASIC error. By storing the message text in the code segment, no data memory is taken from your programs.

The ExeName function reports the full name of your own program, including the drive and path. This lets you easily find configuration files, even when your program was started from a different directory, or found through the PATH setting.

FStamp lets you change the date and time stamp of any file, and Name Dir will rename a directory, which DOS normally does not allow. GetVol and PutVol let you read and write a disk's volume label, and DOSVer reports the DOS version number.

Date and time routines

A full complement of date and time routines are included, to compute time and date differences. The date routines are extremely fast, and require less variable memory than those built into Visual Basic.

Keyboard routines

A set of functions lets you quickly determine or set the status of all keys including Alt, Ctrl, Shift, CapsLock, NumLock, and ScrollLock.

Financial/scientific routines

A full complement of financial and scientific functions is provided, including every function in Lotus 1-2-3.

Strings

A wealth of string manipulation routines are included. There are InStr replacements that allow wildcards, honor or ignore capitalization, look for characters that match those in a table, and even search backward through a string. A sophisticated parsing function lets you easily split strings such as the DOS PATH into their component parts. ParseString is much more powerful than Read and Data, and more than overcomes their omission from Visual Basic.

String encryption routines let you quickly secure data and passwords, using any other string as a key. A unique Sequence routine advances digits and letters for controlling serial numbers and product codes. Special UCASE$ and LCASE$ replacements let our European friends handle the unique capitalization needs of their languages.

Conversion routines translate between Hex, Binary, and Decimal numbers.

A Soundex function lets you compare strings and names based on how they sound.

Miscellaneous routines

Many hardware services are also included to let you determine the CPU type, coprocessor, number and type of drives and if they are on a network server, printer status, monitor type, serial and parallel ports, and more.

Memory services report on the total installed memory, Windows virtual memory, and EMS/XMS memory. Windows-specific routines return the version number and operating mode, free resources, and the Windows and System directories.

Other miscellaneous routines let you manipulate unsigned integers, shift bits, copy blocks of memory, and compare entire Type variables in one operation.

Although Visual Basic doesn't support BASIC's CALL INTERRUPT, QuickPak Professional does. With DosCall you can easily access all of the low-level system services.

Other important Visual Basic omissions are also provided, including the CVi/CVd and MKi$/MKd$ family of functions; Peek and Poke; Inp and Out; and VarSeg, VarPtr, and SAdd. Other VB oversights we provide are Sound and Play, Swap, and Fre. Because these are no longer reserved words, we use the original names so you don't even have to change your code.

Windows-specific services

Routines are included to provide the following Windows services:

- Determine if a particular program is running.
- Get window handles for the whole system, or one application. Although Visual Basic lets you know the handle for your own forms, there's no direct way to pass a control's handle to an API routine.
- Functions that access the Visual Basic API Twips2Pixels and Pixels2 Twips services, to determine the ratio of pixels to twips and vice versa.
- A special function that returns a pointer to a Visual Basic HLS string.
- A subroutine that reports and counts all top windows, children under a given window, all tasks, and all parent tasks.
- A SplitColor subroutine that splits the Windows long integer color into its component Red, Green, and Blue values.

General information

Programmers who already own QuickPak Professional for QuickBasic or BASIC 7 PDS will be pleased to know that the identical calling syntax is used for the Windows version, which simplifies converting existing applications to the Windows environment.

QuickPak Professional for Windows costs $199, including all of the subroutines, functions, custom controls, and fully commented source code.

About Crescent Software

Crescent Software has provided add-on libraries and utilities for BASIC programmers since 1986. With a staff of seven full-time programmers, Crescent is the largest publisher of BASIC support products. Crescent Software tools have received exceptional reviews in all of the major computer publications. Crescent President Ethan Winer is a nationally recognized authority on compiled BASIC, and is a contributing editor for PC Magazine and BASICPro. Ethan has written feature articles for *Programmers Journal*, *Computer Language*, *Microsoft Systems Journal*, *PC Techniques*, and *Inside Microsoft BASIC*.

For further information, call or write:

Crescent Software
32 Seventy Acres
West Redding, CT 06896
(800) 35-BASIC (orders only)
(203) 438-5300 (information)

B
The companion disk

This book has a companion disk that contains the .MAK, .FRM, .BAS, and other files that are mentioned in this book. These files are located in the self-extracting archive file VBXTOOL.EXE. To install and unpack these files perform the following steps:

1. Select the \VB directory or, if you use a different directory to store Visual Basic, select the directory.
2. Create the subdirectory VBXTOOL by executing the following DOS command:

   C> MD VBXTOOL

3. Select the EASYVB subdirectory by executing the following DOS command:

   C> CD VBXTOOL

4. Insert the companion disk in drive A.
5. Unpack the self-extracting archive file by executing the following command from DOS:

   C> A:VBXTOOL

This command unpacks the archive file and installs the files in directory \VB\VBXTOOL.

Index

Other Bestsellers of Related Interest

BUILD YOUR OWN 386/386SX
COMPATIBLE AND SAVE A BUNDLE
—2nd Edition—*Aubrey Pilgrim*

Now, with the latest in Pilgrim's best-selling Build Your Own series, you can assemble an 80386 microcomputer at home using mail-order parts that cost a lot less today than they did several years ago. Absolutely no special technical know-how is required—only a pair of pliers, a couple of screwdrivers, and this detailed, easy-to-follow guide. 248 pages, 79 illustrations. **Book No. 4089, $18.95 paperback, $29.95 hardcover**

BIT-MAPPED GRAPHICS—*Steve Rimmer*

This is one of the first books to cover the specific graphic file formats used by popular paint and desktop publishing packages. It shows you how to pack and unpack bit-map image files so you can import and export them to other applications. And, it also helps you sort through available file formats, standards, patches, and revision levels, using commercial-quality C code to explore bit-mapped graphics and effectively deal with image files. 504 pages, 131 illustrations. **Book No. 3558, $26.95 paperback, $38.95 hardcover**

MACINTOSH SYSTEM 7: The Complete
Sourcebook—*Gordon M. Campbell*

Campbell shows off some fo the exciting new features of System 7 and offers tips for upgrading your hardware and software. This is your best guide to the first major development in the Macintosh since its introduction in 1984. With this book by your keyboard, you can count on clear skies and smooth sailing, for either upgrade or installation. 320 pages, Illustrated. **Book No. 4074, $29.95 paperback only**

MS-DOS® BATCH FILE PROGRAMMING
—3rd Edition—*Ronny Richardson*

Now updated to cover DOS 5.0, this book explores the power of .BAT—the PC user's key to total system control. Richardson shows how to boost productivity dramatically with simple step-saving programs. He discusses two of the most often customized system batch files, AUTOEXEC.BAT and CONFIG.SYS. You can then progress to creating your own batch files in order to make your computer run more smoothly and do exactly what you want it to do. 440 pages, 186 illustrations, 5.25″ disk included. **Book No. 3916, $26.95 paperback, $36.95 hardcover**

MS-DOS® BATCH FILE UTILITIES
—*Ronny Richardson*

Featuring more than 200 of the best batch file programs available for the PC, this is the most complete source of documentation available for batch file utilities currently offered as shareware or in the public domain. Arranged alphabetically and meticulously cross-referenced by category, this valuable reference features detailed descriptions and instructions for ALL commercial batch files on the DOS market today. 368 pages, 275 illustrations, 5.25″ disk included. **Book No. 3915, $26.95 paperback, $36.95 hardcover**

FOXPRO®: The Master Reference
—2nd Edition—*Robin Stark and Shelley Satonin*

Design and run powerful, customized databases in no time using all the exciting new features of FoxPro. This alphabetical guide to every FoxPro command and function covers all versions through 2.0—more than 350 entries in all. Its innovative three-part indexing system leads you quickly to all commands, functions, and examples found in the book. 512 pages, 135 illustrations. **Book No. 4056, $24.95 paperback only**

NORTON UTILITIES® 6.0: An Illustrated Tutorial—*Richard Evans*

Richard Evans shows you how to painlessly perform the most dazzling Norton functions using the all-new features of Norton Utilities 6.0. He also reviews the best from previous releases, providing clear, easy-to-follow instructions and screen illustrations reflecting Norton's new developments. You'll also learn about NDOS, a new configuration and shell program that replaces COMMAND.COM. 464 pages, 277 illustrations. **Book No. 4132, $19.95 paperback, $29.95 hardcover**

101+ FOXPRO® AND dBASE® IV USER-DEFINED FUNCTIONS—*Philip Steele*

Whether you've already written many lines of database code and just want to improve your code or you want to develop more complex applications for distribution in the corporate marketplace, this book's for you. It contains professional guidelines for developing and writing UDFs that will eliminate repetitive database programming tasks. A companion disk, offered on an order form at the end of the book, contains all the UDFs used in the book. 368 pages, 159 illustrations. **Book No. 3951, $18.95 paperback only**

The enclosed double-density 3¹/₂″ disk contains the self-extracting file, VBXTOOL.EXE. This file contains 75 other programs in a compressed format.

Before you can access the programs contained in VBXTOOL.EXE, you must create a directory on your hard drive, copy VBXTOOL.EXE into the new directory, and run the VBXTOOL.EXE file. At the C> prompt, type:

MD C: \ *directory_name*

(where *directory_name* is the name of the directory that you want to create) and press Enter. You have just created a directory on your hard drive to hold all of the programs contained in VBXTOOL.EXE. Now, place the companion diskette in drive A: and copy VBXTOOL.EXE to your newly created directory by typing:

COPY A: \ VBXTOOL.EXE C: \ *directory_name*

(where *directory_name* is the name of the directory that you created earlier) and press Enter. Now, you can safely run VBXTOOL.EXE to extract the other programs. At the C> prompt, type:

VBXTOOL

and press Enter. The program will list the name of each file as it is uncompressed and will return to the DOS prompt when all of the files have been uncompressed.